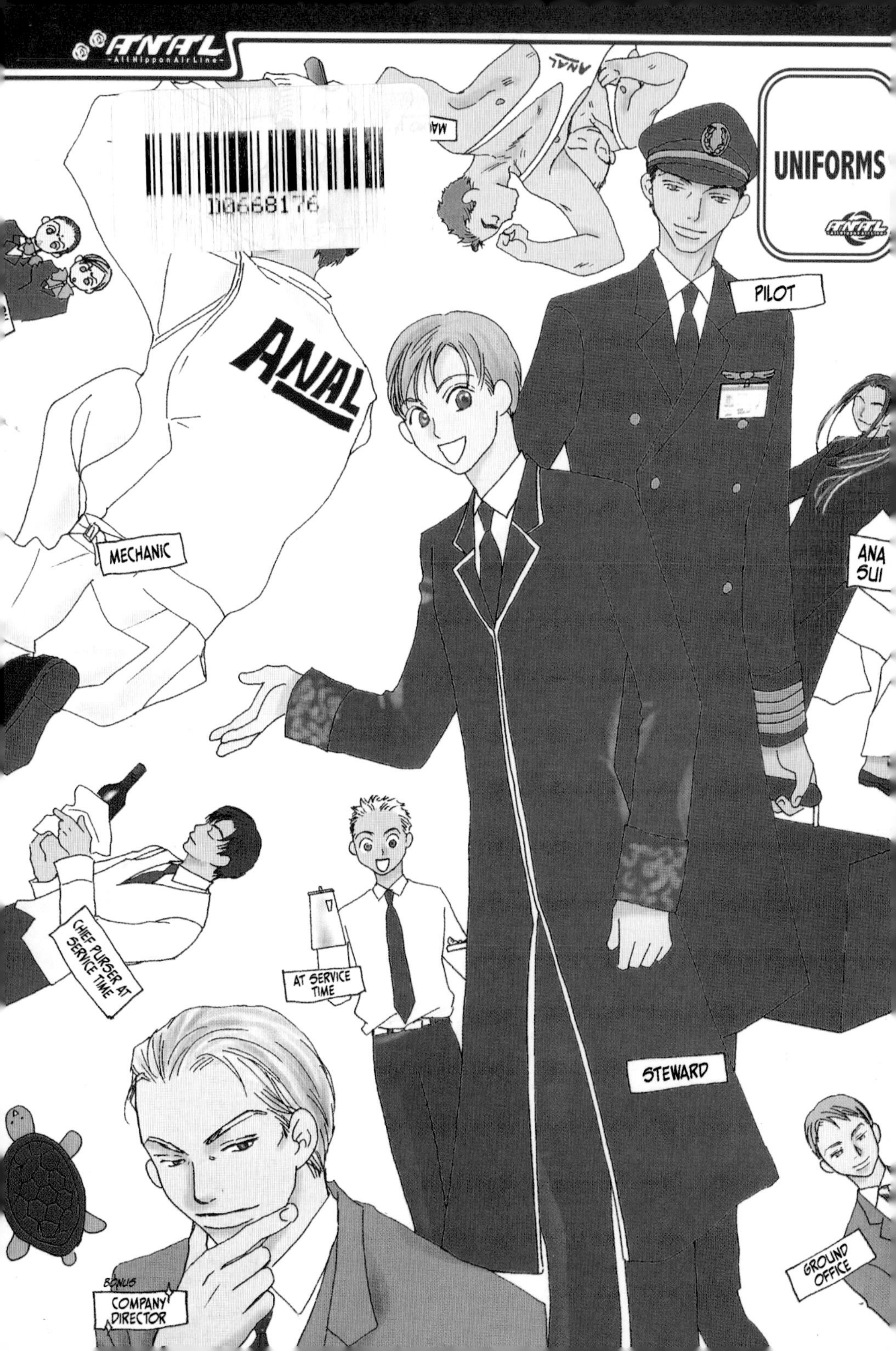
ANAL
-All Nippon AirLine-
UNIFORMS
PILOT
ANAL
MECHANIC
ANA SUI
CHIEF PURSER AT SERVICE TIME
AT SERVICE TIME
STEWARD
GROUND OFFICE
BONUS
COMPANY DIRECTOR

# All Nippon Air Line
PARADISE AT 30,000 FEET




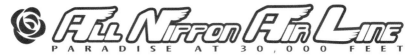

| | |
|---|---|
| Translation | **Sachiko Sato** |
| Lettering | **Eva Han** |
| Layout / Graphic Design | **Fred Lui/Wendy Lee** |
| Editing | **Stephanie Donnelly** |
| Editor in Chief | **Fred Lui** |
| Publisher | **Hikaru Sasahara** |





English Edition Published by
DIGITAL MANGA PUBLISHING
A division of DIGITAL MANGA, Inc.
1487 W 178th Street, Suite 300
Gardena, CA 90248

www.dmpbooks.com

First Edition: February 2008
ISBN-10: 1-56970-748-0
ISBN-13: 978-1-56970-748-7

1 3 5 7 9 10 8 6 4 2

Printed in China

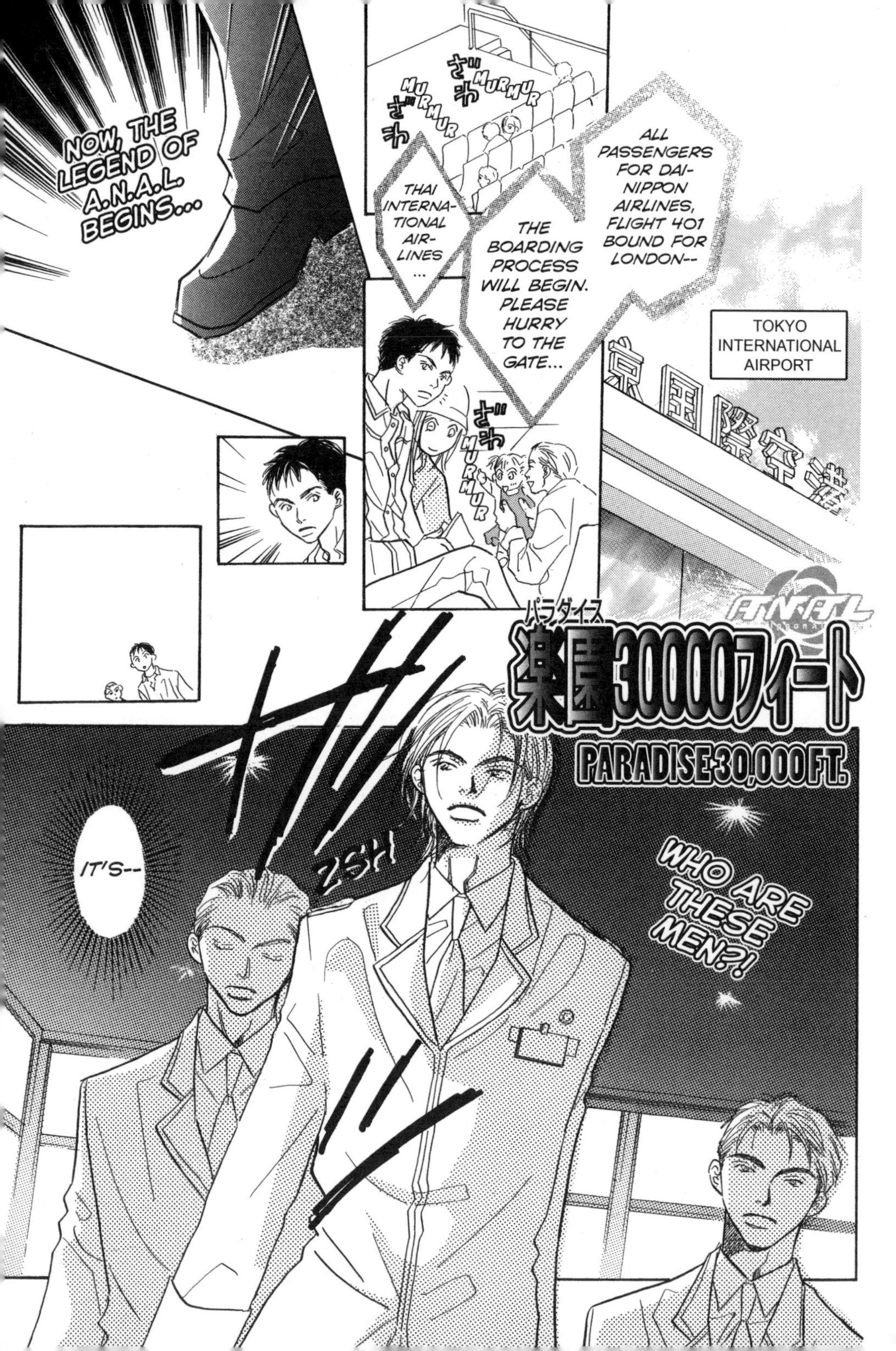
TOKYO INTERNATIONAL AIRPORT
ALL PASSENGERS FOR DAI-NIPPON AIRLINES, FLIGHT 401 BOUND FOR LONDON--
THE BOARDING PROCESS WILL BEGIN. PLEASE HURRY TO THE GATE...
THAI INTERNATIONAL AIR-LINES ...
ざわ MURMUR
ざわ MURMUR
NOW, THE LEGEND OF A.N.A.L. BEGINS...
ざわ MURMUR
楽園(パラダイス)30000フィート
PARADISE 30,000 FT.
WHO ARE THESE MEN?!
ZSH
IT'S--

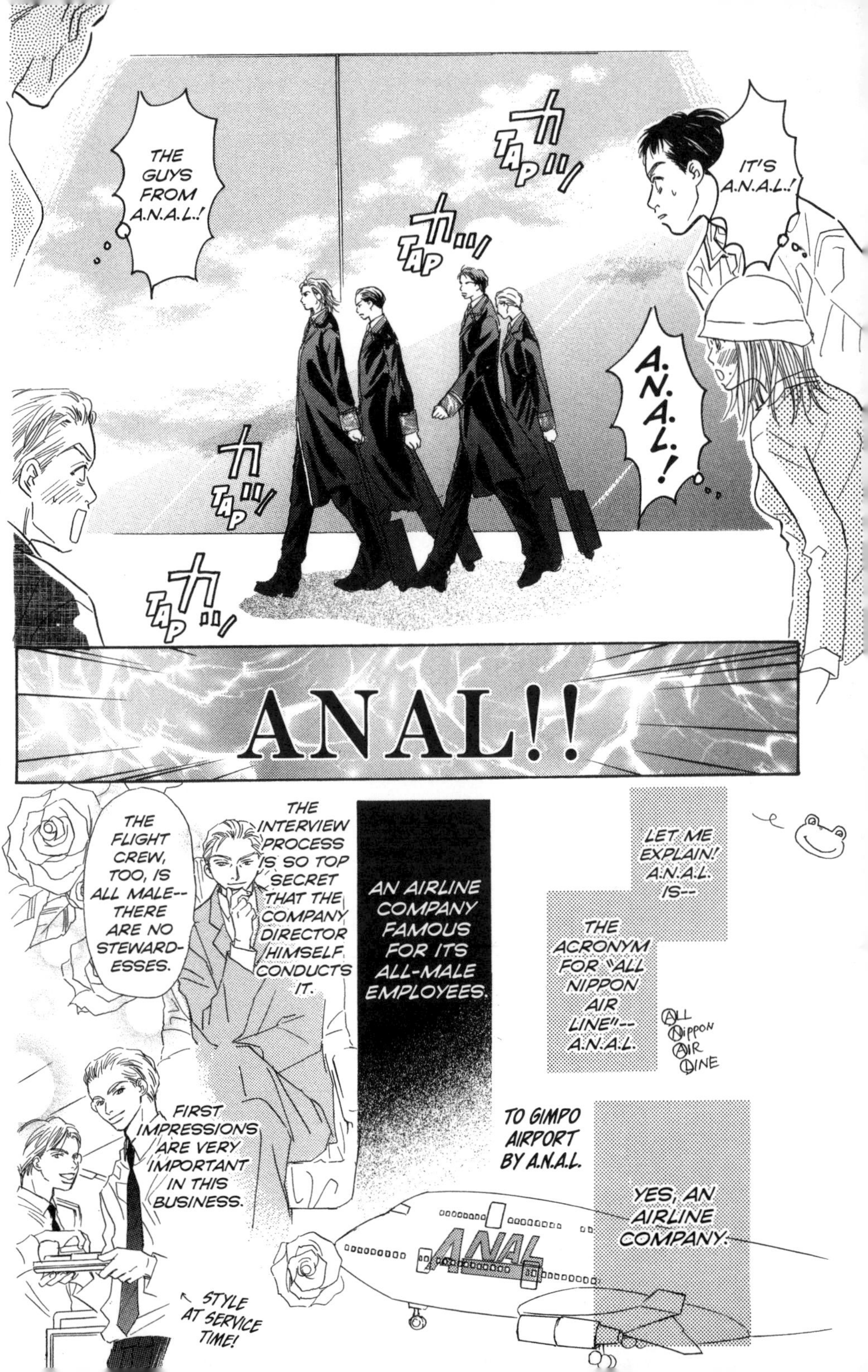

IT'S A.N.A.L..!
TAP
TAP
A.N.A.L.!
TAP
TAP
THE GUYS FROM A.N.A.L..!
ANAL!!
LET ME EXPLAIN! A.N.A.L. IS--
THE ACRONYM FOR "ALL NIPPON AIR LINE"-- A.N.A.L.
ALL NIPPON AIR LINE
AN AIRLINE COMPANY FAMOUS FOR ITS ALL-MALE EMPLOYEES.
THE INTERVIEW PROCESS IS SO TOP SECRET THAT THE COMPANY DIRECTOR HIMSELF CONDUCTS IT.
THE FLIGHT CREW, TOO, IS ALL MALE-- THERE ARE NO STEWARDESSES.
YES, AN AIRLINE COMPANY.
TO GIMPO AIRPORT BY A.N.A.L.
ANAL
FIRST IMPRESSIONS ARE VERY IMPORTANT IN THIS BUSINESS.
STYLE AT SERVICE TIME!

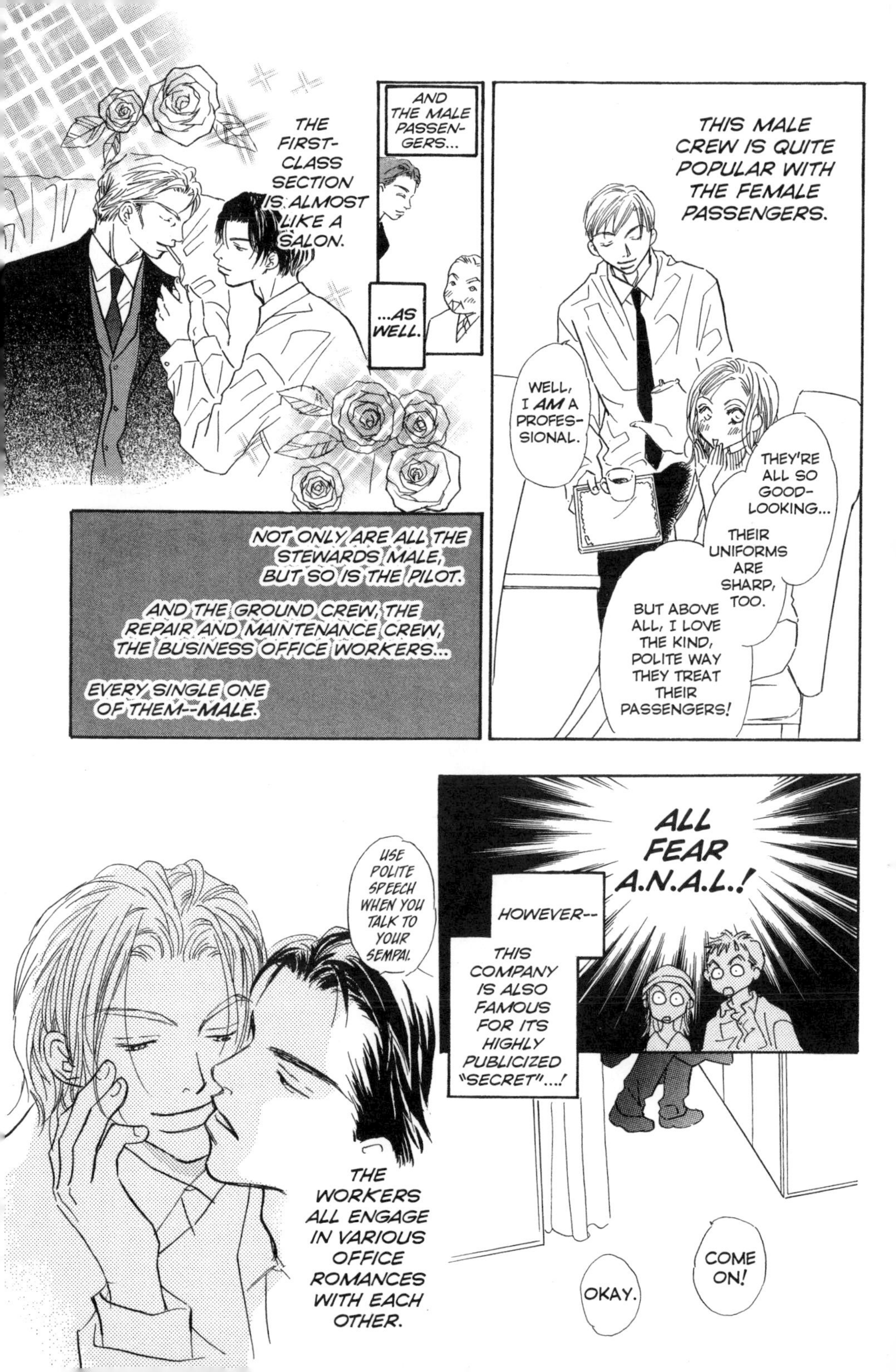
THIS MALE CREW IS QUITE POPULAR WITH THE FEMALE PASSENGERS.
THEY'RE ALL SO GOOD-LOOKING...
THEIR UNIFORMS ARE SHARP, TOO.
BUT ABOVE ALL, I LOVE THE KIND, POLITE WAY THEY TREAT THEIR PASSENGERS!
WELL, I AM A PROFESSIONAL.
THE FIRST-CLASS SECTION IS ALMOST LIKE A SALON.
AND THE MALE PASSENGERS...
...AS WELL.
NOT ONLY ARE ALL THE STEWARDS MALE, BUT SO IS THE PILOT.
AND THE GROUND CREW, THE REPAIR AND MAINTENANCE CREW, THE BUSINESS OFFICE WORKERS...
EVERY SINGLE ONE OF THEM--MALE.
ALL FEAR A.N.A.L.!
HOWEVER--
THIS COMPANY IS ALSO FAMOUS FOR ITS HIGHLY PUBLICIZED "SECRET"...!
COME ON!
OKAY.
USE POLITE SPEECH WHEN YOU TALK TO YOUR SEMPAI.
THE WORKERS ALL ENGAGE IN VARIOUS OFFICE ROMANCES WITH EACH OTHER.

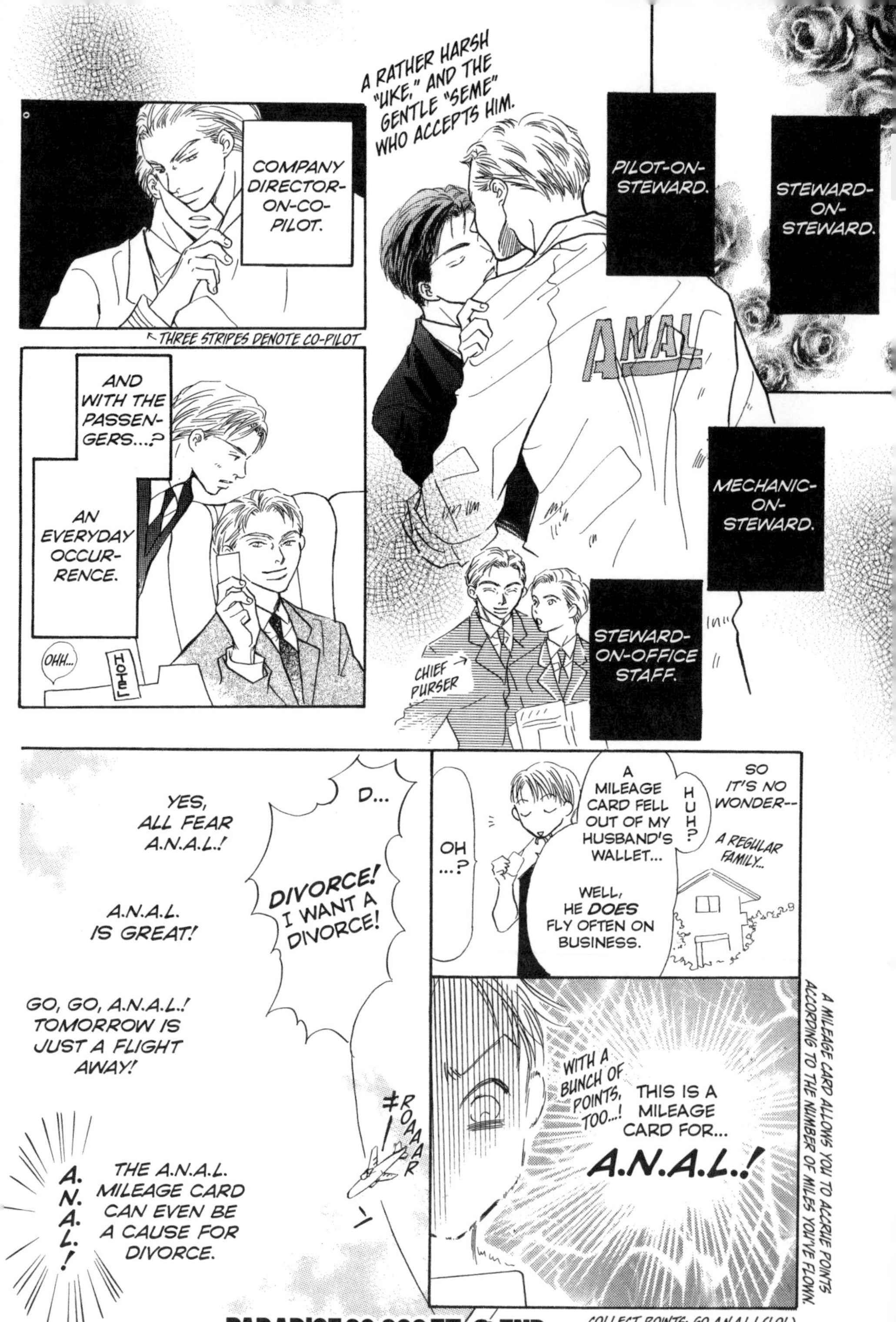
STEWARD-ON-STEWARD.
PILOT-ON-STEWARD.
A RATHER HARSH "UKE," AND THE GENTLE "SEME" WHO ACCEPTS HIM.
ANAL
MECHANIC-ON-STEWARD.
STEWARD-ON-OFFICE STAFF.
CHIEF PURSER
COMPANY DIRECTOR-ON-CO-PILOT.
THREE STRIPES DENOTE CO-PILOT
AND WITH THE PASSENGERS...?
AN EVERYDAY OCCURRENCE.
OHH...
HOTEL
SO IT'S NO WONDER--
A REGULAR FAMILY...
HUH?
A MILEAGE CARD FELL OUT OF MY HUSBAND'S WALLET...
WELL, HE *DOES* FLY OFTEN ON BUSINESS.
OH ...?
A MILEAGE CARD ALLOWS YOU TO ACCRUE POINTS ACCORDING TO THE NUMBER OF MILES YOU'VE FLOWN.
THIS IS A MILEAGE CARD FOR...
A.N.A.L.!
WITH A BUNCH OF POINTS, TOO...!
D...
DIVORCE! I WANT A DIVORCE!
ROAAAR
YES, ALL FEAR A.N.A.L.!
A.N.A.L. IS GREAT!
GO, GO, A.N.A.L.! TOMORROW IS JUST A FLIGHT AWAY!
THE A.N.A.L. MILEAGE CARD CAN EVEN BE A CAUSE FOR DIVORCE.
A.N.A.L.!

COLLECT POINTS; GO A.N.A.L.! (LOL)

**PARADISE 30,000 FT. END**

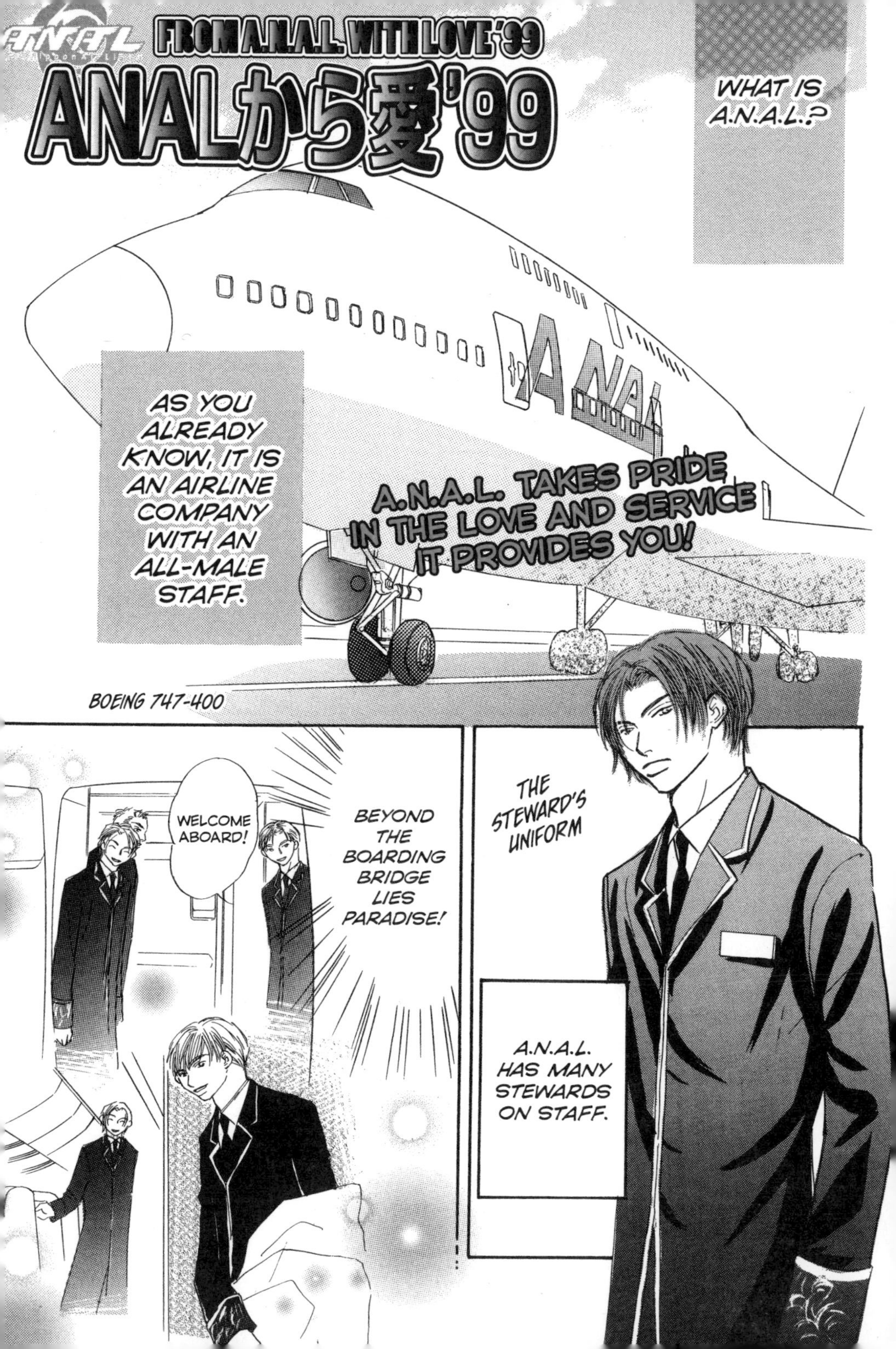
FROM A.N.A.L. WITH LOVE '99
ANALから愛'99
WHAT IS A.N.A.L.?
AS YOU ALREADY KNOW, IT IS AN AIRLINE COMPANY WITH AN ALL-MALE STAFF.
A.N.A.L. TAKES PRIDE IN THE LOVE AND SERVICE IT PROVIDES YOU!
BOEING 747-400
THE STEWARD'S UNIFORM
A.N.A.L. HAS MANY STEWARDS ON STAFF.
BEYOND THE BOARDING BRIDGE LIES PARADISE!
WELCOME ABOARD!

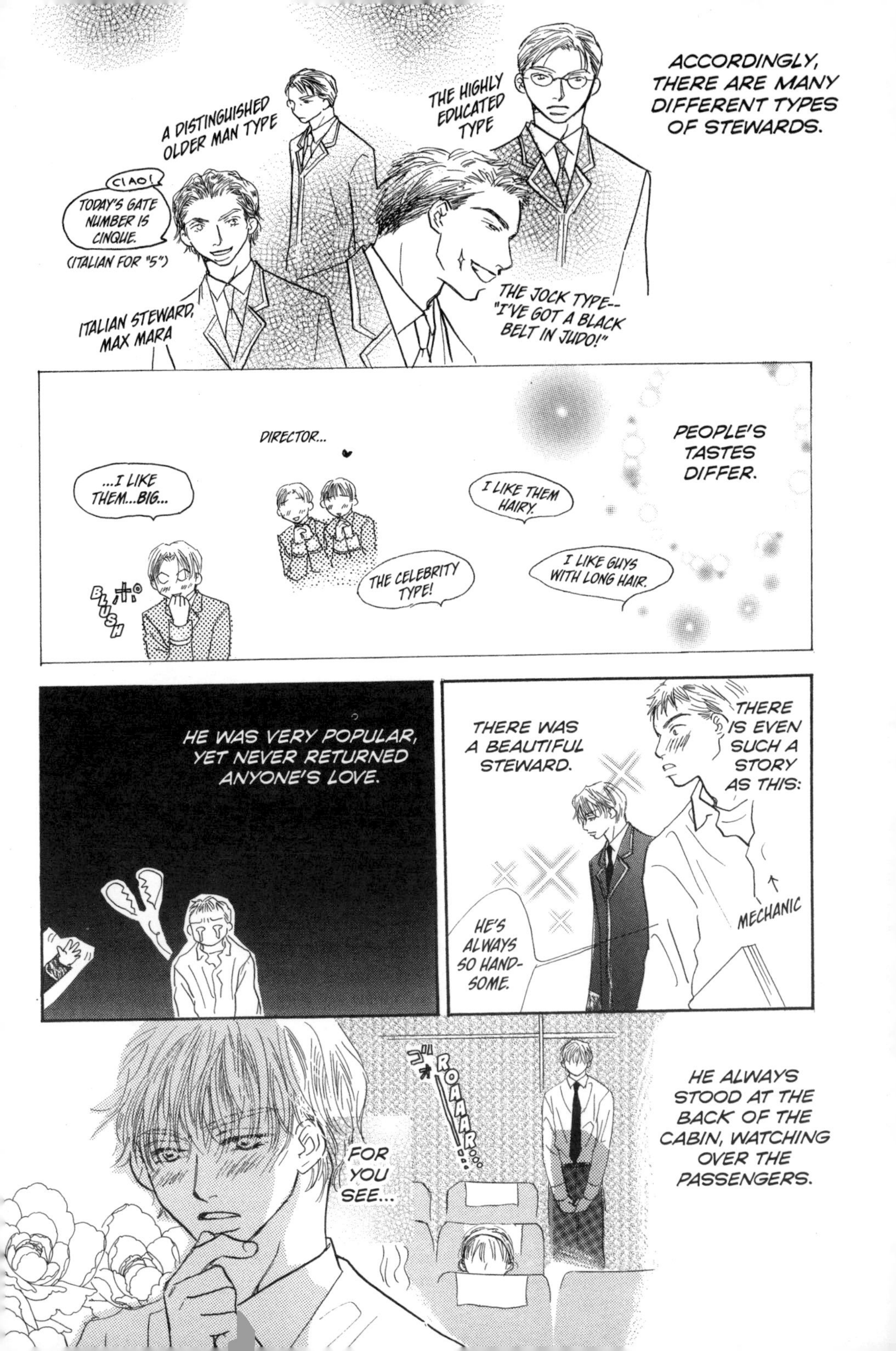
ACCORDINGLY, THERE ARE MANY DIFFERENT TYPES OF STEWARDS.
THE HIGHLY EDUCATED TYPE
A DISTINGUISHED OLDER MAN TYPE
THE JOCK TYPE-- "I'VE GOT A BLACK BELT IN JUDO!"
CIAO!
TODAY'S GATE NUMBER IS CINQUE.
(ITALIAN FOR "5")
ITALIAN STEWARD, MAX MARA
PEOPLE'S TASTES DIFFER.
I LIKE THEM HAIRY.
I LIKE GUYS WITH LONG HAIR.
DIRECTOR...
THE CELEBRITY TYPE!
...I LIKE THEM...BIG...
BLUSH
THERE IS EVEN SUCH A STORY AS THIS:
THERE WAS A BEAUTIFUL STEWARD.
MECHANIC
HE'S ALWAYS SO HANDSOME.
HE WAS VERY POPULAR, YET NEVER RETURNED ANYONE'S LOVE.
HE ALWAYS STOOD AT THE BACK OF THE CABIN, WATCHING OVER THE PASSENGERS.
ゴオ
ROAAAR...
FOR YOU SEE...

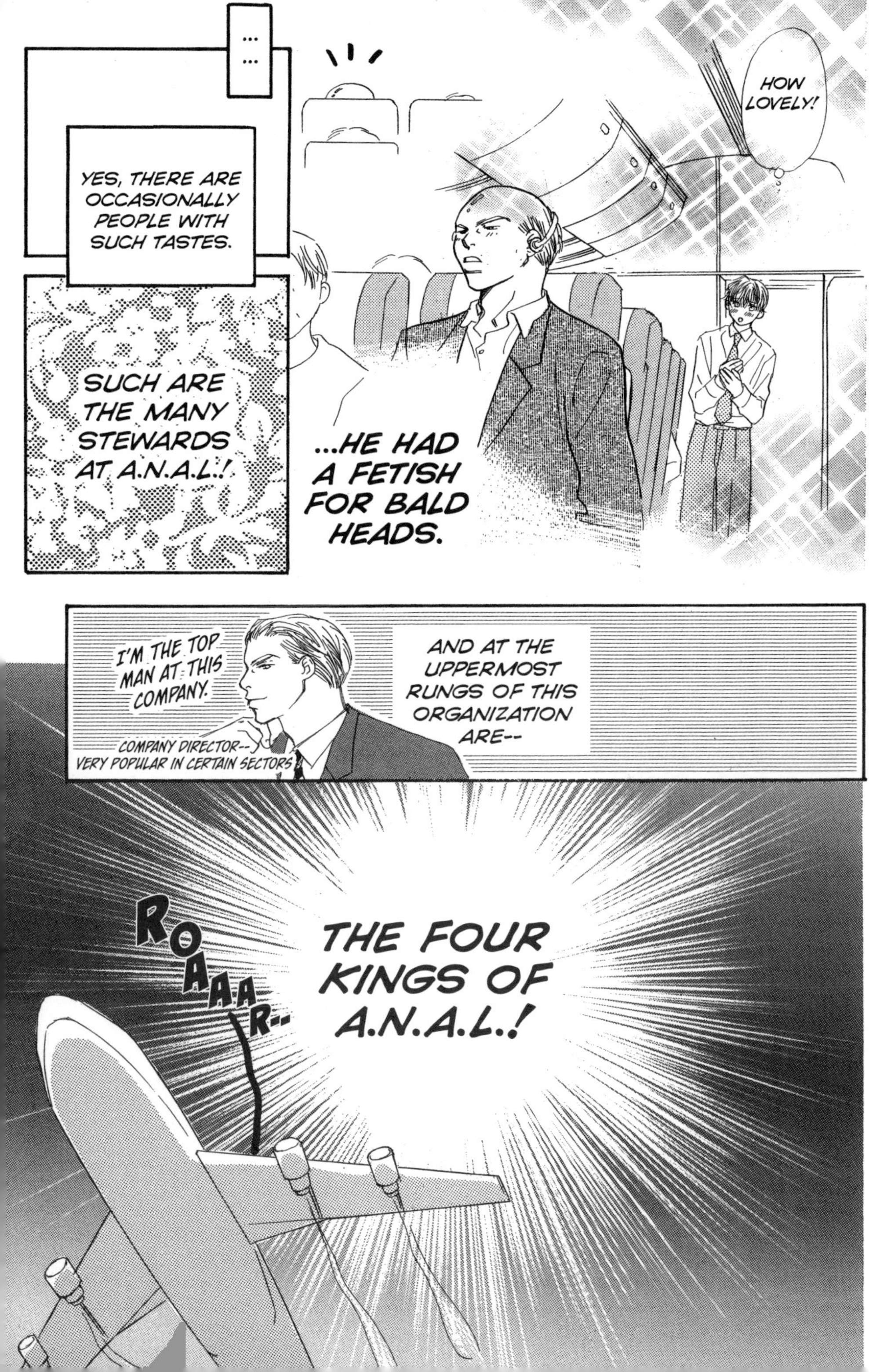
HOW LOVELY!
...HE HAD A FETISH FOR BALD HEADS.
... ...
YES, THERE ARE OCCASIONALLY PEOPLE WITH SUCH TASTES.
SUCH ARE THE MANY STEWARDS AT A.N.A.L.!
AND AT THE UPPERMOST RUNGS OF THIS ORGANIZATION ARE--
I'M THE TOP MAN AT THIS COMPANY.
COMPANY DIRECTOR-- VERY POPULAR IN CERTAIN SECTORS
THE FOUR KINGS OF A.N.A.L.!
ROAAAAR--

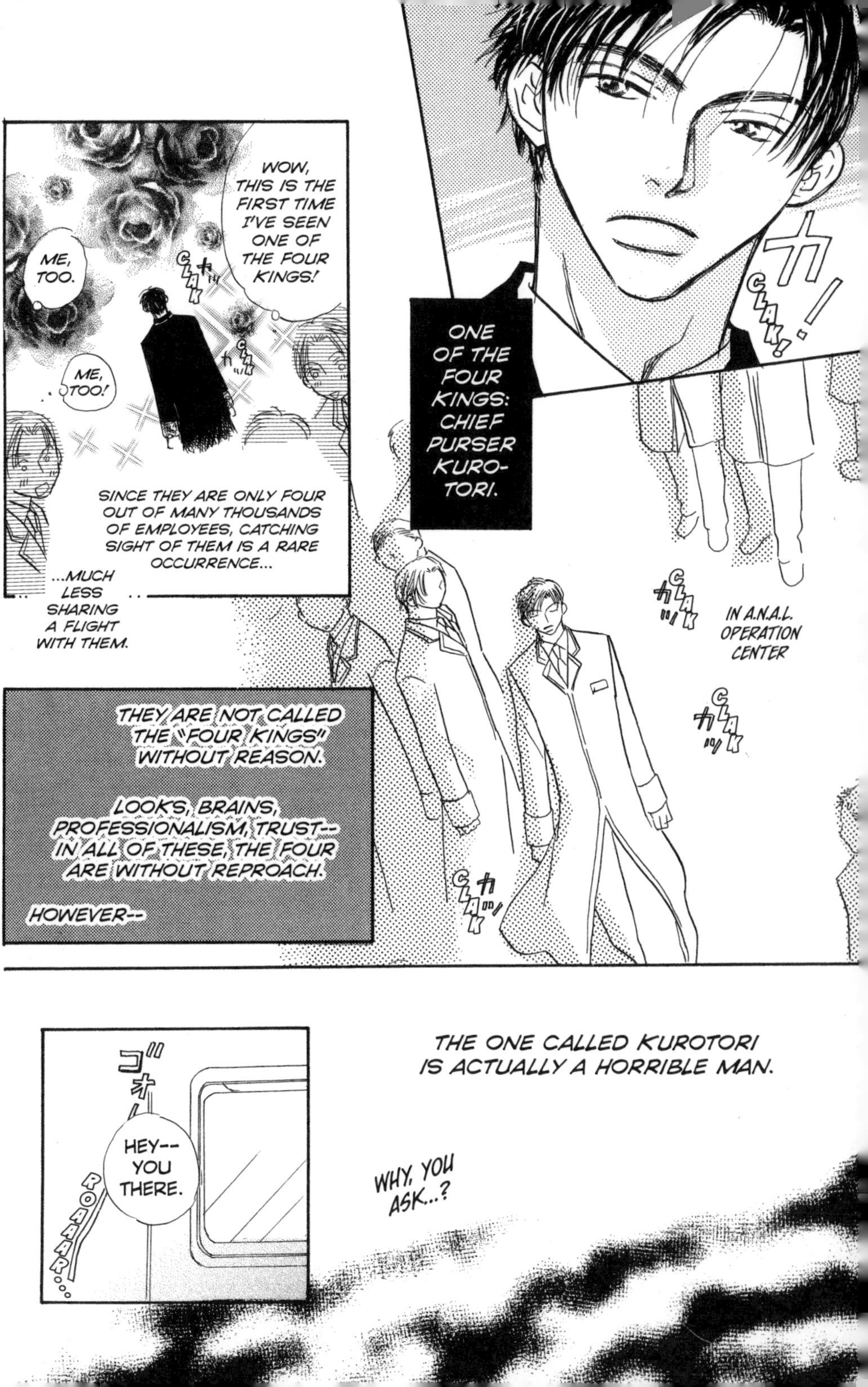
CLAK!
ONE OF THE FOUR KINGS: CHIEF PURSER KURO-TORI.
CLAK
IN A.N.A.L. OPERATION CENTER
CLAK
CLAK
WOW, THIS IS THE FIRST TIME I'VE SEEN ONE OF THE FOUR KINGS!
ME, TOO.
CLAK
CLAK
ME, TOO!
SINCE THEY ARE ONLY FOUR OUT OF MANY THOUSANDS OF EMPLOYEES, CATCHING SIGHT OF THEM IS A RARE OCCURRENCE...
...MUCH LESS SHARING A FLIGHT WITH THEM.
THEY ARE NOT CALLED THE "FOUR KINGS" WITHOUT REASON.
LOOKS, BRAINS, PROFESSIONALISM, TRUST-- IN ALL OF THESE, THE FOUR ARE WITHOUT REPROACH.
HOWEVER--
THE ONE CALLED KUROTORI IS ACTUALLY A HORRIBLE MAN.
WHY, YOU ASK...?
HEY-- YOU THERE.
ROAAAR...

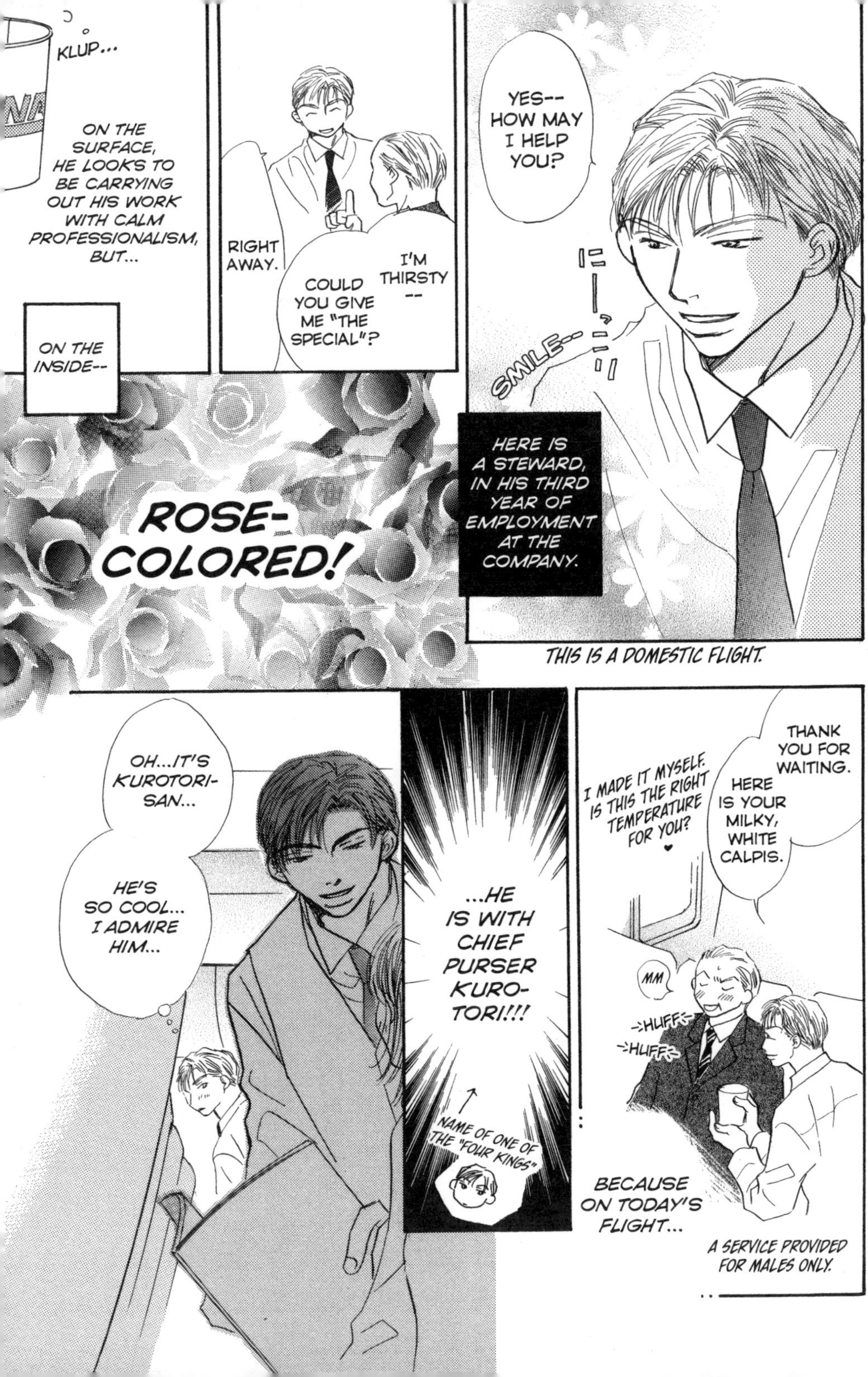

YES-- HOW MAY I HELP YOU?
SMILE--
HERE IS A STEWARD, IN HIS THIRD YEAR OF EMPLOYMENT AT THE COMPANY.
I'M THIRSTY--
COULD YOU GIVE ME "THE SPECIAL"?
RIGHT AWAY.
KLUP...
ON THE SURFACE, HE LOOKS TO BE CARRYING OUT HIS WORK WITH CALM PROFESSIONALISM, BUT...
ON THE INSIDE--
ROSE-COLORED!
THIS IS A DOMESTIC FLIGHT.
THANK YOU FOR WAITING.
HERE IS YOUR MILKY, WHITE CALPIS.
I MADE IT MYSELF. IS THIS THE RIGHT TEMPERATURE FOR YOU? ♥
MM
HUFF
HUFF
BECAUSE ON TODAY'S FLIGHT...
A SERVICE PROVIDED FOR MALES ONLY.
...HE IS WITH CHIEF PURSER KUROTORI!!!
NAME OF ONE OF THE "FOUR KINGS"
OH...IT'S KUROTORI-SAN...
HE'S SO COOL... I ADMIRE HIM...

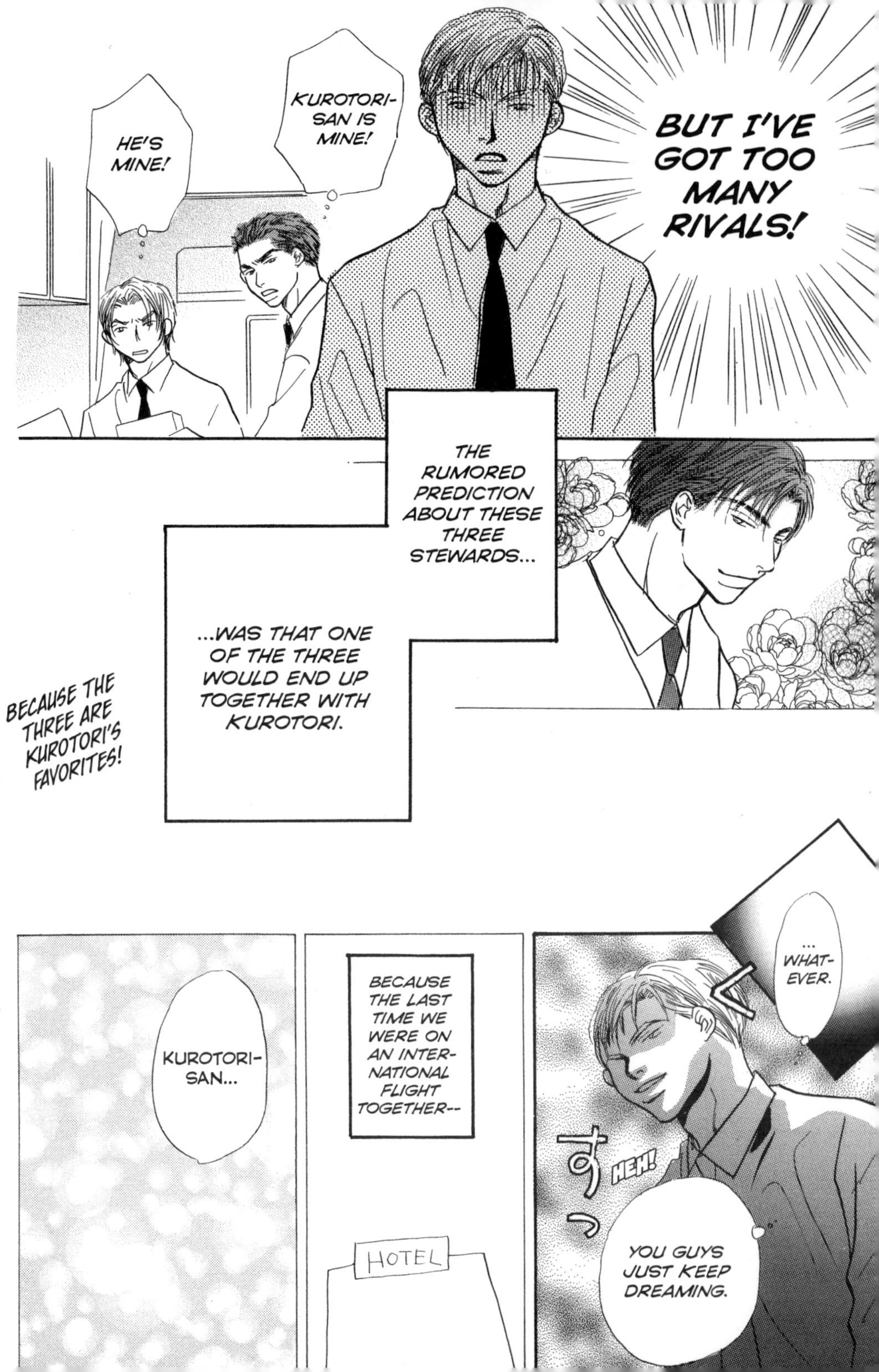
BUT I'VE GOT TOO MANY RIVALS!
KUROTORI-SAN IS MINE!
HE'S MINE!
THE RUMORED PREDICTION ABOUT THESE THREE STEWARDS...
...WAS THAT ONE OF THE THREE WOULD END UP TOGETHER WITH KUROTORI.
BECAUSE THE THREE ARE KUROTORI'S FAVORITES!
...WHATEVER.
HEH!
すっ
YOU GUYS JUST KEEP DREAMING.
BECAUSE THE LAST TIME WE WERE ON AN INTERNATIONAL FLIGHT TOGETHER--
HOTEL
KUROTORI-SAN...

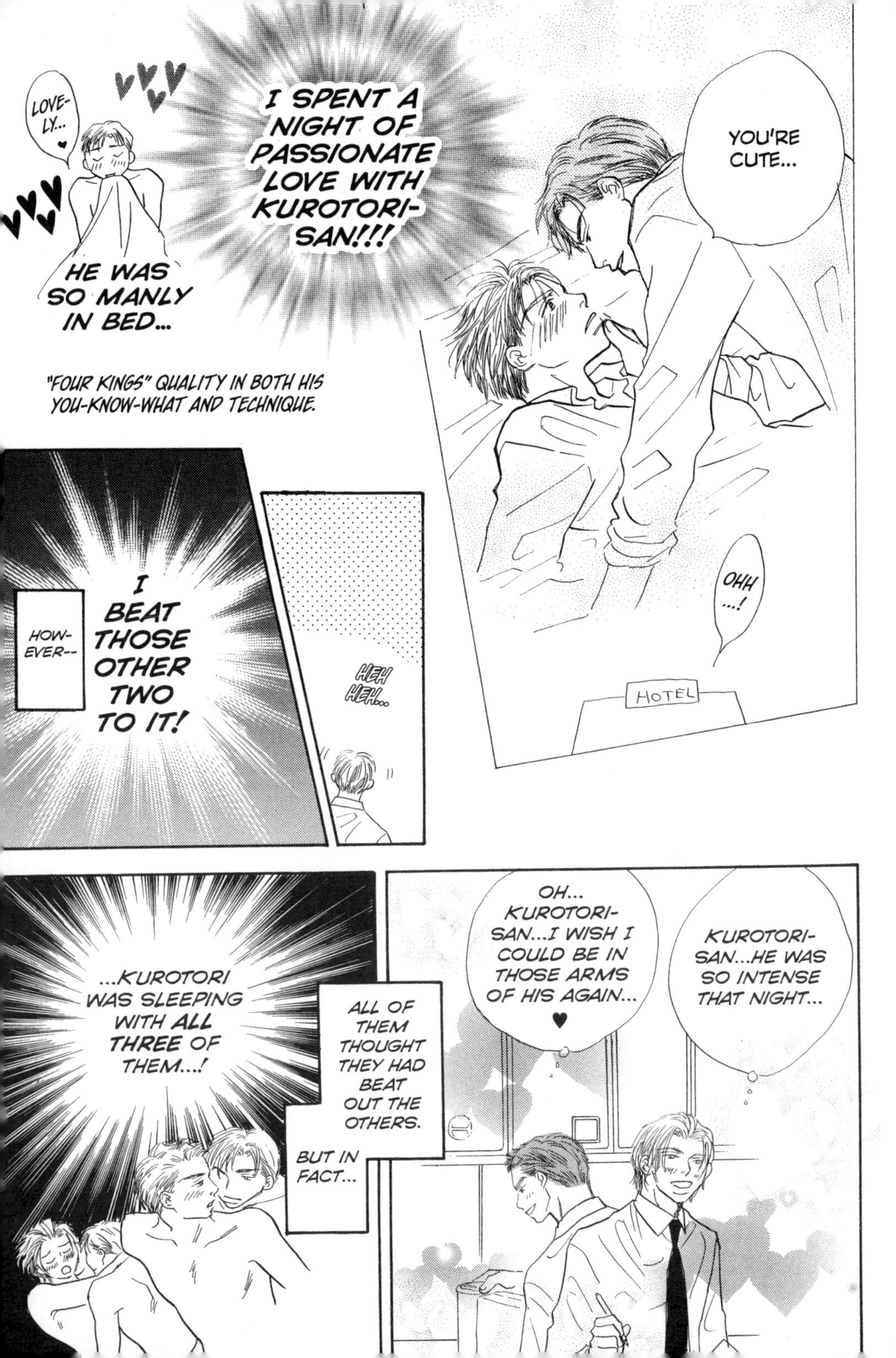
YOU'RE CUTE...
OHH ...!
HOTEL
I SPENT A NIGHT OF PASSIONATE LOVE WITH KUROTORI-SAN!!!
LOVE-LY...
HE WAS SO MANLY IN BED...
"FOUR KINGS" QUALITY IN BOTH HIS YOU-KNOW-WHAT AND TECHNIQUE.
HEH HEH...
HOW-EVER--
I BEAT THOSE OTHER TWO TO IT!
KUROTORI-SAN...HE WAS SO INTENSE THAT NIGHT...
OH... KUROTORI-SAN...I WISH I COULD BE IN THOSE ARMS OF HIS AGAIN...
ALL OF THEM THOUGHT THEY HAD BEAT OUT THE OTHERS.
BUT IN FACT...
...KUROTORI WAS SLEEPING WITH ALL THREE OF THEM...!

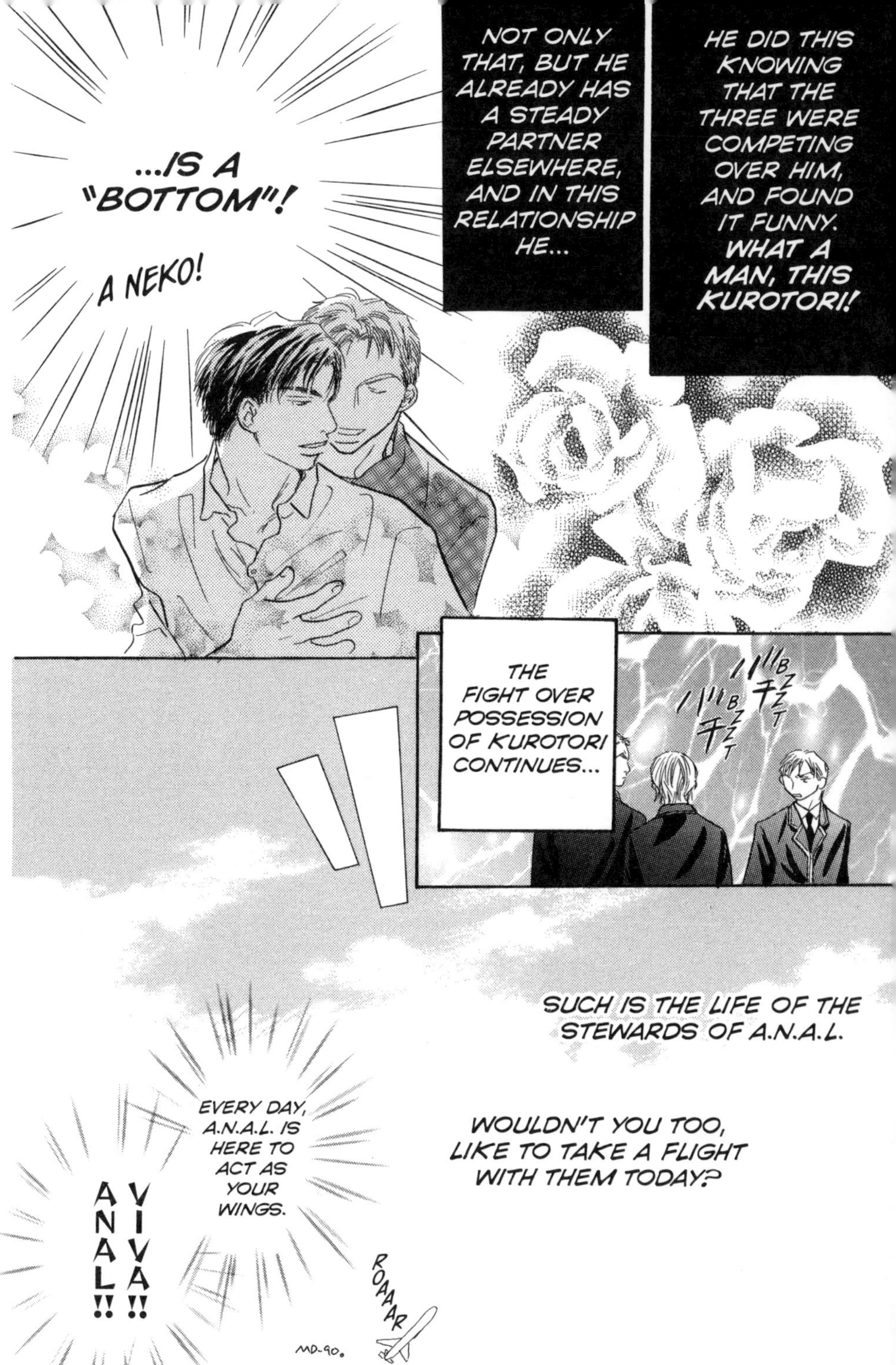
HE DID THIS KNOWING THAT THE THREE WERE COMPETING OVER HIM, AND FOUND IT FUNNY. WHAT A MAN, THIS KUROTORI!
NOT ONLY THAT, BUT HE ALREADY HAS A STEADY PARTNER ELSEWHERE, AND IN THIS RELATIONSHIP HE...
...IS A "BOTTOM"!
A NEKO!
BZZT
BZZT
THE FIGHT OVER POSSESSION OF KUROTORI CONTINUES...
SUCH IS THE LIFE OF THE STEWARDS OF A.N.A.L.
WOULDN'T YOU TOO, LIKE TO TAKE A FLIGHT WITH THEM TODAY?
EVERY DAY, A.N.A.L. IS HERE TO ACT AS YOUR WINGS.
VIVA!!
ANAL!!
ROAAAR
MD-90

**FROM A.N.A.L. WITH LOVE '99 END**

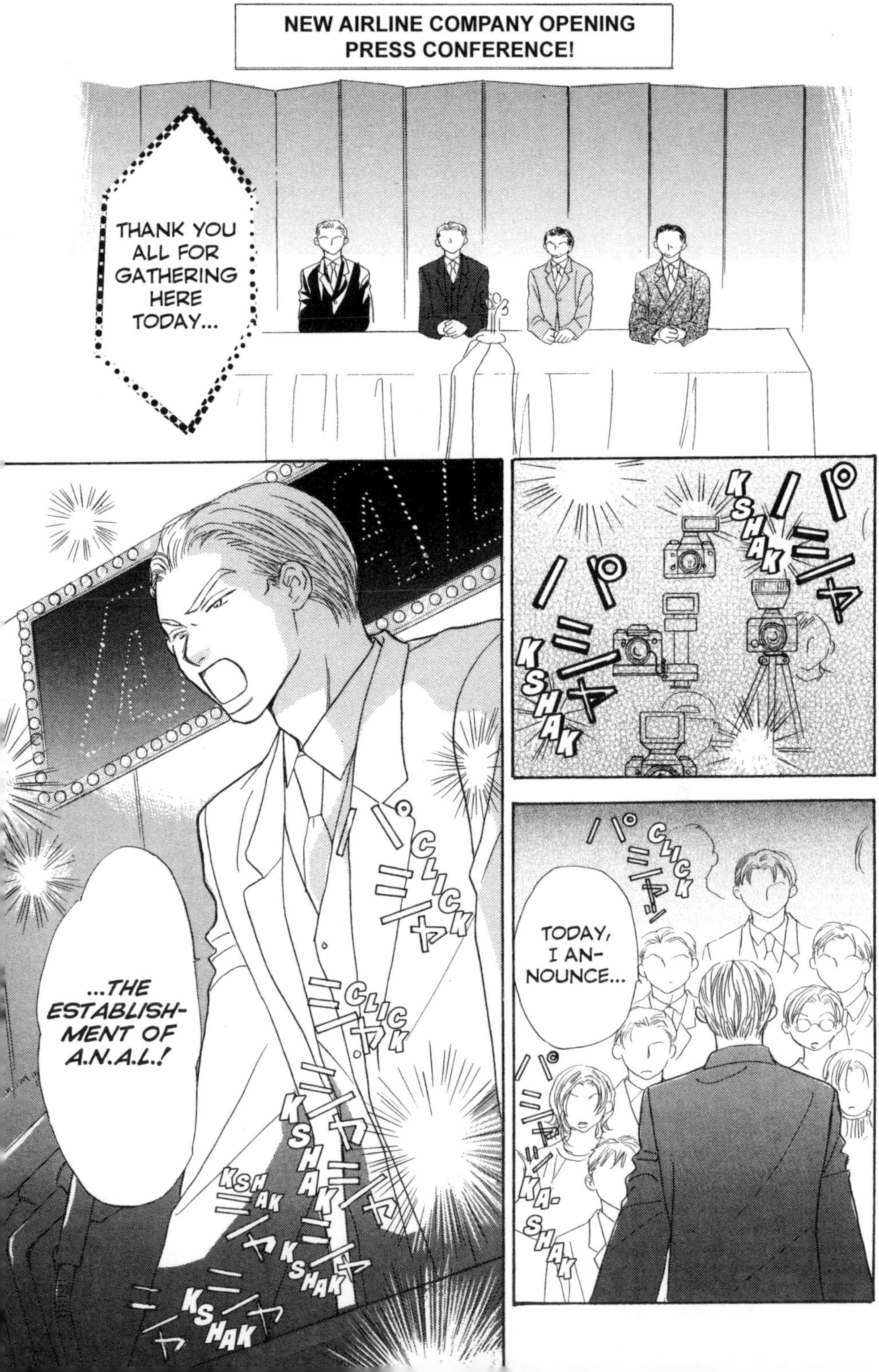
NEW AIRLINE COMPANY OPENING PRESS CONFERENCE!
THANK YOU ALL FOR GATHERING HERE TODAY...
KSHAK
KSHAK
CLICK
TODAY, I ANNOUNCE...
KA-SHAK
CLICK
...THE ESTABLISHMENT OF A.N.A.L.!
CLICK
KSHAK
KSHAK
KSHAK
KSHAK

# THE BIRTH OF A.N.A.L.

# ANAL誕生

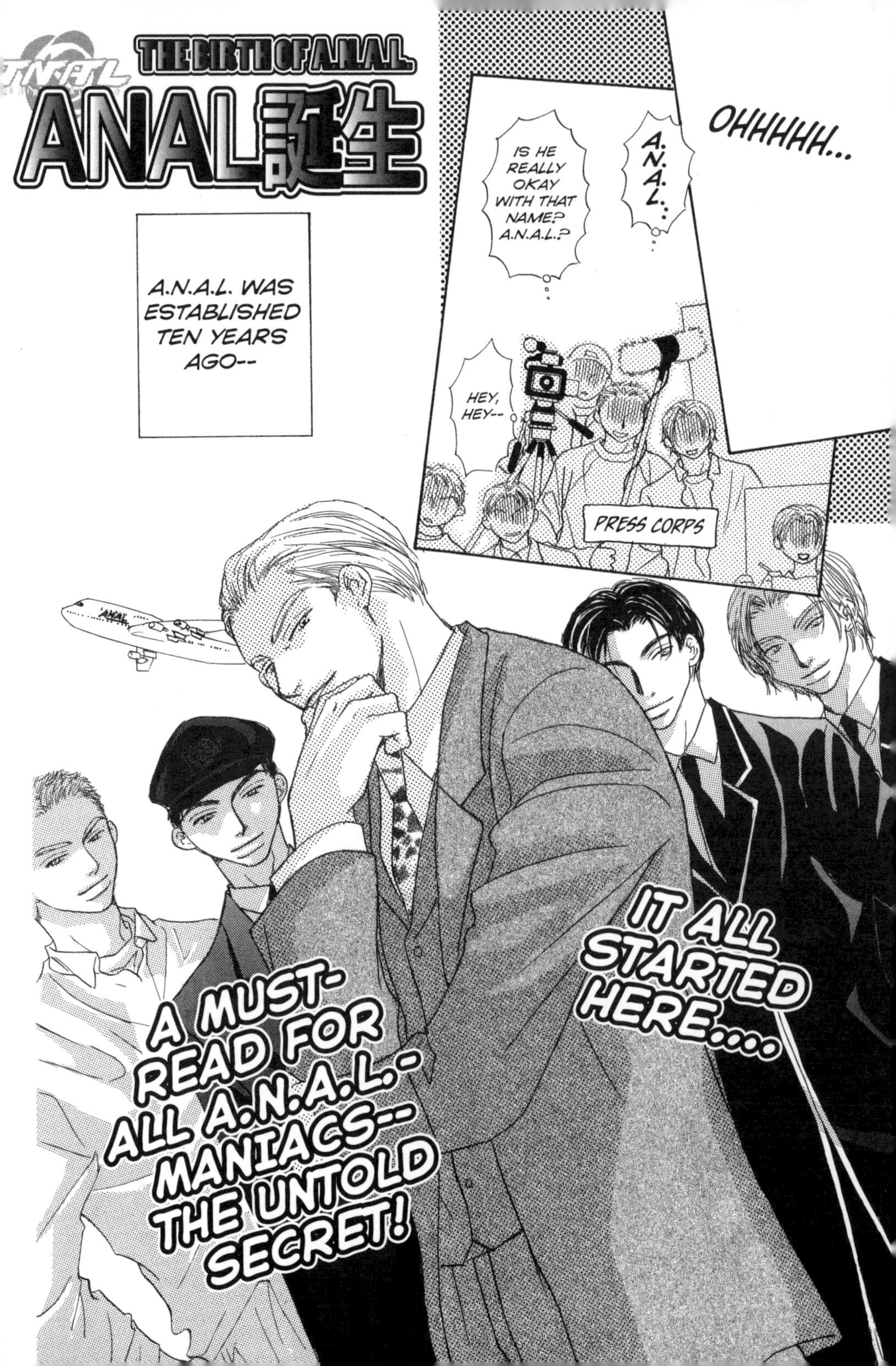
OHHHHH...
A.N.A.L...
IS HE REALLY OKAY WITH THAT NAME? A.N.A.L.?
HEY, HEY--
PRESS CORPS
A.N.A.L. WAS ESTABLISHED TEN YEARS AGO--
IT ALL STARTED HERE....
A MUST-READ FOR ALL A.N.A.L.-MANIACS--THE UNTOLD SECRET!

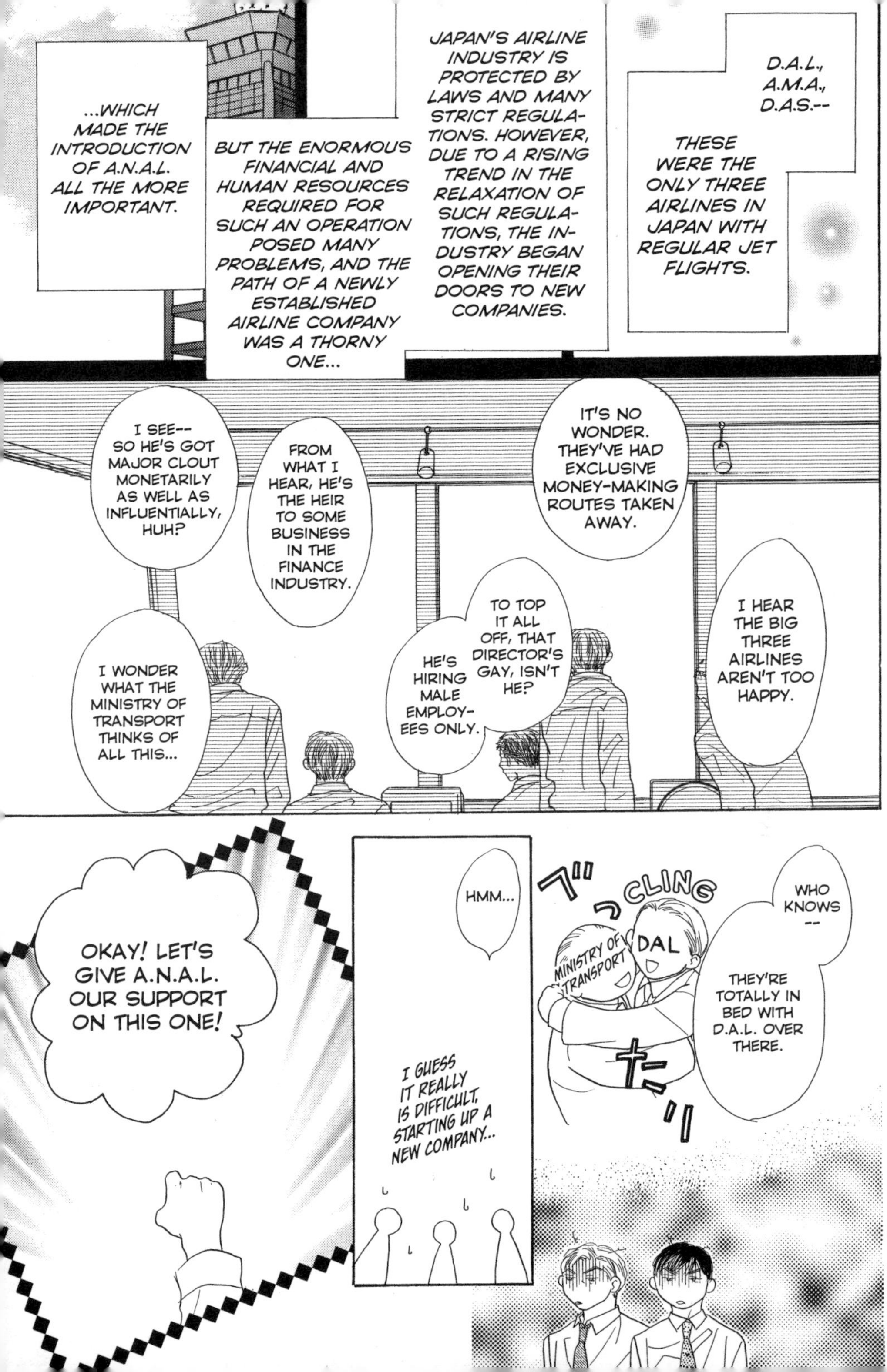
D.A.L., A.M.A., D.A.S.--
THESE WERE THE ONLY THREE AIRLINES IN JAPAN WITH REGULAR JET FLIGHTS.
JAPAN'S AIRLINE INDUSTRY IS PROTECTED BY LAWS AND MANY STRICT REGULATIONS. HOWEVER, DUE TO A RISING TREND IN THE RELAXATION OF SUCH REGULATIONS, THE INDUSTRY BEGAN OPENING THEIR DOORS TO NEW COMPANIES.
BUT THE ENORMOUS FINANCIAL AND HUMAN RESOURCES REQUIRED FOR SUCH AN OPERATION POSED MANY PROBLEMS, AND THE PATH OF A NEWLY ESTABLISHED AIRLINE COMPANY WAS A THORNY ONE...
...WHICH MADE THE INTRODUCTION OF A.N.A.L. ALL THE MORE IMPORTANT.
I HEAR THE BIG THREE AIRLINES AREN'T TOO HAPPY.
IT'S NO WONDER. THEY'VE HAD EXCLUSIVE MONEY-MAKING ROUTES TAKEN AWAY.
FROM WHAT I HEAR, HE'S THE HEIR TO SOME BUSINESS IN THE FINANCE INDUSTRY.
I SEE-- SO HE'S GOT MAJOR CLOUT MONETARILY AS WELL AS INFLUENTIALLY, HUH?
TO TOP IT ALL OFF, THAT DIRECTOR'S GAY, ISN'T HE?
HE'S HIRING MALE EMPLOYEES ONLY.
I WONDER WHAT THE MINISTRY OF TRANSPORT THINKS OF ALL THIS...
WHO KNOWS --
THEY'RE TOTALLY IN BED WITH D.A.L. OVER THERE.
CLING
DAL
MINISTRY OF TRANSPORT
HMM...
I GUESS IT REALLY IS DIFFICULT, STARTING UP A NEW COMPANY...
OKAY! LET'S GIVE A.N.A.L. OUR SUPPORT ON THIS ONE!

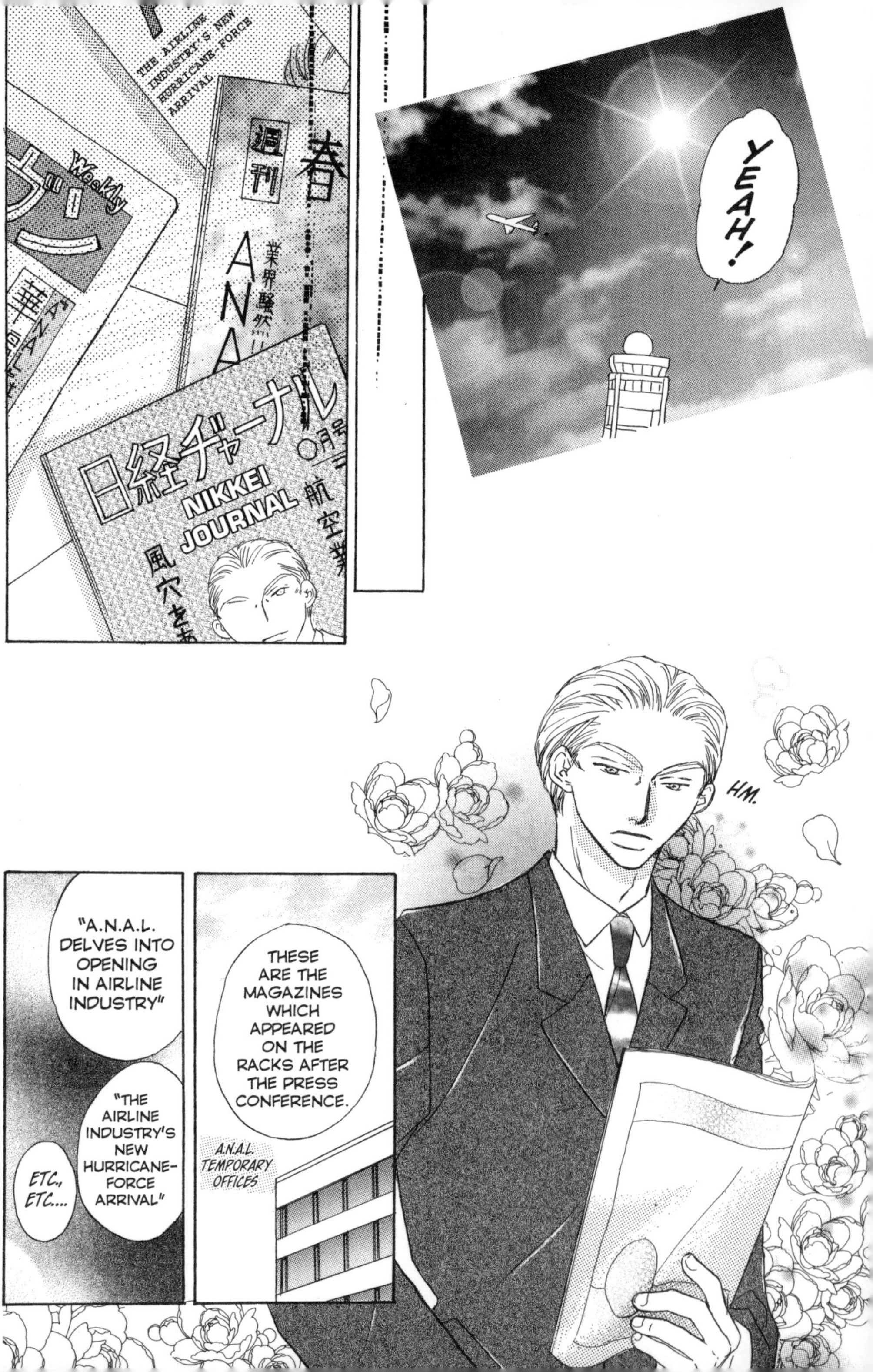
YEAH!
THE AIRLINE INDUSTRY'S NEW HURRICANE-FORCE ARRIVAL
Weekly
週刊
春
業界騒然!!
日経ジャーナル
NIKKEI JOURNAL
航空業
HM.
THESE ARE THE MAGAZINES WHICH APPEARED ON THE RACKS AFTER THE PRESS CONFERENCE.
A.N.A.L. TEMPORARY OFFICES
"A.N.A.L. DELVES INTO OPENING IN AIRLINE INDUSTRY"
"THE AIRLINE INDUSTRY'S NEW HURRICANE-FORCE ARRIVAL"
ETC., ETC....

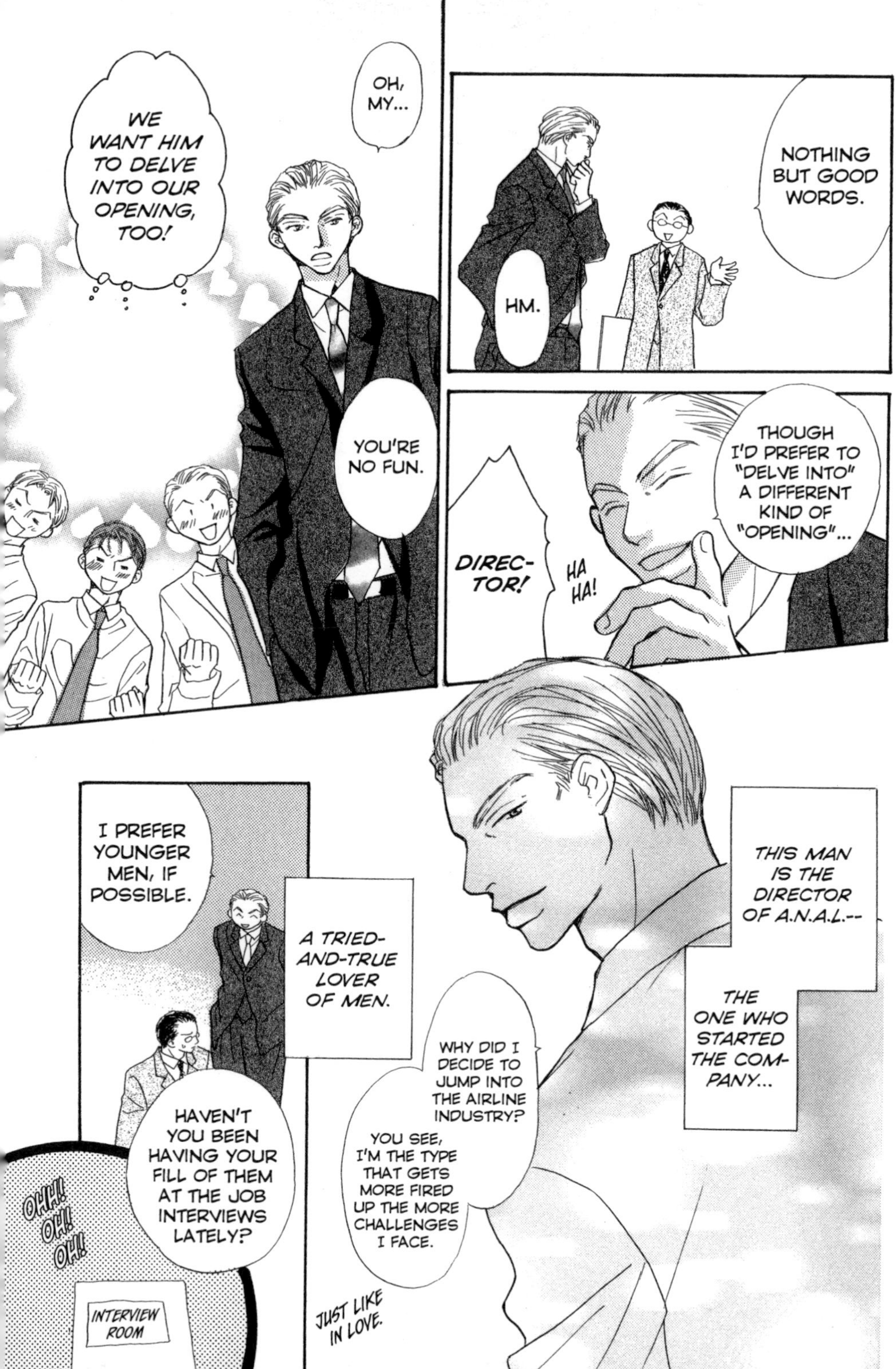

NOTHING BUT GOOD WORDS.
HM.
THOUGH I'D PREFER TO "DELVE INTO" A DIFFERENT KIND OF "OPENING"...
HA HA!
DIREC- TOR!
OH, MY...
WE WANT HIM TO DELVE INTO OUR OPENING, TOO!
YOU'RE NO FUN.
THIS MAN IS THE DIRECTOR OF A.N.A.L.--
THE ONE WHO STARTED THE COM- PANY...
WHY DID I DECIDE TO JUMP INTO THE AIRLINE INDUSTRY?
YOU SEE, I'M THE TYPE THAT GETS MORE FIRED UP THE MORE CHALLENGES I FACE.
JUST LIKE IN LOVE.
A TRIED- AND-TRUE LOVER OF MEN.
I PREFER YOUNGER MEN, IF POSSIBLE.
HAVEN'T YOU BEEN HAVING YOUR FILL OF THEM AT THE JOB INTERVIEWS LATELY?
OHH! OH! OH!
INTERVIEW ROOM

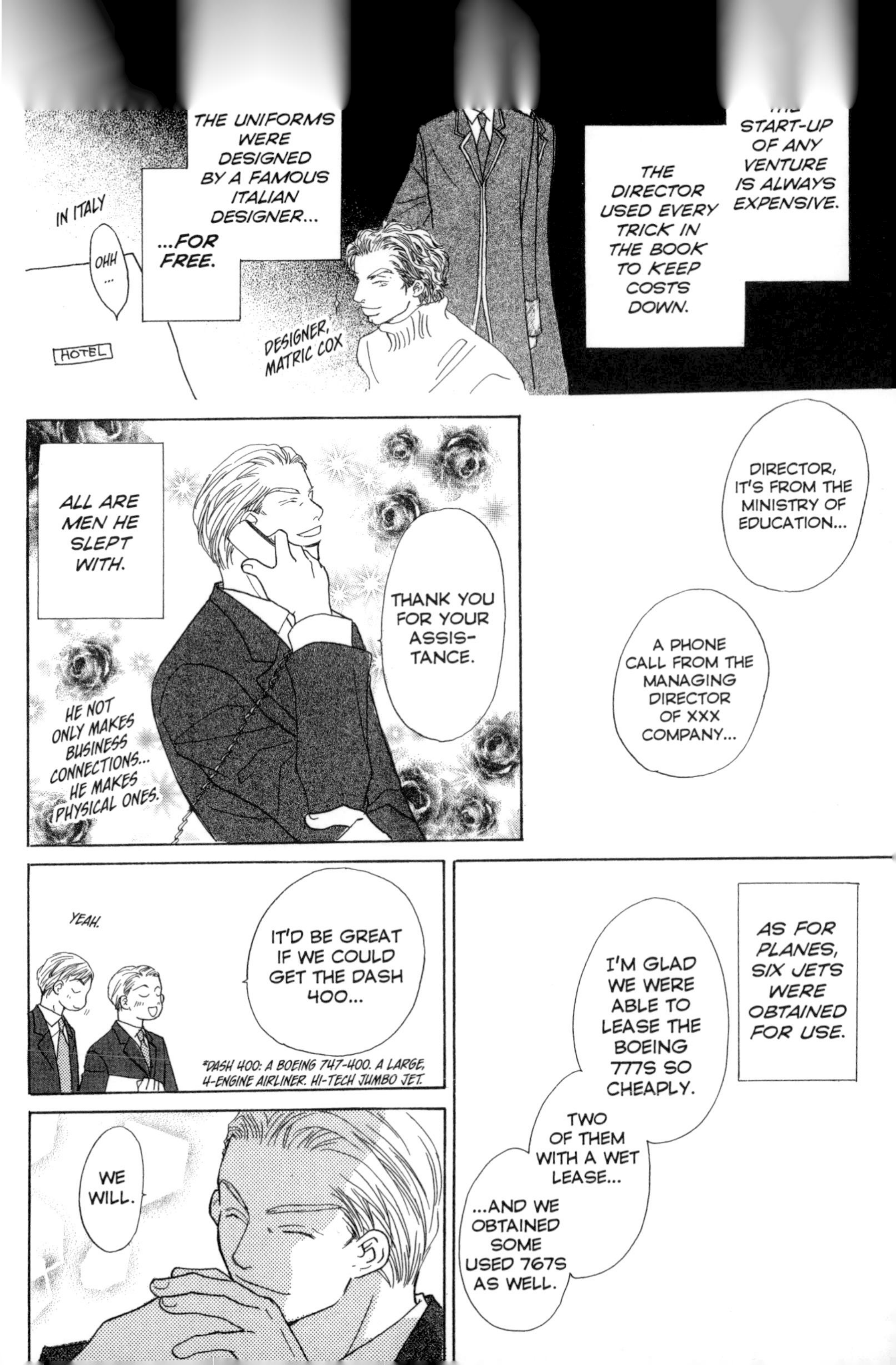
START-UP OF ANY VENTURE IS ALWAYS EXPENSIVE.
THE DIRECTOR USED EVERY TRICK IN THE BOOK TO KEEP COSTS DOWN.
THE UNIFORMS WERE DESIGNED BY A FAMOUS ITALIAN DESIGNER...
...FOR FREE.
DESIGNER, MATRIC COX
IN ITALY
OHH ...
HOTEL
DIRECTOR, IT'S FROM THE MINISTRY OF EDUCATION...
A PHONE CALL FROM THE MANAGING DIRECTOR OF XXX COMPANY...
THANK YOU FOR YOUR ASSIS-TANCE.
ALL ARE MEN HE SLEPT WITH.
HE NOT ONLY MAKES BUSINESS CONNECTIONS... HE MAKES PHYSICAL ONES.
AS FOR PLANES, SIX JETS WERE OBTAINED FOR USE.
I'M GLAD WE WERE ABLE TO LEASE THE BOEING 777S SO CHEAPLY.
TWO OF THEM WITH A WET LEASE...
...AND WE OBTAINED SOME USED 767S AS WELL.
IT'D BE GREAT IF WE COULD GET THE DASH 400...
YEAH.
*DASH 400: A BOEING 747-400. A LARGE, 4-ENGINE AIRLINER. HI-TECH JUMBO JET.
WE WILL.

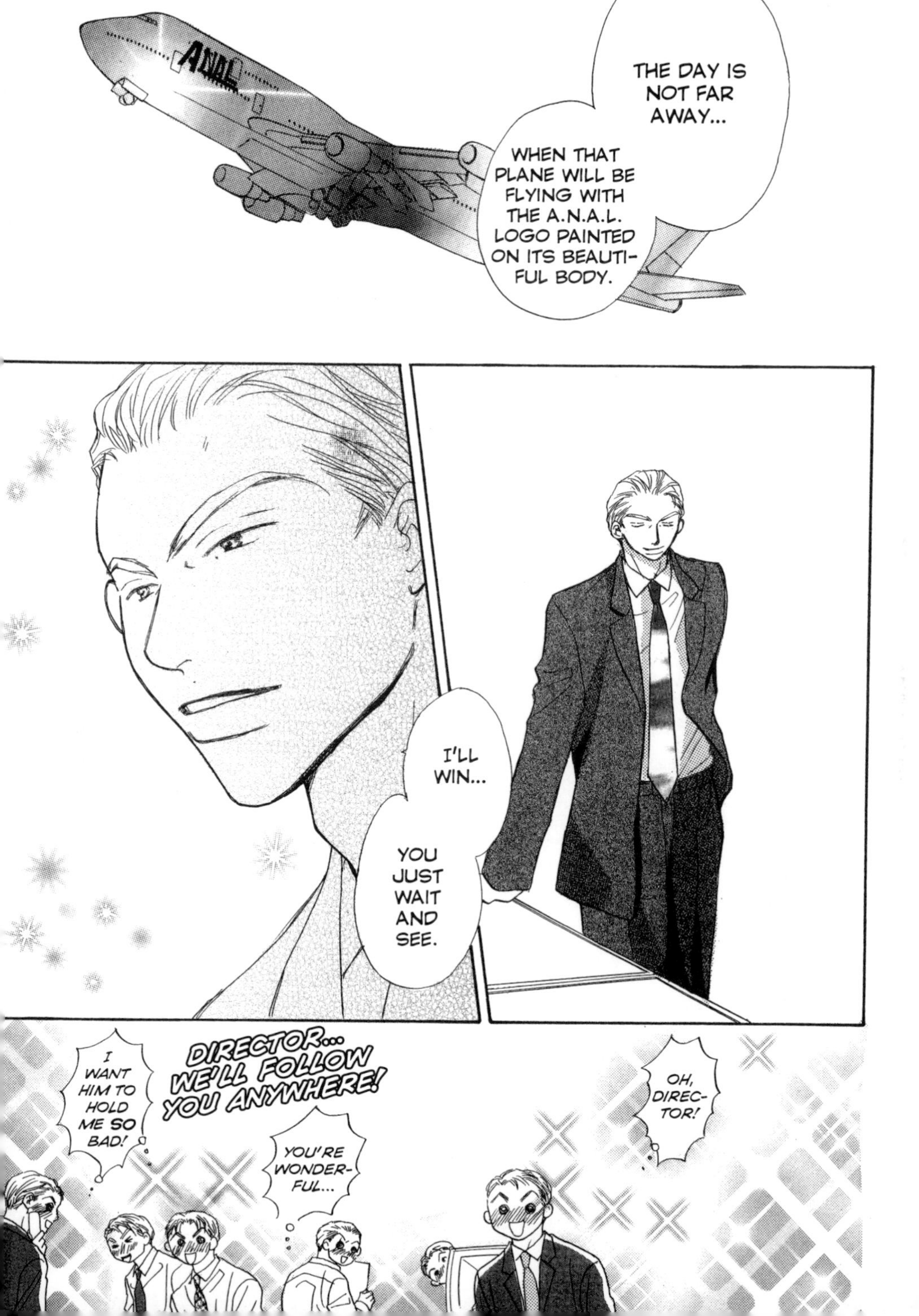
THE DAY IS NOT FAR AWAY...
WHEN THAT PLANE WILL BE FLYING WITH THE A.N.A.L. LOGO PAINTED ON ITS BEAUTIFUL BODY.
I'LL WIN...
YOU JUST WAIT AND SEE.
OH, DIRECTOR!
DIRECTOR... WE'LL FOLLOW YOU ANYWHERE!
I WANT HIM TO HOLD ME SO BAD!
YOU'RE WONDERFUL...

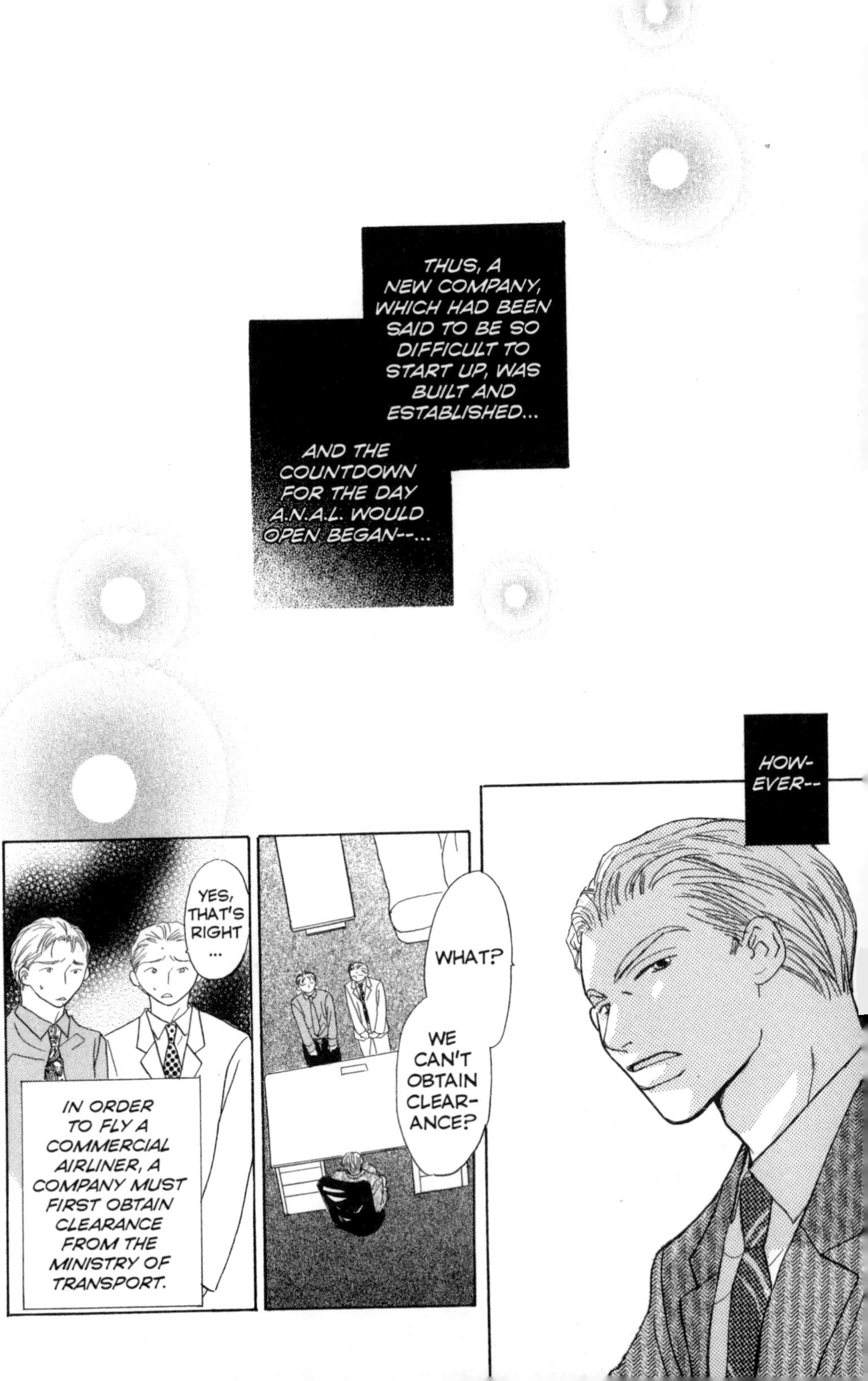
THUS, A NEW COMPANY, WHICH HAD BEEN SAID TO BE SO DIFFICULT TO START UP, WAS BUILT AND ESTABLISHED...
AND THE COUNTDOWN FOR THE DAY A.N.A.L. WOULD OPEN BEGAN--...
HOW-EVER--
WHAT?
WE CAN'T OBTAIN CLEAR-ANCE?
YES, THAT'S RIGHT ...
IN ORDER TO FLY A COMMERCIAL AIRLINER, A COMPANY MUST FIRST OBTAIN CLEARANCE FROM THE MINISTRY OF TRANSPORT.

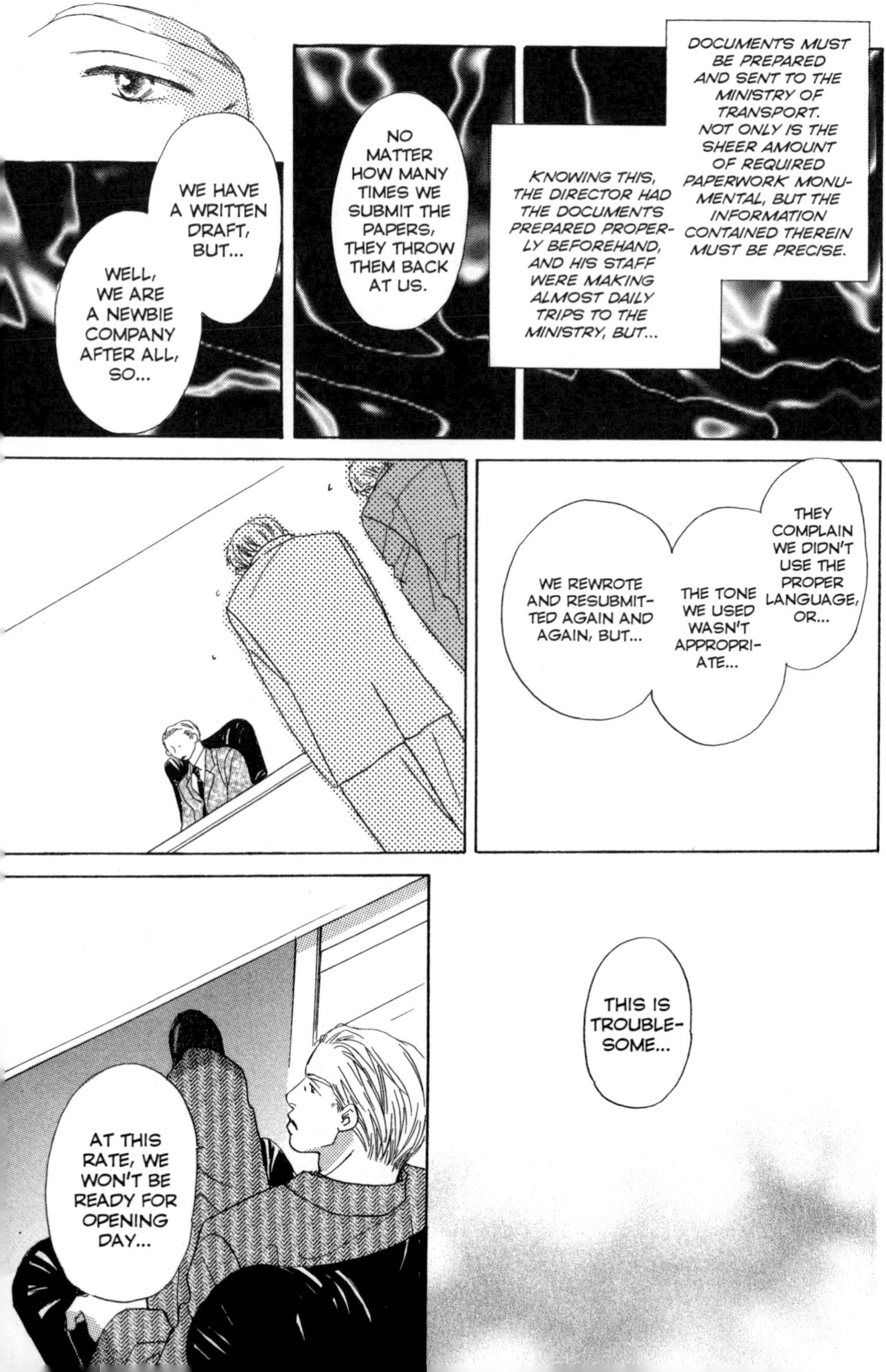
DOCUMENTS MUST BE PREPARED AND SENT TO THE MINISTRY OF TRANSPORT. NOT ONLY IS THE SHEER AMOUNT OF REQUIRED PAPERWORK MONU-MENTAL, BUT THE INFORMATION CONTAINED THEREIN MUST BE PRECISE.
KNOWING THIS, THE DIRECTOR HAD THE DOCUMENTS PREPARED PROPER-LY BEFOREHAND, AND HIS STAFF WERE MAKING ALMOST DAILY TRIPS TO THE MINISTRY, BUT...
NO MATTER HOW MANY TIMES WE SUBMIT THE PAPERS, THEY THROW THEM BACK AT US.
WE HAVE A WRITTEN DRAFT, BUT...
WELL, WE ARE A NEWBIE COMPANY AFTER ALL, SO...
THEY COMPLAIN WE DIDN'T USE THE PROPER LANGUAGE, OR...
THE TONE WE USED WASN'T APPROPRI-ATE...
WE REWROTE AND RESUBMIT-TED AGAIN AND AGAIN, BUT...
THIS IS TROUBLE-SOME...
AT THIS RATE, WE WON'T BE READY FOR OPENING DAY...

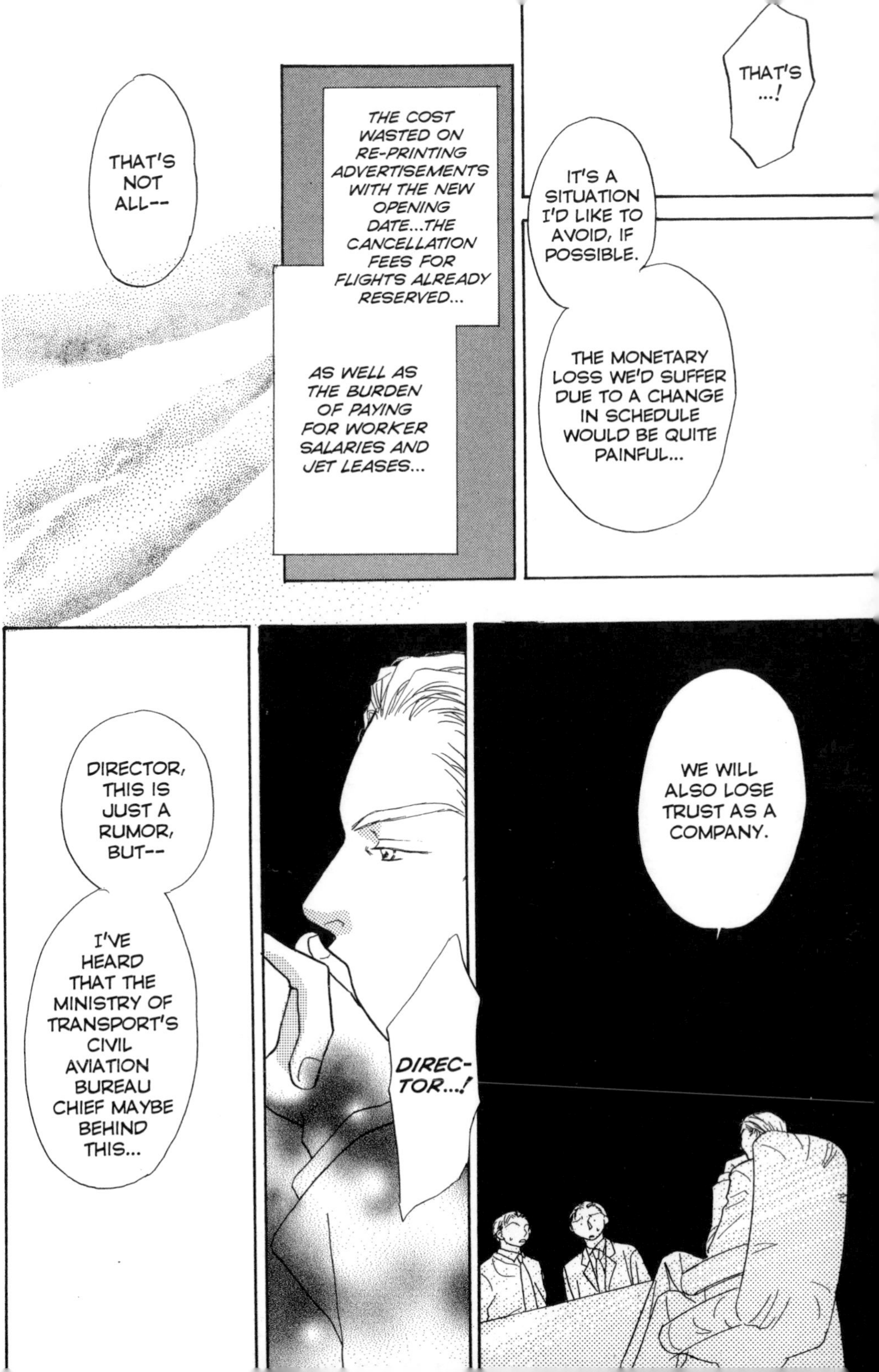
THAT'S ...!
IT'S A SITUATION I'D LIKE TO AVOID, IF POSSIBLE.
THE MONETARY LOSS WE'D SUFFER DUE TO A CHANGE IN SCHEDULE WOULD BE QUITE PAINFUL...
THE COST WASTED ON RE-PRINTING ADVERTISEMENTS WITH THE NEW OPENING DATE...THE CANCELLATION FEES FOR FLIGHTS ALREADY RESERVED...
AS WELL AS THE BURDEN OF PAYING FOR WORKER SALARIES AND JET LEASES...
THAT'S NOT ALL--
WE WILL ALSO LOSE TRUST AS A COMPANY.
DIRECTOR...!
DIRECTOR, THIS IS JUST A RUMOR, BUT--
I'VE HEARD THAT THE MINISTRY OF TRANSPORT'S CIVIL AVIATION BUREAU CHIEF MAYBE BEHIND THIS...

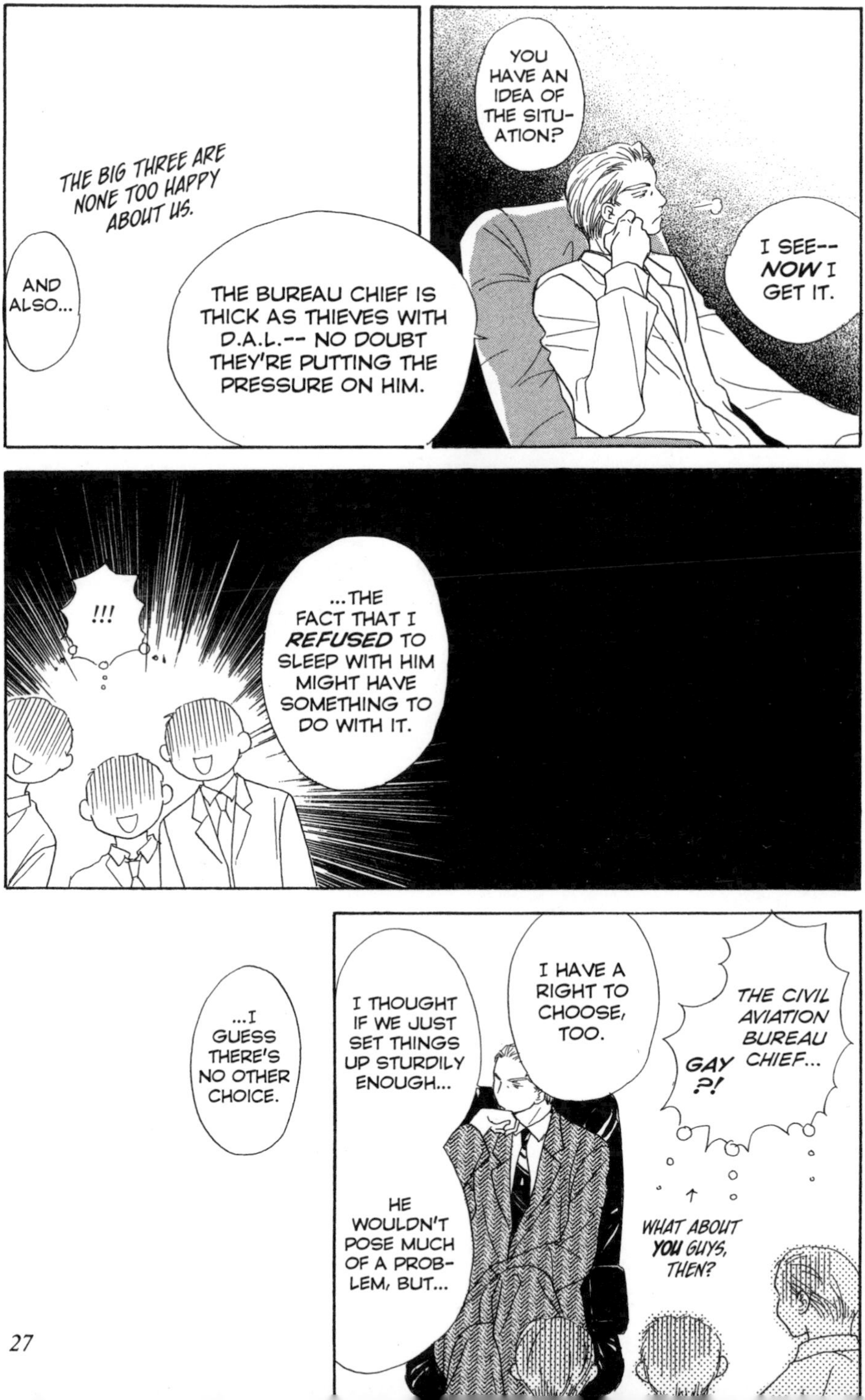
I SEE-- **NOW** I GET IT.
YOU HAVE AN IDEA OF THE SITUATION?
THE BIG THREE ARE NONE TOO HAPPY ABOUT US.
THE BUREAU CHIEF IS THICK AS THIEVES WITH D.A.L.-- NO DOUBT THEY'RE PUTTING THE PRESSURE ON HIM.
AND ALSO...
...THE FACT THAT I **REFUSED** TO SLEEP WITH HIM MIGHT HAVE SOMETHING TO DO WITH IT.
!!!
THE CIVIL AVIATION BUREAU CHIEF...
GAY ?!
WHAT ABOUT **YOU** GUYS, THEN?
I HAVE A RIGHT TO CHOOSE, TOO.
I THOUGHT IF WE JUST SET THINGS UP STURDILY ENOUGH...
HE WOULDN'T POSE MUCH OF A PROB-LEM, BUT...
...I GUESS THERE'S NO OTHER CHOICE.

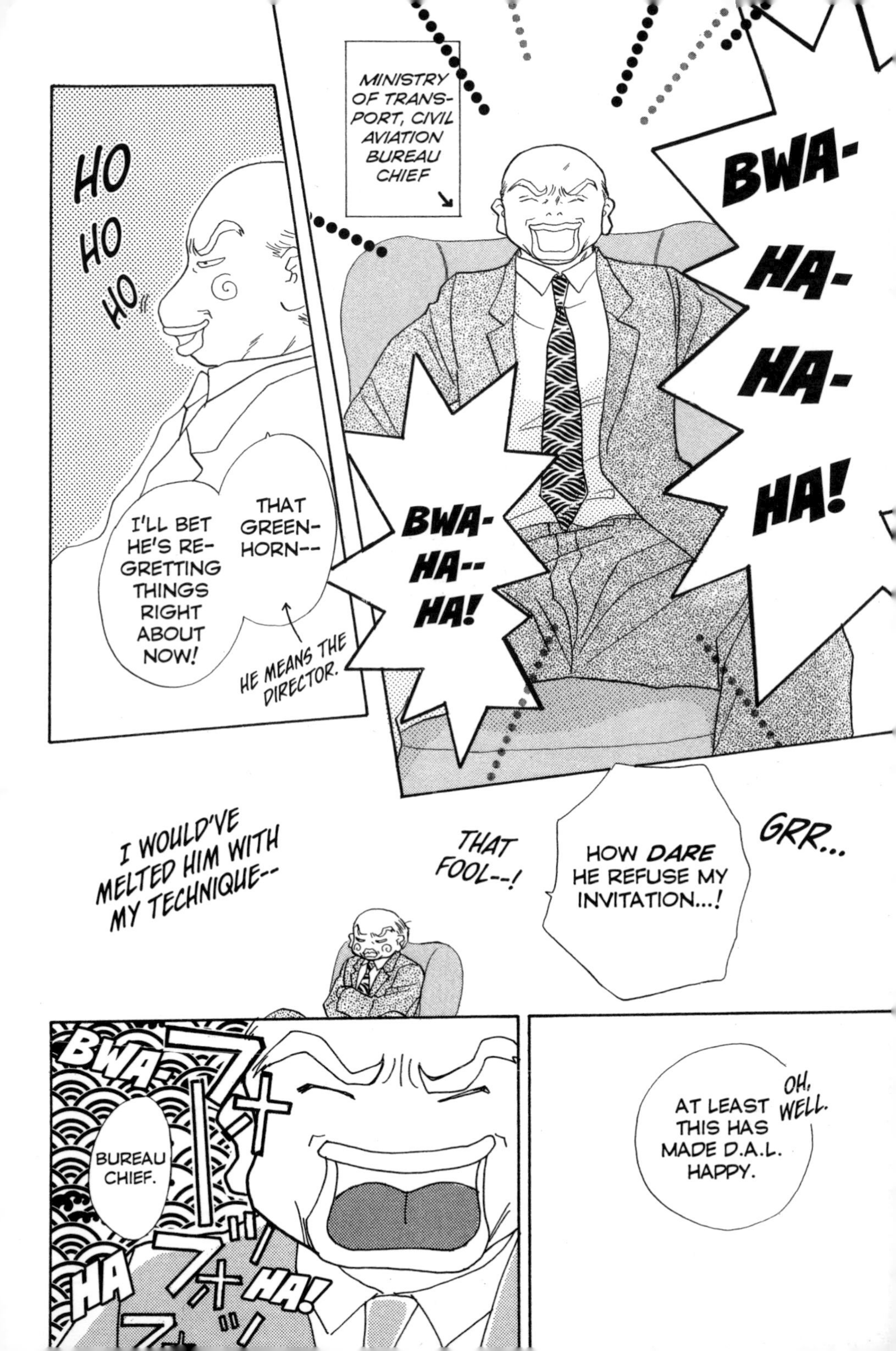
MINISTRY OF TRANSPORT, CIVIL AVIATION BUREAU CHIEF
BWA-HA-HA-HA!
BWA-HA--HA!
HO HO HO
THAT GREENHORN--
I'LL BET HE'S REGRETTING THINGS RIGHT ABOUT NOW!
HE MEANS THE DIRECTOR.
GRR...
HOW DARE HE REFUSE MY INVITATION...!
THAT FOOL--!
I WOULD'VE MELTED HIM WITH MY TECHNIQUE--
OH, WELL.
AT LEAST THIS HAS MADE D.A.L. HAPPY.
BWA-
BUREAU CHIEF.
HA
HA!

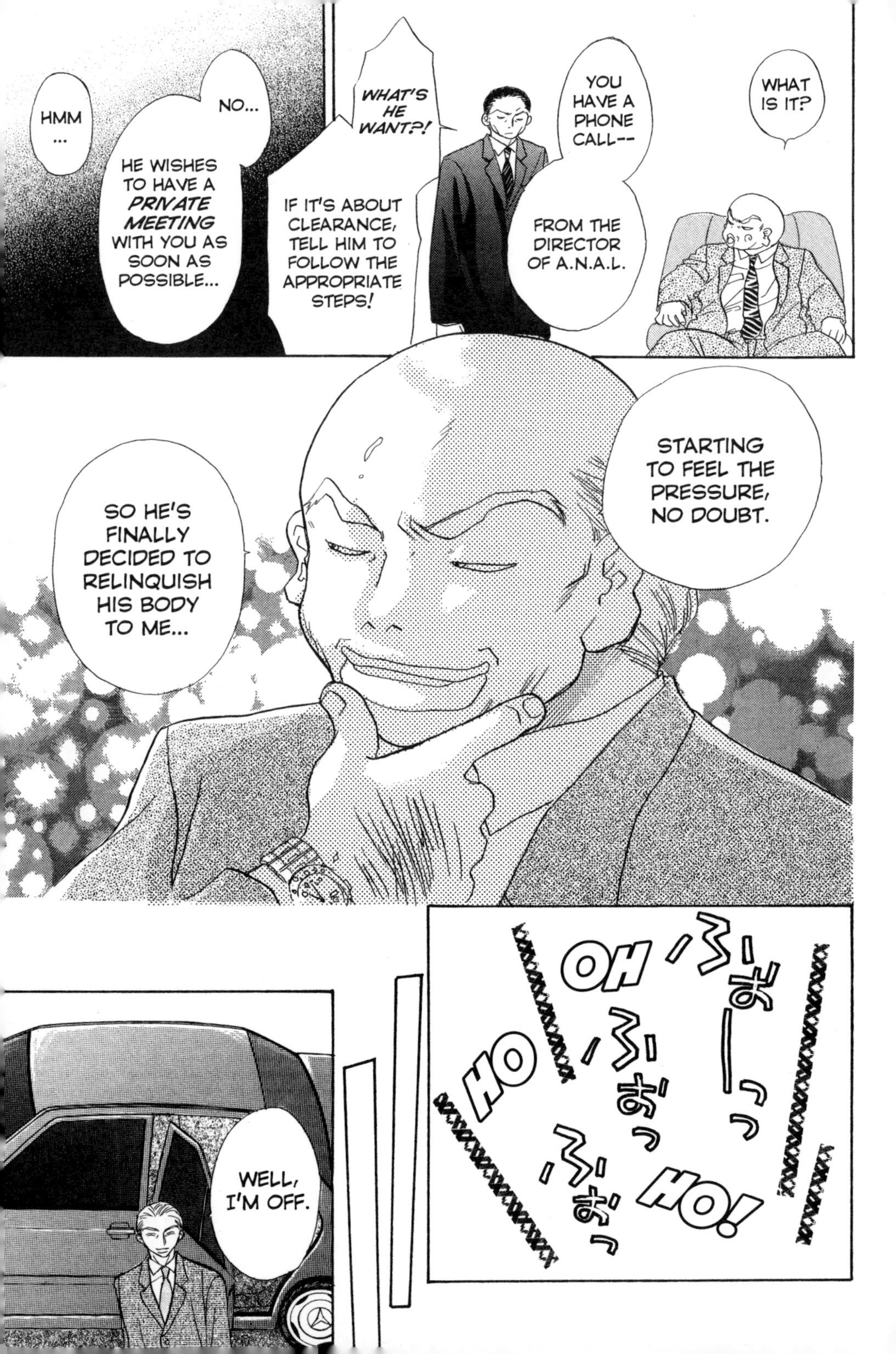
WHAT IS IT?
YOU HAVE A PHONE CALL--
FROM THE DIRECTOR OF A.N.A.L.
WHAT'S HE WANT?!
IF IT'S ABOUT CLEARANCE, TELL HIM TO FOLLOW THE APPROPRIATE STEPS!
NO...
HE WISHES TO HAVE A PRIVATE MEETING WITH YOU AS SOON AS POSSIBLE...
HMM...
STARTING TO FEEL THE PRESSURE, NO DOUBT.
SO HE'S FINALLY DECIDED TO RELINQUISH HIS BODY TO ME...
ふぉーっ
ふぉっ
ふぉっ
HO HO HO!
WELL, I'M OFF.

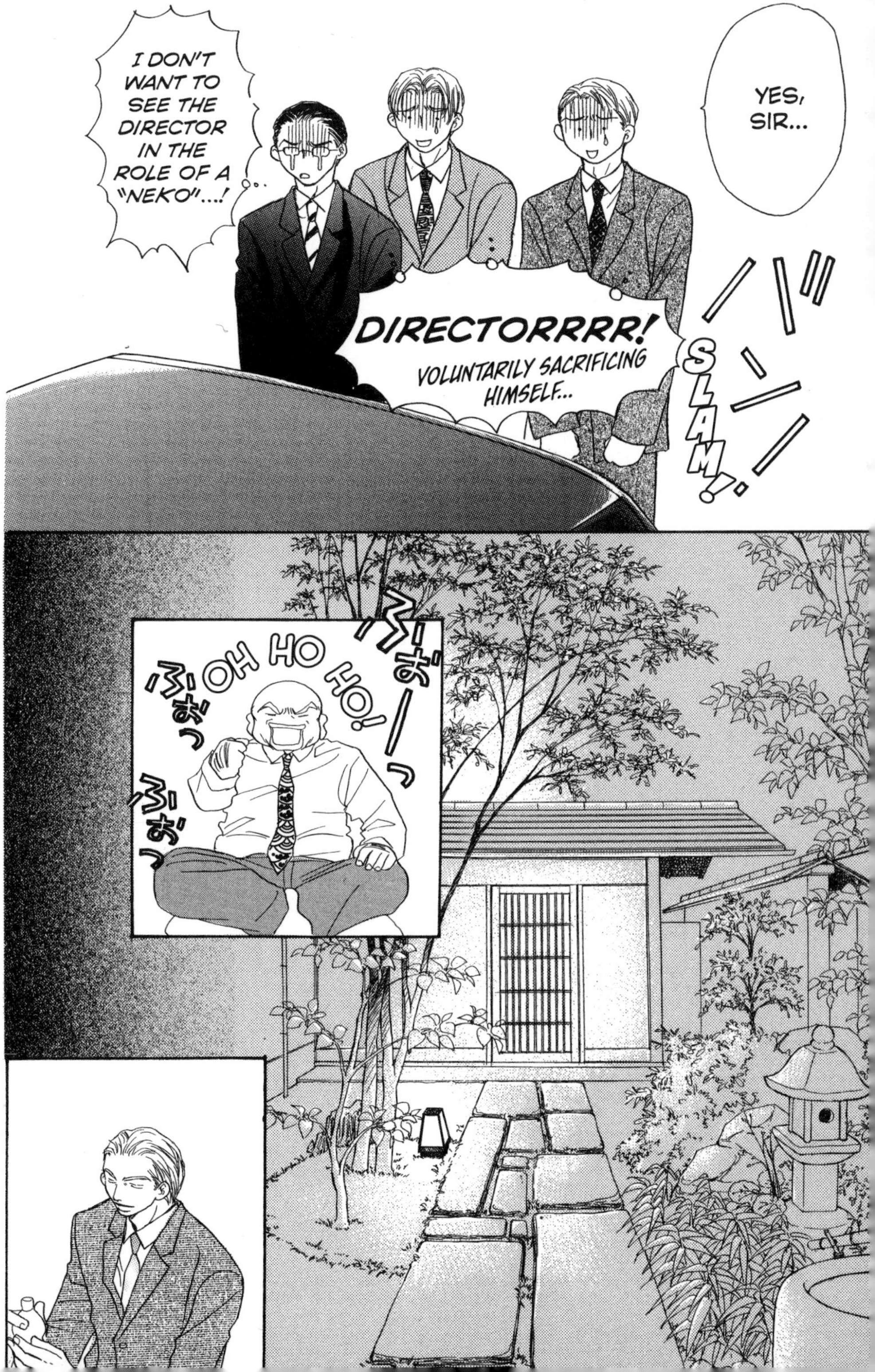
YES, SIR...
I DON'T WANT TO SEE THE DIRECTOR IN THE ROLE OF A "NEKO"...!
DIRECTORRRR!
VOLUNTARILY SACRIFICING HIMSELF...
SLAM!
ふぉーっ
OH HO HO!
ふぉっ
ふぉっ

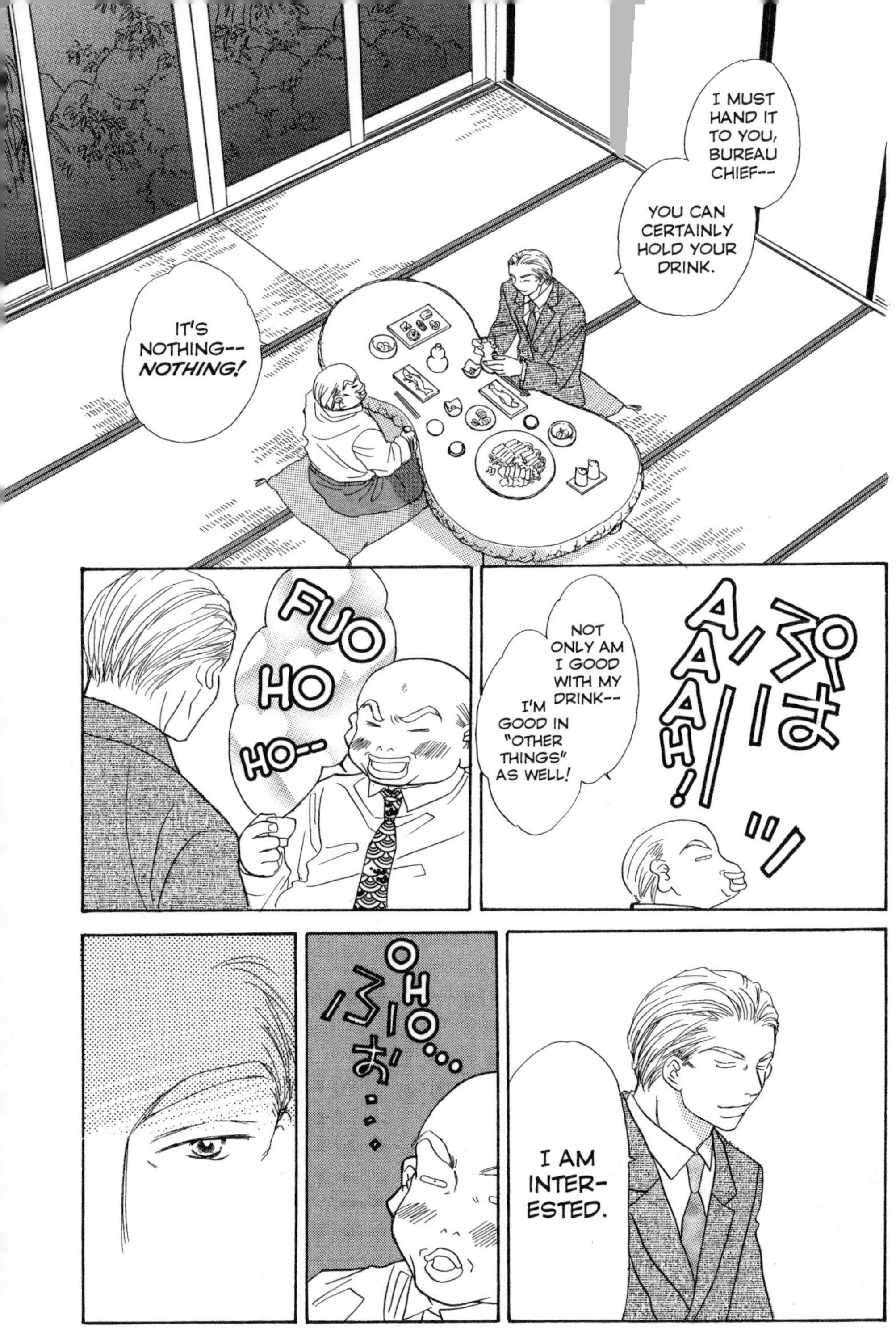
I MUST HAND IT TO YOU, BUREAU CHIEF--
YOU CAN CERTAINLY HOLD YOUR DRINK.
IT'S NOTHING-- *NOTHING!*
ぷはーーッ
AAAH!
NOT ONLY AM I GOOD WITH MY DRINK--
I'M GOOD IN "OTHER THINGS" AS WELL!
FUO HO HO--
I AM INTER-ESTED.
OHO...
ふーお...

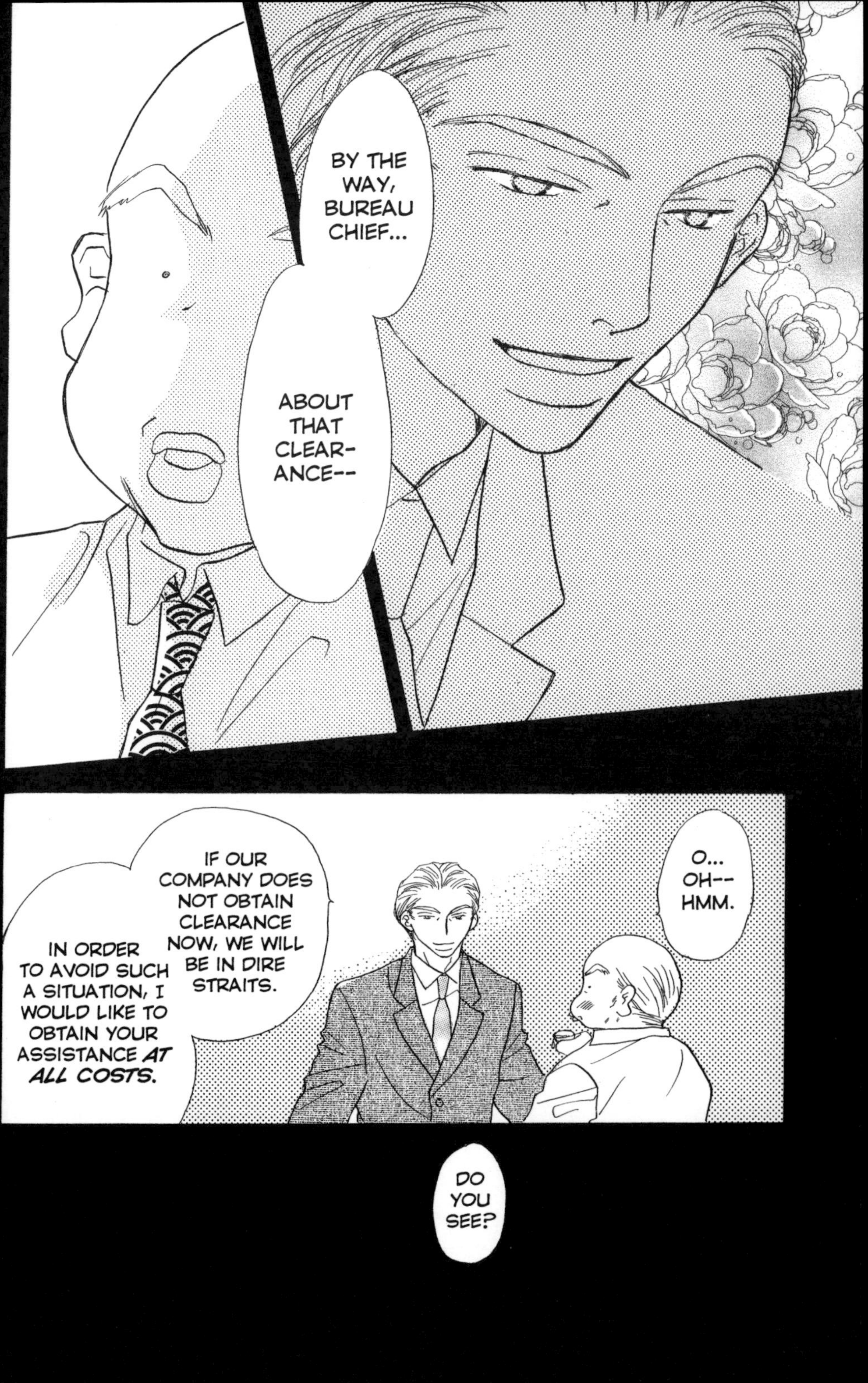
BY THE WAY, BUREAU CHIEF...
ABOUT THAT CLEARANCE--
O... OH-- HMM.
IF OUR COMPANY DOES NOT OBTAIN CLEARANCE NOW, WE WILL BE IN DIRE STRAITS.
IN ORDER TO AVOID SUCH A SITUATION, I WOULD LIKE TO OBTAIN YOUR ASSISTANCE *AT ALL COSTS*.
DO YOU SEE?

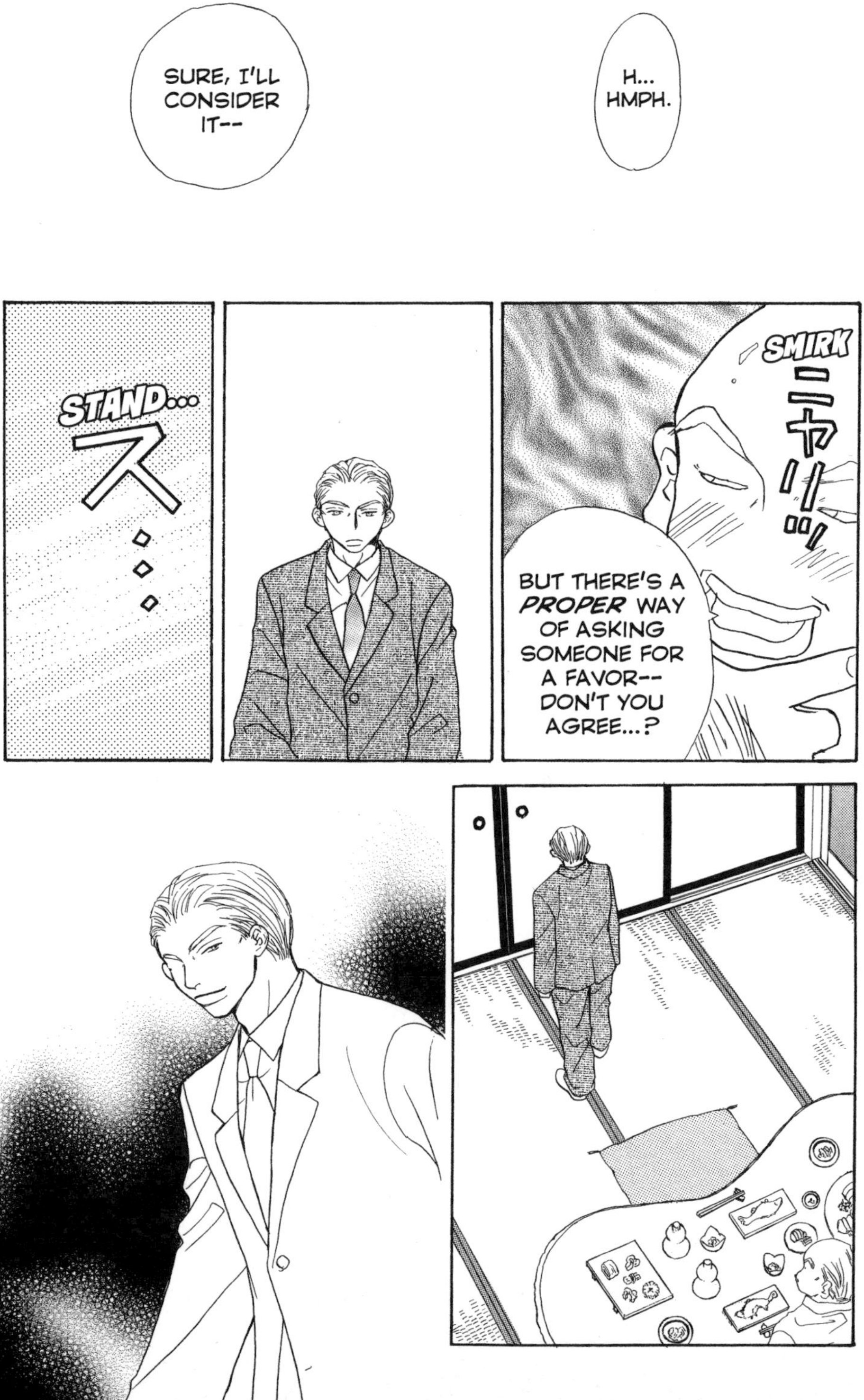
H... HMPH.
SURE, I'LL CONSIDER IT--
SMIRK
ニヤリ
BUT THERE'S A ***PROPER*** WAY OF ASKING SOMEONE FOR A FAVOR-- DON'T YOU AGREE...?
STAND...
ス...

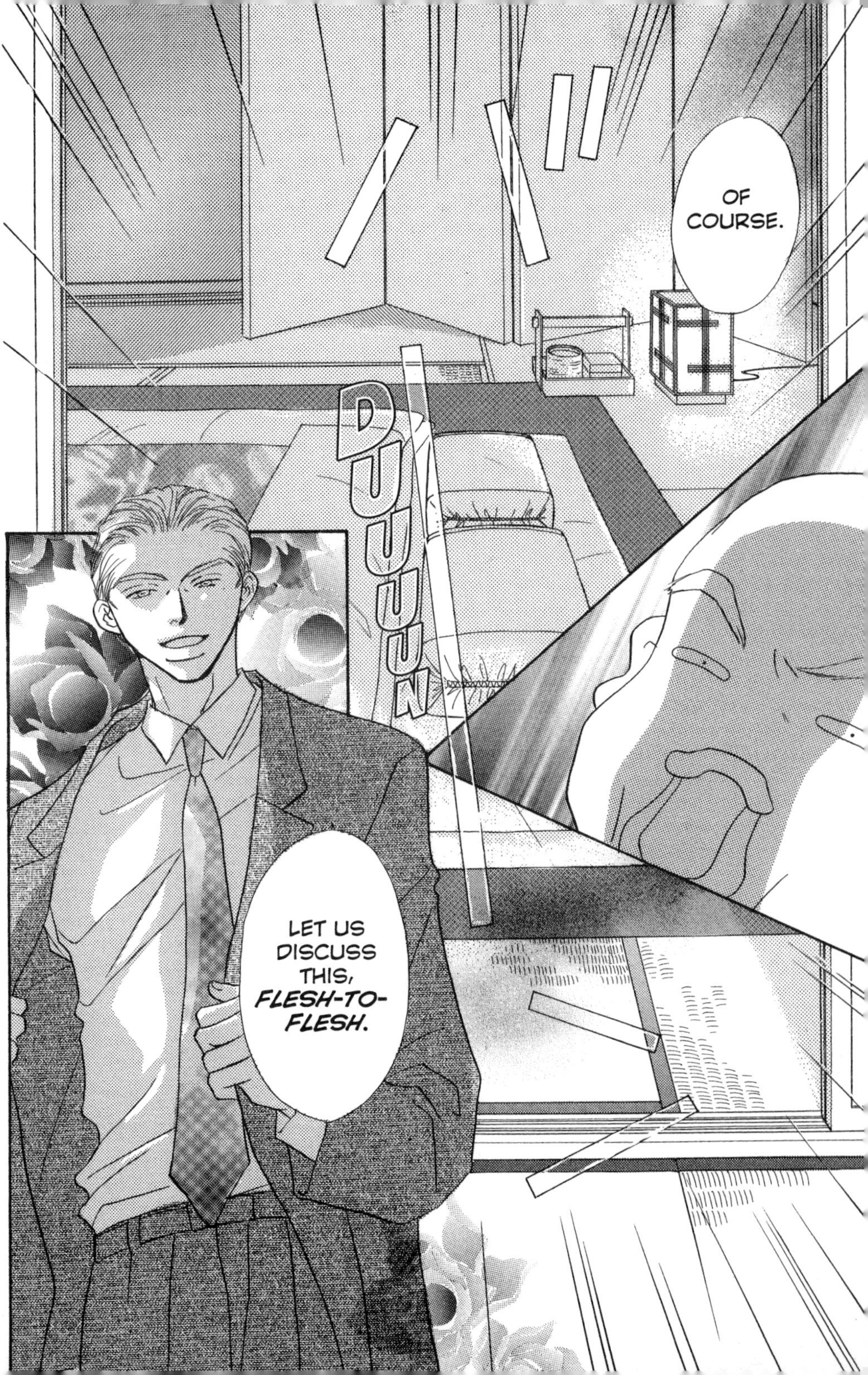
OF COURSE.
DUUUUUN
LET US DISCUSS THIS, *FLESH-TO-FLESH*.

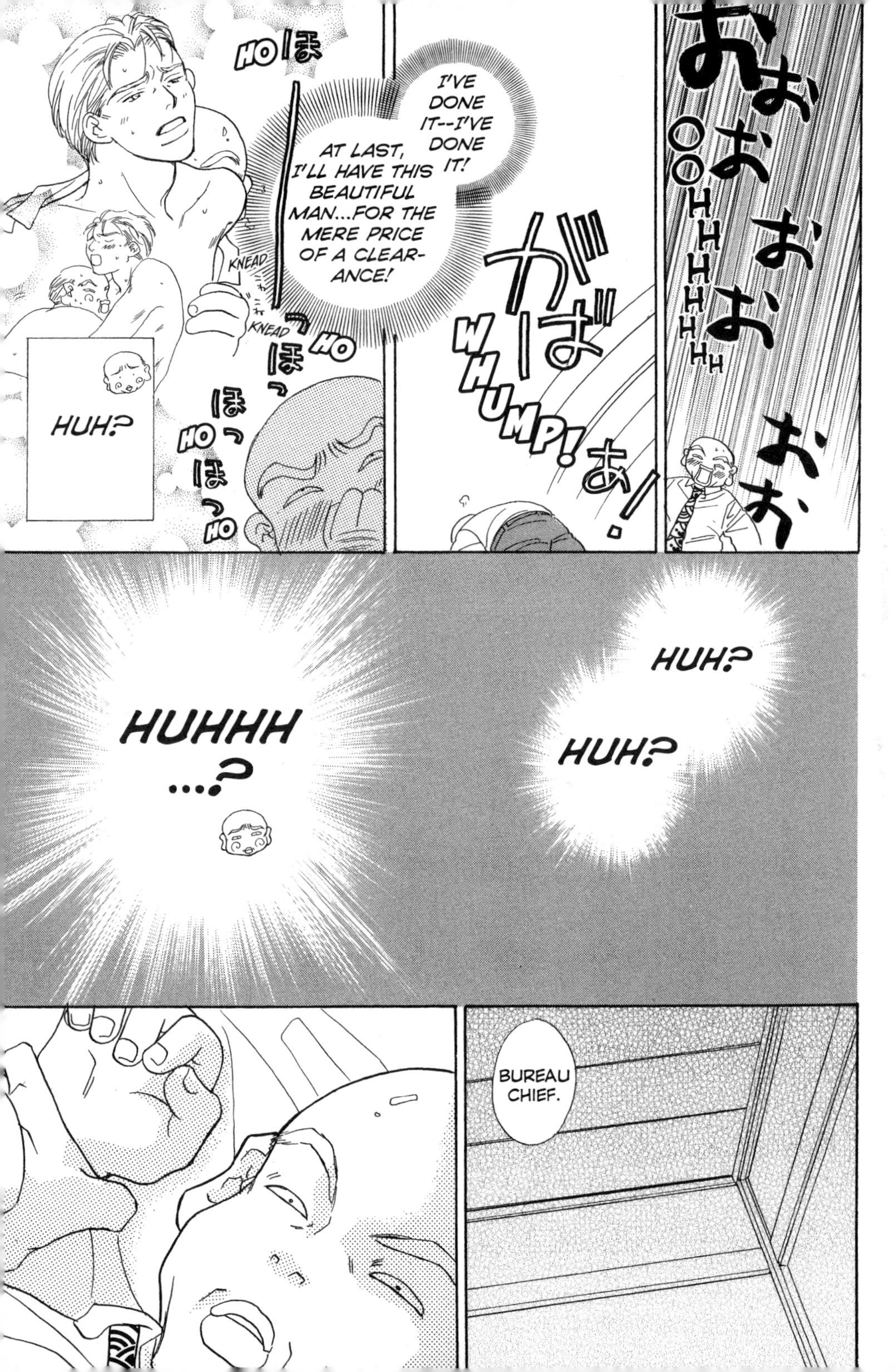

おぉおおぉおお
OOHHHHHHHHH
おお
がばっ
WHUMP!
あ!
I'VE DONE IT--I'VE DONE IT!
AT LAST, I'LL HAVE THIS BEAUTIFUL MAN...FOR THE MERE PRICE OF A CLEARANCE!
HO ほ
KNEAD
KNEAD
HO ほっ
HO ほっ
HO ほっ
HUH?
HUH?
HUH?
HUHHH ...?
BUREAU CHIEF.

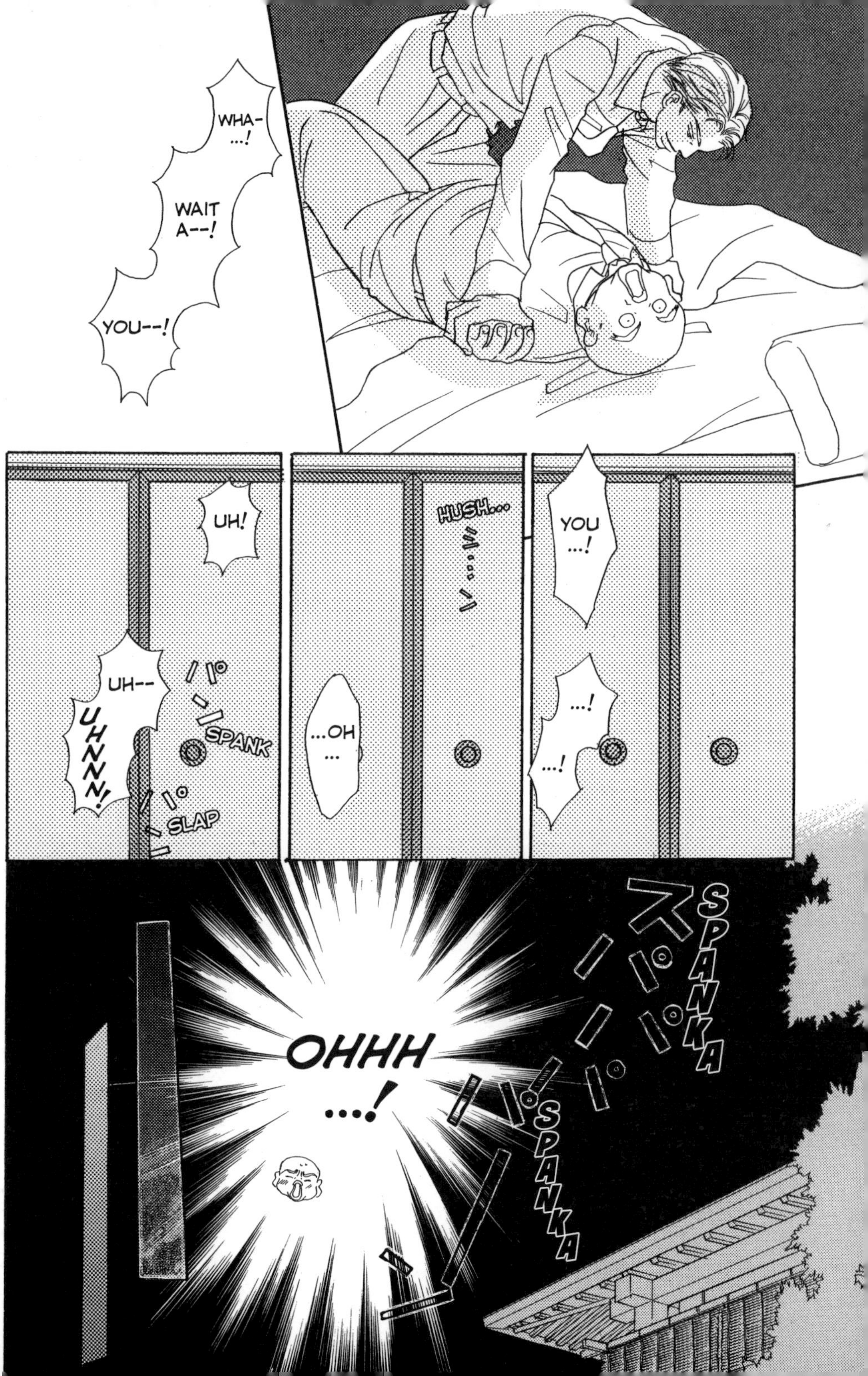
WHA-...!
WAIT A--!
YOU--!
YOU...!
...!
...!
HUSH...
...OH...
UH!
UH--
UHNNN!
SPANK
SLAP
SPANKA
SPANKA
OHHH...!

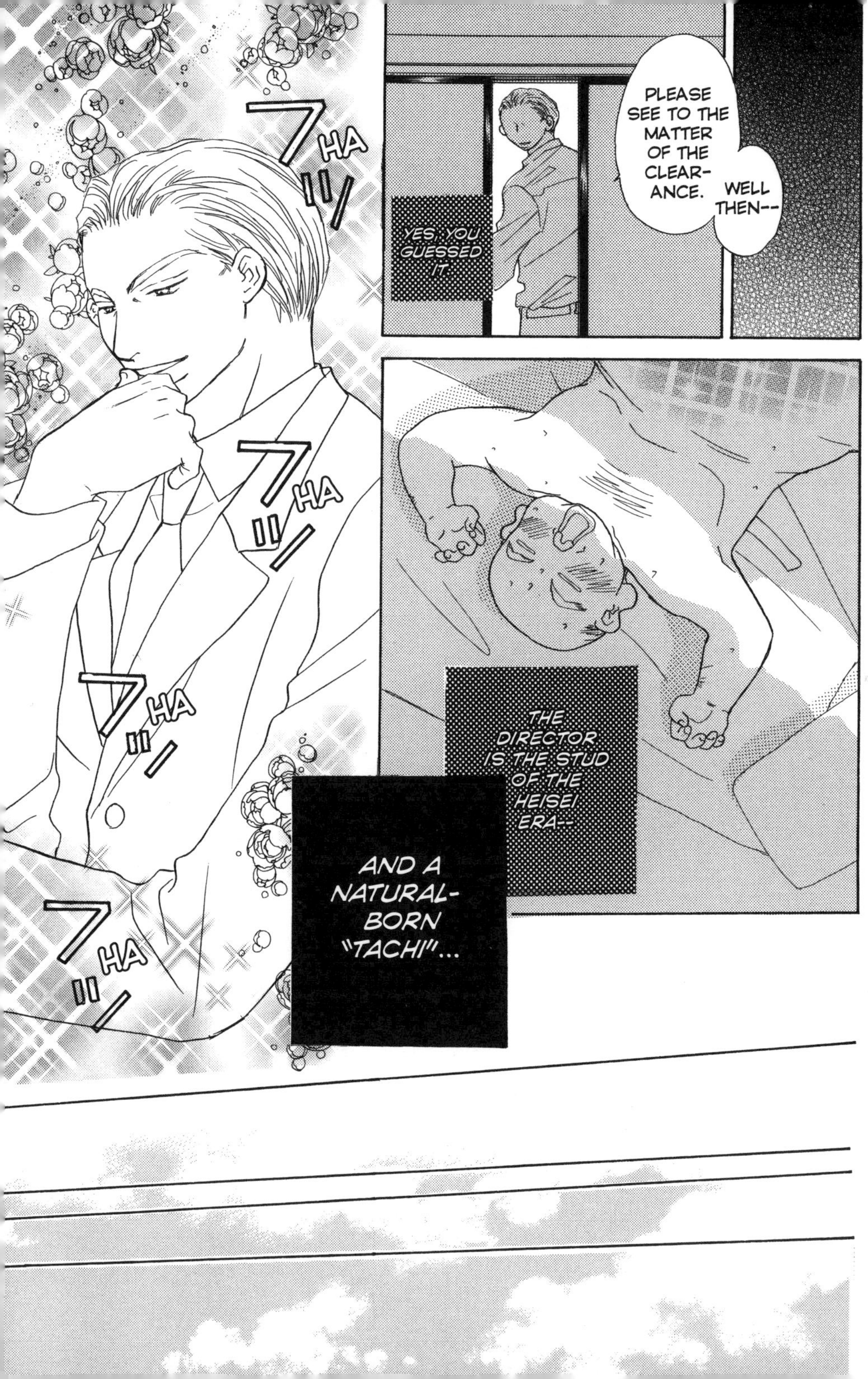

PLEASE SEE TO THE MATTER OF THE CLEAR-ANCE.
WELL THEN--
YES, YOU GUESSED IT.
THE DIRECTOR IS THE STUD OF THE HEISEI ERA--
HA
HA
HA
HA
AND A NATURAL-BORN "TACHI"...

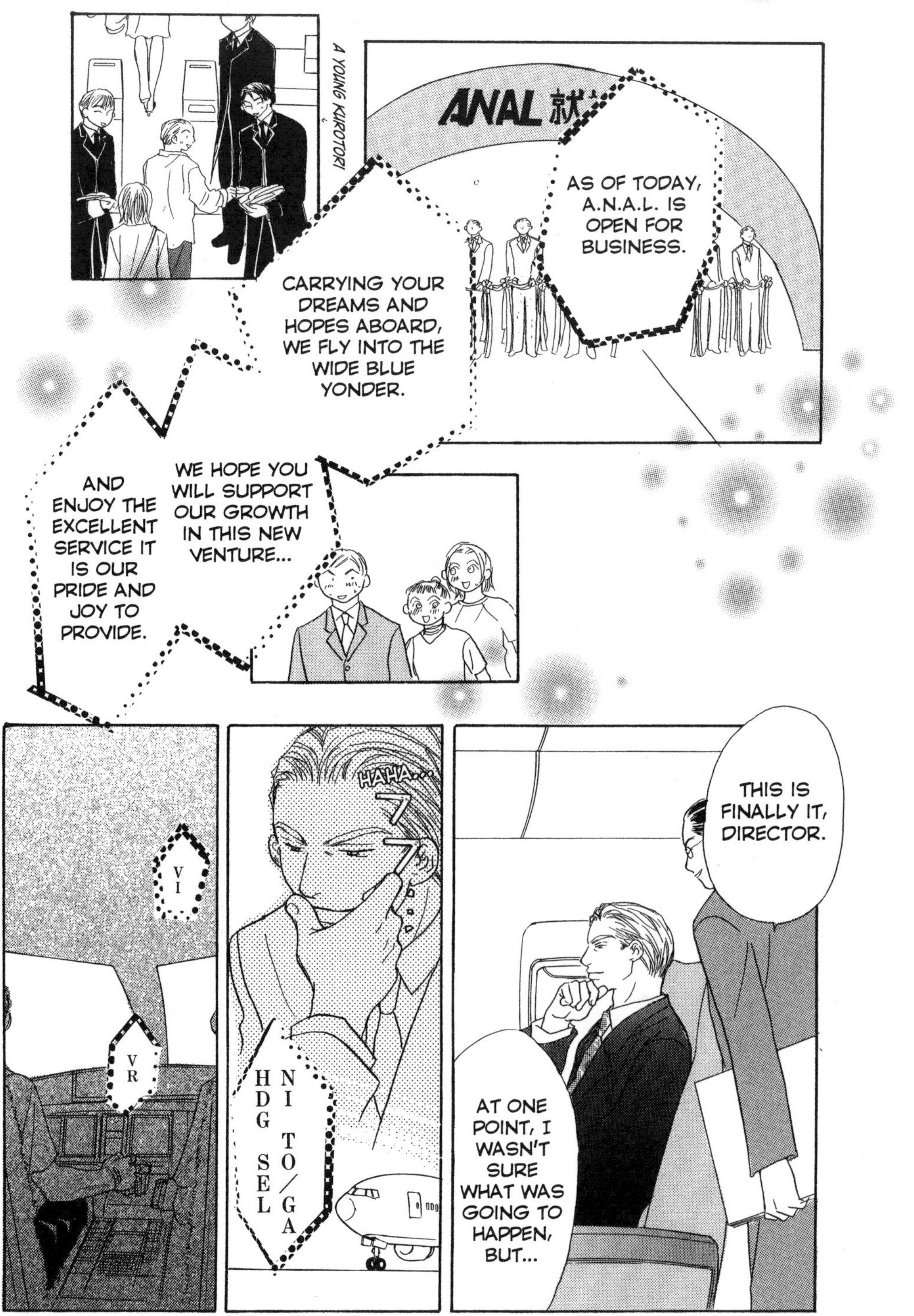
ANAL
AS OF TODAY, A.N.A.L. IS OPEN FOR BUSINESS.
CARRYING YOUR DREAMS AND HOPES ABOARD, WE FLY INTO THE WIDE BLUE YONDER.
A YOUNG KUROTORI
WE HOPE YOU WILL SUPPORT OUR GROWTH IN THIS NEW VENTURE...
AND ENJOY THE EXCELLENT SERVICE IT IS OUR PRIDE AND JOY TO PROVIDE.
THIS IS FINALLY IT, DIRECTOR.
AT ONE POINT, I WASN'T SURE WHAT WAS GOING TO HAPPEN, BUT...
HAHA...
NI TO/GA
HDG SEL
VI
VR

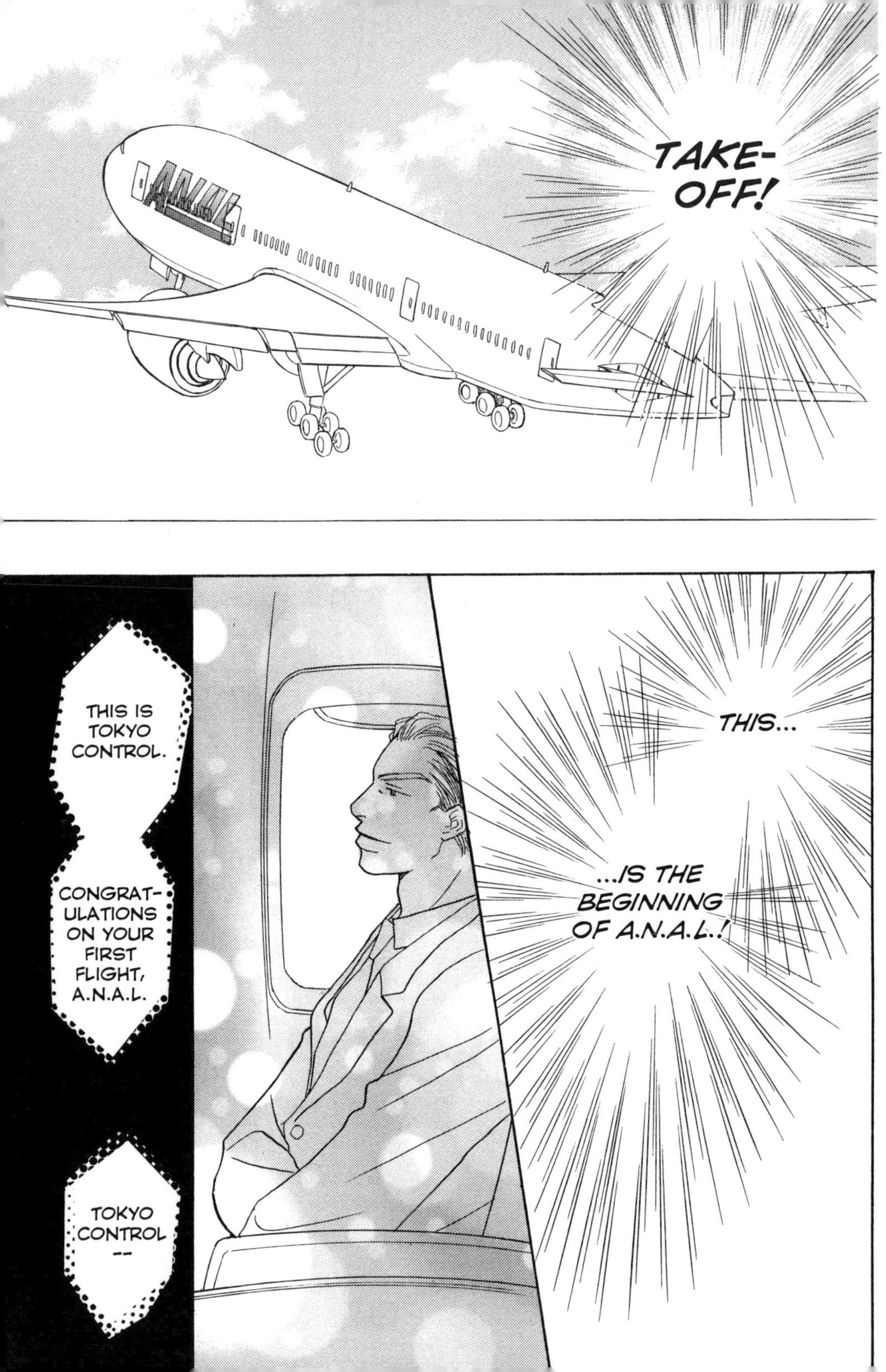
TAKE-OFF!
THIS...
...IS THE BEGINNING OF A.N.A.L.!
THIS IS TOKYO CONTROL.
CONGRATULATIONS ON YOUR FIRST FLIGHT, A.N.A.L.
TOKYO CONTROL --

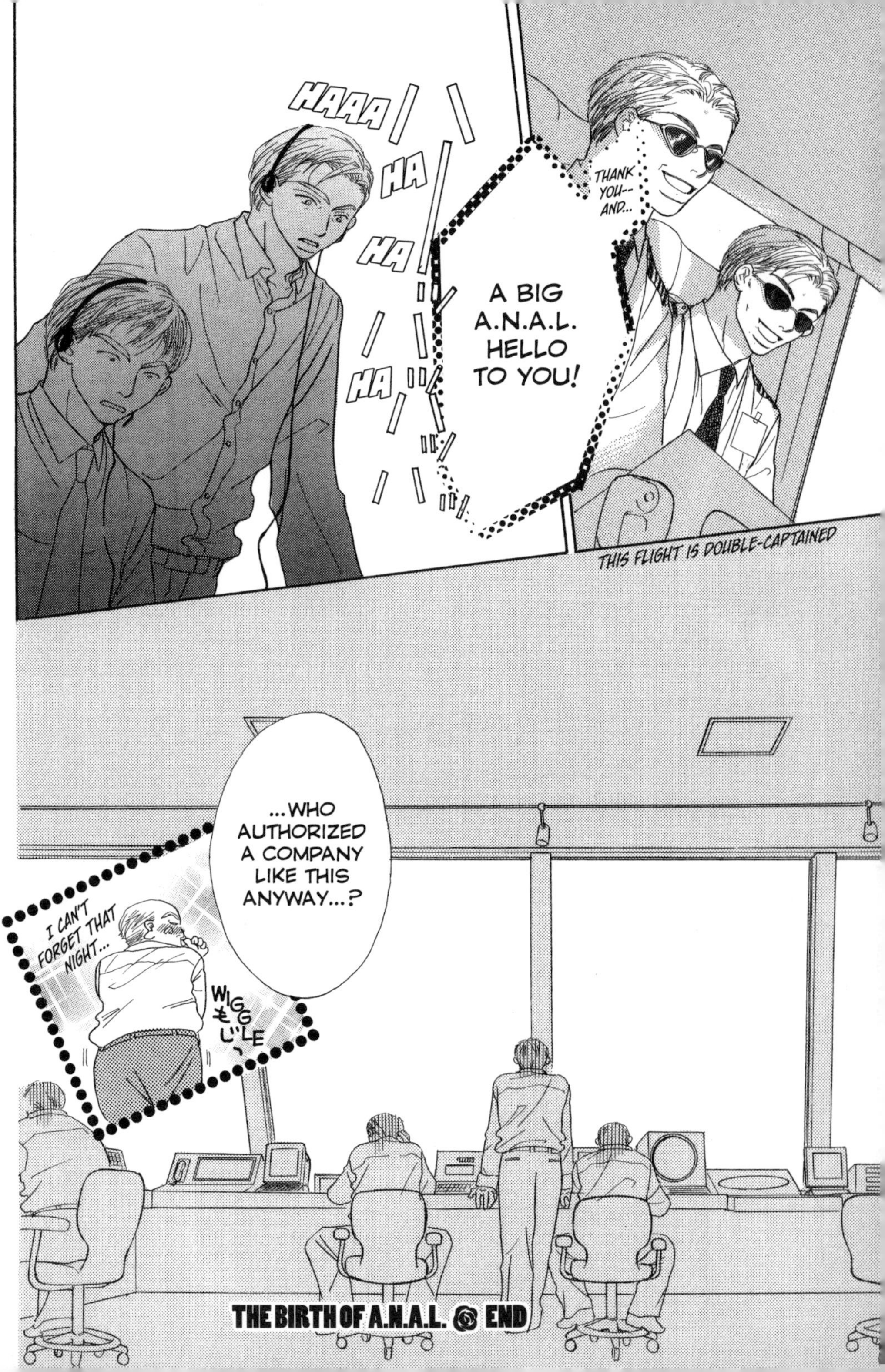
THANK YOU-- AND...
A BIG A.N.A.L. HELLO TO YOU!
HAAA
HA
HA
HA
THIS FLIGHT IS DOUBLE-CAPTAINED
...WHO AUTHORIZED A COMPANY LIKE THIS ANYWAY...?
I CAN'T FORGET THAT NIGHT...
WIGGLE
THE BIRTH OF A.N.A.L. END

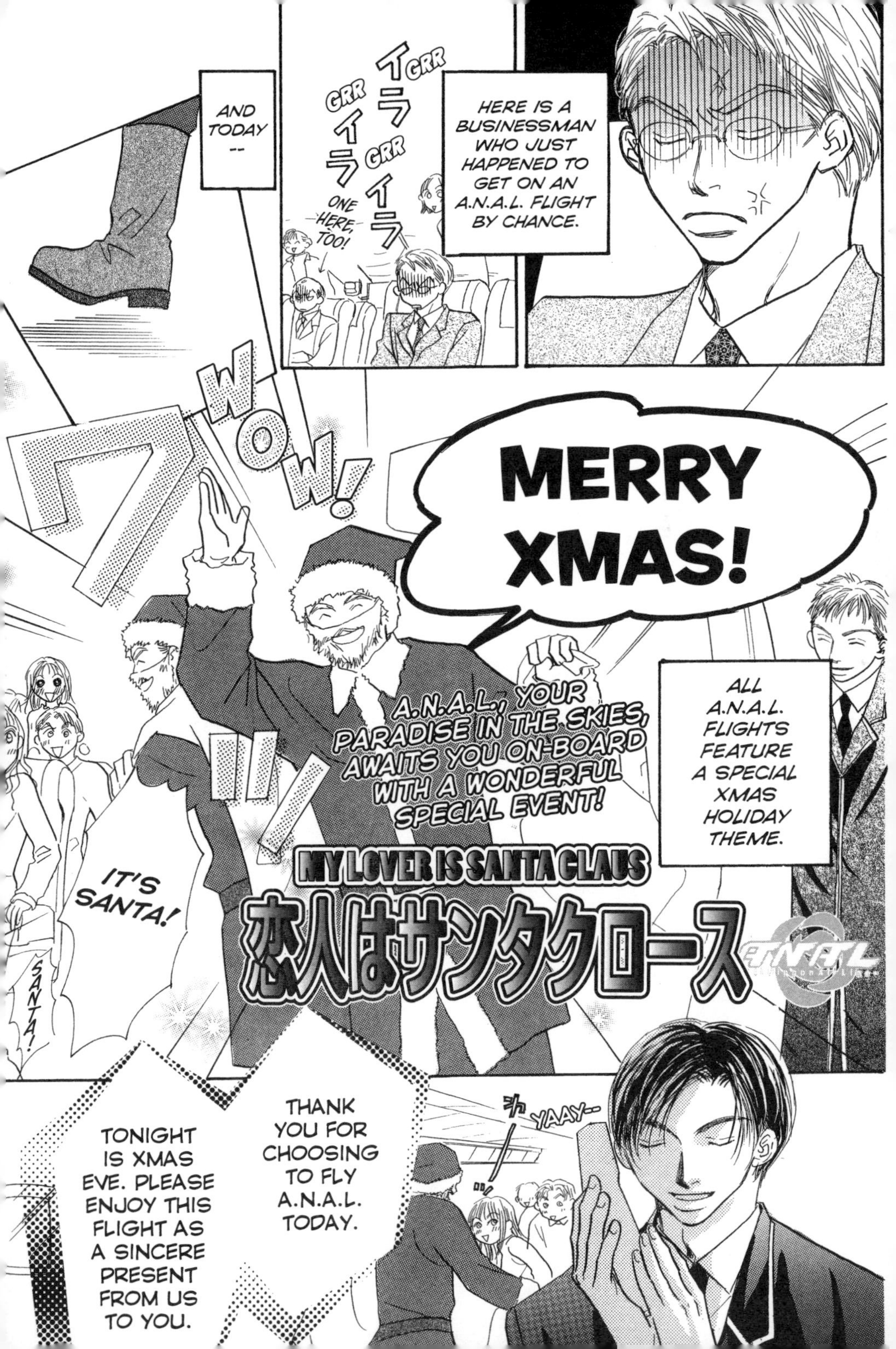
HERE IS A BUSINESSMAN WHO JUST HAPPENED TO GET ON AN A.N.A.L. FLIGHT BY CHANCE.
イライラ
GRR GRR GRR
ONE HERE, TOO!
AND TODAY --
MERRY XMAS!
WOW!
ALL A.N.A.L. FLIGHTS FEATURE A SPECIAL XMAS HOLIDAY THEME.
A.N.A.L., YOUR PARADISE IN THE SKIES, AWAITS YOU ON-BOARD WITH A WONDERFUL SPECIAL EVENT!
MY LOVER IS SANTA CLAUS
恋人はサンタクロース
IT'S SANTA!
SANTA!
YAAAY--
THANK YOU FOR CHOOSING TO FLY A.N.A.L. TODAY.
TONIGHT IS XMAS EVE. PLEASE ENJOY THIS FLIGHT AS A SINCERE PRESENT FROM US TO YOU.

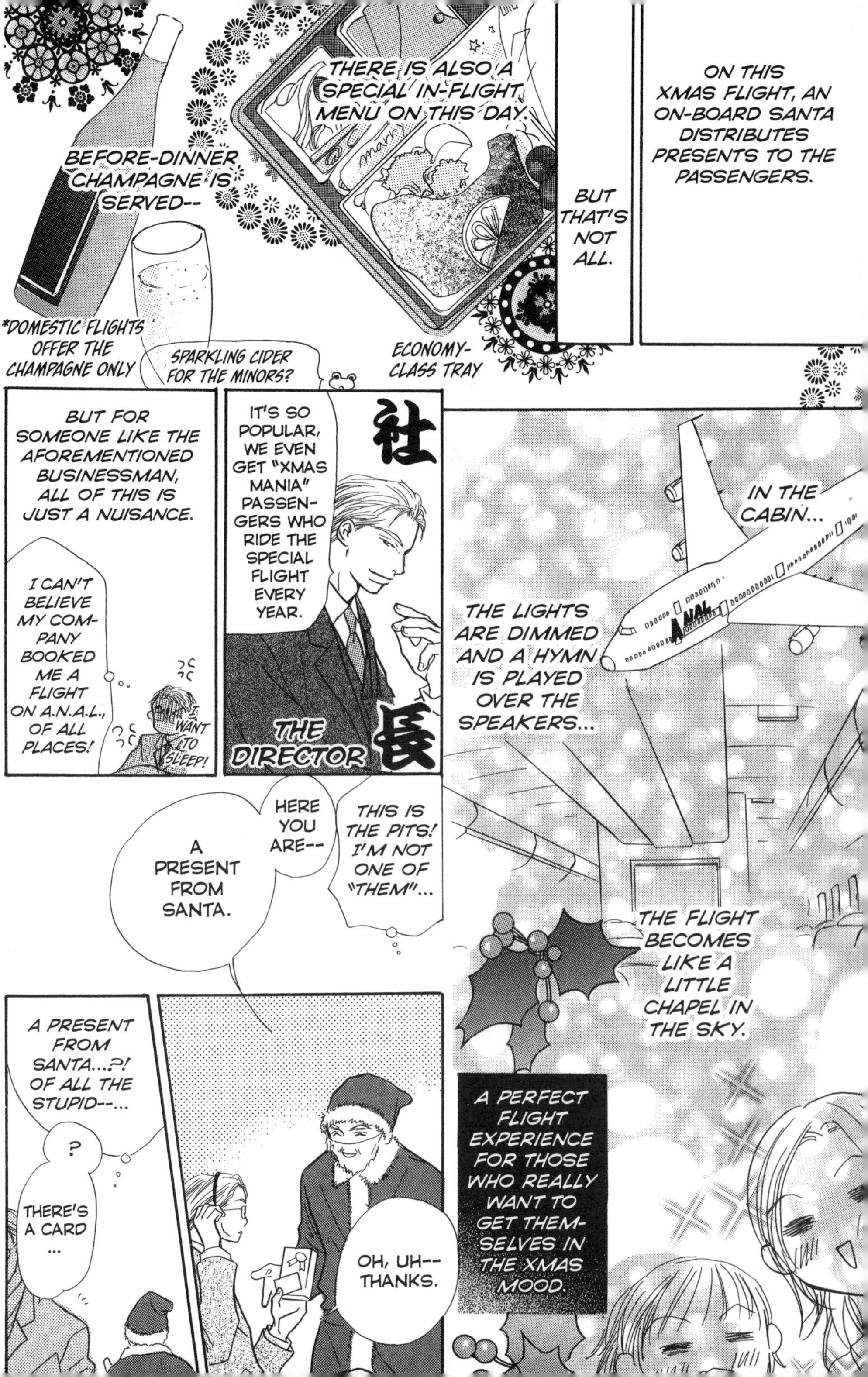

ON THIS XMAS FLIGHT, AN ON-BOARD SANTA DISTRIBUTES PRESENTS TO THE PASSENGERS.
BUT THAT'S NOT ALL.
THERE IS ALSO A SPECIAL IN-FLIGHT MENU ON THIS DAY.
BEFORE-DINNER CHAMPAGNE IS SERVED--
ECONOMY-CLASS TRAY
SPARKLING CIDER FOR THE MINORS?
*DOMESTIC FLIGHTS OFFER THE CHAMPAGNE ONLY
IN THE CABIN...
THE LIGHTS ARE DIMMED AND A HYMN IS PLAYED OVER THE SPEAKERS...
THE FLIGHT BECOMES LIKE A LITTLE CHAPEL IN THE SKY.
A PERFECT FLIGHT EXPERIENCE FOR THOSE WHO REALLY WANT TO GET THEMSELVES IN THE XMAS MOOD.
社長
IT'S SO POPULAR, WE EVEN GET "XMAS MANIA" PASSENGERS WHO RIDE THE SPECIAL FLIGHT EVERY YEAR.
THE DIRECTOR
BUT FOR SOMEONE LIKE THE AFOREMENTIONED BUSINESSMAN, ALL OF THIS IS JUST A NUISANCE.
I CAN'T BELIEVE MY COMPANY BOOKED ME A FLIGHT ON A.N.A.L., OF ALL PLACES!
I WANT TO SLEEP!
HERE YOU ARE--
A PRESENT FROM SANTA.
THIS IS THE PITS! I'M NOT ONE OF "THEM"...
OH, UH-- THANKS.
A PRESENT FROM SANTA...?! OF ALL THE STUPID--...
?
THERE'S A CARD ...

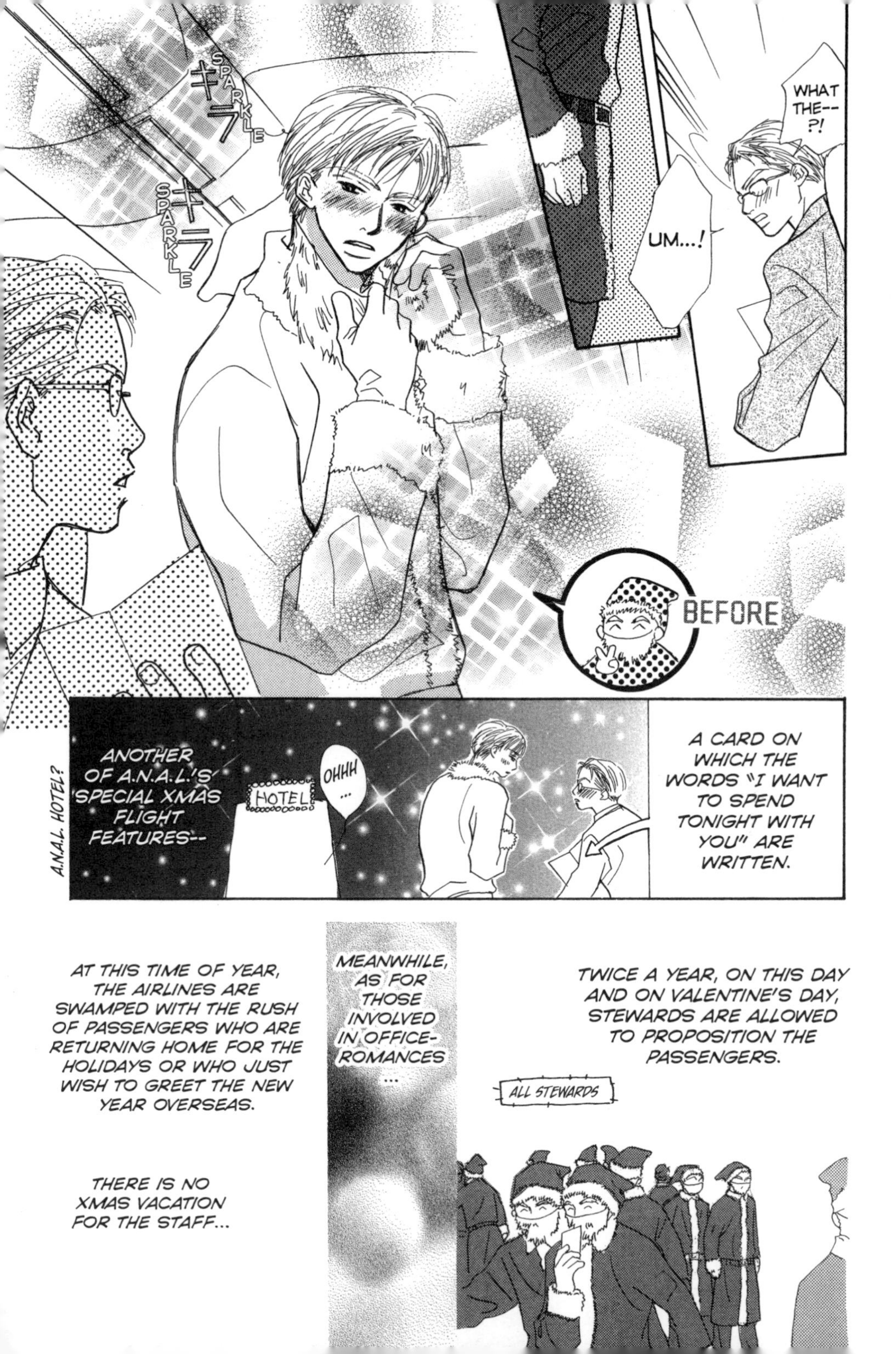

SPARKLE
SPARKLE
BEFORE
UM...!
WHAT THE--?!
A.N.A.L. HOTEL?
ANOTHER OF A.N.A.L.'S SPECIAL XMAS FLIGHT FEATURES--
HOTEL
OHHH ...
A CARD ON WHICH THE WORDS "I WANT TO SPEND TONIGHT WITH YOU" ARE WRITTEN.
AT THIS TIME OF YEAR, THE AIRLINES ARE SWAMPED WITH THE RUSH OF PASSENGERS WHO ARE RETURNING HOME FOR THE HOLIDAYS OR WHO JUST WISH TO GREET THE NEW YEAR OVERSEAS.
THERE IS NO XMAS VACATION FOR THE STAFF...
MEANWHILE, AS FOR THOSE INVOLVED IN OFFICE-ROMANCES ...
TWICE A YEAR, ON THIS DAY AND ON VALENTINE'S DAY, STEWARDS ARE ALLOWED TO PROPOSITION THE PASSENGERS.
ALL STEWARDS

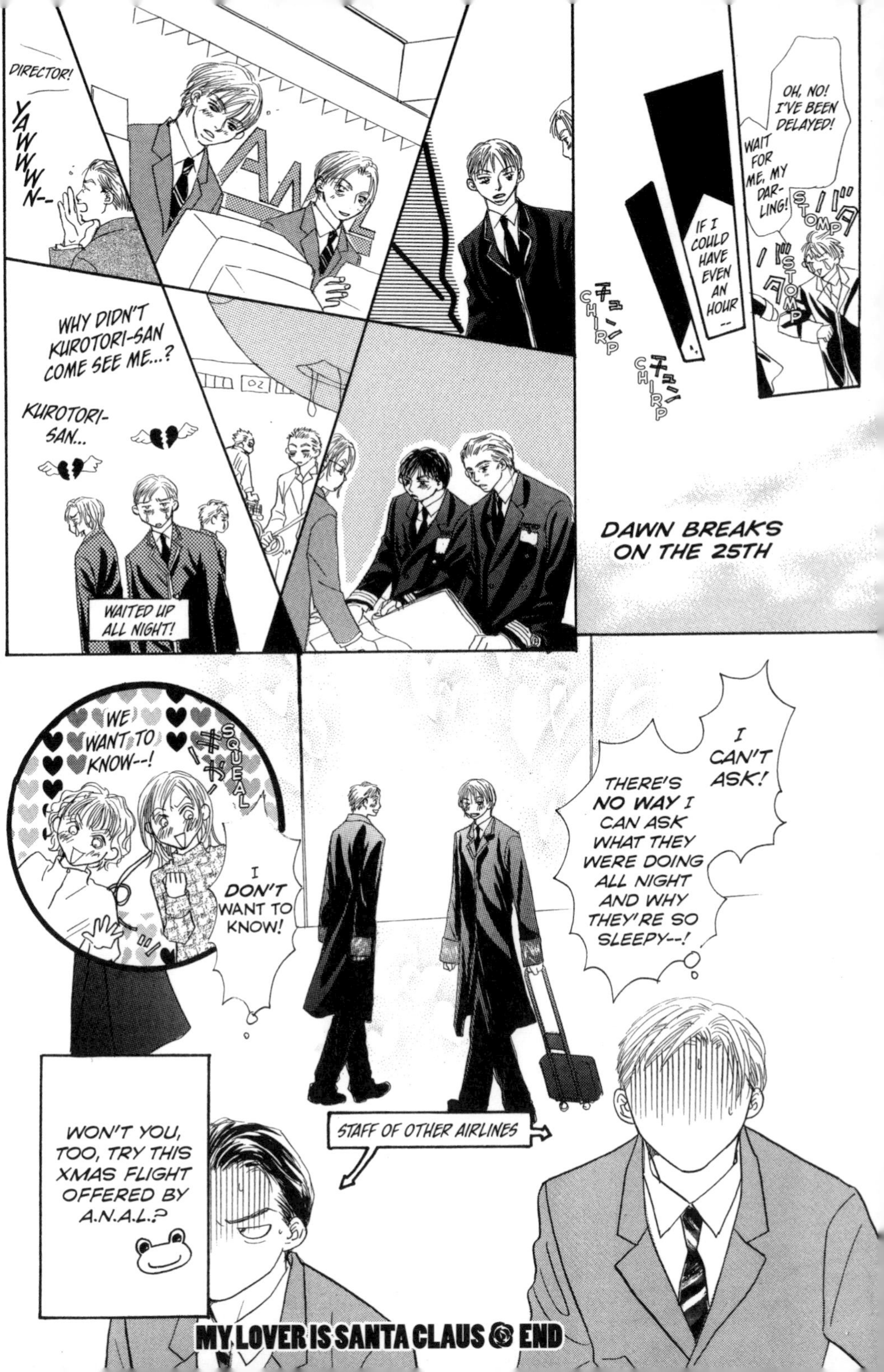
OH, NO! I'VE BEEN DELAYED!
WAIT FOR ME, MY DARLING!
STOMP
STOMP
IF I COULD HAVE EVEN AN HOUR --
CHIRP
CHIRP
DAWN BREAKS ON THE 25TH
DIRECTOR!
YAWWWN--
WHY DIDN'T KUROTORI-SAN COME SEE ME...?
KUROTORI-SAN...
WAITED UP ALL NIGHT!
I CAN'T ASK!
THERE'S NO WAY I CAN ASK WHAT THEY WERE DOING ALL NIGHT AND WHY THEY'RE SO SLEEPY--!
I DON'T WANT TO KNOW!
WE WANT TO KNOW--!
SQUEAL
STAFF OF OTHER AIRLINES
WON'T YOU, TOO, TRY THIS XMAS FLIGHT OFFERED BY A.N.A.L.?
MY LOVER IS SANTA CLAUS END

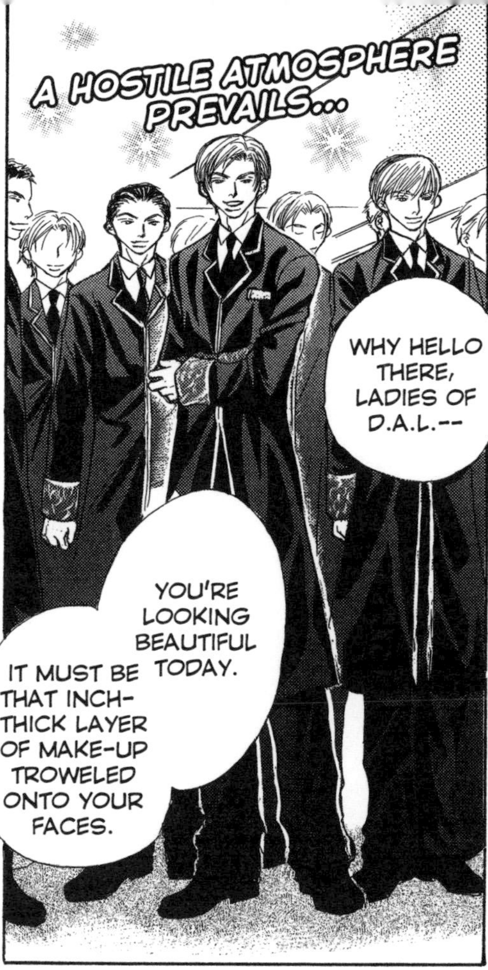
A HOSTILE ATMOSPHERE PREVAILS...
WHY HELLO THERE, LADIES OF D.A.L.--
YOU'RE LOOKING BEAUTIFUL TODAY.
IT MUST BE THAT INCH-THICK LAYER OF MAKE-UP TROWELED ONTO YOUR FACES.
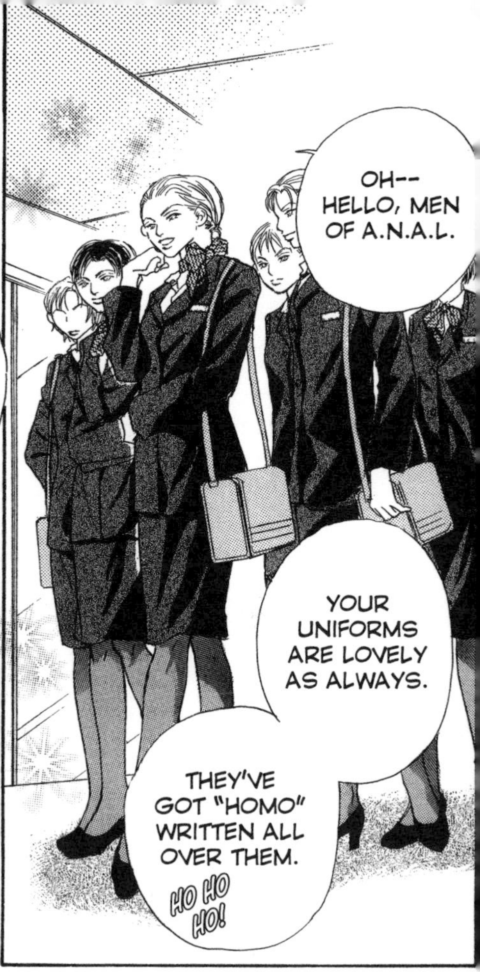
OH-- HELLO, MEN OF A.N.A.L.
YOUR UNIFORMS ARE LOVELY AS ALWAYS.
THEY'VE GOT "HOMO" WRITTEN ALL OVER THEM.
HO HO HO!
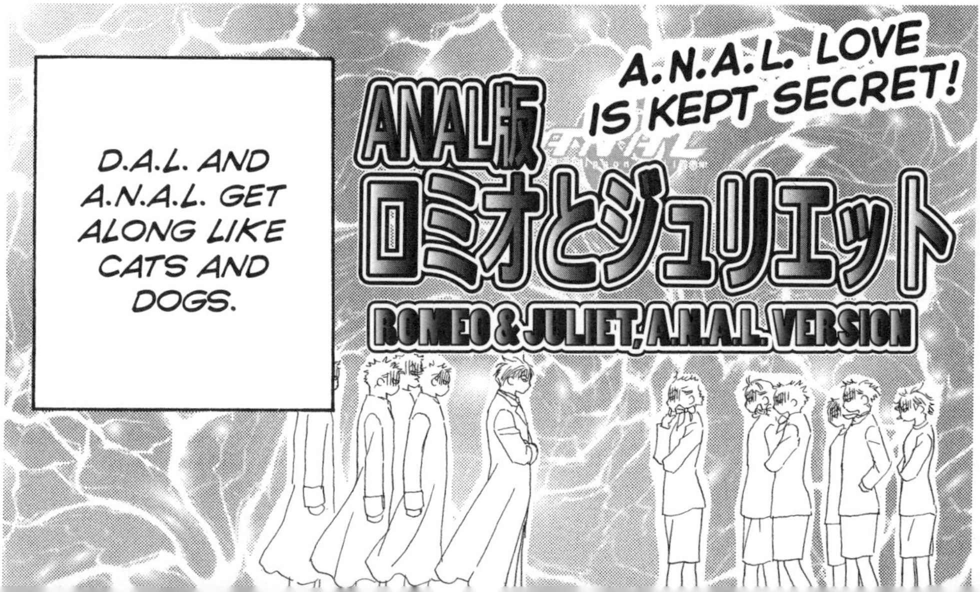
D.A.L. AND A.N.A.L. GET ALONG LIKE CATS AND DOGS.
A.N.A.L. LOVE IS KEPT SECRET!
ANAL版
ロミオとジュリエット
ROMEO & JULIET, A.N.A.L. VERSION

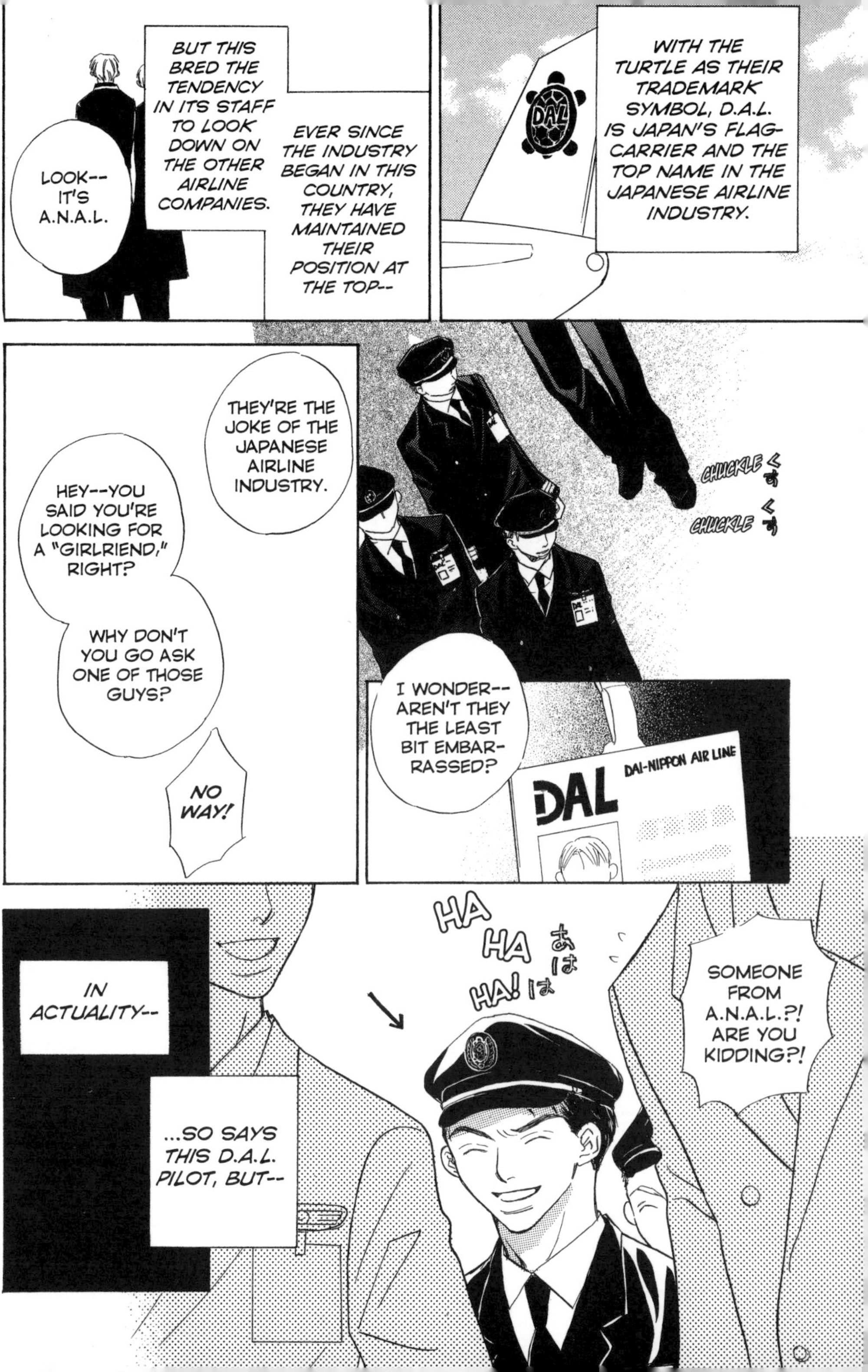

DAL
WITH THE TURTLE AS THEIR TRADEMARK SYMBOL, D.A.L. IS JAPAN'S FLAG-CARRIER AND THE TOP NAME IN THE JAPANESE AIRLINE INDUSTRY.
EVER SINCE THE INDUSTRY BEGAN IN THIS COUNTRY, THEY HAVE MAINTAINED THEIR POSITION AT THE TOP--
BUT THIS BRED THE TENDENCY IN ITS STAFF TO LOOK DOWN ON THE OTHER AIRLINE COMPANIES.
LOOK-- IT'S A.N.A.L.
CHUCKLE くす
CHUCKLE くす
I WONDER-- AREN'T THEY THE LEAST BIT EMBAR-RASSED?
DAI-NIPPON AIR LINE
DAL
THEY'RE THE JOKE OF THE JAPANESE AIRLINE INDUSTRY.
HEY--YOU SAID YOU'RE LOOKING FOR A "GIRLRIEND," RIGHT?
WHY DON'T YOU GO ASK ONE OF THOSE GUYS?
NO WAY!
SOMEONE FROM A.N.A.L.?! ARE YOU KIDDING?!
HA HA HA! あはは
...SO SAYS THIS D.A.L. PILOT, BUT--
IN ACTUALITY--

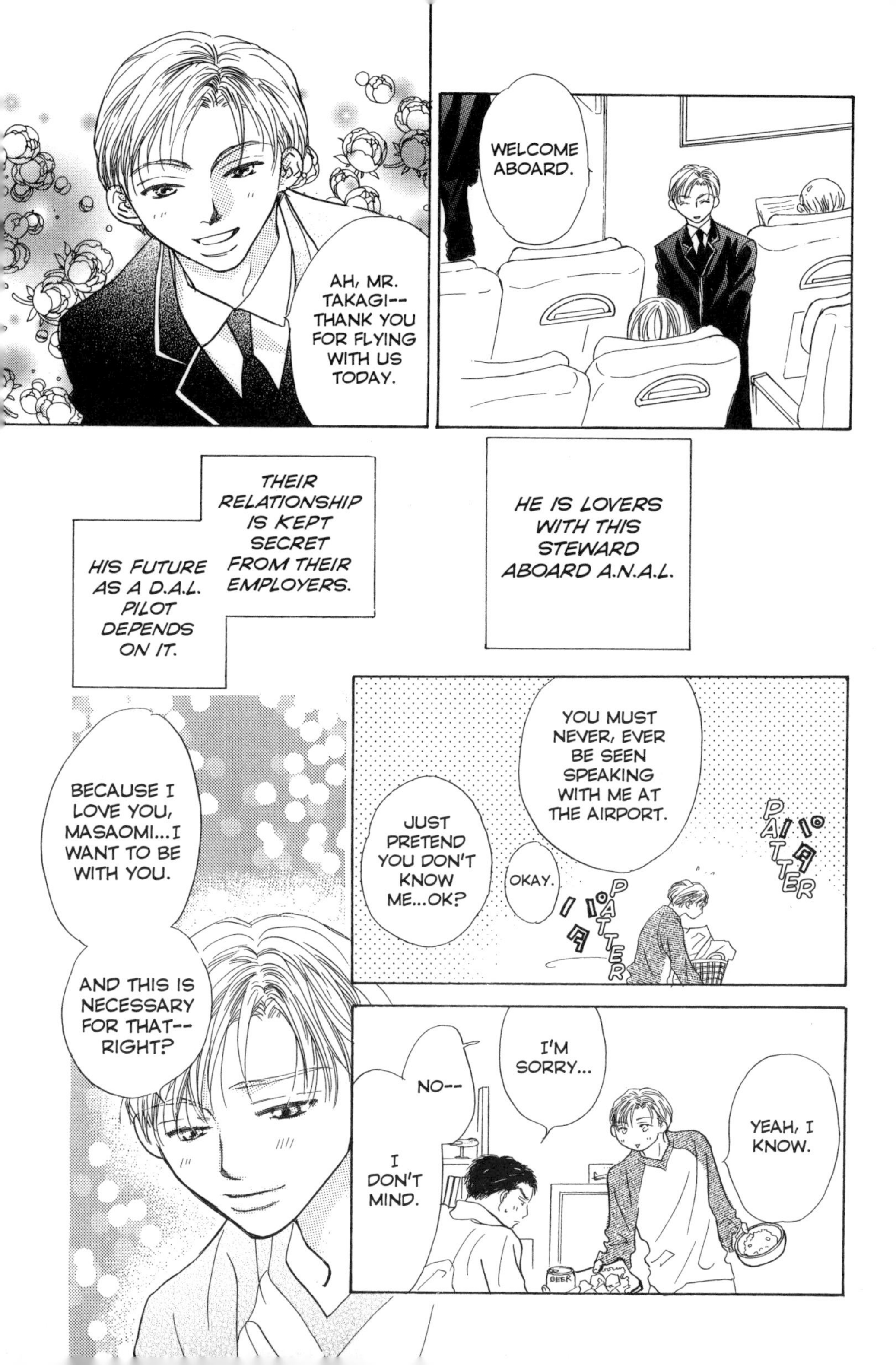
WELCOME ABOARD.
AH, MR. TAKAGI-- THANK YOU FOR FLYING WITH US TODAY.
HE IS LOVERS WITH THIS STEWARD ABOARD A.N.A.L.
THEIR RELATIONSHIP IS KEPT SECRET FROM THEIR EMPLOYERS.
HIS FUTURE AS A D.A.L. PILOT DEPENDS ON IT.
YOU MUST NEVER, EVER BE SEEN SPEAKING WITH ME AT THE AIRPORT.
JUST PRETEND YOU DON'T KNOW ME...OK?
PATTER
OKAY.
PATTER
I'M SORRY...
YEAH, I KNOW.
NO--
I DON'T MIND.
BEER
BECAUSE I LOVE YOU, MASAOMI...I WANT TO BE WITH YOU.
AND THIS IS NECESSARY FOR THAT-- RIGHT?

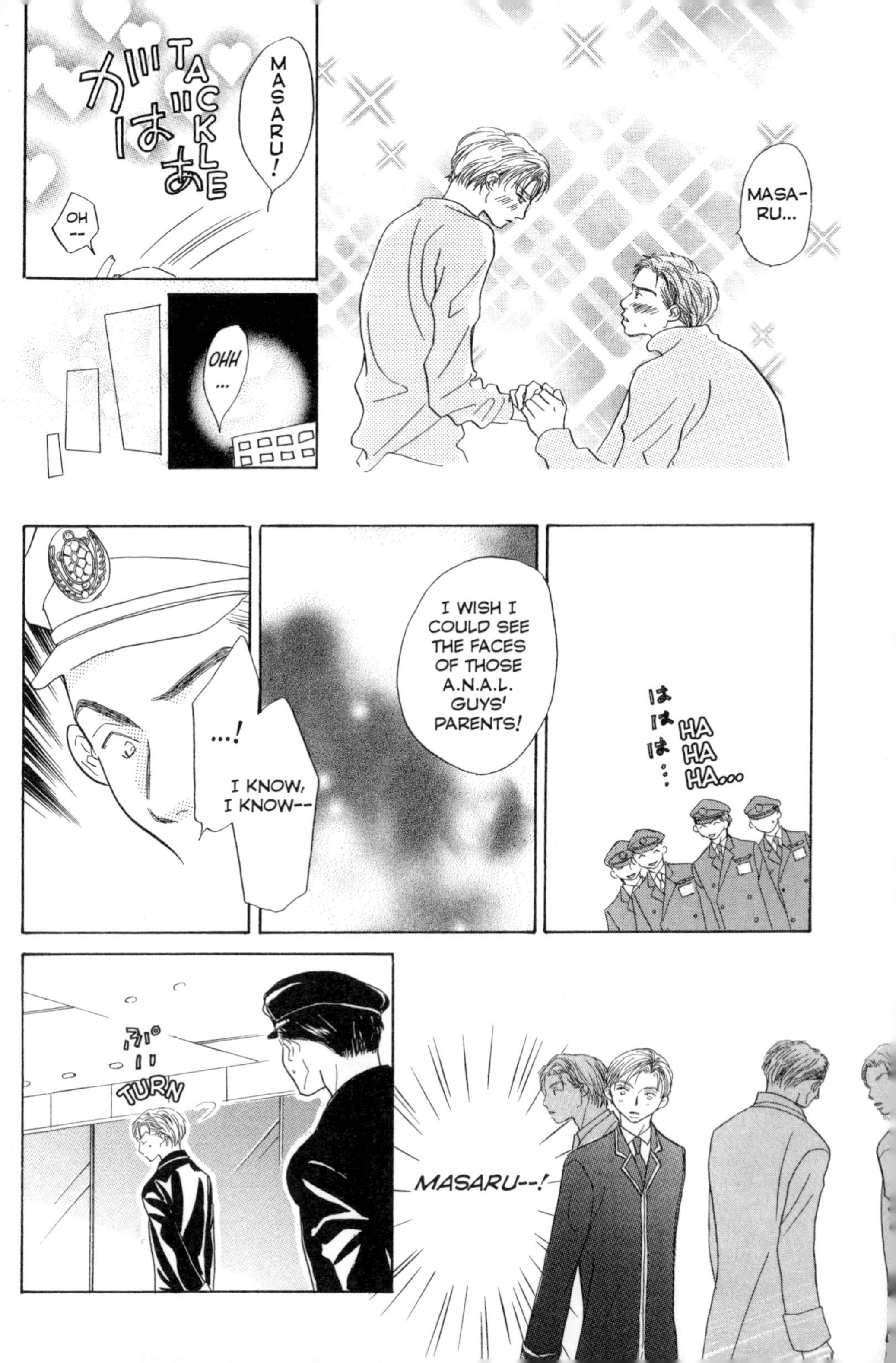
MASA-RU...
MASARU!
TACKLE
OH --
OHH ...
ははは...
HA HA HA...
I WISH I COULD SEE THE FACES OF THOSE A.N.A.L. GUYS' PARENTS!
...!
I KNOW, I KNOW--
MASARU--!
ぷい
TURN

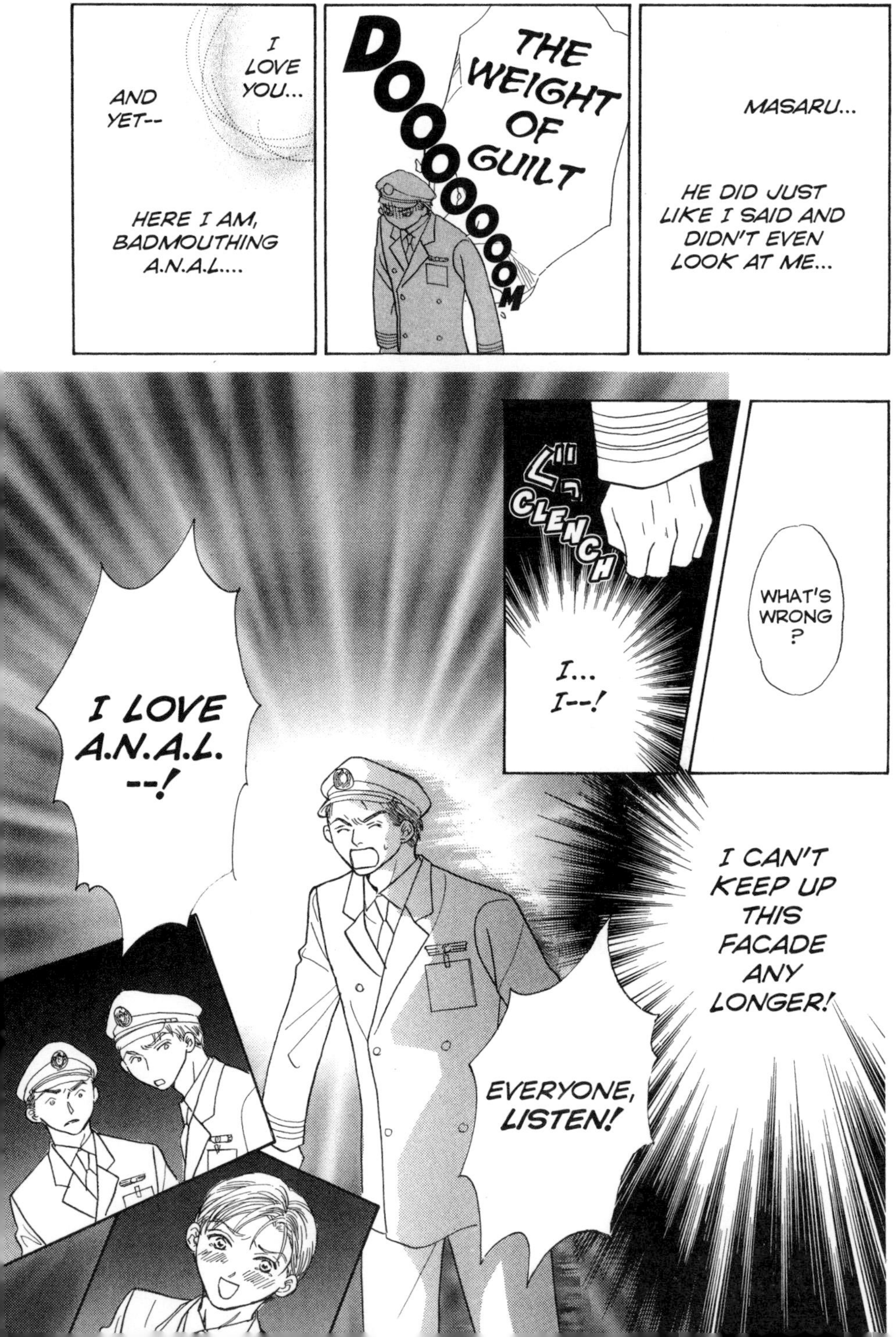
MASARU...
HE DID JUST LIKE I SAID AND DIDN'T EVEN LOOK AT ME...
THE WEIGHT OF GUILT
DOOOOOOOOM
I LOVE YOU...
AND YET--
HERE I AM, BADMOUTHING A.N.A.L....
WHAT'S WRONG?
CLENCH
I... I--!
I CAN'T KEEP UP THIS FACADE ANY LONGER!
EVERYONE, LISTEN!
I LOVE A.N.A.L. --!

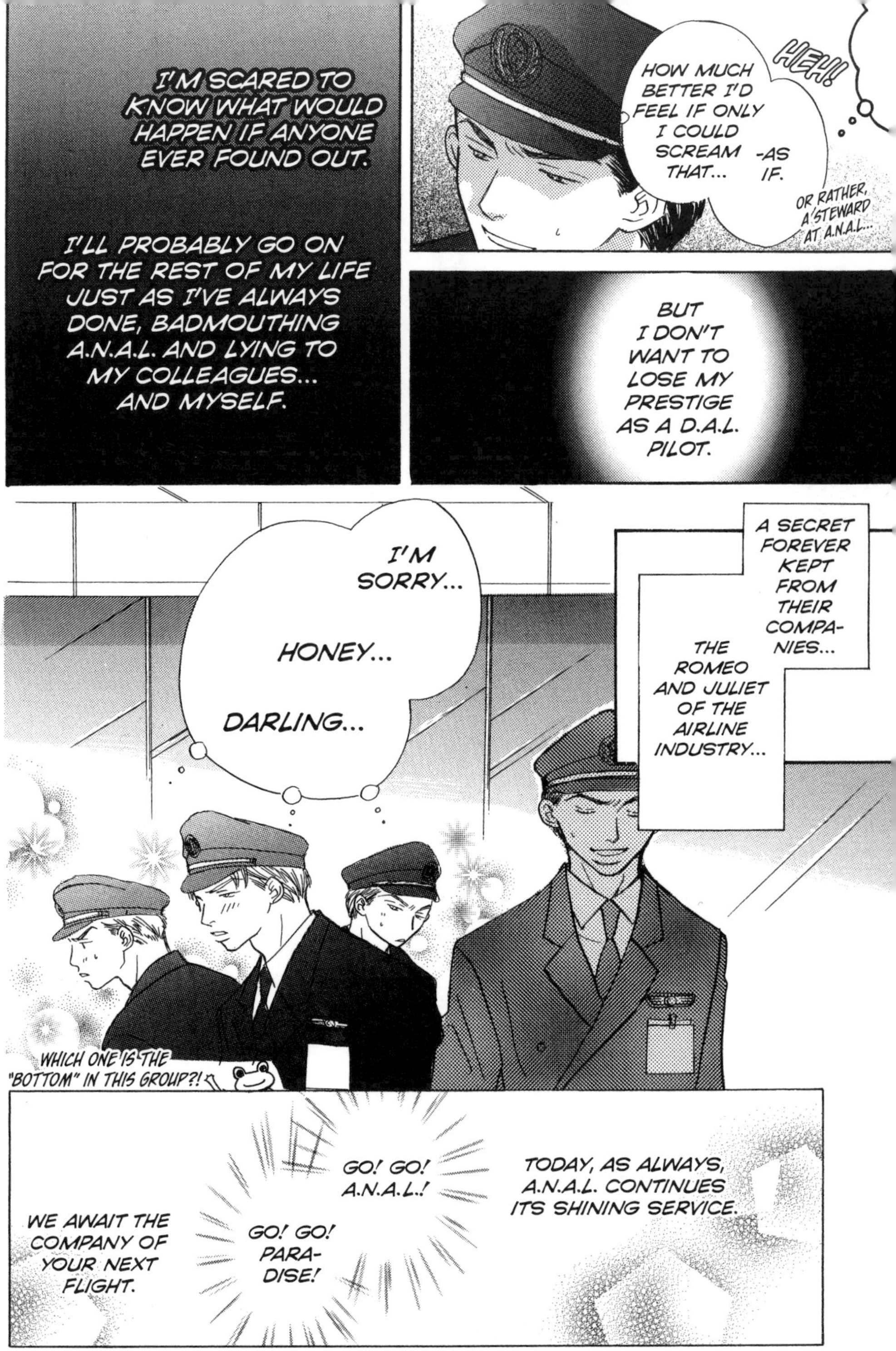

HEH!!
HOW MUCH BETTER I'D FEEL IF ONLY I COULD SCREAM THAT... -AS IF.
OR RATHER, A STEWARD AT A.N.A.L...
BUT I DON'T WANT TO LOSE MY PRESTIGE AS A D.A.L. PILOT.
I'M SCARED TO KNOW WHAT WOULD HAPPEN IF ANYONE EVER FOUND OUT.
I'LL PROBABLY GO ON FOR THE REST OF MY LIFE JUST AS I'VE ALWAYS DONE, BADMOUTHING A.N.A.L. AND LYING TO MY COLLEAGUES... AND MYSELF.
A SECRET FOREVER KEPT FROM THEIR COMPA-NIES...
THE ROMEO AND JULIET OF THE AIRLINE INDUSTRY...
I'M SORRY... HONEY... DARLING...
WHICH ONE IS THE "BOTTOM" IN THIS GROUP?!
TODAY, AS ALWAYS, A.N.A.L. CONTINUES ITS SHINING SERVICE.
GO! GO! A.N.A.L.!
GO! GO! PARA-DISE!
WE AWAIT THE COMPANY OF YOUR NEXT FLIGHT.


**ROMEO & JULIET, A.N.A.L. VERSION ◎ END**

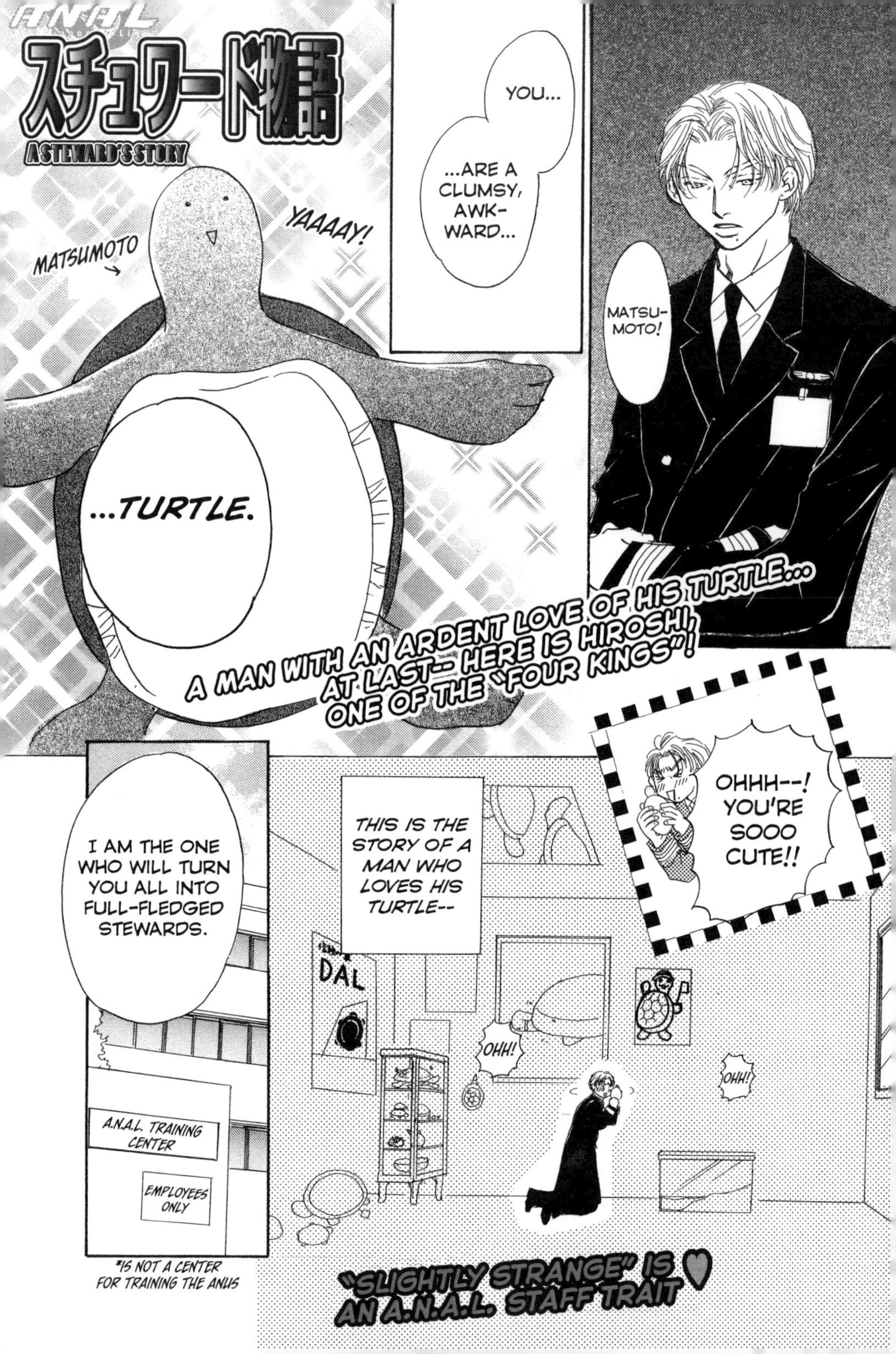
ANAL
スチュワード物語
A STEWARD'S STORY
MATSU-MOTO!
YOU...
...ARE A CLUMSY, AWKWARD...
YAAAAY!
MATSUMOTO →
...TURTLE.
A MAN WITH AN ARDENT LOVE OF HIS TURTLE... AT LAST-- HERE IS HIROSHI, ONE OF THE "FOUR KINGS"!
OHHH--! YOU'RE SOOO CUTE!!
THIS IS THE STORY OF A MAN WHO LOVES HIS TURTLE--
DAL
OHH!
OHH!
I AM THE ONE WHO WILL TURN YOU ALL INTO FULL-FLEDGED STEWARDS.
A.N.A.L. TRAINING CENTER
EMPLOYEES ONLY
*IS NOT A CENTER FOR TRAINING THE ANUS
"SLIGHTLY STRANGE" IS AN A.N.A.L. STAFF TRAIT ♥

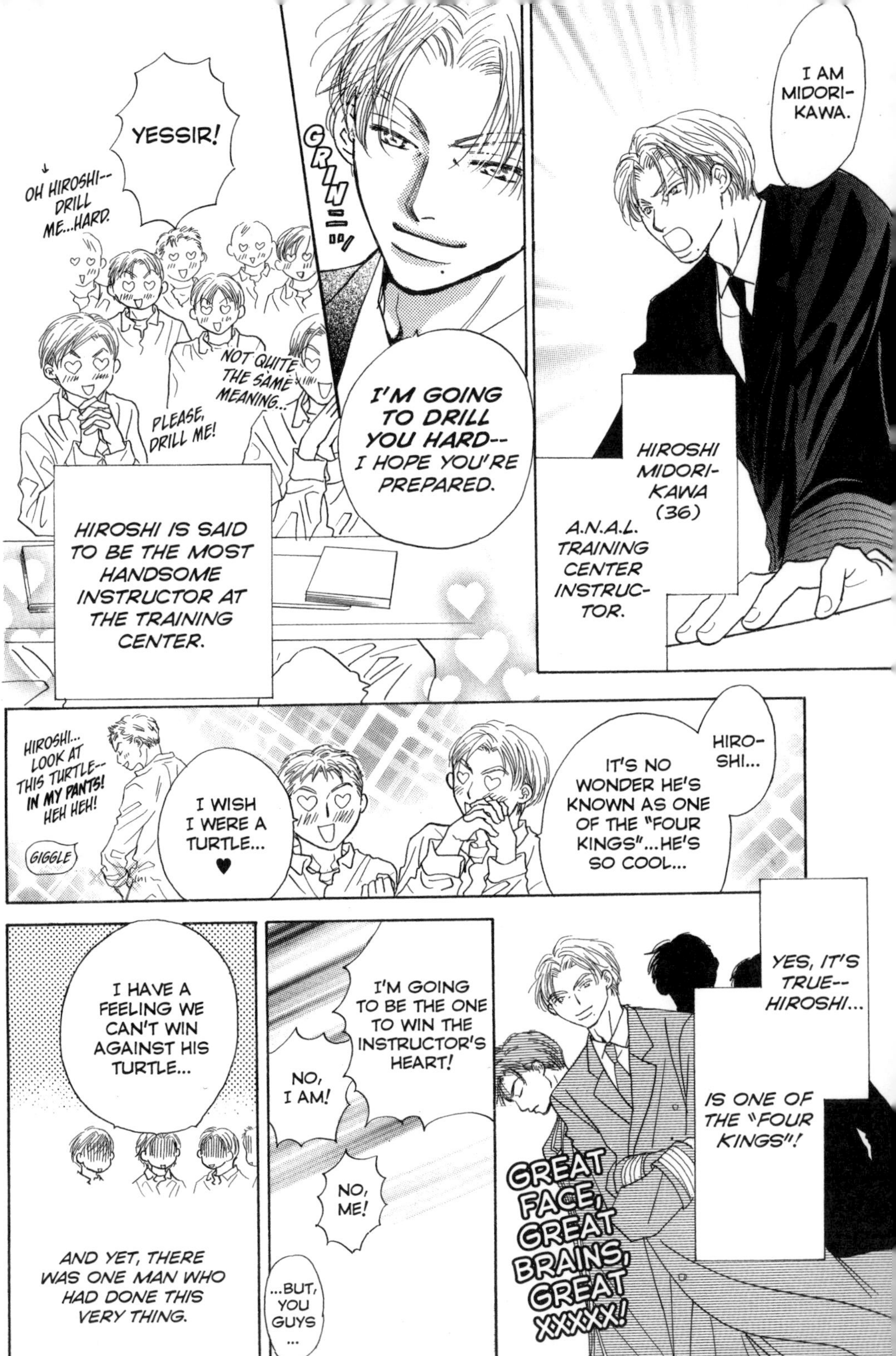
I AM MIDORI-KAWA.
HIROSHI MIDORI-KAWA (36)
A.N.A.L. TRAINING CENTER INSTRUC-TOR.
GRIN==!
I'M GOING TO DRILL YOU HARD-- I HOPE YOU'RE PREPARED.
YESSIR!
OH HIROSHI-- DRILL ME...HARD.
NOT QUITE THE SAME MEANING...
PLEASE, DRILL ME!
HIROSHI IS SAID TO BE THE MOST HANDSOME INSTRUCTOR AT THE TRAINING CENTER.
HIRO-SHI...
IT'S NO WONDER HE'S KNOWN AS ONE OF THE "FOUR KINGS"...HE'S SO COOL...
I WISH I WERE A TURTLE... ♥
HIROSHI... LOOK AT THIS TURTLE-- IN MY PANTS! HEH HEH!
GIGGLE
YES, IT'S TRUE-- HIROSHI...
IS ONE OF THE "FOUR KINGS"!
GREAT FACE, GREAT BRAINS, GREAT XXXXX!
I'M GOING TO BE THE ONE TO WIN THE INSTRUCTOR'S HEART!
NO, I AM!
NO, ME!
...BUT, YOU GUYS ...
I HAVE A FEELING WE CAN'T WIN AGAINST HIS TURTLE...
AND YET, THERE WAS ONE MAN WHO HAD DONE THIS VERY THING.

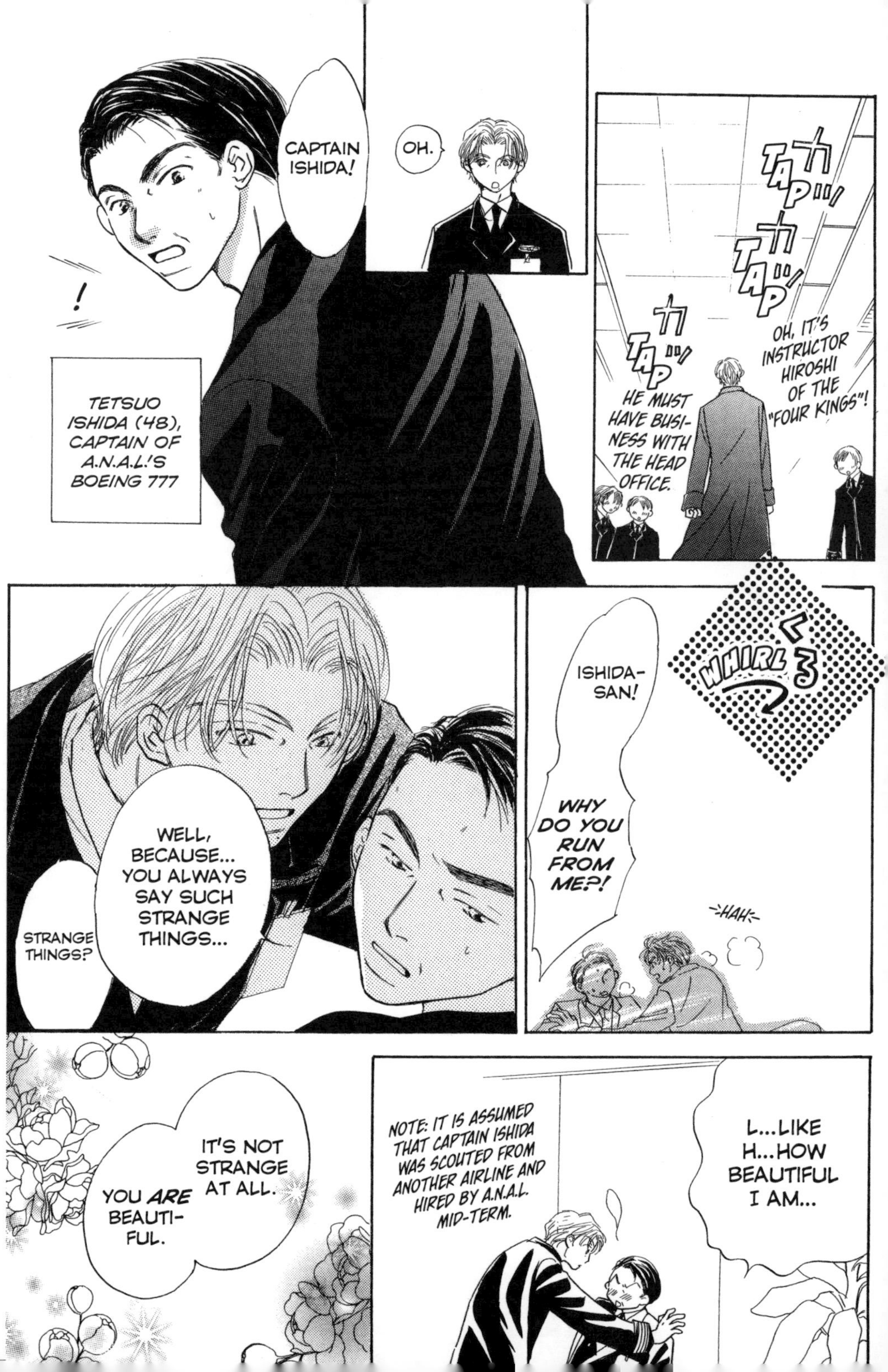
TAP TAP TAP
OH, IT'S INSTRUCTOR HIROSHI OF THE "FOUR KINGS"!
HE MUST HAVE BUSINESS WITH THE HEAD OFFICE.
OH.
CAPTAIN ISHIDA!
!
TETSUO ISHIDA (48), CAPTAIN OF A.N.A.L.'S BOEING 777
WHIRL
ISHIDA-SAN!
WHY DO YOU RUN FROM ME?!
HAH
WELL, BECAUSE... YOU ALWAYS SAY SUCH STRANGE THINGS...
STRANGE THINGS?
L...LIKE H...HOW BEAUTIFUL I AM...
NOTE: IT IS ASSUMED THAT CAPTAIN ISHIDA WAS SCOUTED FROM ANOTHER AIRLINE AND HIRED BY A.N.A.L. MID-TERM.
IT'S NOT STRANGE AT ALL.
YOU ARE BEAUTIFUL.

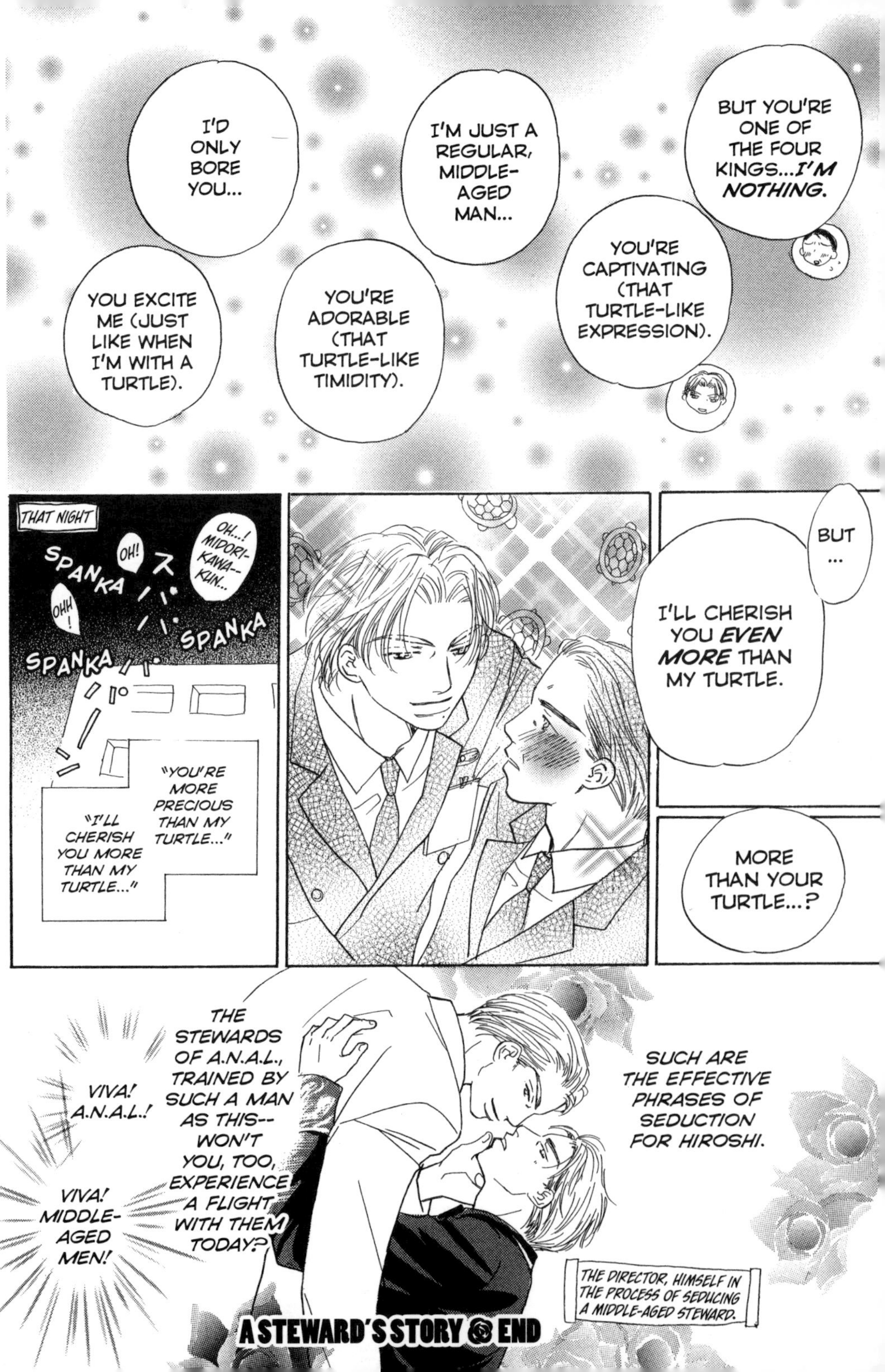
BUT YOU'RE ONE OF THE FOUR KINGS...I'M NOTHING.
I'M JUST A REGULAR, MIDDLE-AGED MAN...
I'D ONLY BORE YOU...
YOU'RE CAPTIVATING (THAT TURTLE-LIKE EXPRESSION).
YOU'RE ADORABLE (THAT TURTLE-LIKE TIMIDITY).
YOU EXCITE ME (JUST LIKE WHEN I'M WITH A TURTLE).
BUT...
I'LL CHERISH YOU EVEN MORE THAN MY TURTLE.
MORE THAN YOUR TURTLE...?
THAT NIGHT
OH...! MIDORI-KAWA-KUN...
OH!
ス
SPANKA
OHH!
SPANKA
SPANKA
"YOU'RE MORE PRECIOUS THAN MY TURTLE..."
"I'LL CHERISH YOU MORE THAN MY TURTLE..."
SUCH ARE THE EFFECTIVE PHRASES OF SEDUCTION FOR HIROSHI.
THE STEWARDS OF A.N.A.L., TRAINED BY SUCH A MAN AS THIS-- WON'T YOU, TOO, EXPERIENCE A FLIGHT WITH THEM TODAY?
VIVA! A.N.A.L.!
VIVA! MIDDLE-AGED MEN!
THE DIRECTOR, HIMSELF IN THE PROCESS OF SEDUCING A MIDDLE-AGED STEWARD.
A STEWARD'S STORY END

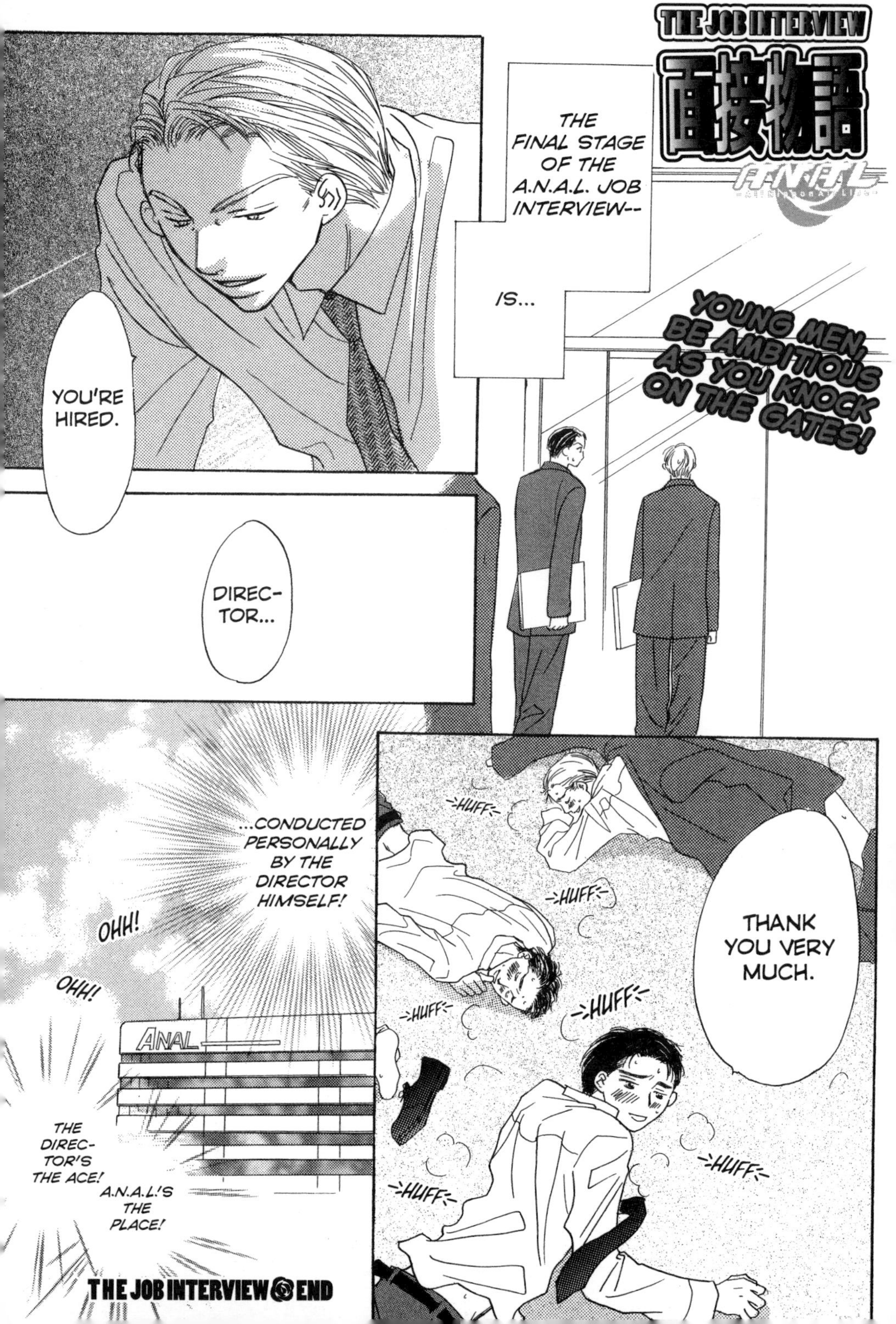
THE JOB INTERVIEW
面接物語
THE FINAL STAGE OF THE A.N.A.L. JOB INTERVIEW--
IS...
YOUNG MEN, BE AMBITIOUS AS YOU KNOCK ON THE GATES!
YOU'RE HIRED.
DIRECTOR...
THANK YOU VERY MUCH.
HUFF
HUFF
HUFF
HUFF
HUFF
HUFF
...CONDUCTED PERSONALLY BY THE DIRECTOR HIMSELF!
OHH!
OHH!
ANAL
THE DIRECTOR'S THE ACE!
A.N.A.L.'S THE PLACE!
THE JOB INTERVIEW END

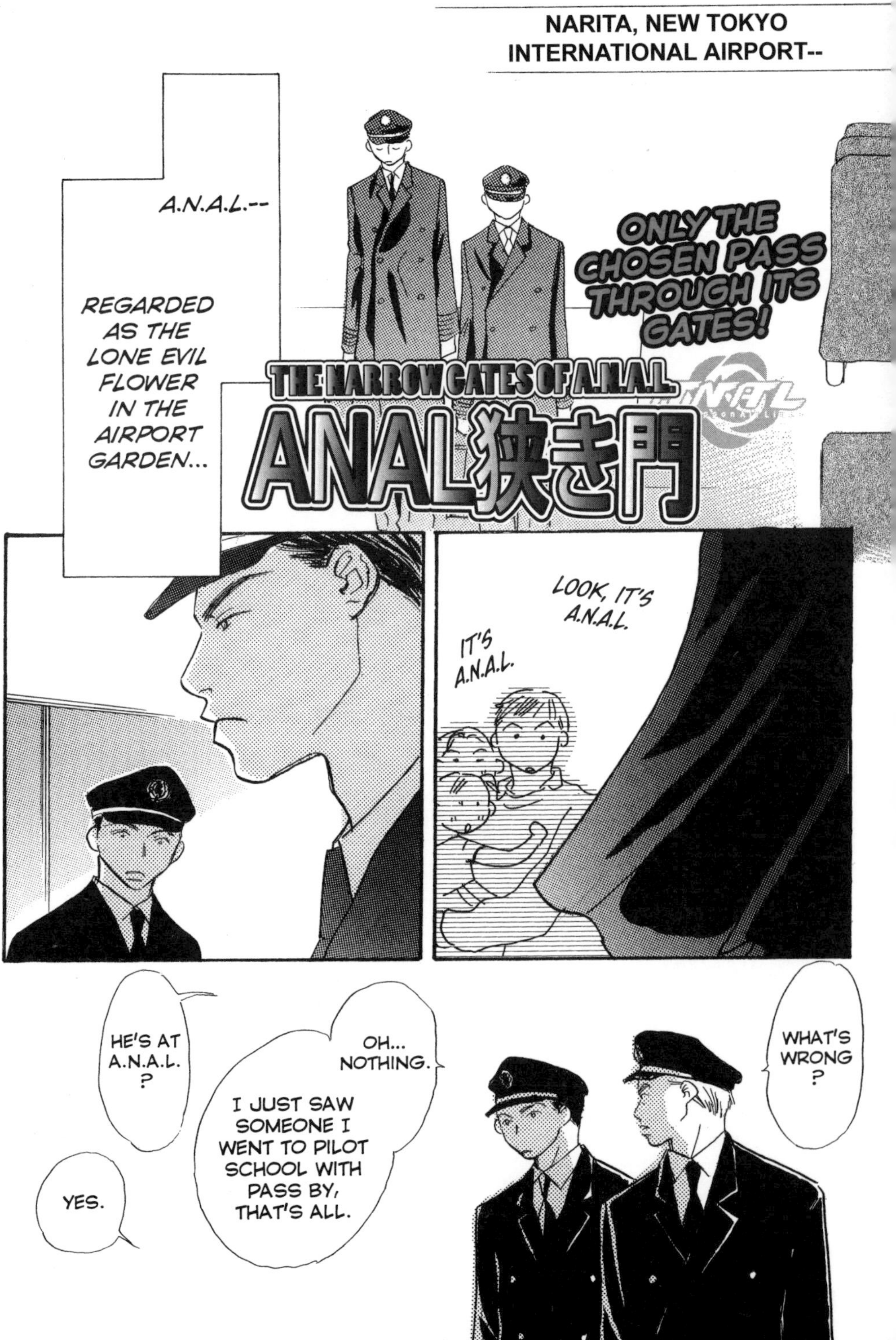
NARITA, NEW TOKYO INTERNATIONAL AIRPORT--
ONLY THE CHOSEN PASS THROUGH ITS GATES!
THE NARROW GATES OF A.N.A.L.
ANAL狭き門
A.N.A.L.--
REGARDED AS THE LONE EVIL FLOWER IN THE AIRPORT GARDEN...
LOOK, IT'S A.N.A.L.
IT'S A.N.A.L.
WHAT'S WRONG?
OH... NOTHING.
I JUST SAW SOMEONE I WENT TO PILOT SCHOOL WITH PASS BY, THAT'S ALL.
HE'S AT A.N.A.L.?
YES.

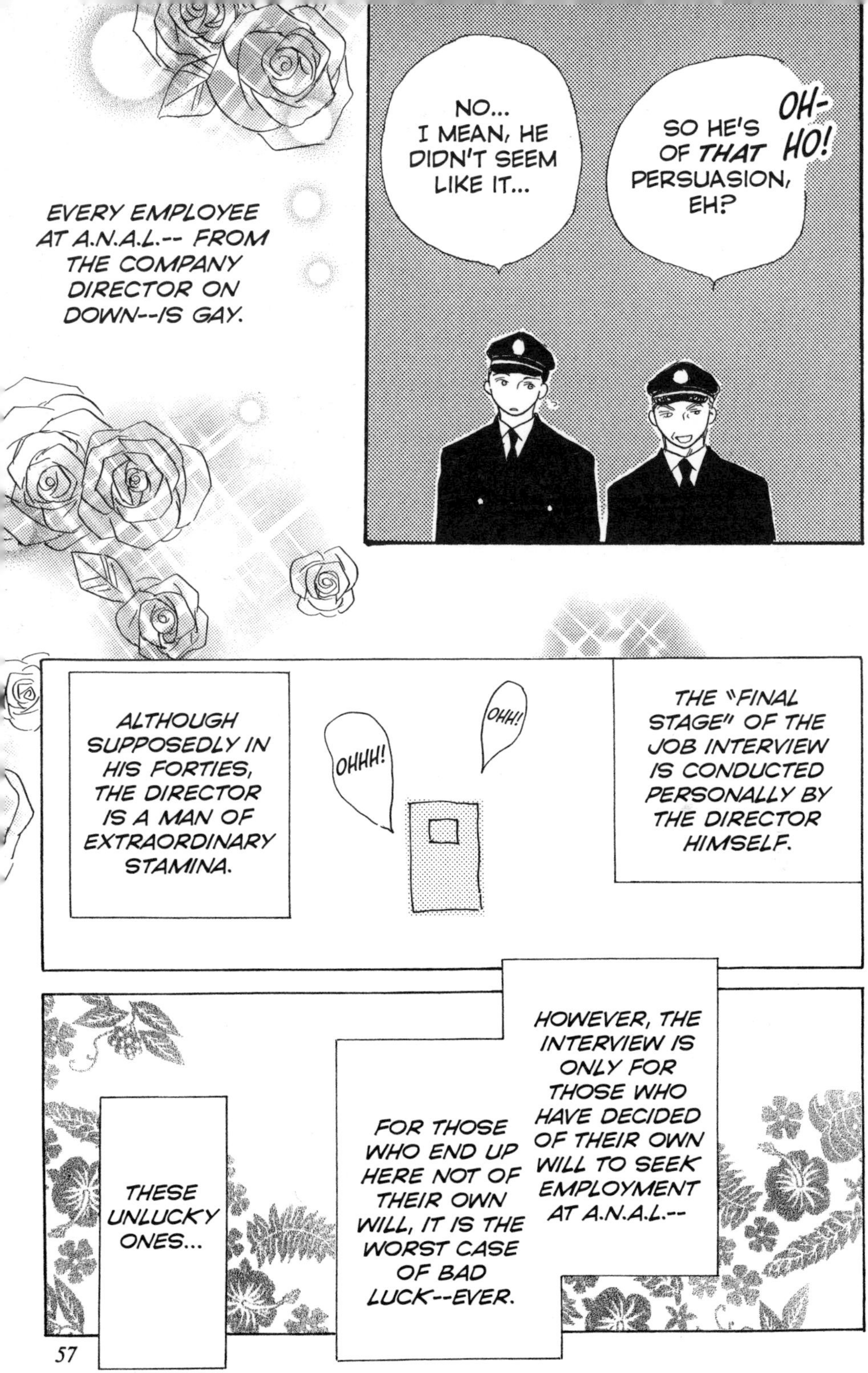
OH-HO!
SO HE'S OF THAT PERSUASION, EH?
NO... I MEAN, HE DIDN'T SEEM LIKE IT...
EVERY EMPLOYEE AT A.N.A.L.-- FROM THE COMPANY DIRECTOR ON DOWN--IS GAY.
THE "FINAL STAGE" OF THE JOB INTERVIEW IS CONDUCTED PERSONALLY BY THE DIRECTOR HIMSELF.
OHH!
OHHH!
ALTHOUGH SUPPOSEDLY IN HIS FORTIES, THE DIRECTOR IS A MAN OF EXTRAORDINARY STAMINA.
HOWEVER, THE INTERVIEW IS ONLY FOR THOSE WHO HAVE DECIDED OF THEIR OWN WILL TO SEEK EMPLOYMENT AT A.N.A.L.--
FOR THOSE WHO END UP HERE NOT OF THEIR OWN WILL, IT IS THE WORST CASE OF BAD LUCK--EVER.
THESE UNLUCKY ONES...

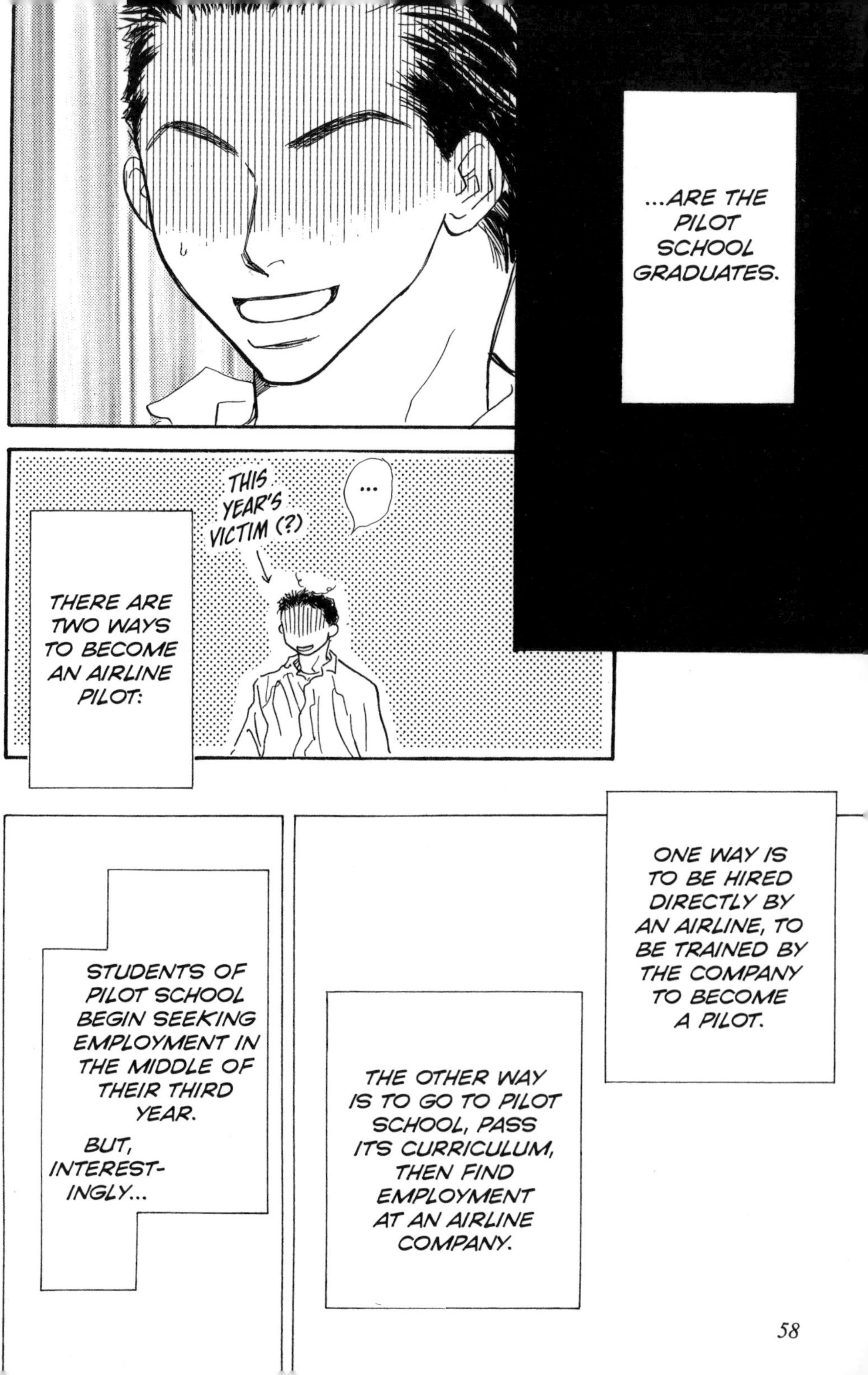
...ARE THE PILOT SCHOOL GRADUATES.
...
THIS YEAR'S VICTIM (?)
THERE ARE TWO WAYS TO BECOME AN AIRLINE PILOT:
ONE WAY IS TO BE HIRED DIRECTLY BY AN AIRLINE, TO BE TRAINED BY THE COMPANY TO BECOME A PILOT.
THE OTHER WAY IS TO GO TO PILOT SCHOOL, PASS ITS CURRICULUM, THEN FIND EMPLOYMENT AT AN AIRLINE COMPANY.
STUDENTS OF PILOT SCHOOL BEGIN SEEKING EMPLOYMENT IN THE MIDDLE OF THEIR THIRD YEAR.
BUT, INTEREST-INGLY...

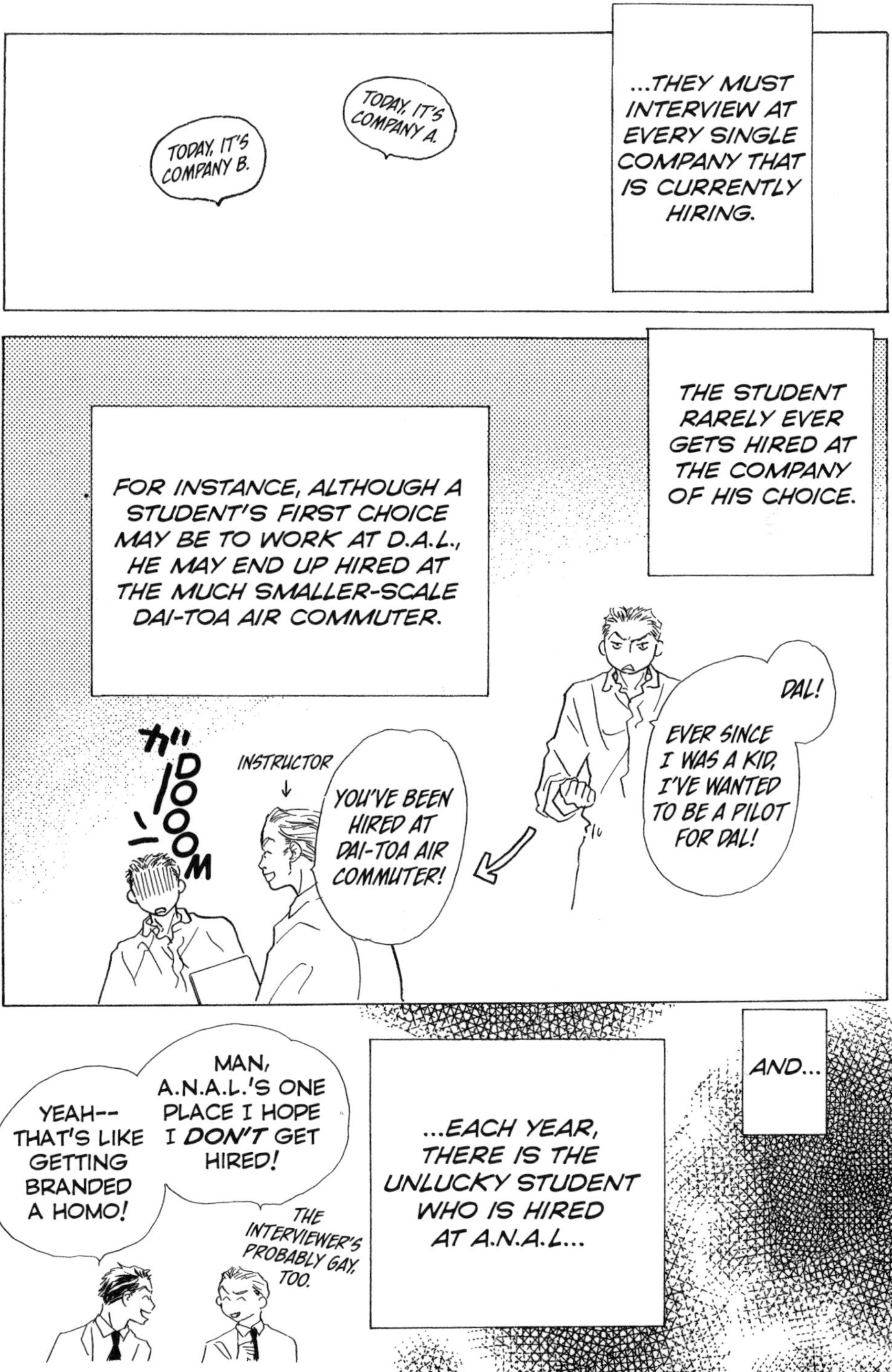
...THEY MUST INTERVIEW AT EVERY SINGLE COMPANY THAT IS CURRENTLY HIRING.
TODAY, IT'S COMPANY A.
TODAY, IT'S COMPANY B.
THE STUDENT RARELY EVER GETS HIRED AT THE COMPANY OF HIS CHOICE.
FOR INSTANCE, ALTHOUGH A STUDENT'S FIRST CHOICE MAY BE TO WORK AT D.A.L., HE MAY END UP HIRED AT THE MUCH SMALLER-SCALE DAI-TOA AIR COMMUTER.
DAL!
EVER SINCE I WAS A KID, I'VE WANTED TO BE A PILOT FOR DAL!
INSTRUCTOR
YOU'VE BEEN HIRED AT DAI-TOA AIR COMMUTER!
DOOOOM
AND...
...EACH YEAR, THERE IS THE UNLUCKY STUDENT WHO IS HIRED AT A.N.A.L...
MAN, A.N.A.L.'S ONE PLACE I HOPE I *DON'T* GET HIRED!
YEAH--THAT'S LIKE GETTING BRANDED A HOMO!
THE INTERVIEWER'S PROBABLY GAY, TOO.

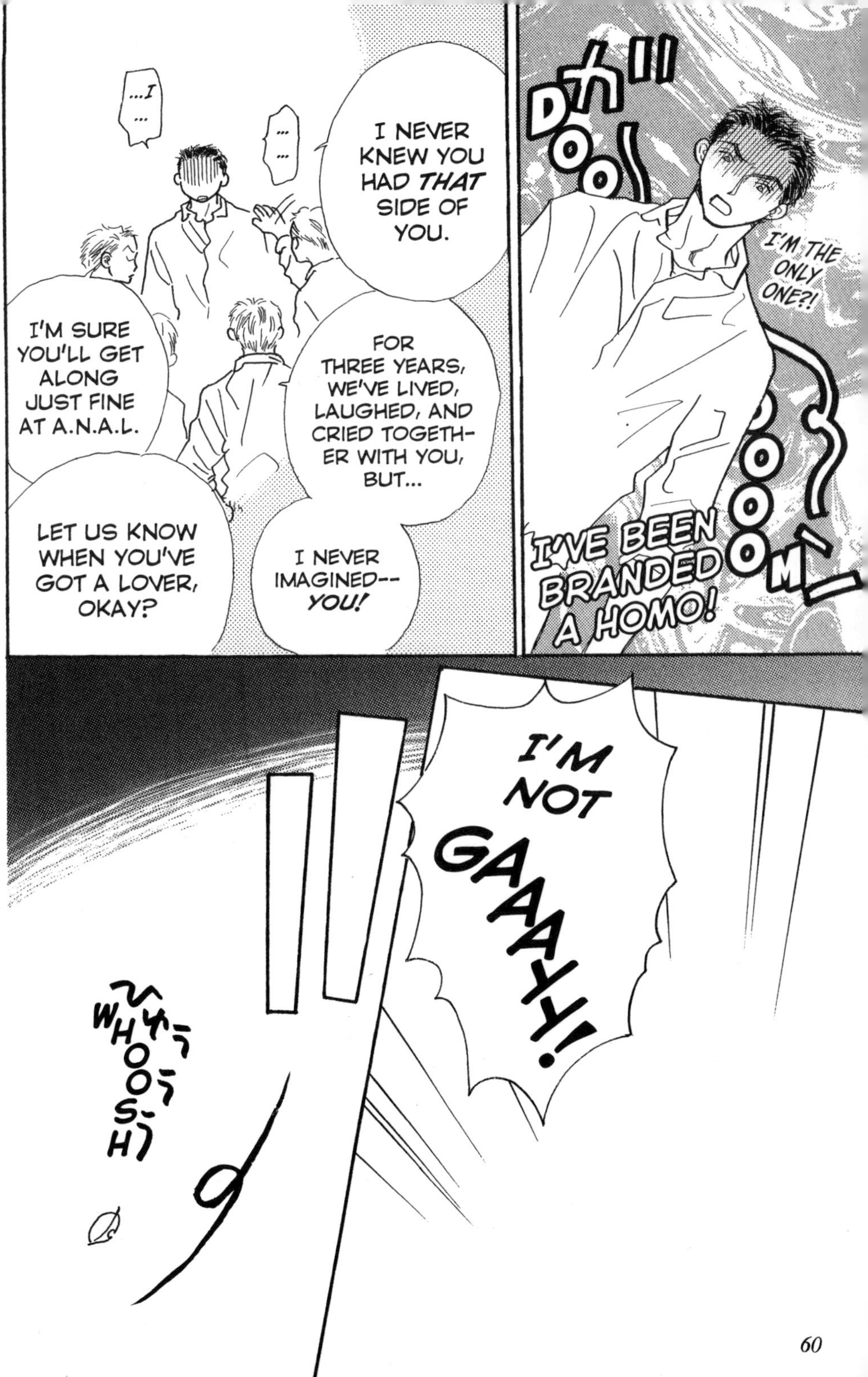

I'M THE ONLY ONE?!
DOOOOOOOM
I'VE BEEN BRANDED A HOMO!
I NEVER KNEW YOU HAD *THAT* SIDE OF YOU.
... ...
...I ...
FOR THREE YEARS, WE'VE LIVED, LAUGHED, AND CRIED TOGETHER WITH YOU, BUT...
I NEVER IMAGINED-- *YOU!*
I'M SURE YOU'LL GET ALONG JUST FINE AT A.N.A.L.
LET US KNOW WHEN YOU'VE GOT A LOVER, OKAY?
I'M NOT GAAAYY!
WHOOSH

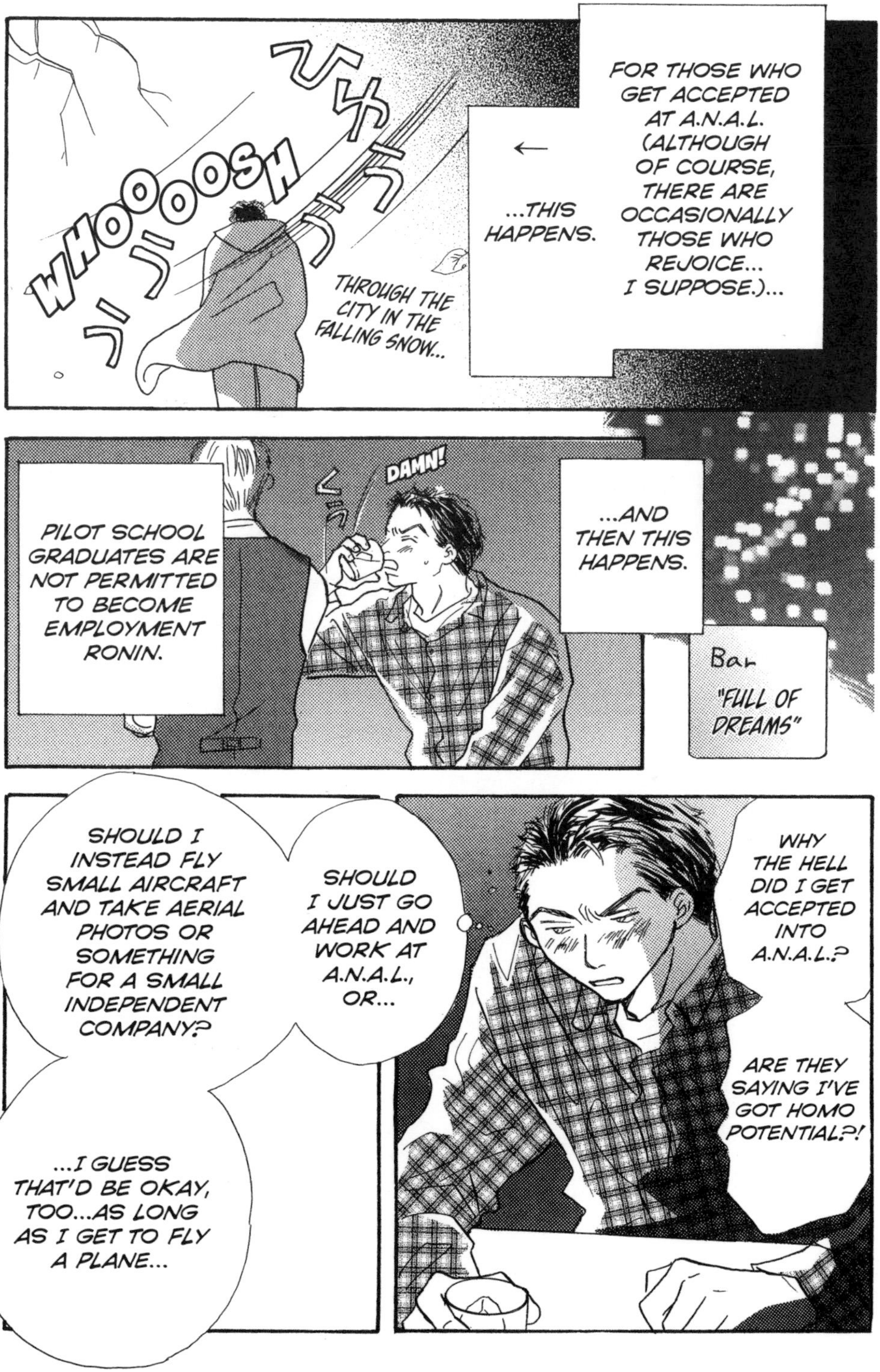
FOR THOSE WHO GET ACCEPTED AT A.N.A.L. (ALTHOUGH OF COURSE, THERE ARE OCCASIONALLY THOSE WHO REJOICE... I SUPPOSE.)...
←
...THIS HAPPENS.
THROUGH THE CITY IN THE FALLING SNOW...
WHOOOOSH
Bar
"FULL OF DREAMS"
...AND THEN THIS HAPPENS.
DAMN!
PILOT SCHOOL GRADUATES ARE NOT PERMITTED TO BECOME EMPLOYMENT RONIN.
WHY THE HELL DID I GET ACCEPTED INTO A.N.A.L.?
ARE THEY SAYING I'VE GOT HOMO POTENTIAL?!
SHOULD I JUST GO AHEAD AND WORK AT A.N.A.L., OR...
SHOULD I INSTEAD FLY SMALL AIRCRAFT AND TAKE AERIAL PHOTOS OR SOMETHING FOR A SMALL INDEPENDENT COMPANY?
...I GUESS THAT'D BE OKAY, TOO...AS LONG AS I GET TO FLY A PLANE...

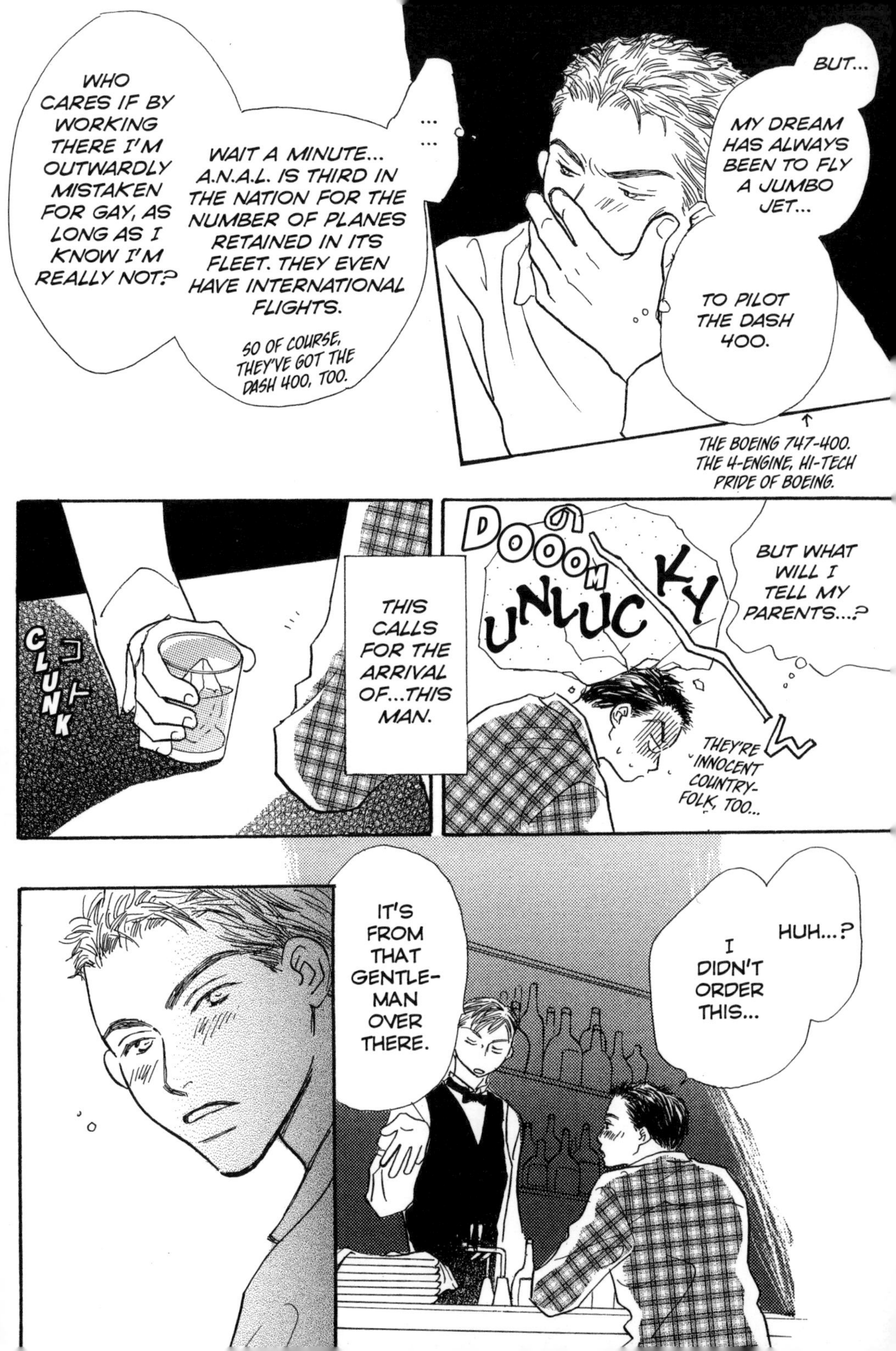
BUT...
MY DREAM HAS ALWAYS BEEN TO FLY A JUMBO JET...
TO PILOT THE DASH 400.
THE BOEING 747-400. THE 4-ENGINE, HI-TECH PRIDE OF BOEING.
... ...
WAIT A MINUTE... A.N.A.L. IS THIRD IN THE NATION FOR THE NUMBER OF PLANES RETAINED IN ITS FLEET. THEY EVEN HAVE INTERNATIONAL FLIGHTS.
SO OF COURSE, THEY'VE GOT THE DASH 400, TOO.
WHO CARES IF BY WORKING THERE I'M OUTWARDLY MISTAKEN FOR GAY, AS LONG AS I KNOW I'M REALLY NOT?
DOOOOM
UNLUCKY
BUT WHAT WILL I TELL MY PARENTS...?
THEY'RE INNOCENT COUNTRY-FOLK, TOO...
THIS CALLS FOR THE ARRIVAL OF...THIS MAN.
CLUNK
HUH...?
I DIDN'T ORDER THIS...
IT'S FROM THAT GENTLEMAN OVER THERE.

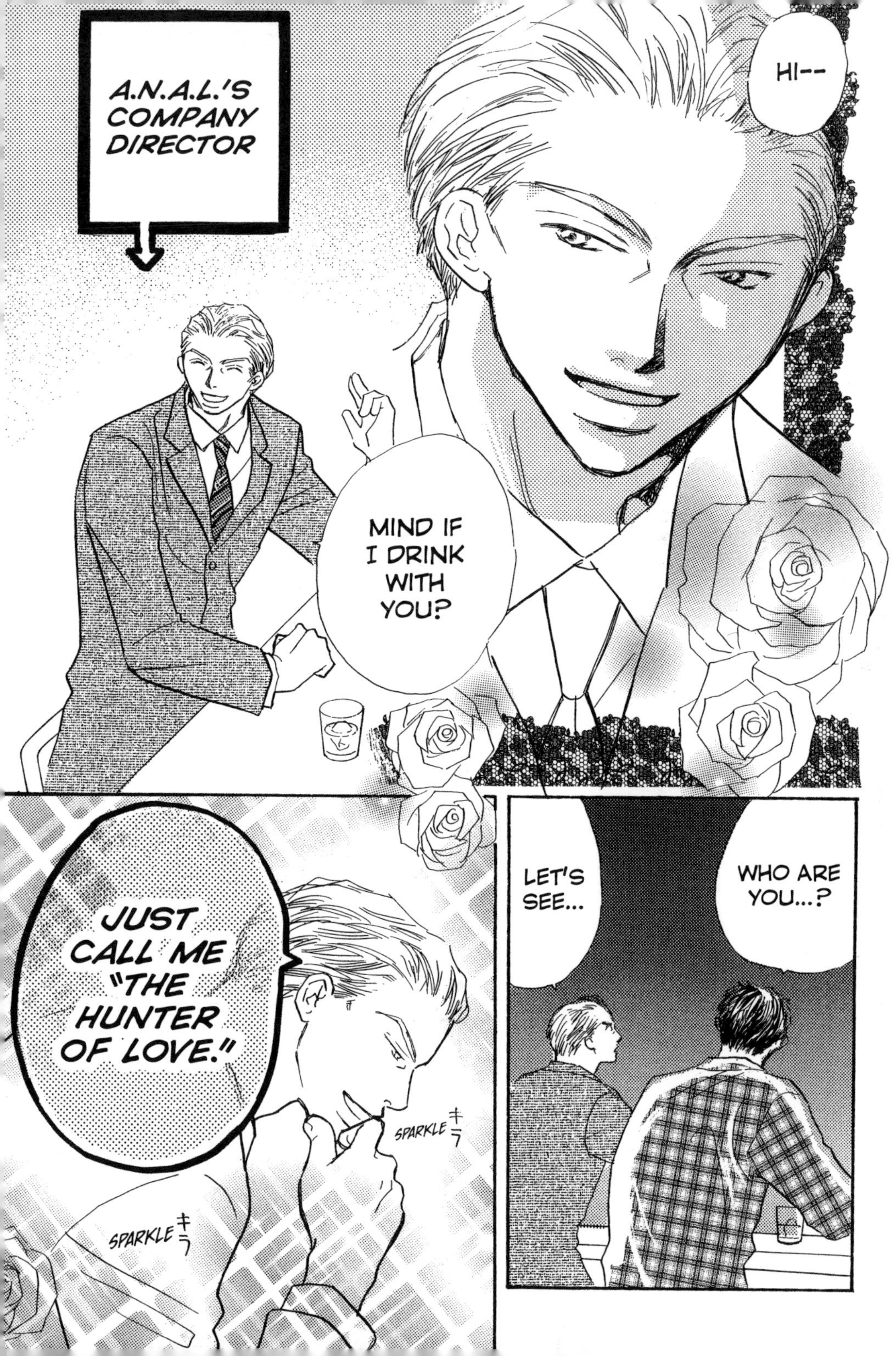
HI--
MIND IF I DRINK WITH YOU?
A.N.A.L.'S COMPANY DIRECTOR
WHO ARE YOU...?
LET'S SEE...
JUST CALL ME "THE HUNTER OF LOVE."
SPARKLE キラ
SPARKLE キラ

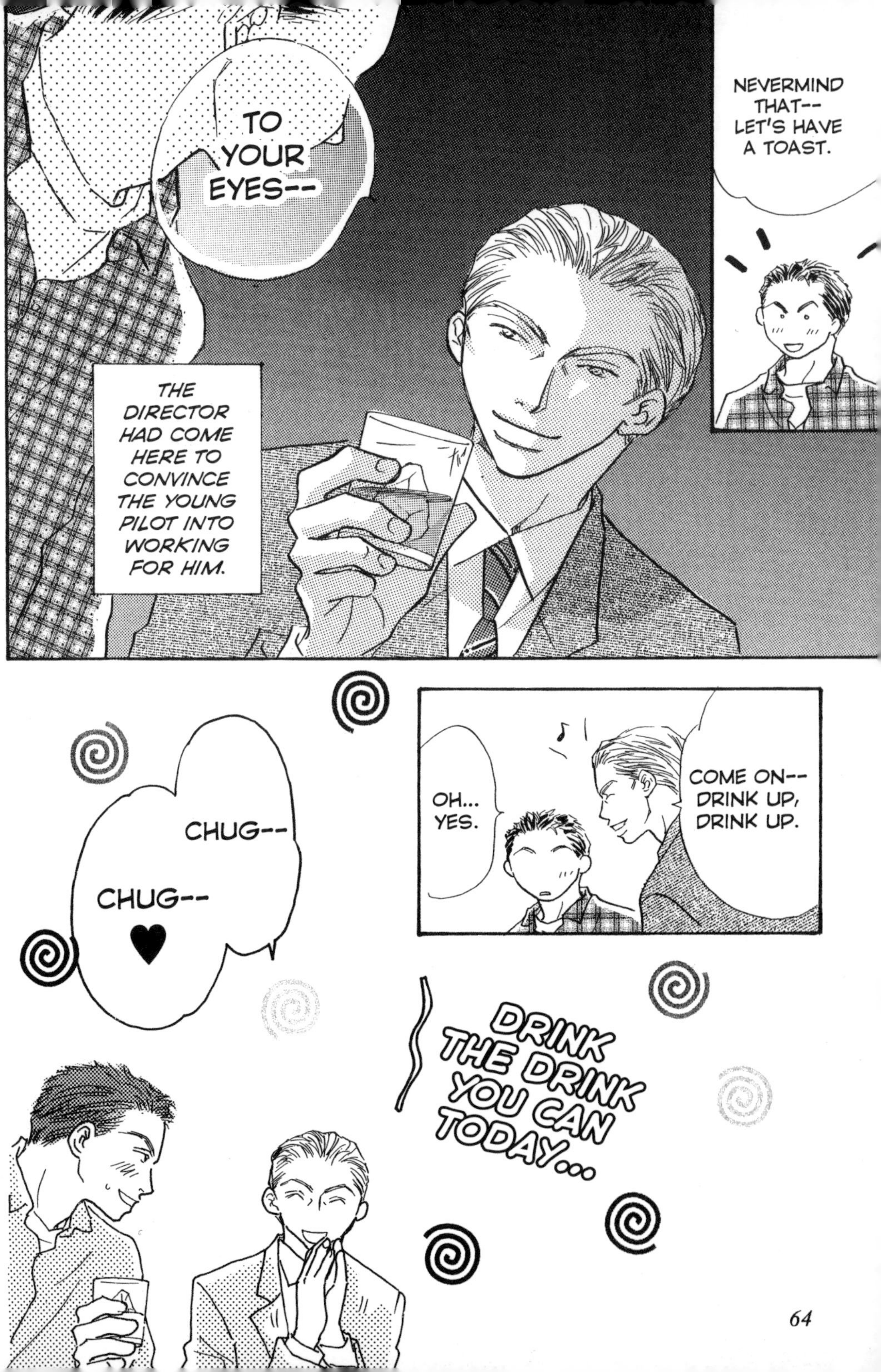

NEVERMIND THAT-- LET'S HAVE A TOAST.
TO YOUR EYES--
THE DIRECTOR HAD COME HERE TO CONVINCE THE YOUNG PILOT INTO WORKING FOR HIM.
COME ON-- DRINK UP, DRINK UP.
OH... YES.
CHUG-- CHUG-- ♥
DRINK THE DRINK YOU CAN TODAY...

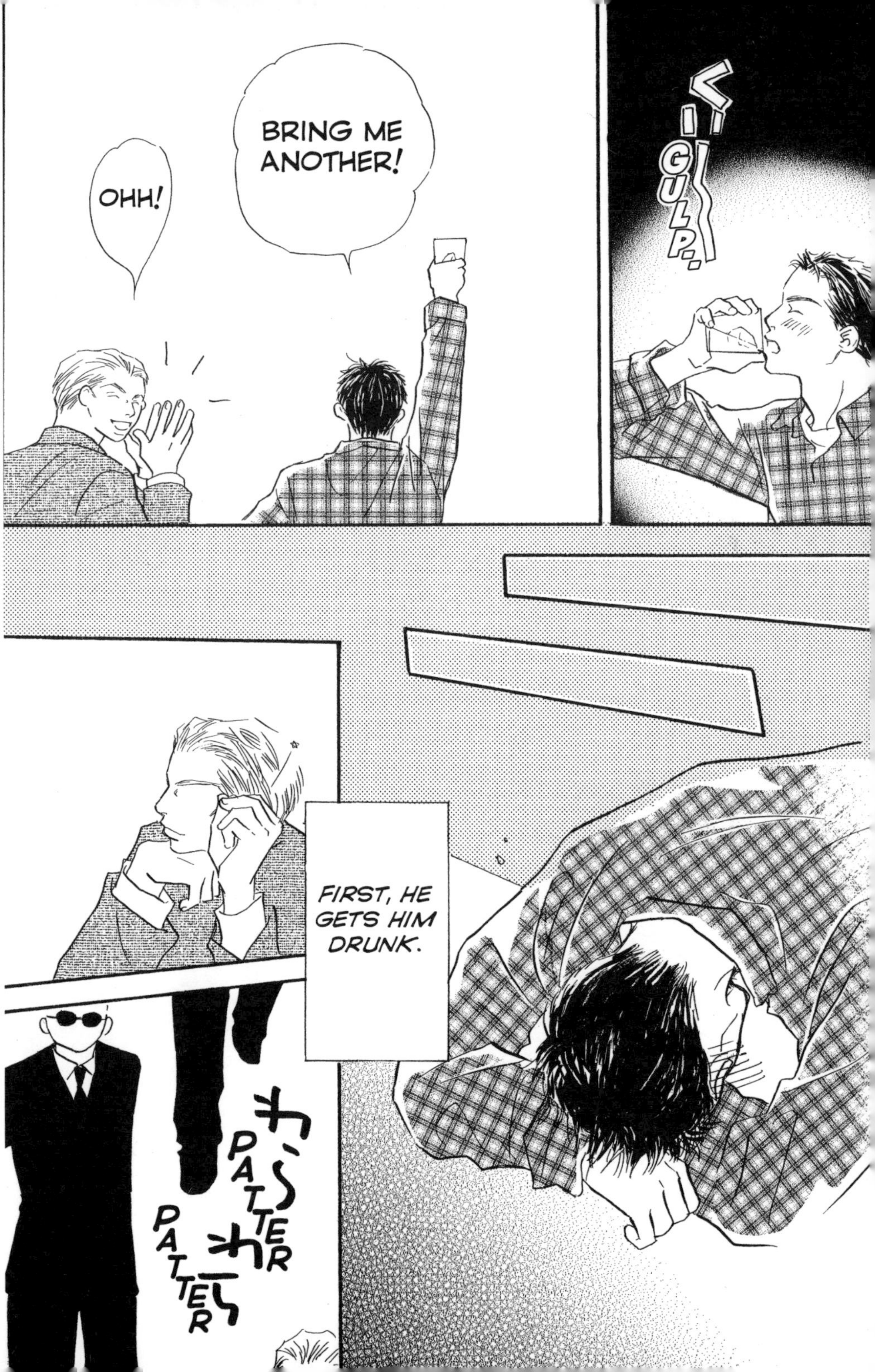

GULP..
BRING ME ANOTHER!
OHH!
FIRST, HE GETS HIM DRUNK.
PATTER
PATTER

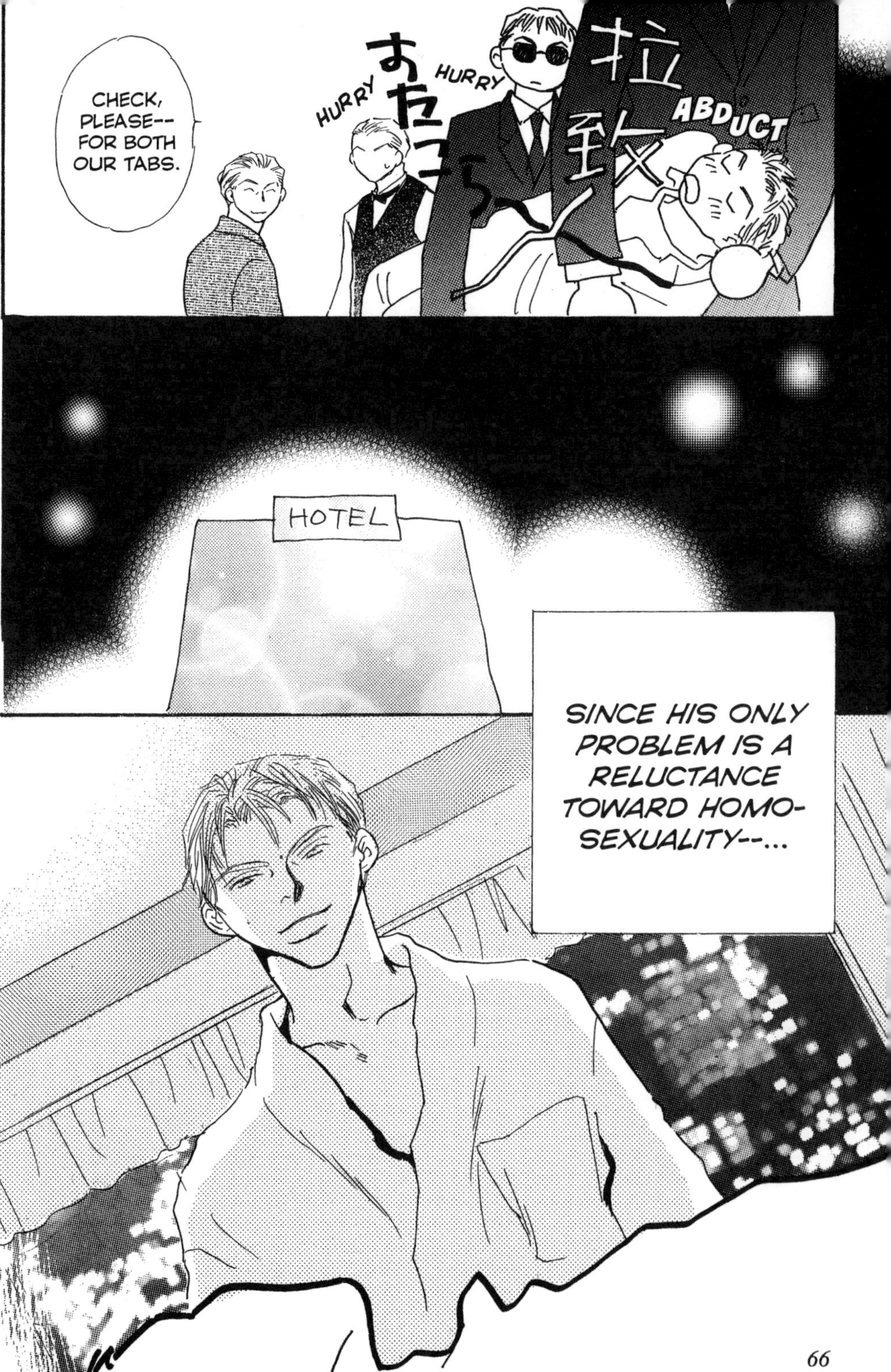
拉致
ABDUCT
HURRY
HURRY
CHECK, PLEASE-- FOR BOTH OUR TABS.
HOTEL
SINCE HIS ONLY PROBLEM IS A RELUCTANCE TOWARD HOMO-SEXUALITY--...

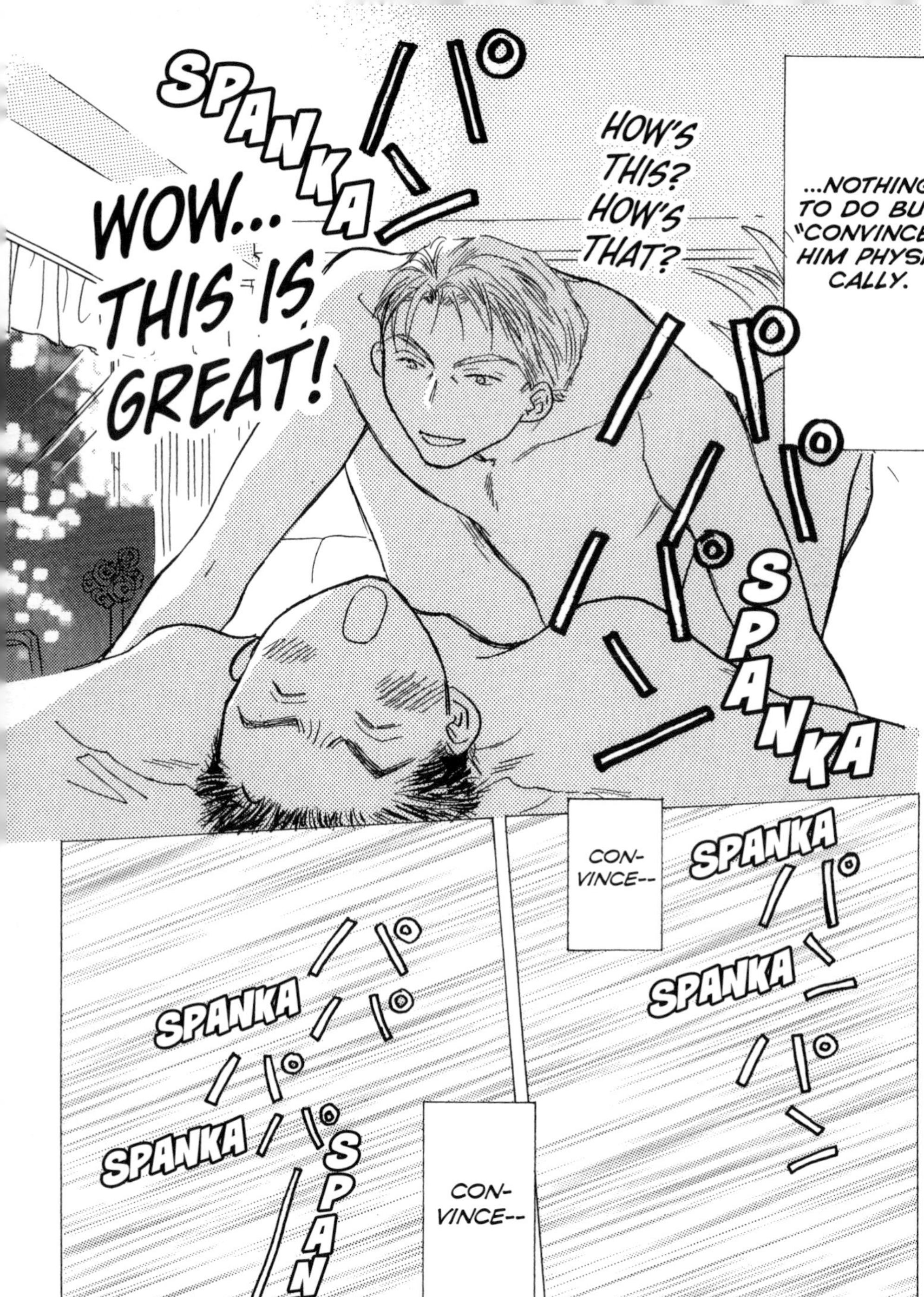
...NOTHING TO DO BUT "CONVINCE" HIM PHYSICALLY.
SPANKA
HOW'S THIS? HOW'S THAT?
SPANKA
WOW... THIS IS GREAT!
CON-VINCE--
SPANKA
SPANKA
CON-VINCE--
SPANKA
SPANKA
SPANK!

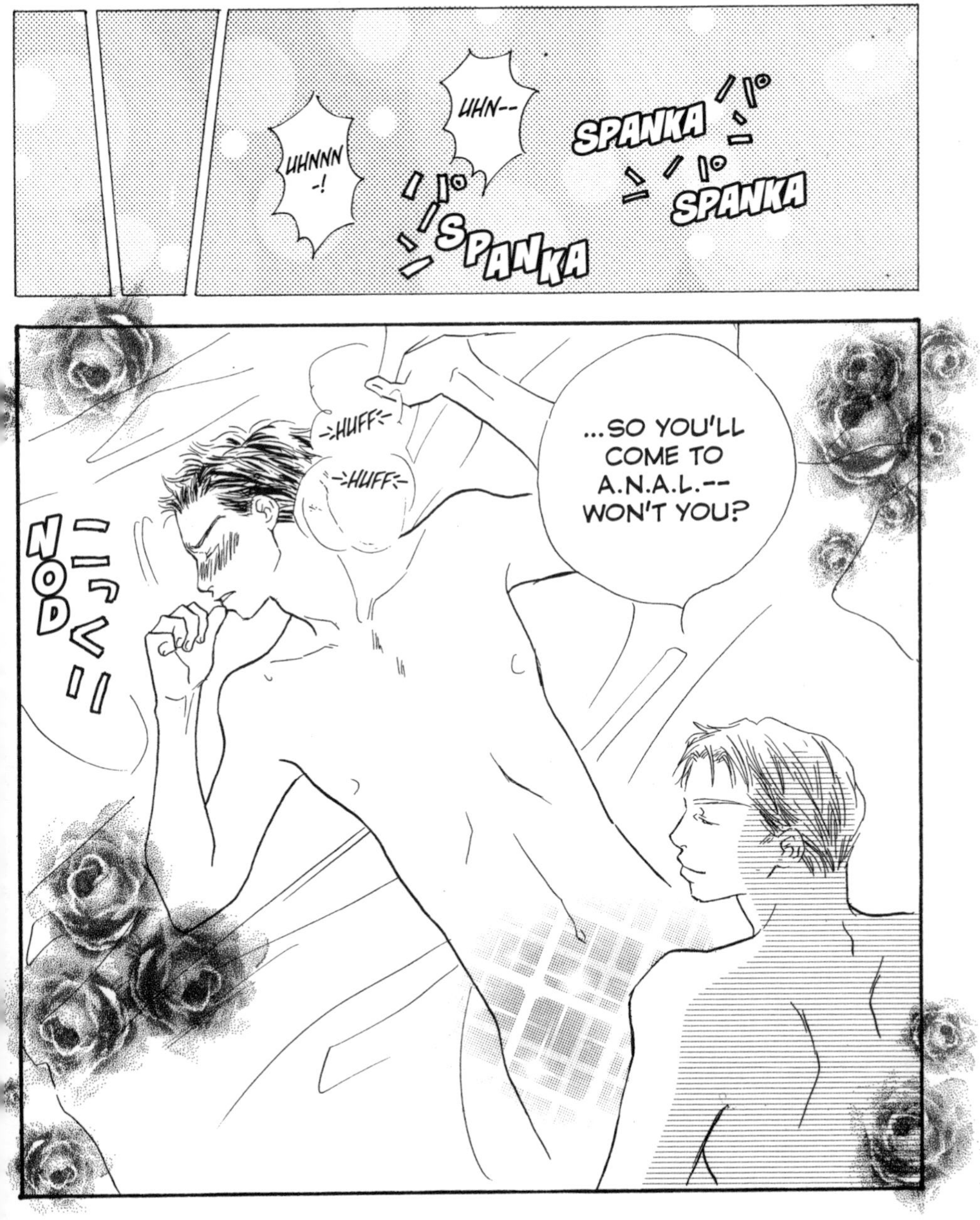
SPANKA
SPANKA
UHN--
SPANKA
UHNNN -!
...SO YOU'LL COME TO A.N.A.L.-- WON'T YOU?
HUFF
HUFF
NOD

AND SO--THIS IS HOW, EACH YEAR, THE DIRECTOR "CONVINCES" THE (STRAIGHT) PILOT CANDIDATES...

99.9% SUCCESS RATE

**THE NARROW GATES OF A.N.A.L. END**

THE END.

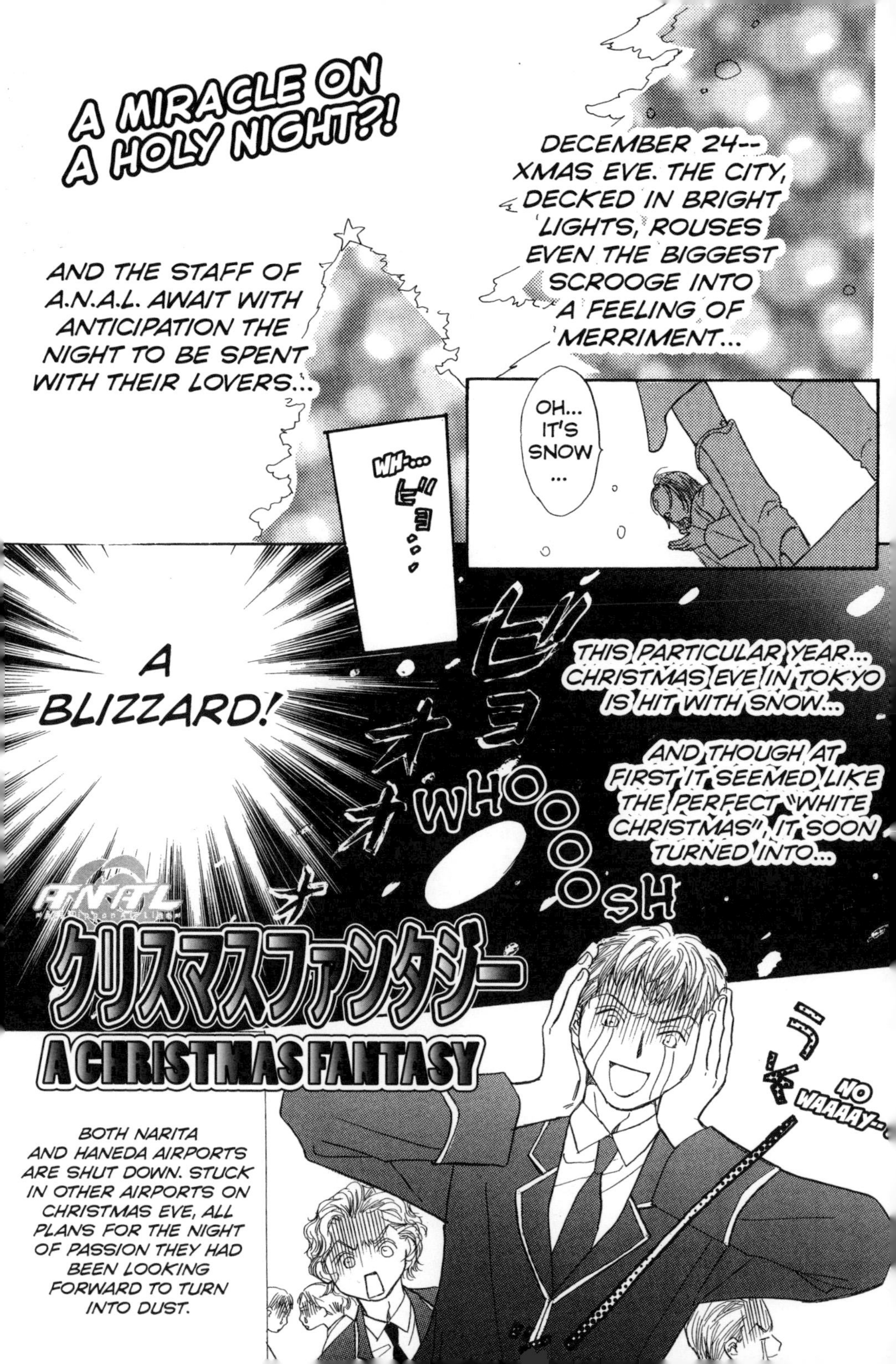
A MIRACLE ON A HOLY NIGHT?!
DECEMBER 24-- XMAS EVE. THE CITY, DECKED IN BRIGHT LIGHTS, ROUSES EVEN THE BIGGEST SCROOGE INTO A FEELING OF MERRIMENT...
AND THE STAFF OF A.N.A.L. AWAIT WITH ANTICIPATION THE NIGHT TO BE SPENT WITH THEIR LOVERS...
OH... IT'S SNOW ...
WH-...
THIS PARTICULAR YEAR... CHRISTMAS EVE IN TOKYO IS HIT WITH SNOW...
AND THOUGH AT FIRST IT SEEMED LIKE THE PERFECT "WHITE CHRISTMAS", IT SOON TURNED INTO...
A BLIZZARD!
WHOOOOOSH
クリスマスファンタジー
A CHRISTMAS FANTASY
NO WAAAAY--
BOTH NARITA AND HANEDA AIRPORTS ARE SHUT DOWN. STUCK IN OTHER AIRPORTS ON CHRISTMAS EVE, ALL PLANS FOR THE NIGHT OF PASSION THEY HAD BEEN LOOKING FORWARD TO TURN INTO DUST.

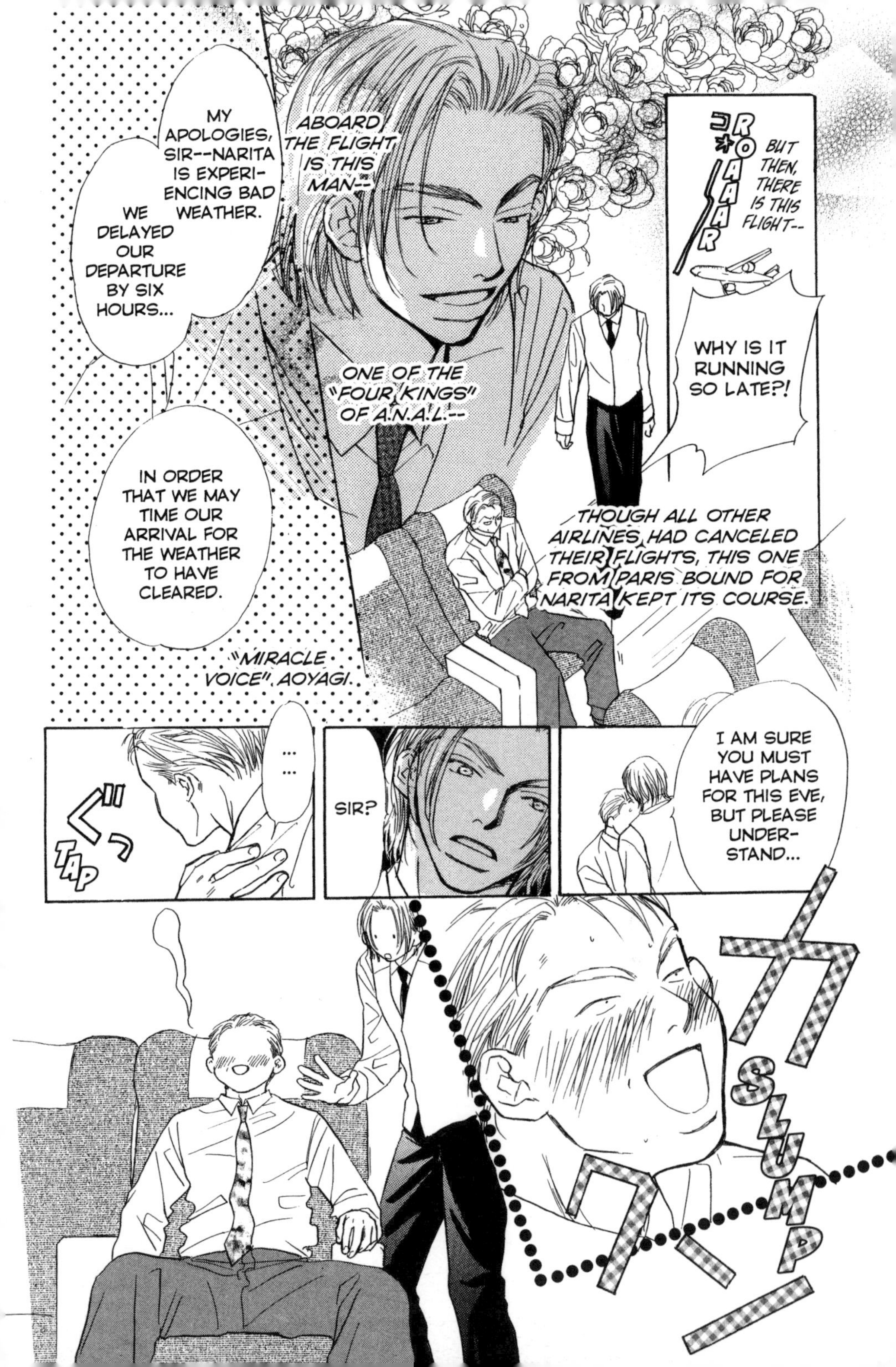
ROAAAR
BUT THEN, THERE IS THIS FLIGHT--
WHY IS IT RUNNING SO LATE?!
THOUGH ALL OTHER AIRLINES HAD CANCELED THEIR FLIGHTS, THIS ONE FROM PARIS BOUND FOR NARITA KEPT ITS COURSE.
ABOARD THE FLIGHT IS THIS MAN--
ONE OF THE "FOUR KINGS" OF A.N.A.L.--
MY APOLOGIES, SIR--NARITA IS EXPERIENCING BAD WEATHER.
WE DELAYED OUR DEPARTURE BY SIX HOURS...
IN ORDER THAT WE MAY TIME OUR ARRIVAL FOR THE WEATHER TO HAVE CLEARED.
"MIRACLE VOICE" AOYAGI.
I AM SURE YOU MUST HAVE PLANS FOR THIS EVE, BUT PLEASE UNDERSTAND...
SIR?
... ...
TAP
SLUMP

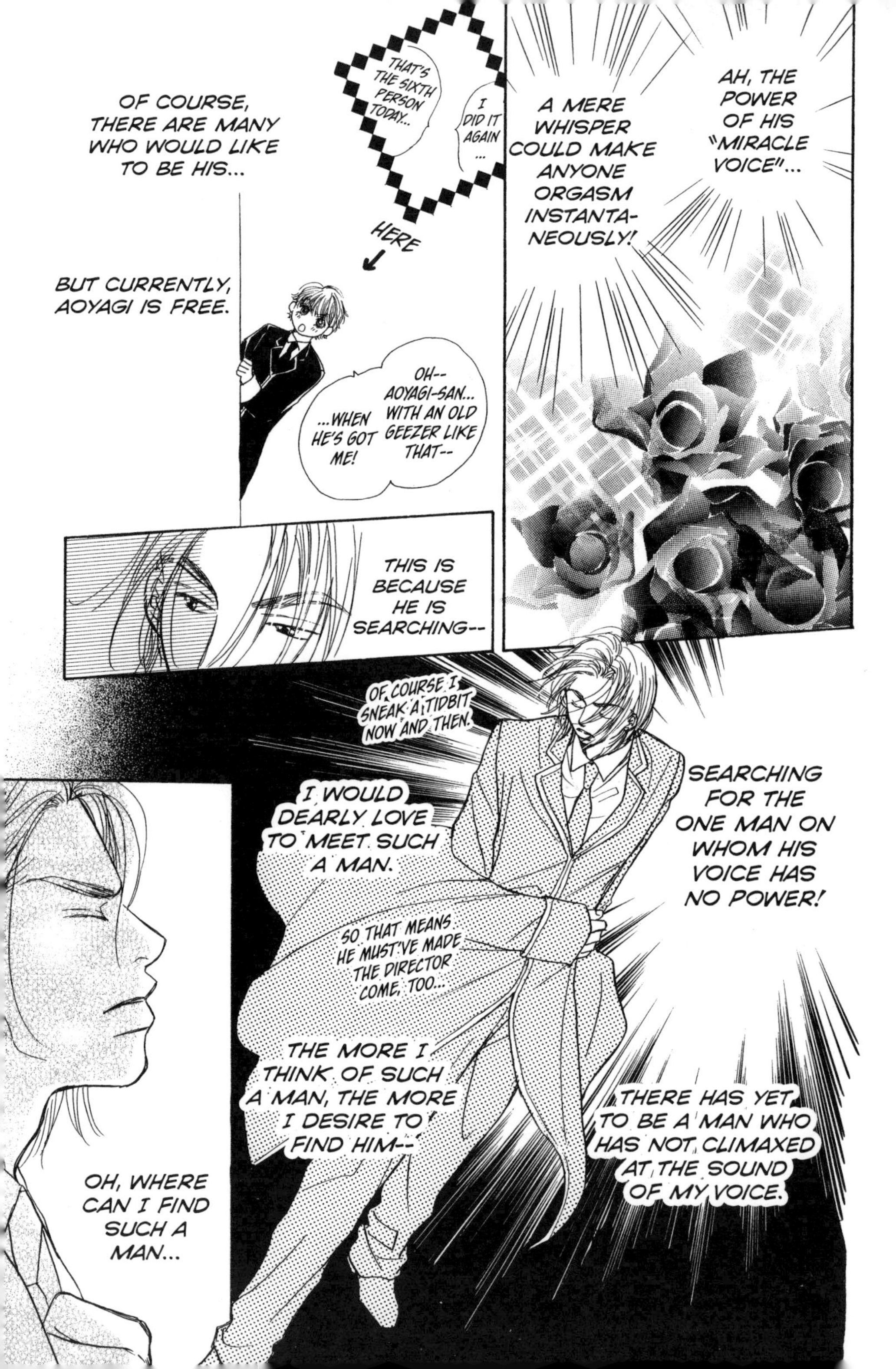
AH, THE POWER OF HIS "MIRACLE VOICE"...
A MERE WHISPER COULD MAKE ANYONE ORGASM INSTANTANEOUSLY!
I DID IT AGAIN...
THAT'S THE SIXTH PERSON TODAY...
OF COURSE, THERE ARE MANY WHO WOULD LIKE TO BE HIS...
HERE
BUT CURRENTLY, AOYAGI IS FREE.
OH-- AOYAGI-SAN... WITH AN OLD GEEZER LIKE THAT--
...WHEN HE'S GOT ME!
THIS IS BECAUSE HE IS SEARCHING--
SEARCHING FOR THE ONE MAN ON WHOM HIS VOICE HAS NO POWER!
OF COURSE I SNEAK A TIDBIT NOW AND THEN.
I WOULD DEARLY LOVE TO MEET SUCH A MAN.
SO THAT MEANS HE MUST'VE MADE THE DIRECTOR COME, TOO...
THERE HAS YET TO BE A MAN WHO HAS NOT CLIMAXED AT THE SOUND OF MY VOICE.
THE MORE I THINK OF SUCH A MAN, THE MORE I DESIRE TO FIND HIM--
OH, WHERE CAN I FIND SUCH A MAN...

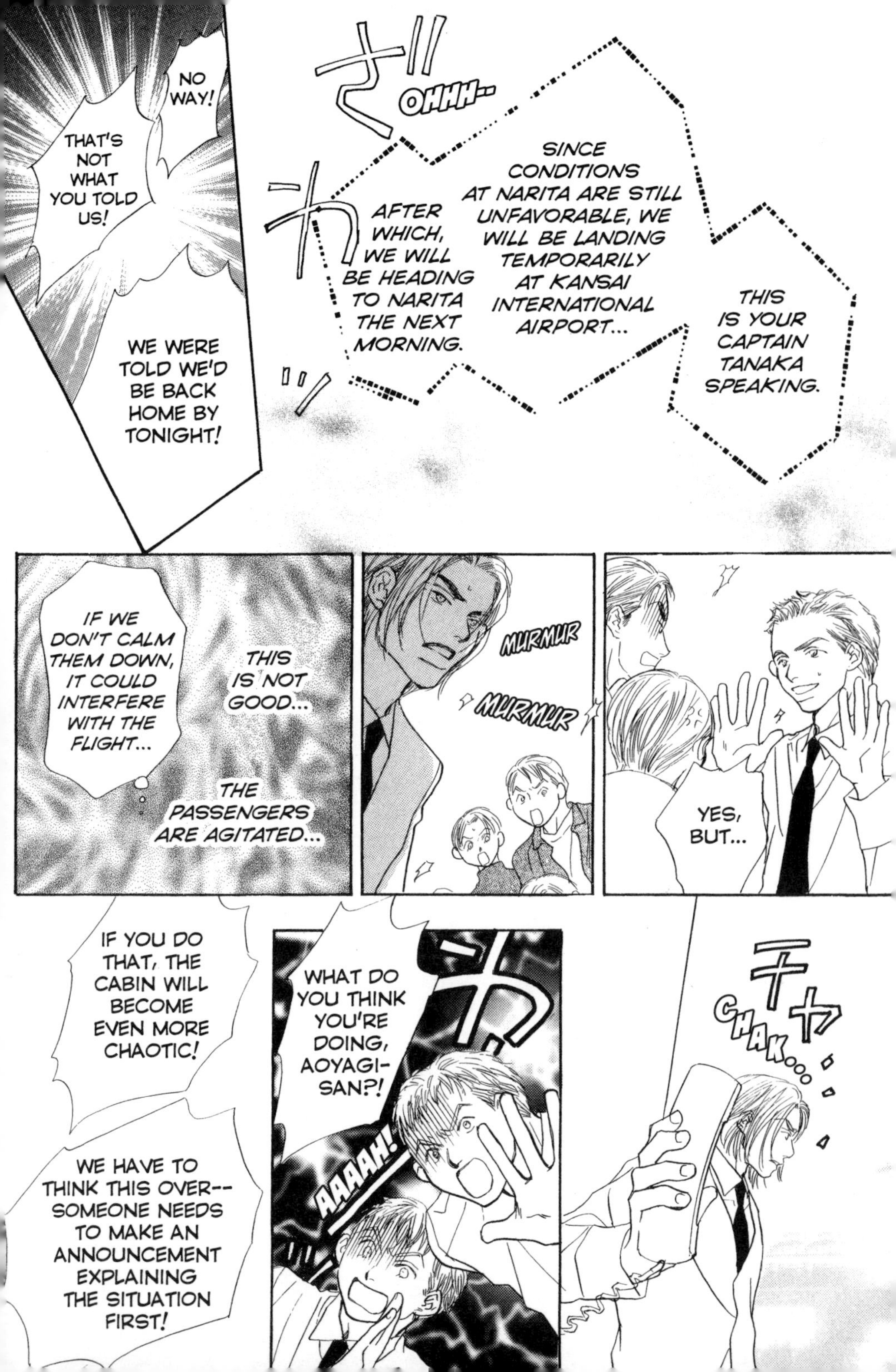
THIS IS YOUR CAPTAIN TANAKA SPEAKING.
SINCE CONDITIONS AT NARITA ARE STILL UNFAVORABLE, WE WILL BE LANDING TEMPORARILY AT KANSAI INTERNATIONAL AIRPORT...
AFTER WHICH, WE WILL BE HEADING TO NARITA THE NEXT MORNING.
OHHH--
NO WAY!
THAT'S NOT WHAT YOU TOLD US!
WE WERE TOLD WE'D BE BACK HOME BY TONIGHT!
YES, BUT...
MURMUR
MURMUR
THE PASSENGERS ARE AGITATED...
THIS IS NOT GOOD...
IF WE DON'T CALM THEM DOWN, IT COULD INTERFERE WITH THE FLIGHT...
CHAK
WHAT DO YOU THINK YOU'RE DOING, AOYAGI-SAN?!
AAAAH!
IF YOU DO THAT, THE CABIN WILL BECOME EVEN MORE CHAOTIC!
WE HAVE TO THINK THIS OVER-- SOMEONE NEEDS TO MAKE AN ANNOUNCEMENT EXPLAINING THE SITUATION FIRST!

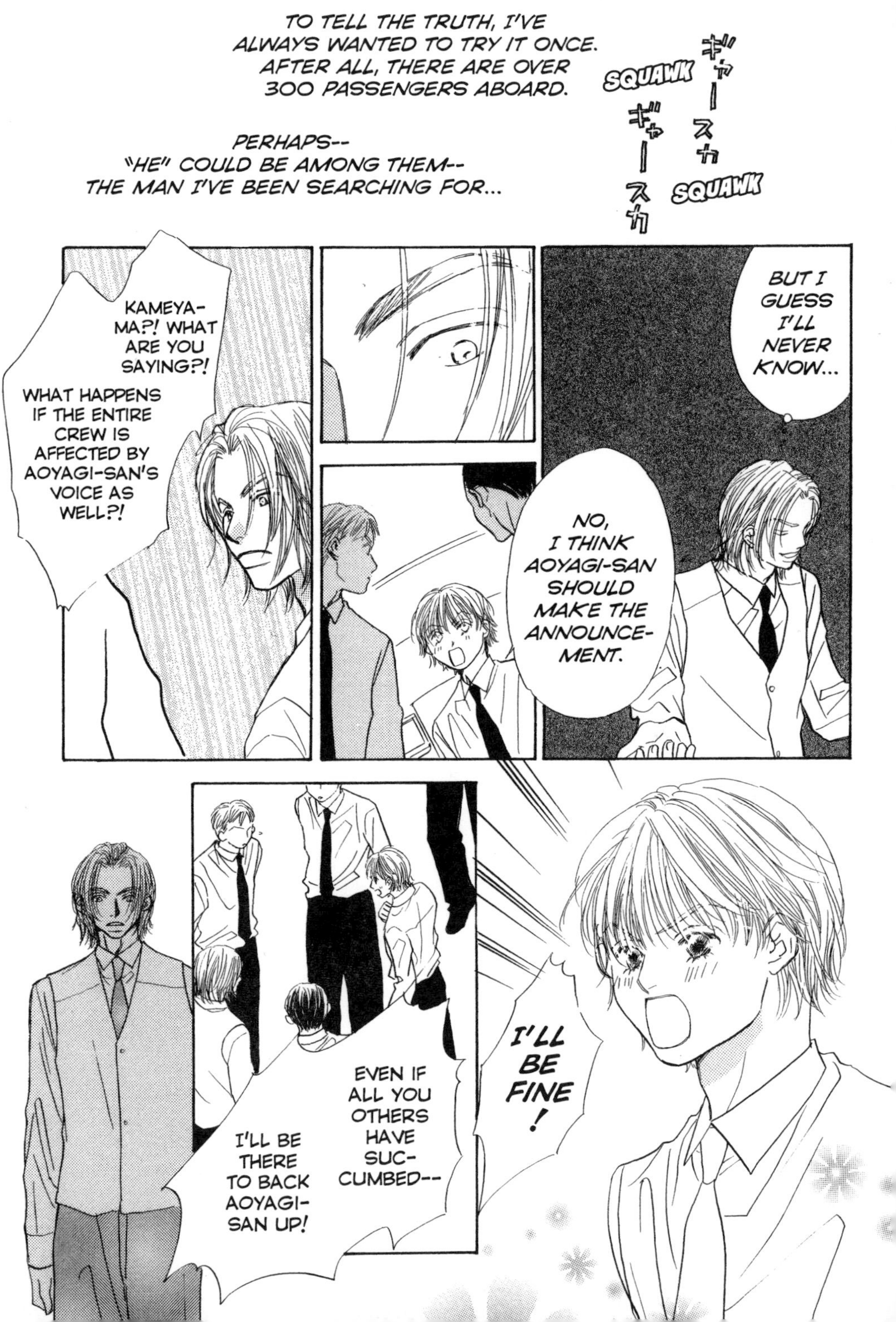
ギャースカ
SQUAWK
ギャースカ
SQUAWK
TO TELL THE TRUTH, I'VE ALWAYS WANTED TO TRY IT ONCE. AFTER ALL, THERE ARE OVER 300 PASSENGERS ABOARD.
PERHAPS-- "HE" COULD BE AMONG THEM-- THE MAN I'VE BEEN SEARCHING FOR...
BUT I GUESS I'LL NEVER KNOW...
NO, I THINK AOYAGI-SAN SHOULD MAKE THE ANNOUNCE-MENT.
KAMEYA-MA?! WHAT ARE YOU SAYING?!
WHAT HAPPENS IF THE ENTIRE CREW IS AFFECTED BY AOYAGI-SAN'S VOICE AS WELL?!
I'LL BE FINE!
EVEN IF ALL YOU OTHERS HAVE SUC-CUMBED--
I'LL BE THERE TO BACK AOYAGI-SAN UP!

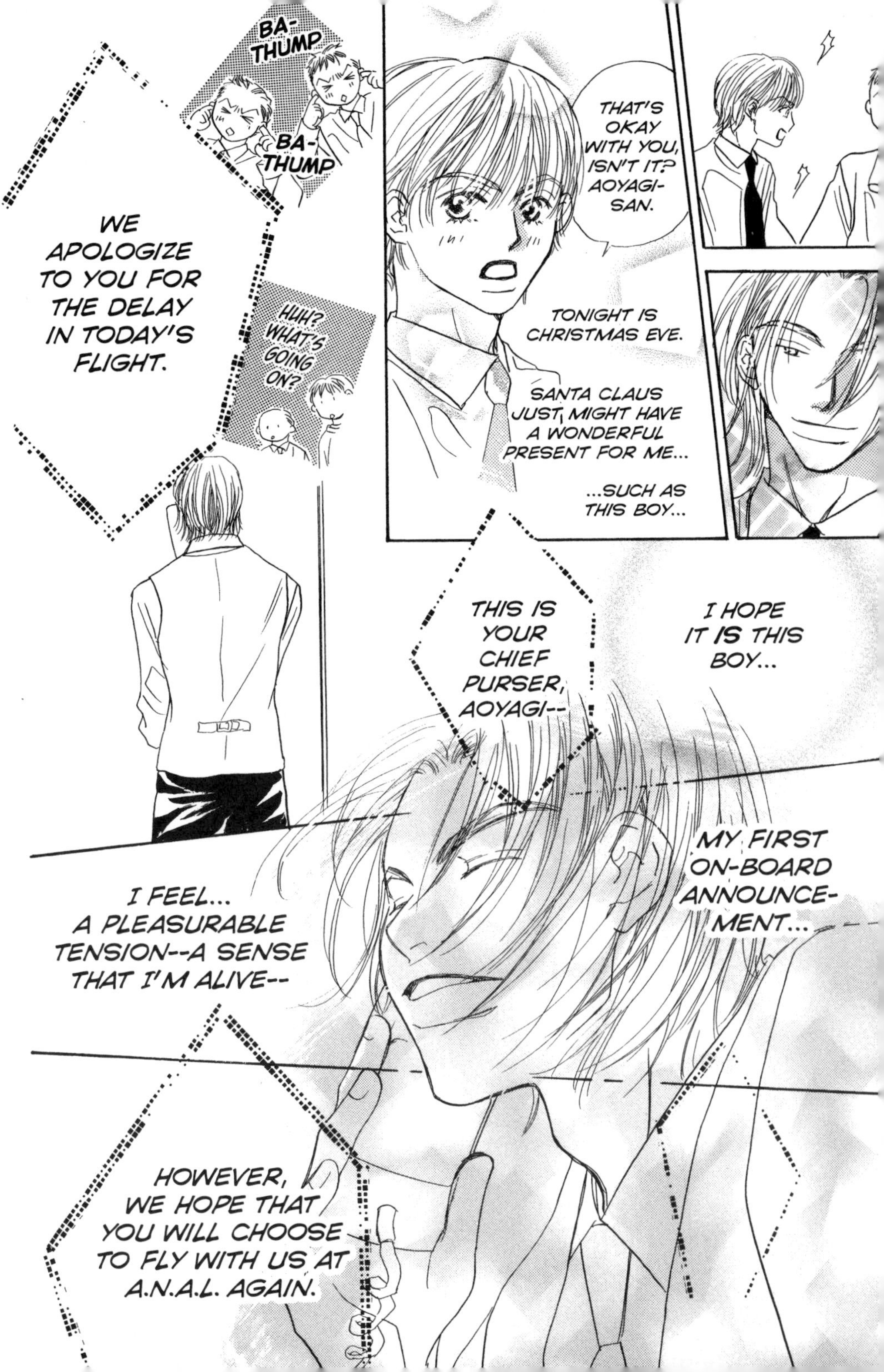
THAT'S OKAY WITH YOU, ISN'T IT? AOYAGI-SAN.
TONIGHT IS CHRISTMAS EVE.
SANTA CLAUS JUST MIGHT HAVE A WONDERFUL PRESENT FOR ME...
...SUCH AS THIS BOY...
BA-THUMP
BA-THUMP
WE APOLOGIZE TO YOU FOR THE DELAY IN TODAY'S FLIGHT.
HUH? WHAT'S GOING ON?
I HOPE IT **IS** THIS BOY...
THIS IS YOUR CHIEF PURSER, AOYAGI--
MY FIRST ON-BOARD ANNOUNCEMENT...
I FEEL... A PLEASURABLE TENSION--A SENSE THAT I'M ALIVE--
HOWEVER, WE HOPE THAT YOU WILL CHOOSE TO FLY WITH US AT A.N.A.L. AGAIN.

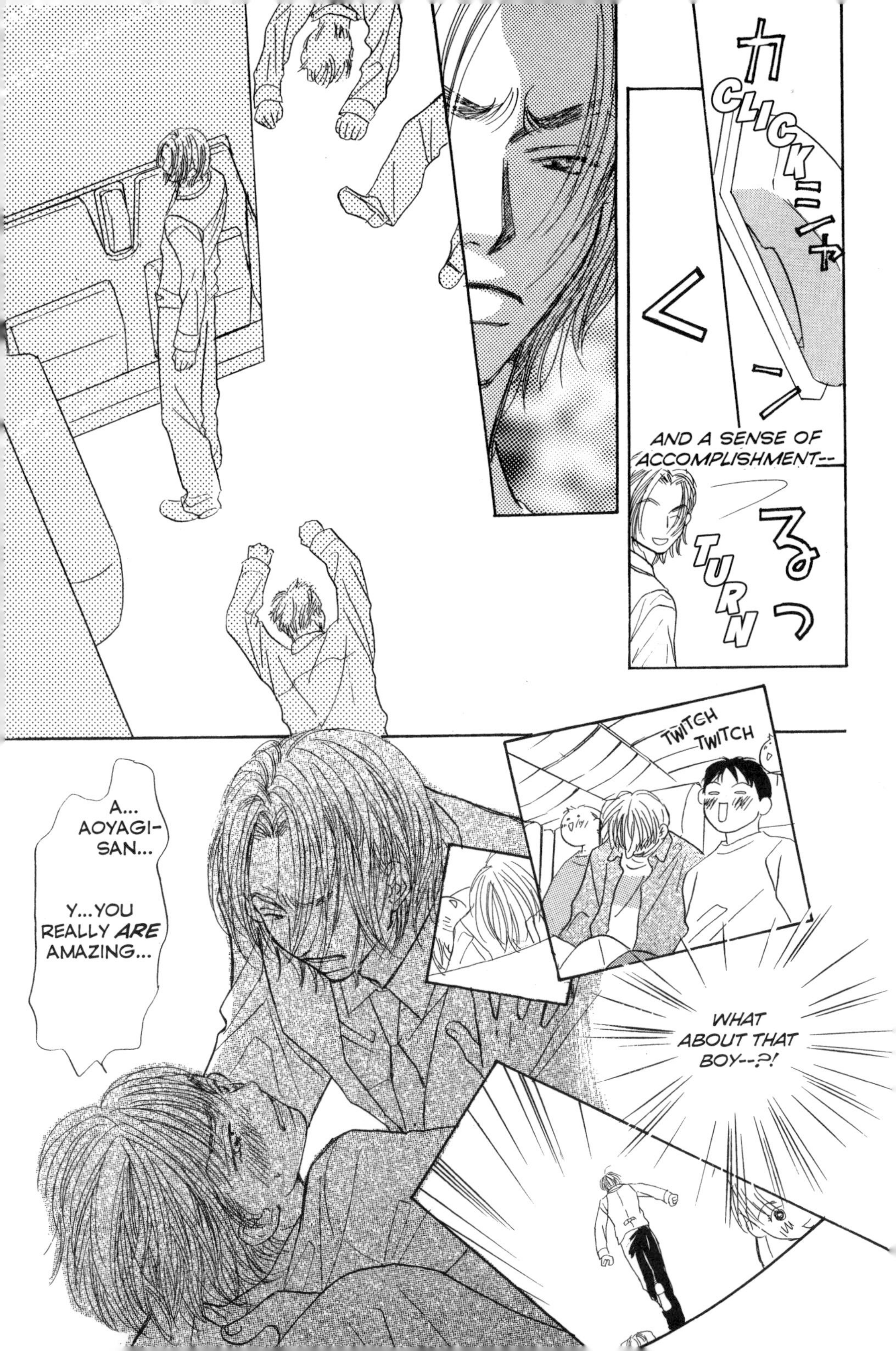
CLICK
AND A SENSE OF ACCOMPLISHMENT--
TURN
TWITCH TWITCH
WHAT ABOUT THAT BOY--?!
A... AOYAGI-SAN...
Y...YOU REALLY ARE AMAZING...

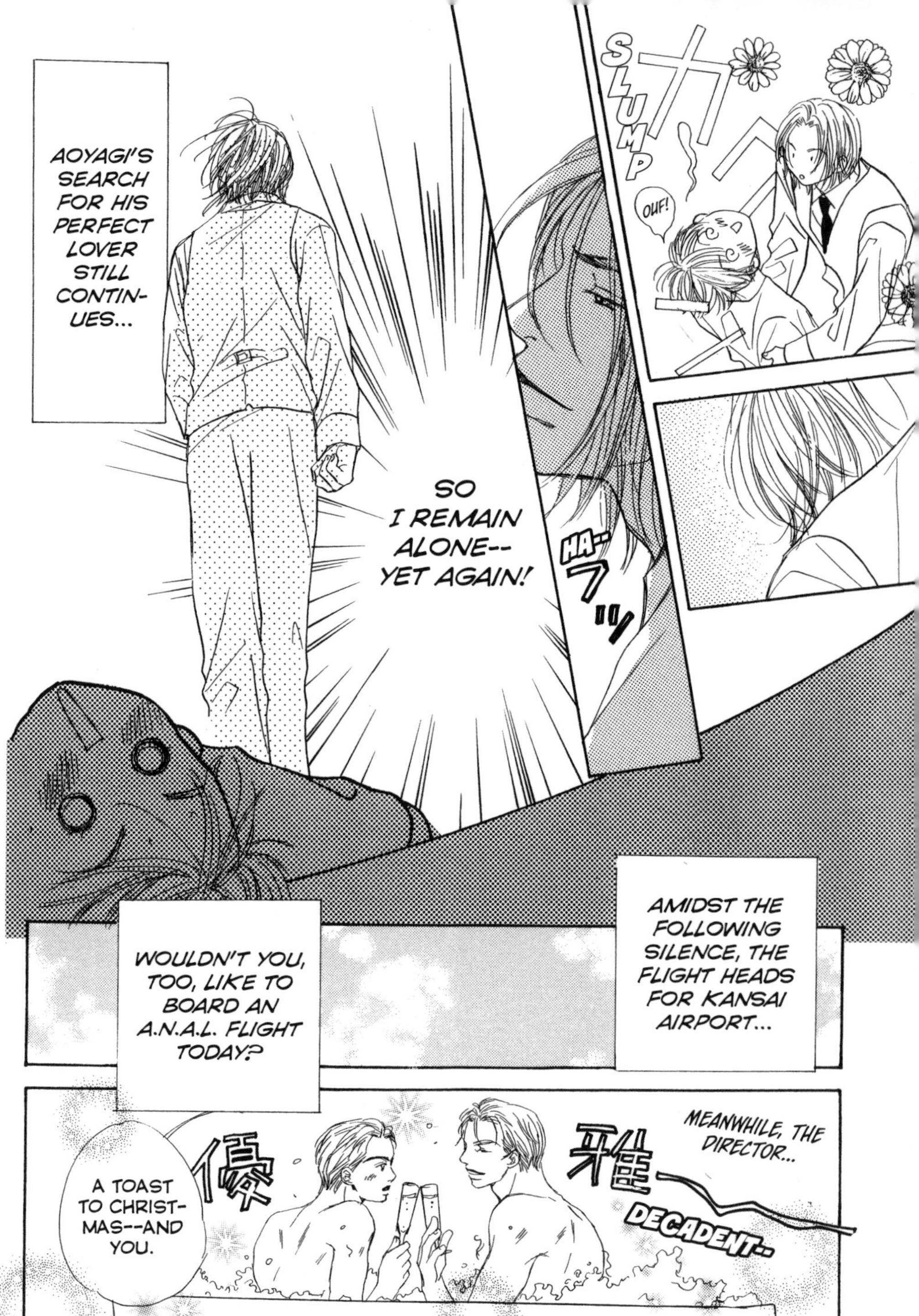
SLUMP
OUF!
HA--
SO I REMAIN ALONE-- YET AGAIN!
AOYAGI'S SEARCH FOR HIS PERFECT LOVER STILL CONTIN-UES...
AMIDST THE FOLLOWING SILENCE, THE FLIGHT HEADS FOR KANSAI AIRPORT...
WOULDN'T YOU, TOO, LIKE TO BOARD AN A.N.A.L. FLIGHT TODAY?
MEANWHILE, THE DIRECTOR...
DECADENT--
A TOAST TO CHRIST-MAS--AND YOU.

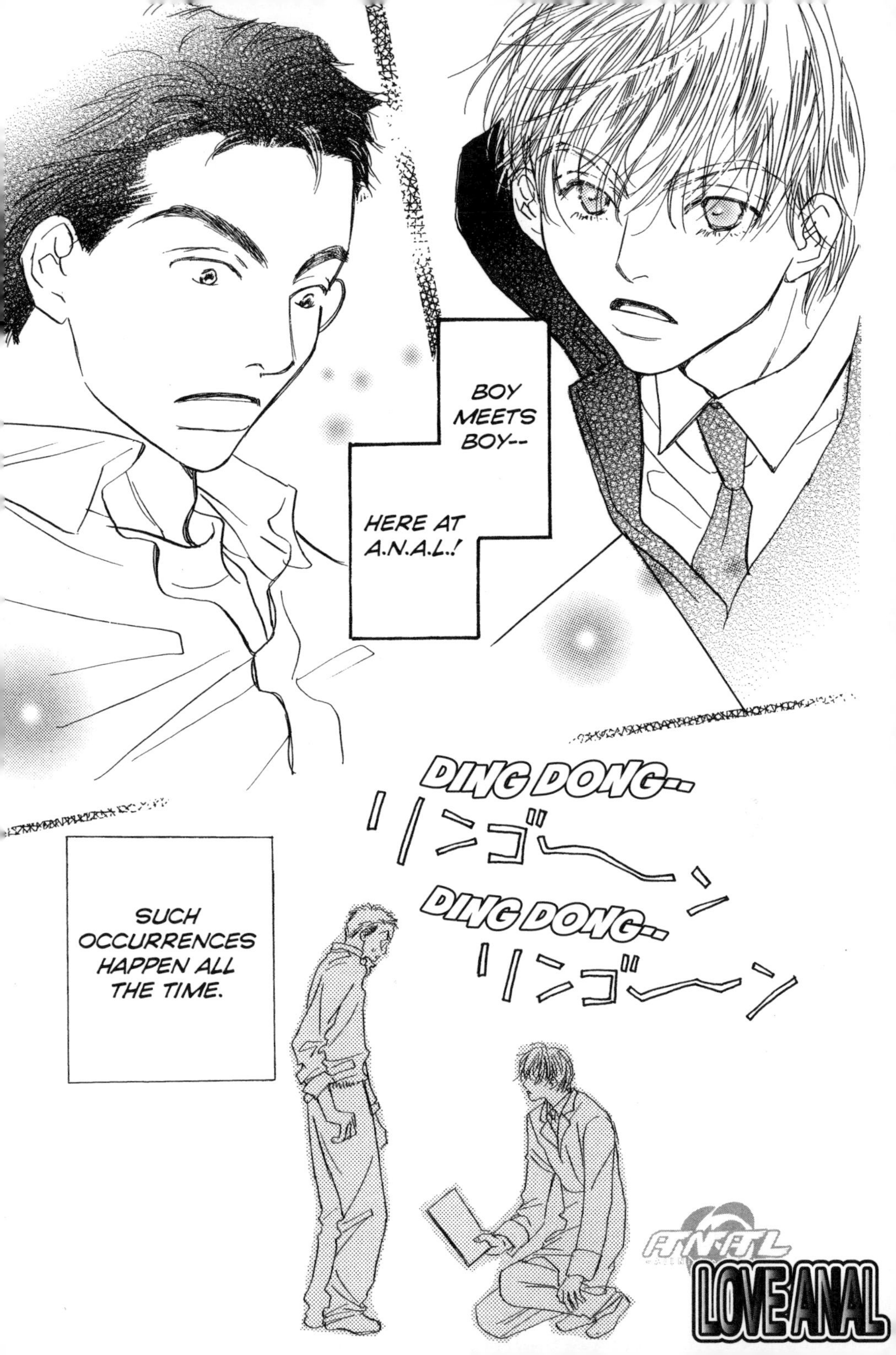
BOY MEETS BOY--
HERE AT A.N.A.L.!
DING DONG--
リンゴーン
DING DONG--
リンゴーン
SUCH OCCURRENCES HAPPEN ALL THE TIME.
LOVE ANAL

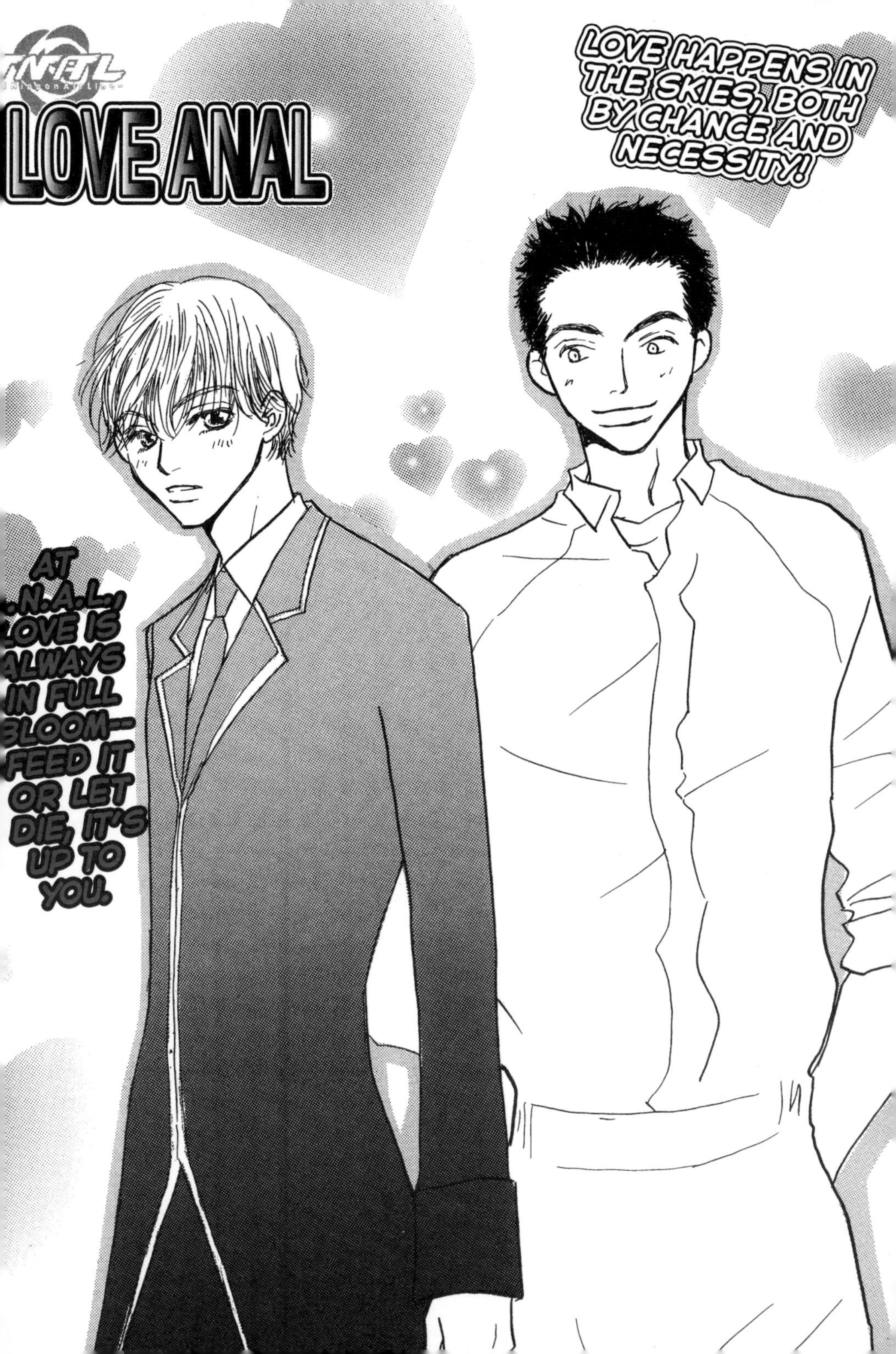

LOVE ANAL
LOVE HAPPENS IN THE SKIES, BOTH BY CHANCE AND NECESSITY!
AT N.A.L., LOVE IS ALWAYS IN FULL BLOOM--FEED IT OR LET DIE, IT'S UP TO YOU.

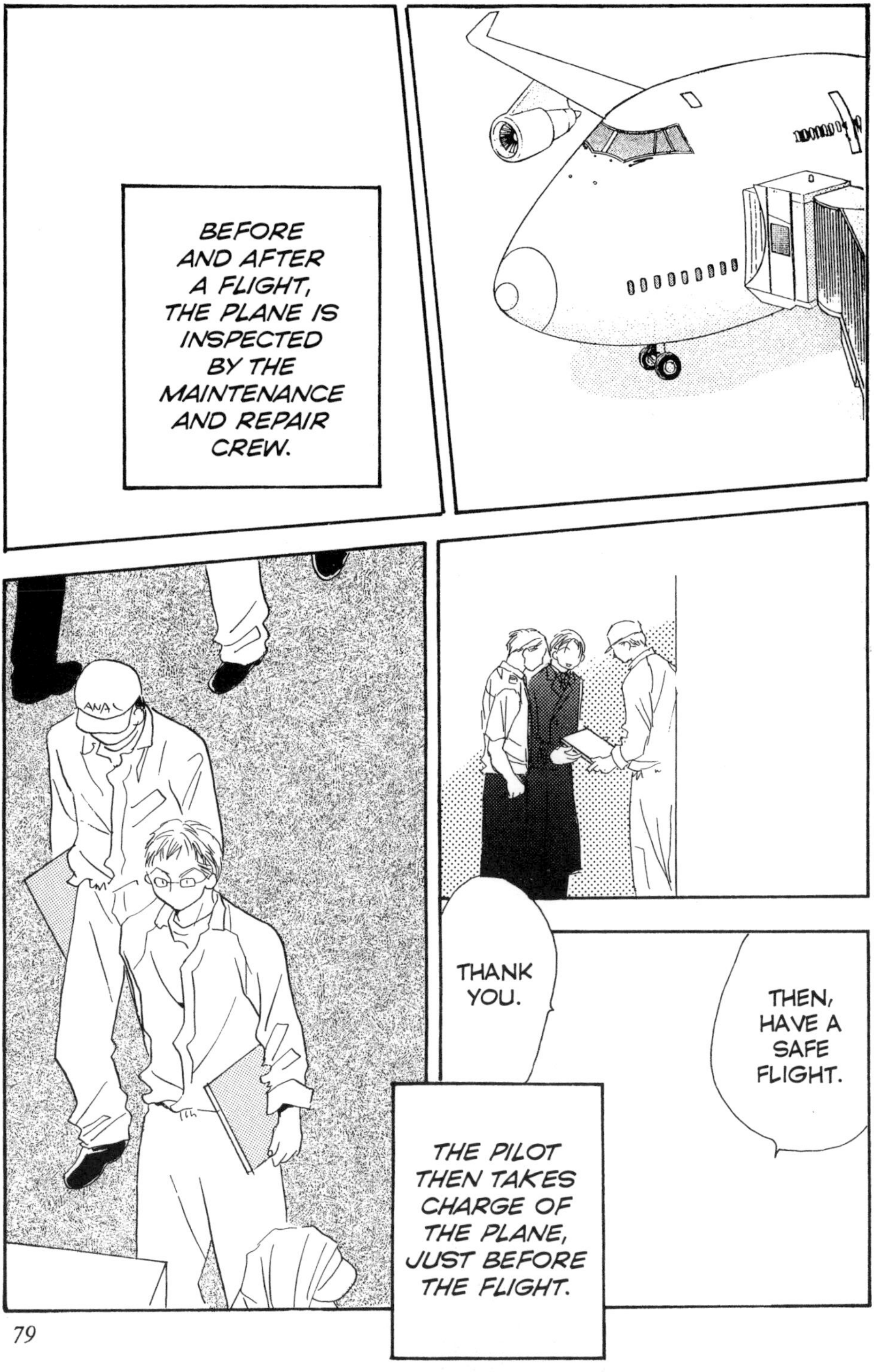
BEFORE AND AFTER A FLIGHT, THE PLANE IS INSPECTED BY THE MAINTENANCE AND REPAIR CREW.
THEN, HAVE A SAFE FLIGHT.
THANK YOU.
THE PILOT THEN TAKES CHARGE OF THE PLANE, JUST BEFORE THE FLIGHT.
ANA

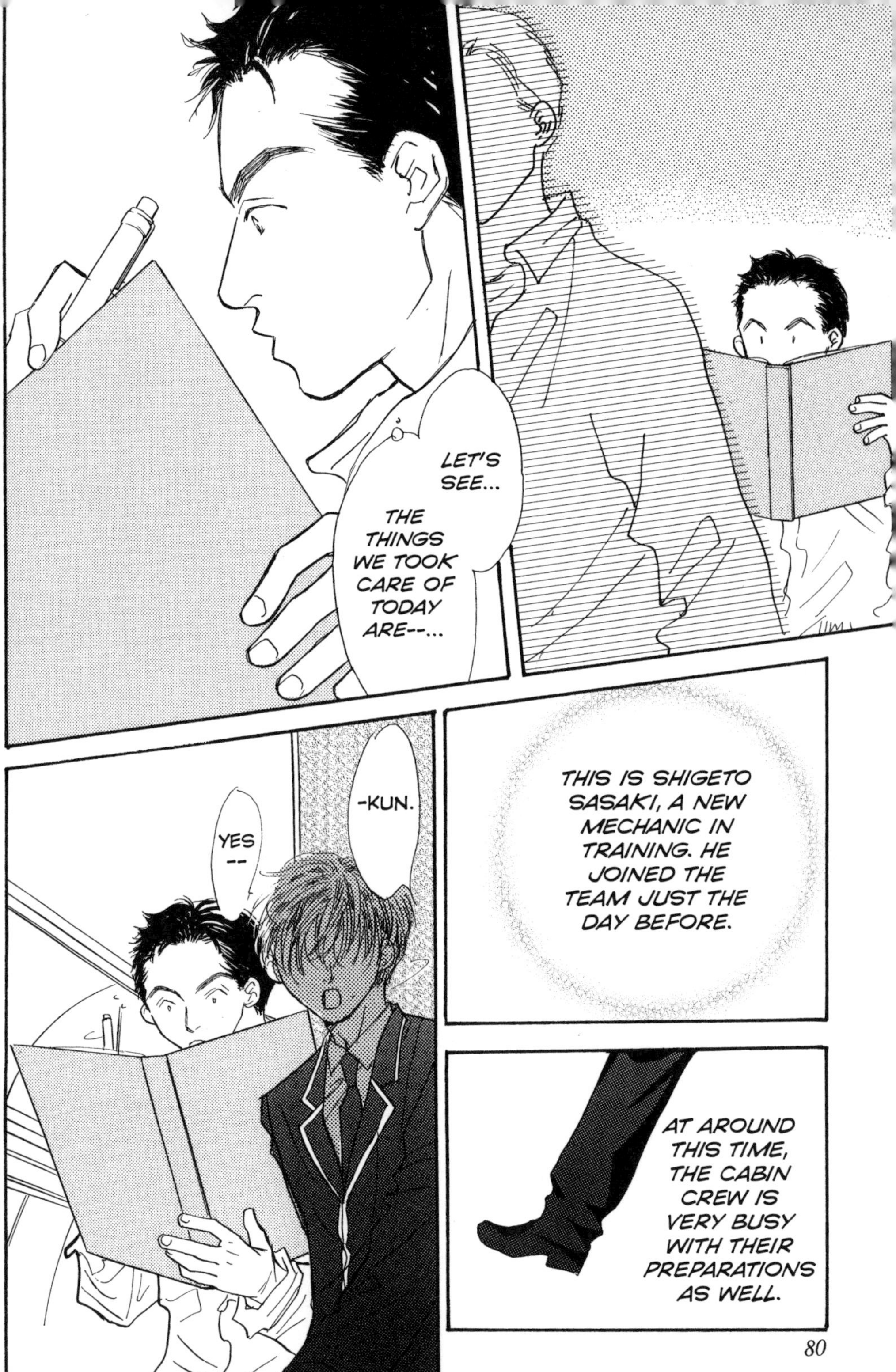
LET'S SEE...
THE THINGS WE TOOK CARE OF TODAY ARE--...
THIS IS SHIGETO SASAKI, A NEW MECHANIC IN TRAINING. HE JOINED THE TEAM JUST THE DAY BEFORE.
AT AROUND THIS TIME, THE CABIN CREW IS VERY BUSY WITH THEIR PREPARATIONS AS WELL.
-KUN.
YES --

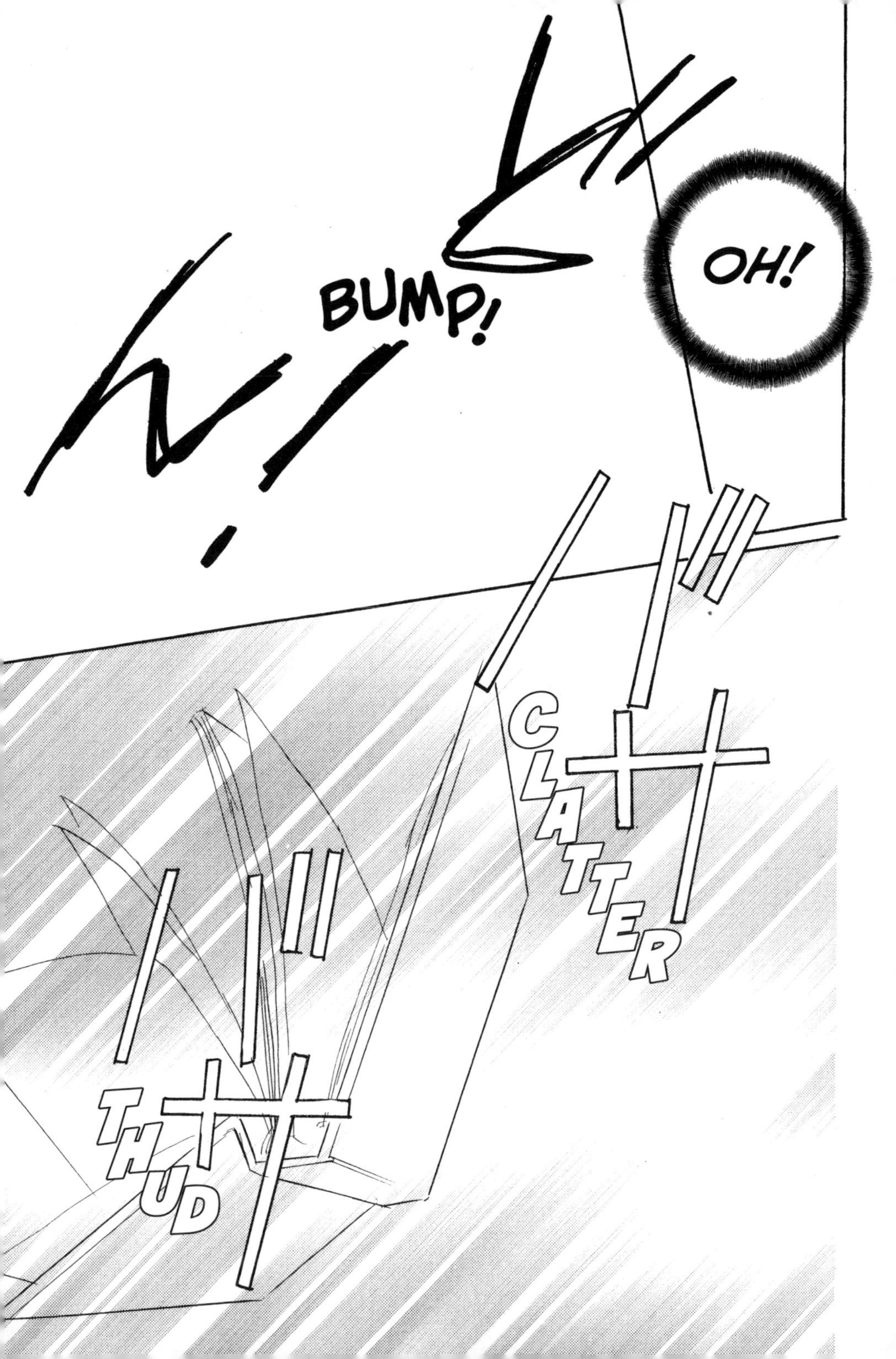
OH!
BUMP!
CLATTER
THUD

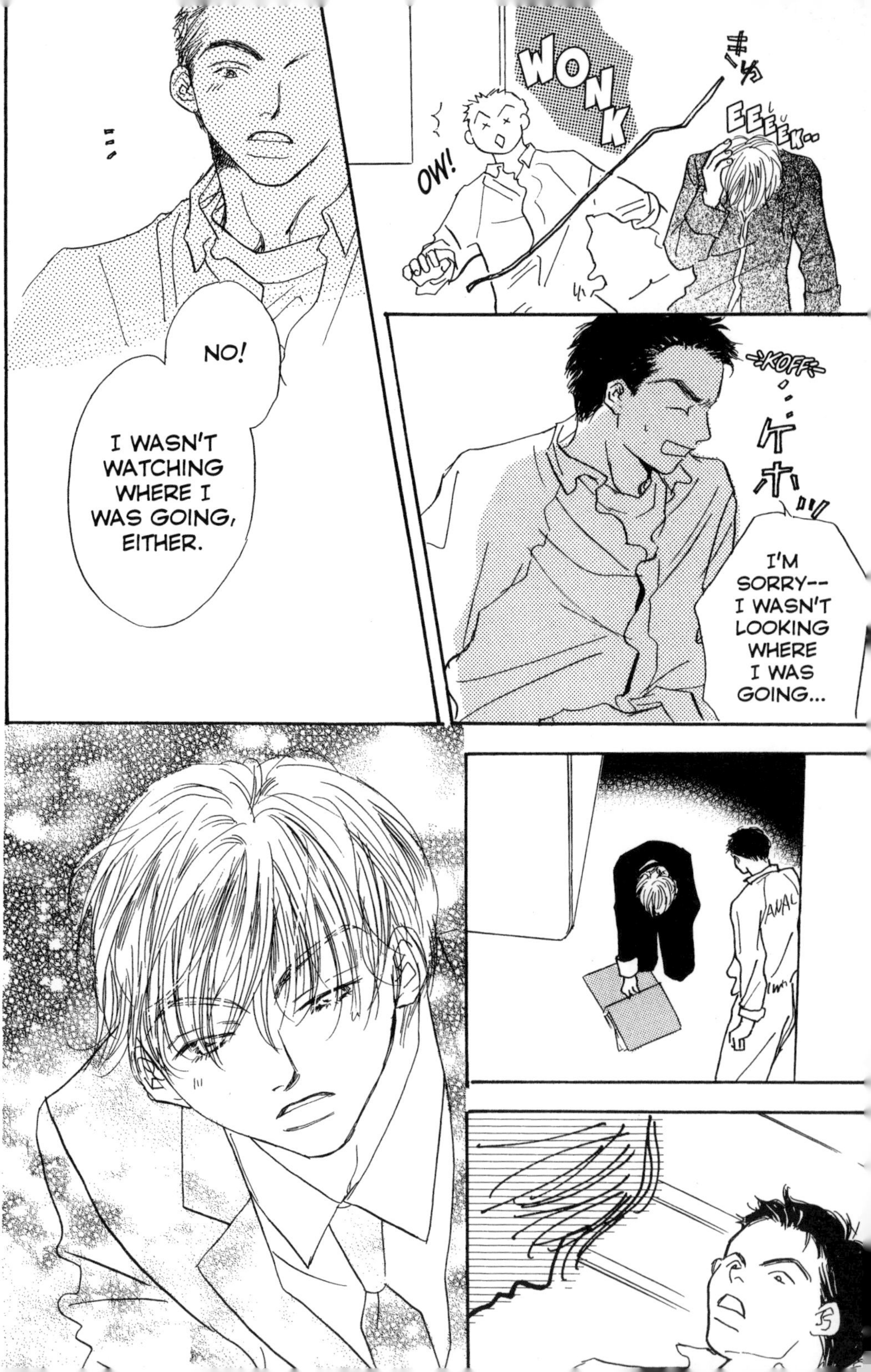
WONK
EEEEK..
OW!
KOFF
I'M SORRY-- I WASN'T LOOKING WHERE I WAS GOING...
...
NO!
I WASN'T WATCHING WHERE I WAS GOING, EITHER.

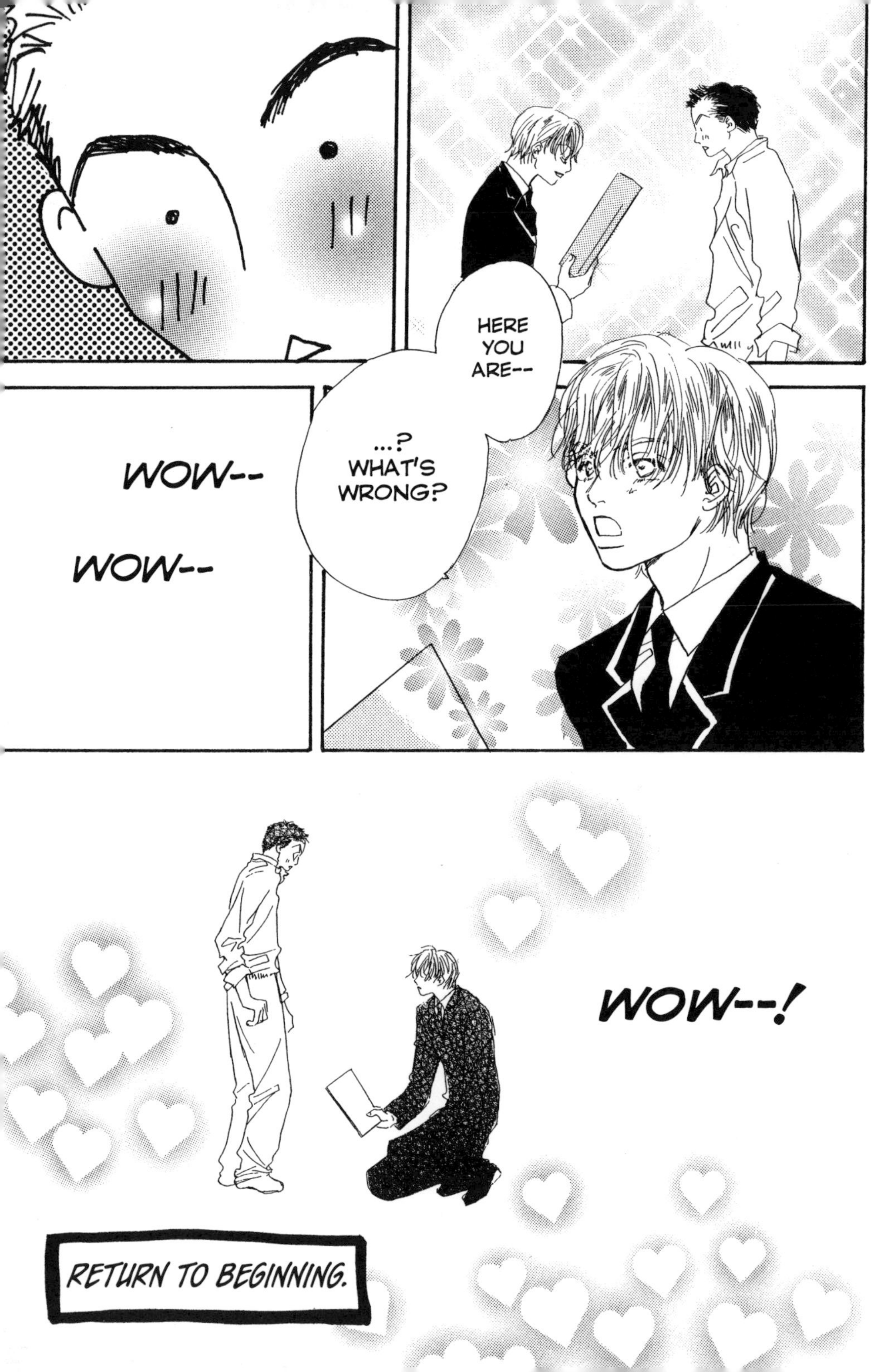

HERE YOU ARE--
...? WHAT'S WRONG?
WOW--
WOW--
WOW--!
RETURN TO BEGINNING.

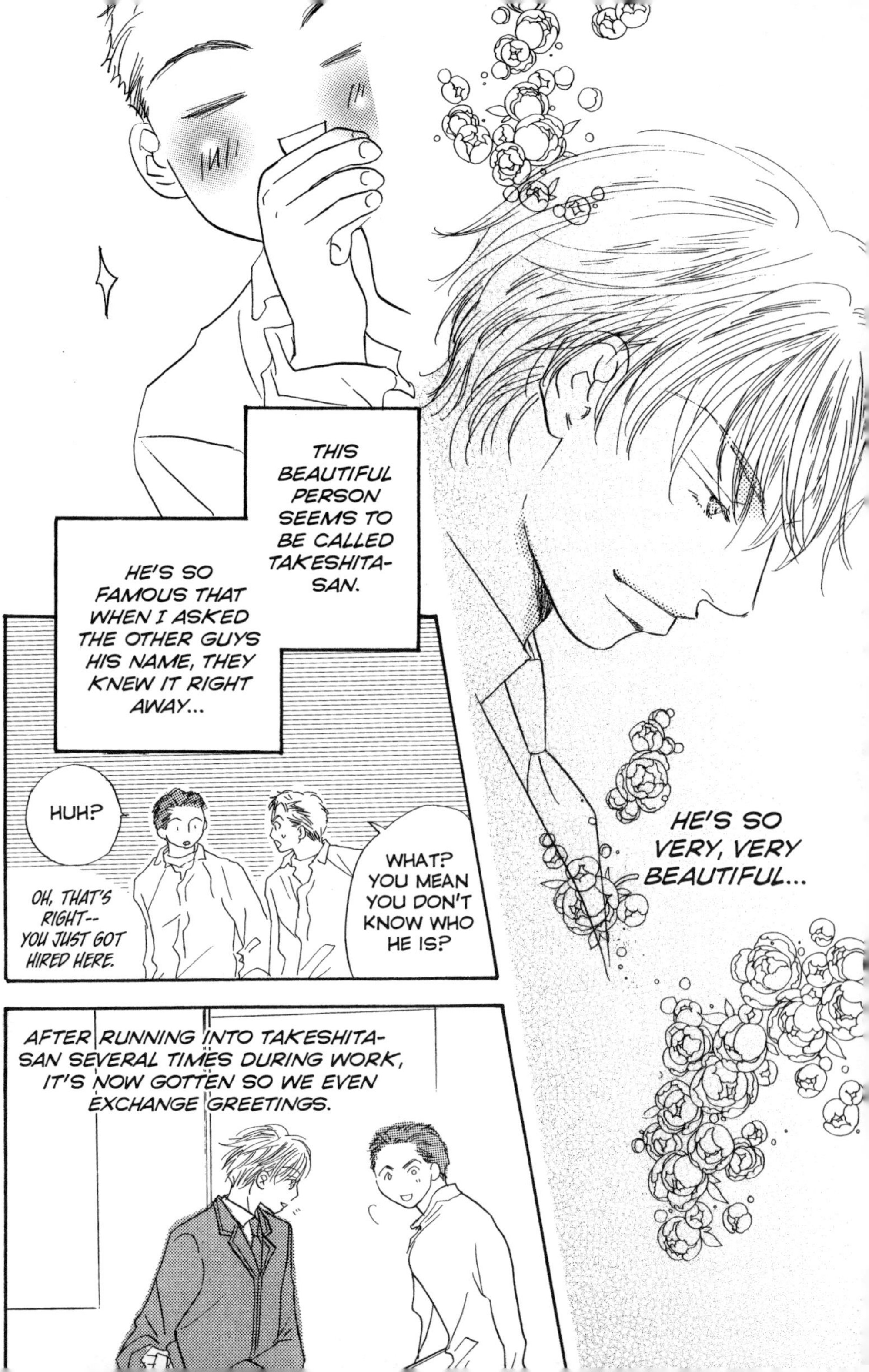
HE'S SO VERY, VERY BEAUTIFUL...
THIS BEAUTIFUL PERSON SEEMS TO BE CALLED TAKESHITA-SAN.
HE'S SO FAMOUS THAT WHEN I ASKED THE OTHER GUYS HIS NAME, THEY KNEW IT RIGHT AWAY...
WHAT? YOU MEAN YOU DON'T KNOW WHO HE IS?
HUH?
OH, THAT'S RIGHT-- YOU JUST GOT HIRED HERE.
AFTER RUNNING INTO TAKESHITA-SAN SEVERAL TIMES DURING WORK, IT'S NOW GOTTEN SO WE EVEN EXCHANGE GREETINGS.

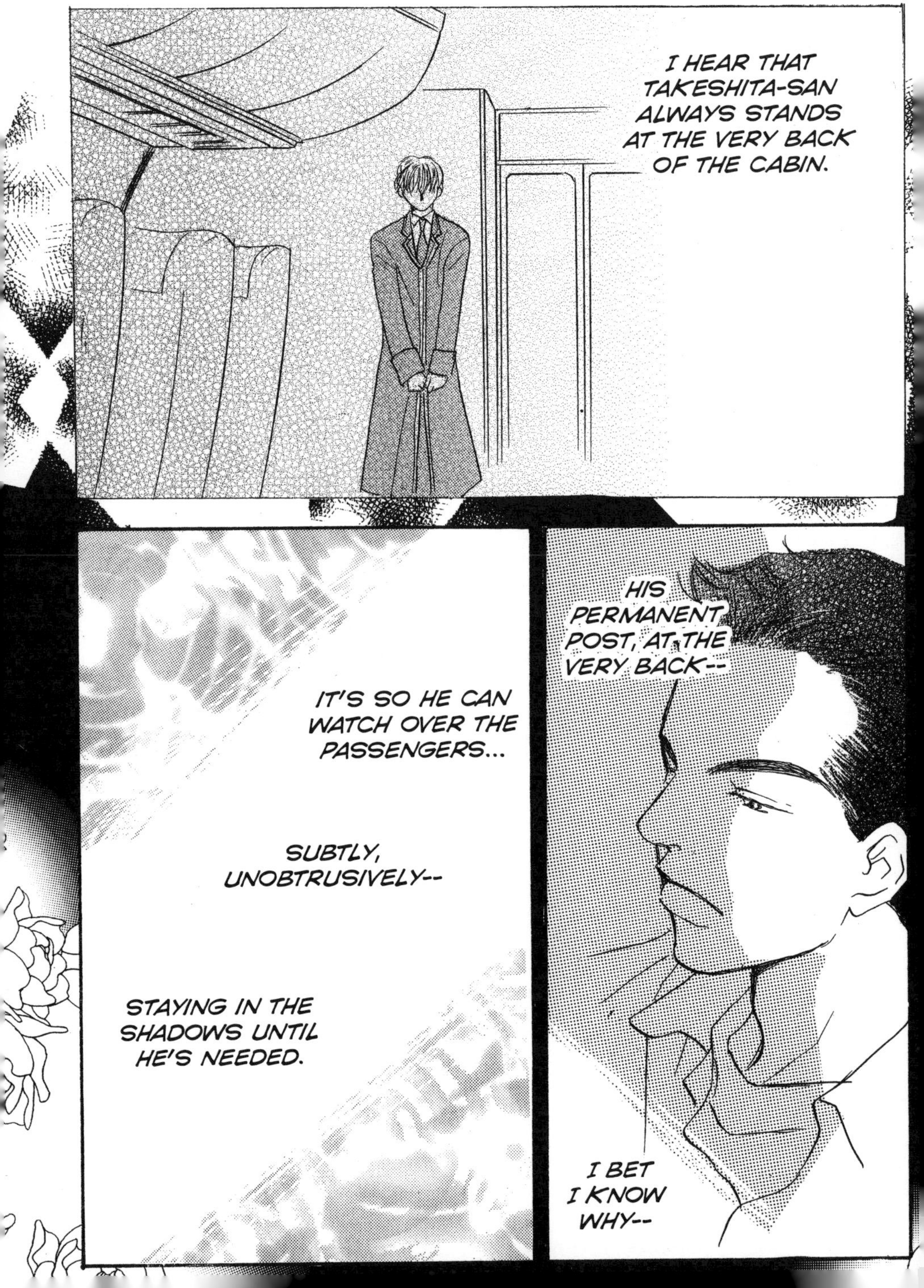
I HEAR THAT TAKESHITA-SAN ALWAYS STANDS AT THE VERY BACK OF THE CABIN.
HIS PERMANENT POST, AT THE VERY BACK--
I BET I KNOW WHY--
IT'S SO HE CAN WATCH OVER THE PASSENGERS...
SUBTLY, UNOBTRUSIVELY--
STAYING IN THE SHADOWS UNTIL HE'S NEEDED.

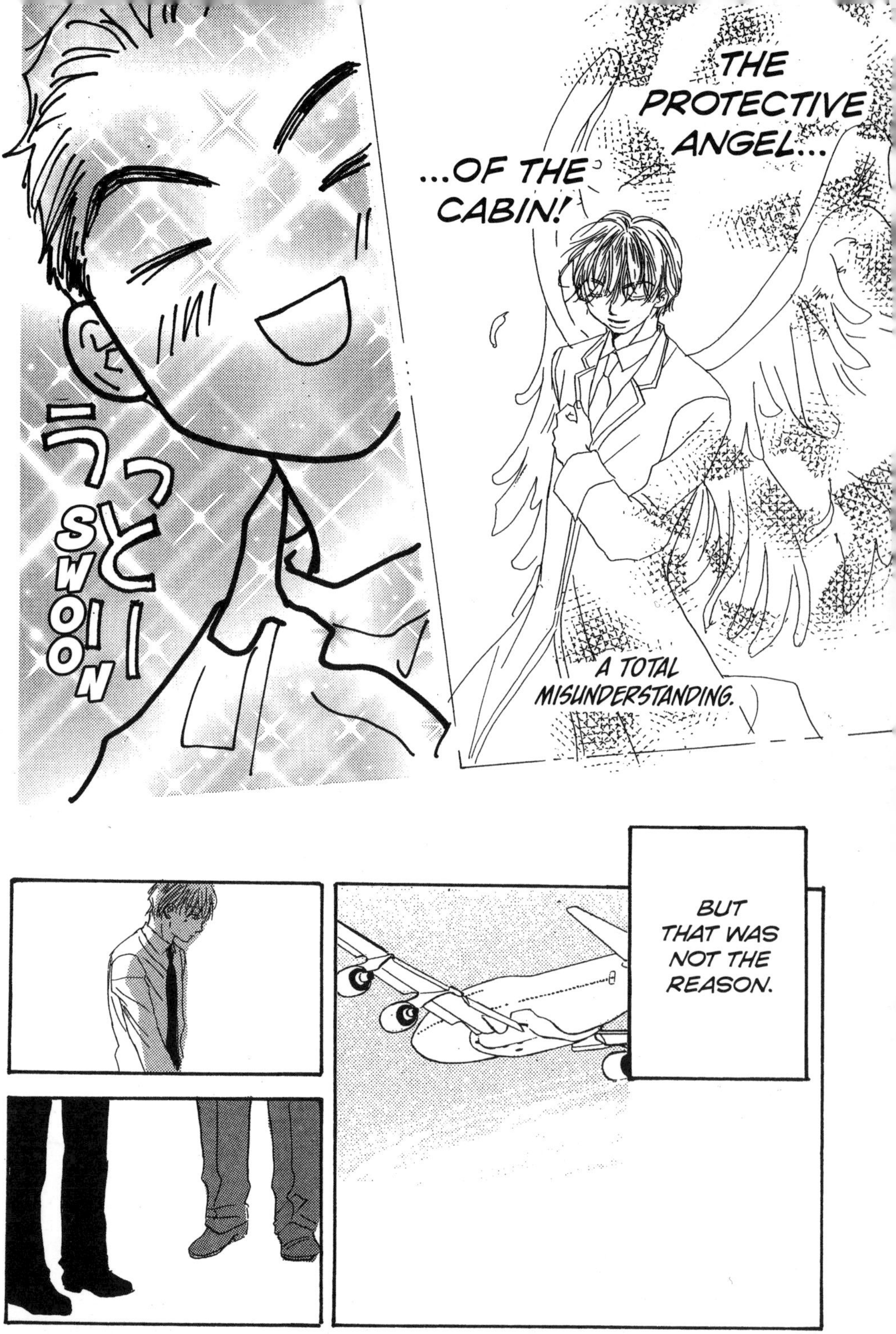
THE PROTECTIVE ANGEL...
...OF THE CABIN!
A TOTAL MISUNDERSTANDING.
うっとーり
SWOOON
BUT THAT WAS NOT THE REASON.

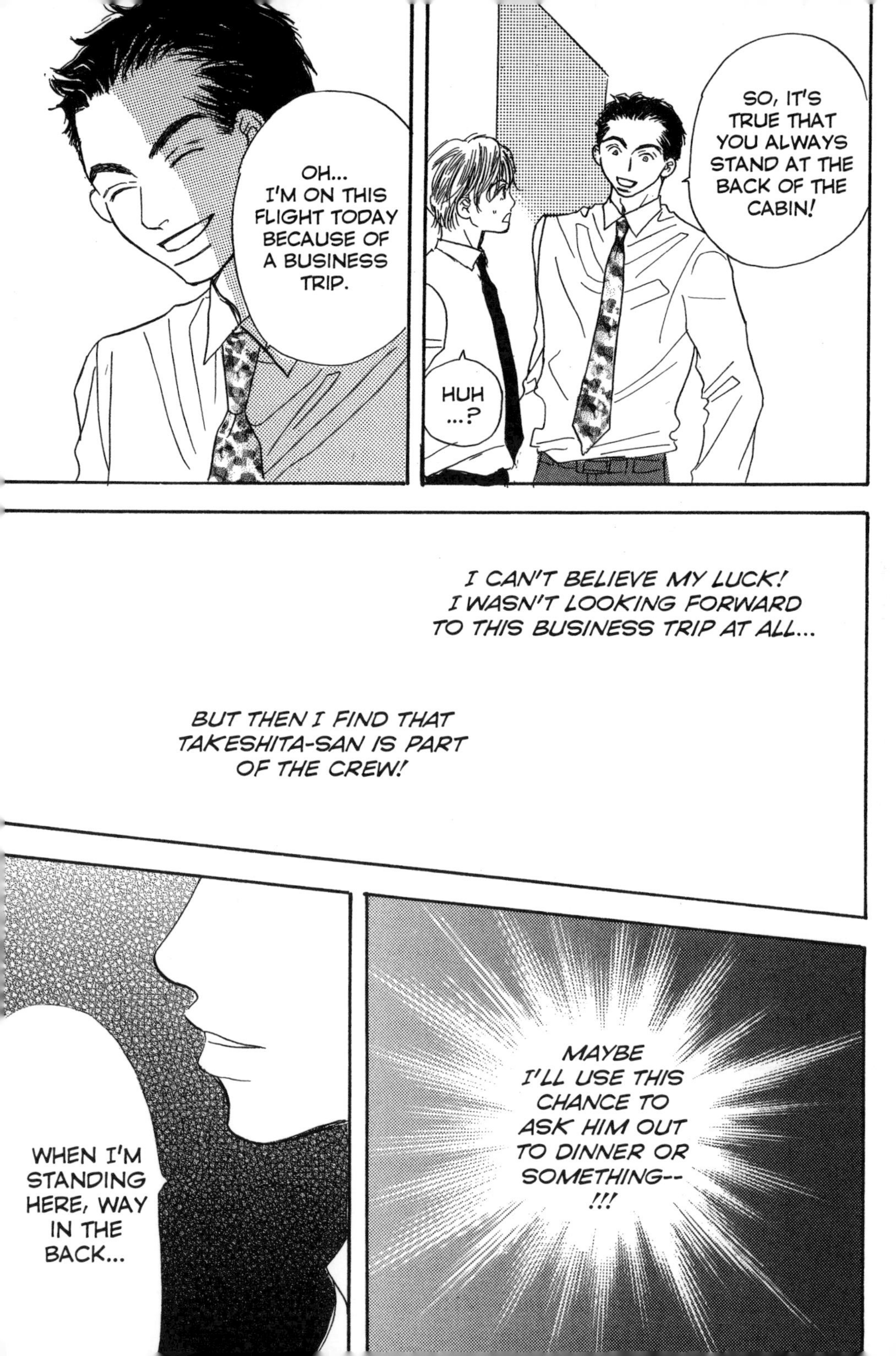
SO, IT'S TRUE THAT YOU ALWAYS STAND AT THE BACK OF THE CABIN!
HUH ...?
OH... I'M ON THIS FLIGHT TODAY BECAUSE OF A BUSINESS TRIP.
I CAN'T BELIEVE MY LUCK! I WASN'T LOOKING FORWARD TO THIS BUSINESS TRIP AT ALL...
BUT THEN I FIND THAT TAKESHITA-SAN IS PART OF THE CREW!
MAYBE I'LL USE THIS CHANCE TO ASK HIM OUT TO DINNER OR SOMETHING-- !!!
WHEN I'M STANDING HERE, WAY IN THE BACK...

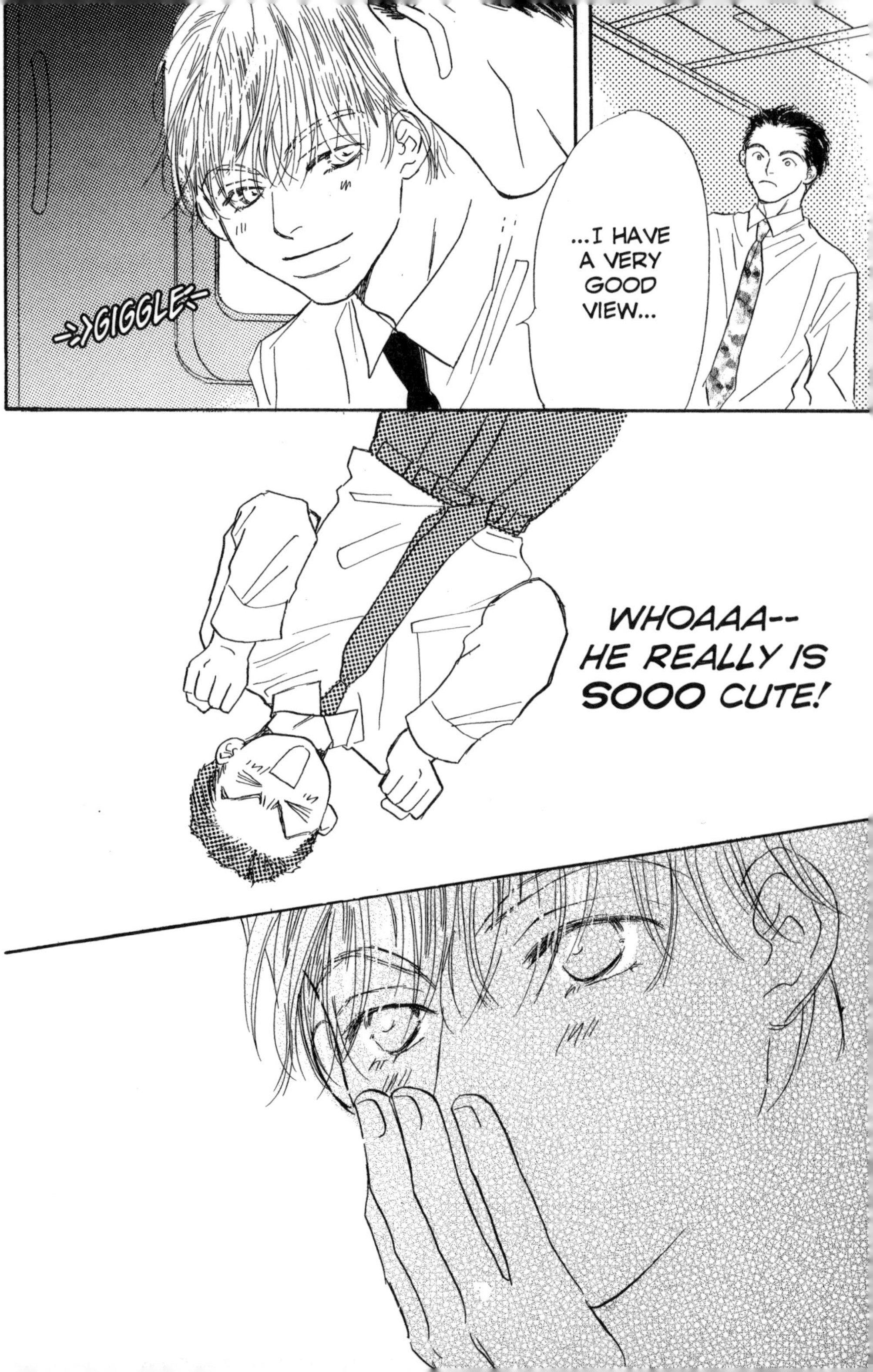
...I HAVE A VERY GOOD VIEW...
GIGGLE
WHOAAA-- HE REALLY IS SOOO CUTE!

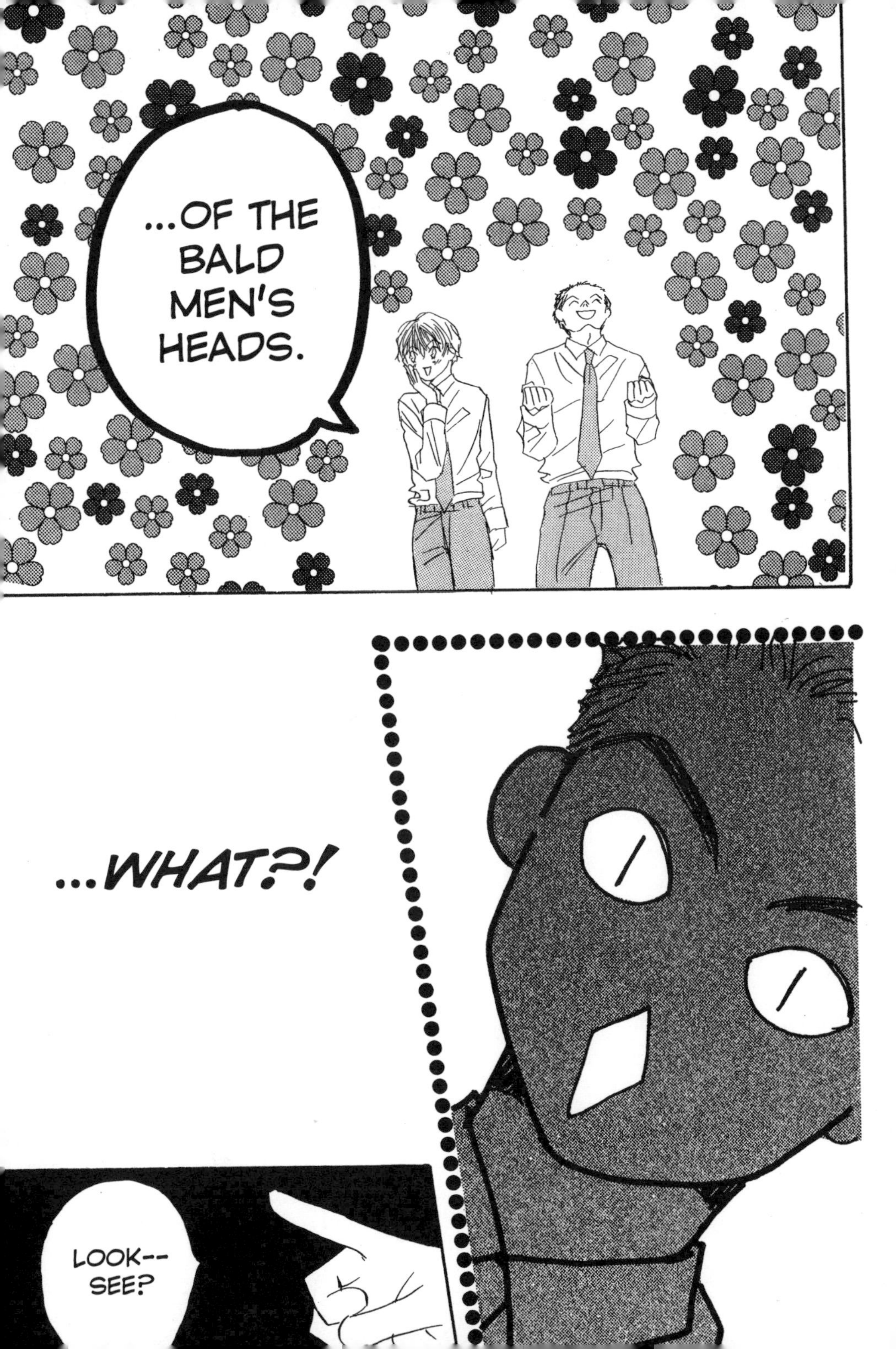
...OF THE BALD MEN'S HEADS.
...WHAT?!
LOOK-- SEE?

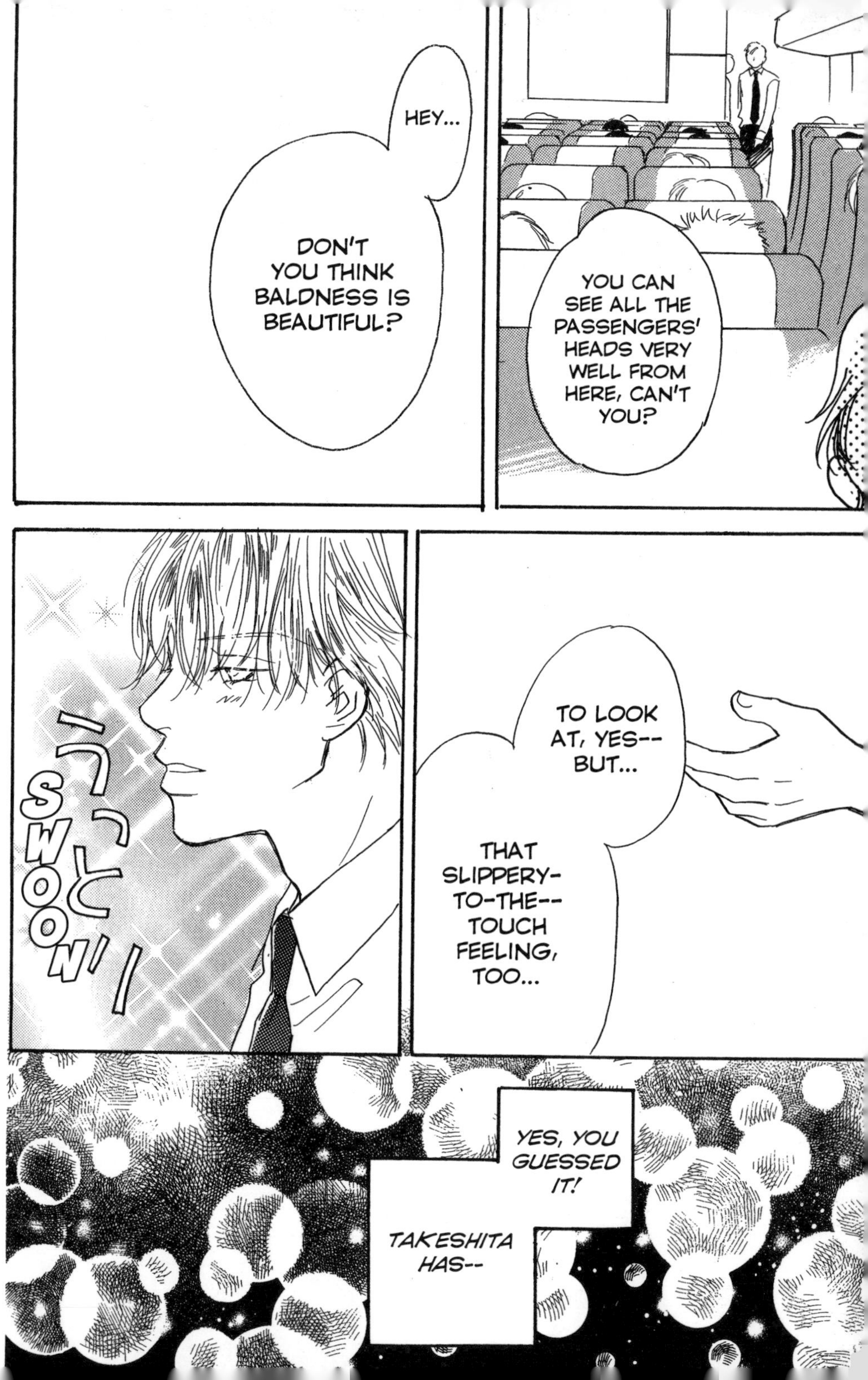
YOU CAN SEE ALL THE PASSENGERS' HEADS VERY WELL FROM HERE, CAN'T YOU?
HEY...
DON'T YOU THINK BALDNESS IS BEAUTIFUL?
TO LOOK AT, YES-- BUT...
THAT SLIPPERY-TO-THE--TOUCH FEELING, TOO...
SWOON
YES, YOU GUESSED IT!
TAKESHITA HAS--

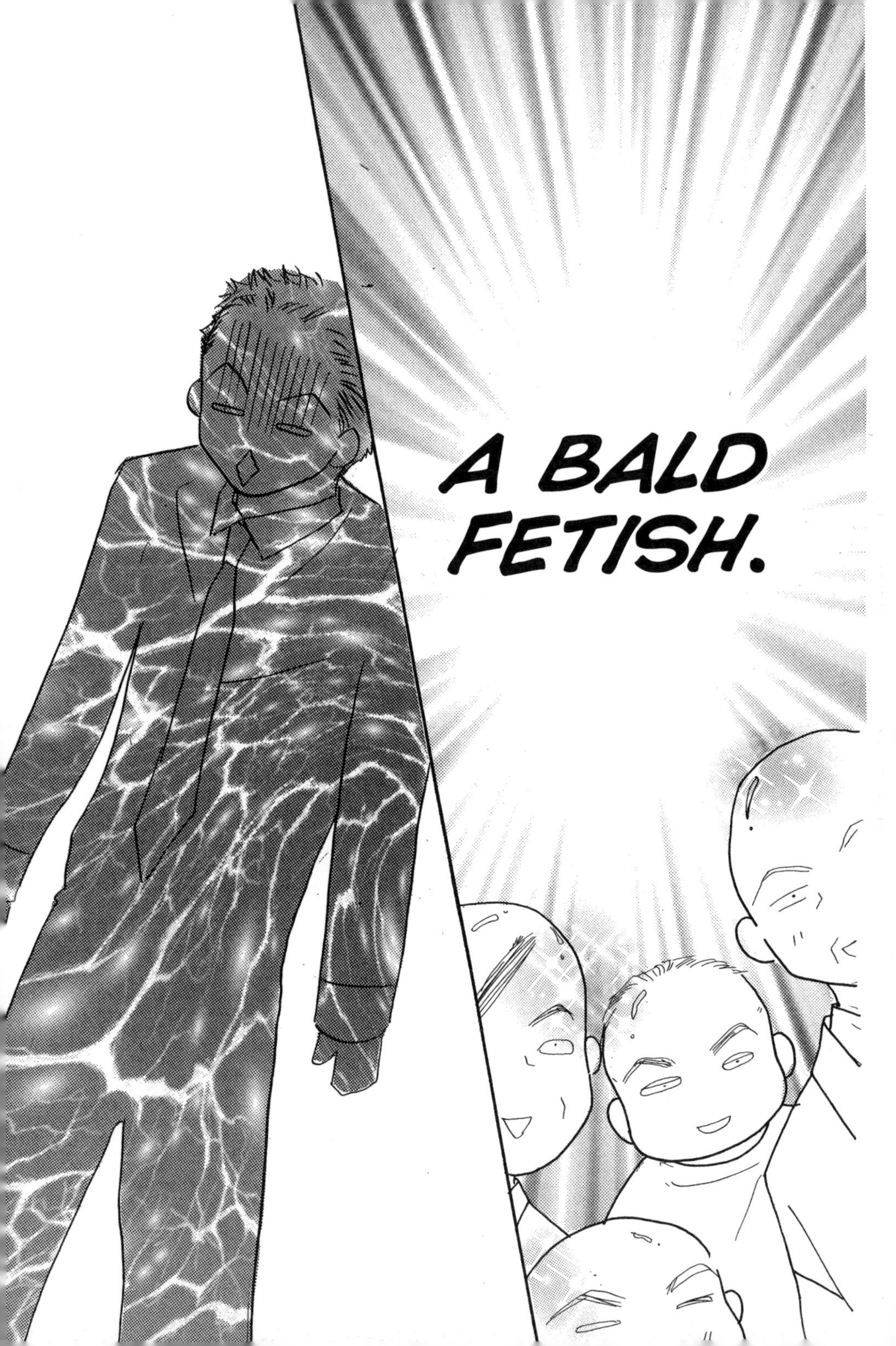
A BALD FETISH.

HE STANDS AT THE BACK, NOT BECAUSE OF ANY ANGELIC HEART...

...BUT SO HE CAN OBSERVE THE BALD PASSENGERS' HEADS FOR THE WHOLE FLIGHT!

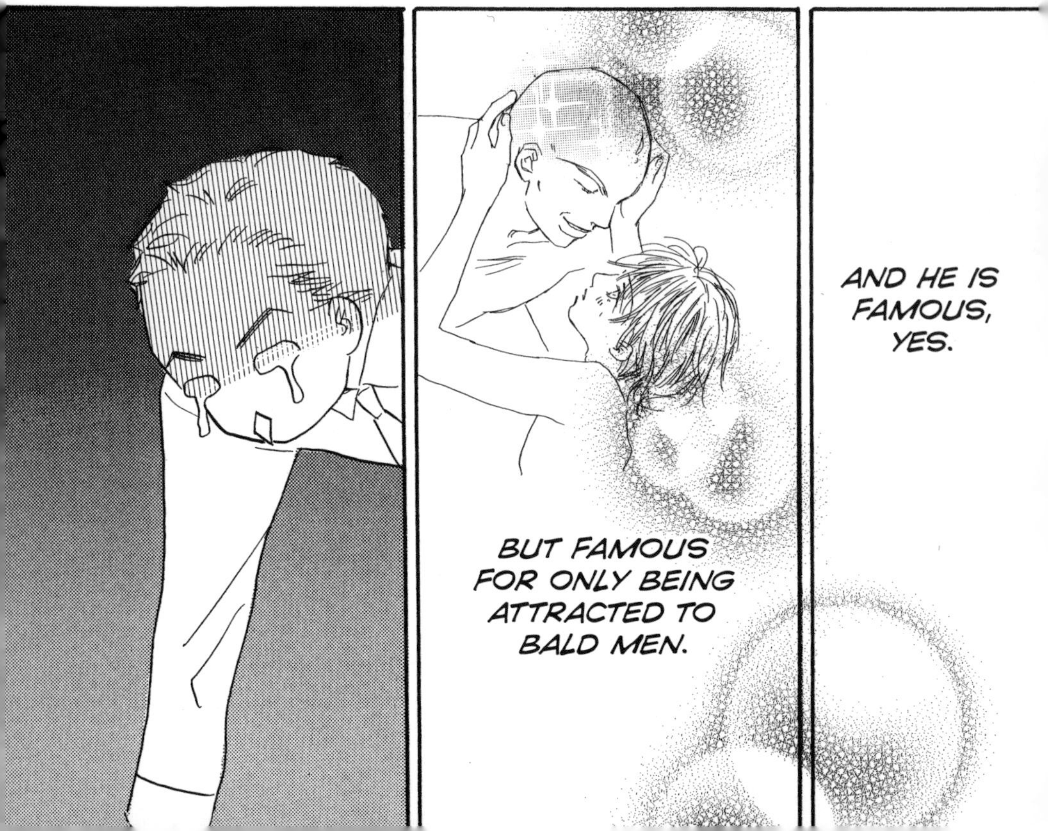
AND HE IS FAMOUS, YES.
BUT FAMOUS FOR ONLY BEING ATTRACTED TO BALD MEN.

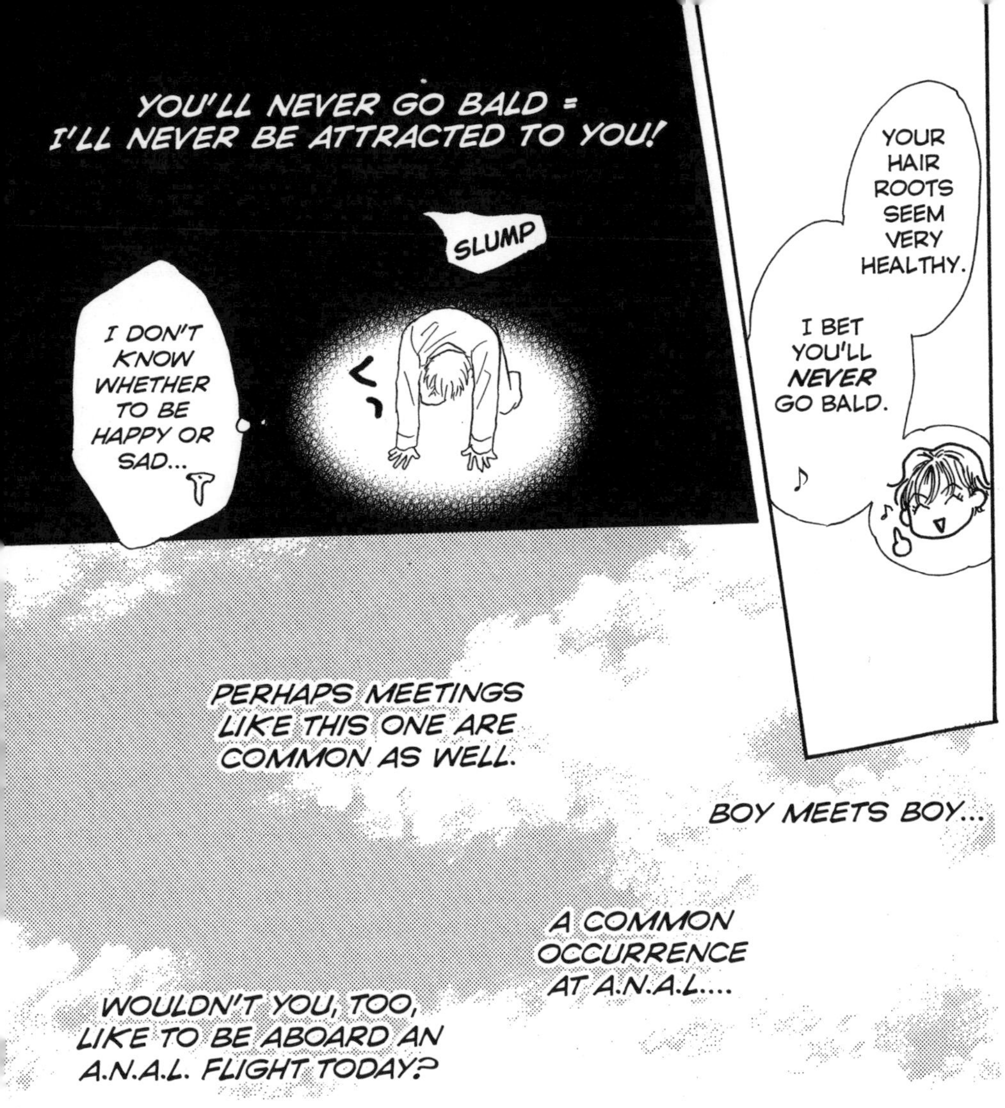
YOUR HAIR ROOTS SEEM VERY HEALTHY.
I BET YOU'LL NEVER GO BALD.
YOU'LL NEVER GO BALD = I'LL NEVER BE ATTRACTED TO YOU!
SLUMP
I DON'T KNOW WHETHER TO BE HAPPY OR SAD...
BOY MEETS BOY...
PERHAPS MEETINGS LIKE THIS ONE ARE COMMON AS WELL.
A COMMON OCCURRENCE AT A.N.A.L....
WOULDN'T YOU, TOO, LIKE TO BE ABOARD AN A.N.A.L. FLIGHT TODAY?

VIVA!! ANAL!!

**LOVE A.N.A.L. END**

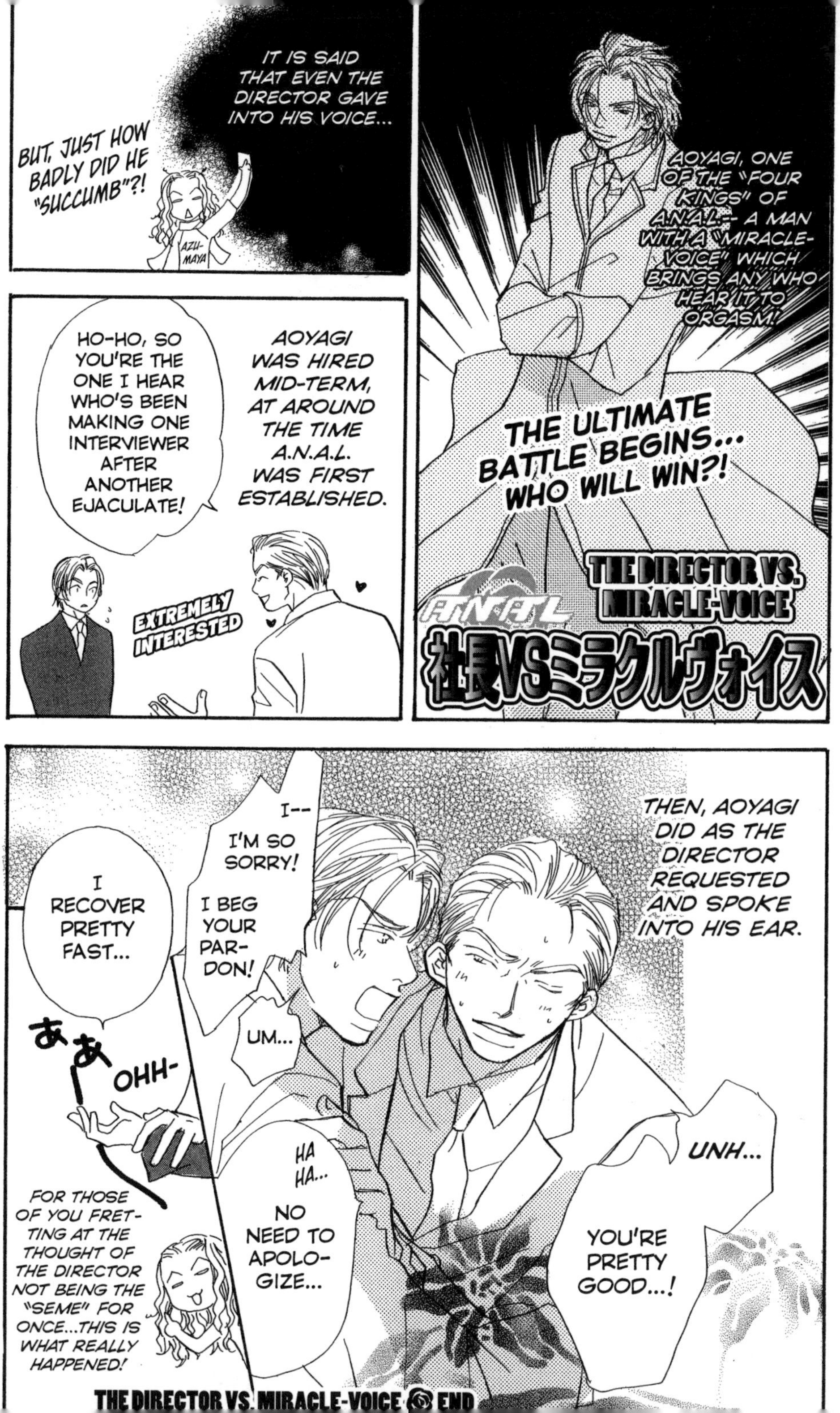
AOYAGI, ONE OF THE "FOUR KINGS" OF A.N.A.L.-- A MAN WITH A "MIRACLE-VOICE" WHICH BRINGS ANY WHO HEAR IT TO ORGASM!
THE ULTIMATE BATTLE BEGINS... WHO WILL WIN?!
THE DIRECTOR VS. MIRACLE-VOICE
A.N.A.L
社長VSミラクルヴォイス
IT IS SAID THAT EVEN THE DIRECTOR GAVE INTO HIS VOICE...
BUT, JUST HOW BADLY DID HE "SUCCUMB"?!
AZU-MAYA
AOYAGI WAS HIRED MID-TERM, AT AROUND THE TIME A.N.A.L. WAS FIRST ESTABLISHED.
HO-HO, SO YOU'RE THE ONE I HEAR WHO'S BEEN MAKING ONE INTERVIEWER AFTER ANOTHER EJACULATE!
EXTREMELY INTERESTED
THEN, AOYAGI DID AS THE DIRECTOR REQUESTED AND SPOKE INTO HIS EAR.
I-- I'M SO SORRY!
I BEG YOUR PAR-DON!
I RECOVER PRETTY FAST...
UNH...
UM...
YOU'RE PRETTY GOOD...!
HA HA...
NO NEED TO APOLO-GIZE...
あぁ
OHH-
FOR THOSE OF YOU FRET-TING AT THE THOUGHT OF THE DIRECTOR NOT BEING THE "SEME" FOR ONCE...THIS IS WHAT REALLY HAPPENED!
THE DIRECTOR VS. MIRACLE-VOICE END

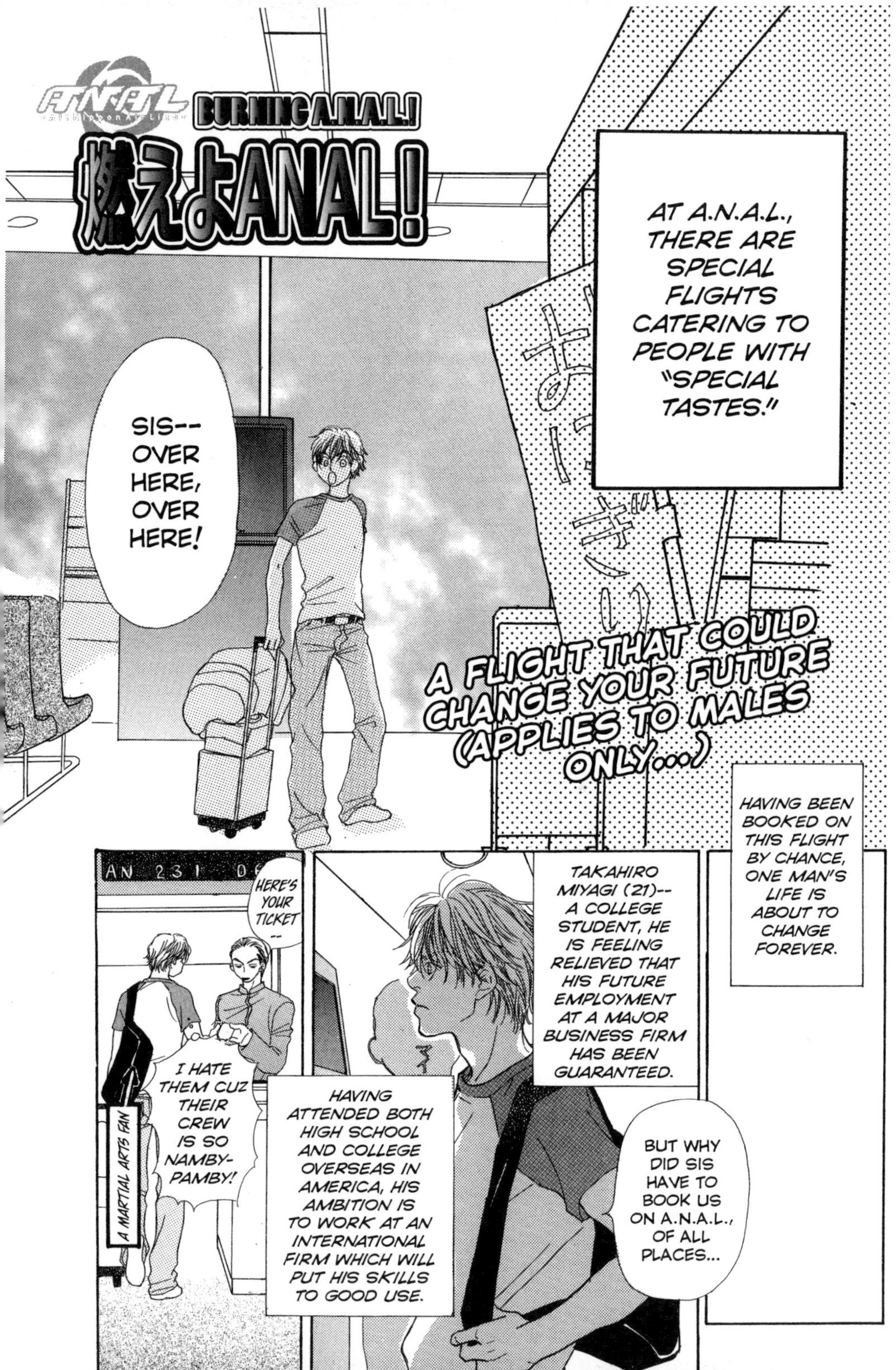
BURNING A.N.A.L.!
燃えよANAL！
AT A.N.A.L., THERE ARE SPECIAL FLIGHTS CATERING TO PEOPLE WITH "SPECIAL TASTES."
A FLIGHT THAT COULD CHANGE YOUR FUTURE (APPLIES TO MALES ONLY...)
SIS-- OVER HERE, OVER HERE!
HAVING BEEN BOOKED ON THIS FLIGHT BY CHANCE, ONE MAN'S LIFE IS ABOUT TO CHANGE FOREVER.
TAKAHIRO MIYAGI (21)-- A COLLEGE STUDENT, HE IS FEELING RELIEVED THAT HIS FUTURE EMPLOYMENT AT A MAJOR BUSINESS FIRM HAS BEEN GUARANTEED.
HAVING ATTENDED BOTH HIGH SCHOOL AND COLLEGE OVERSEAS IN AMERICA, HIS AMBITION IS TO WORK AT AN INTERNATIONAL FIRM WHICH WILL PUT HIS SKILLS TO GOOD USE.
BUT WHY DID SIS HAVE TO BOOK US ON A.N.A.L., OF ALL PLACES...
AN 231 06
HERE'S YOUR TICKET --
I HATE THEM CUZ THEIR CREW IS SO NAMBY-PAMBY!
A MARTIAL ARTS FAN

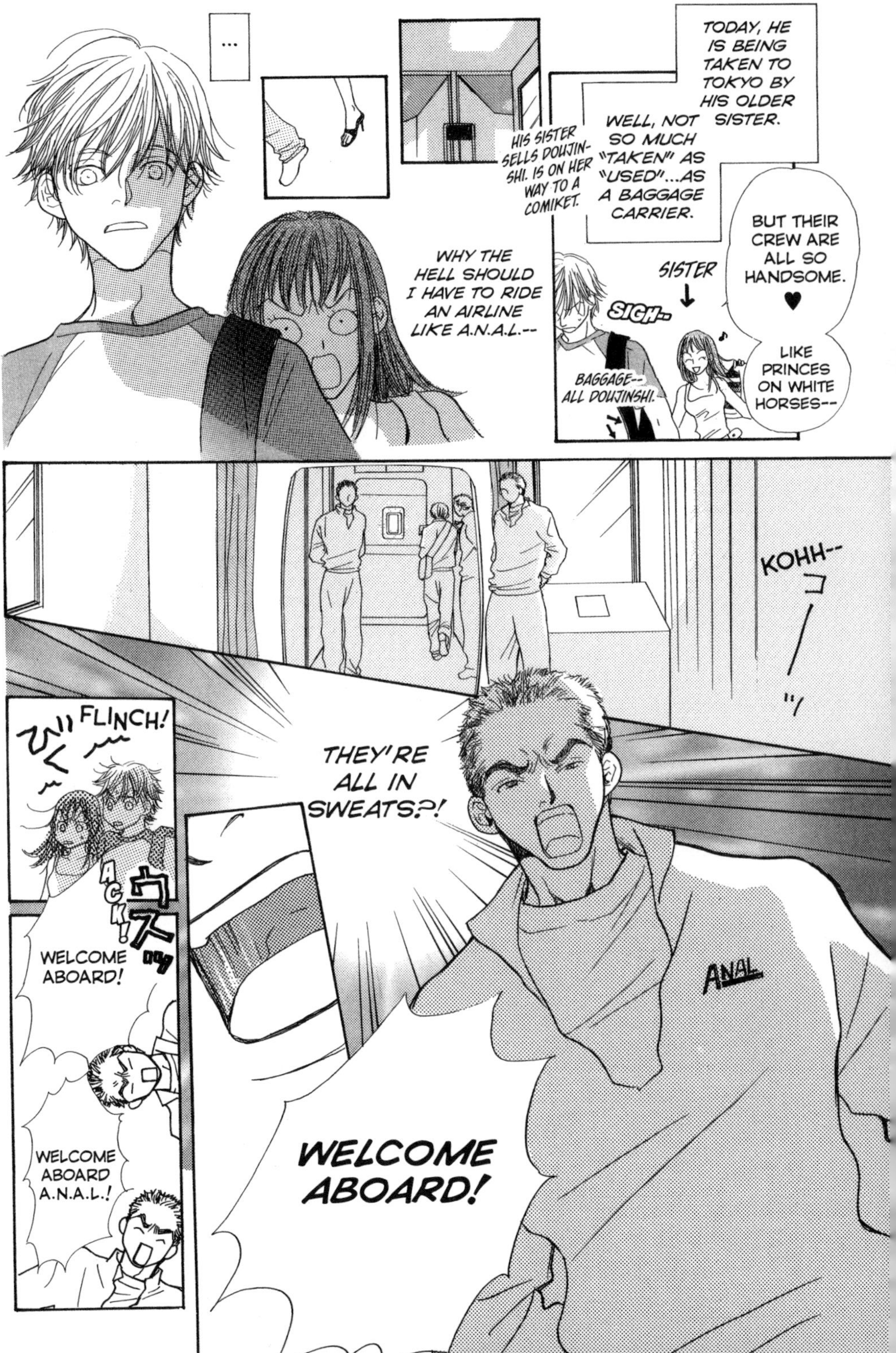
TODAY, HE IS BEING TAKEN TO TOKYO BY HIS OLDER SISTER.
WELL, NOT SO MUCH "TAKEN" AS "USED"...AS A BAGGAGE CARRIER.
HIS SISTER SELLS DOUJINSHI. IS ON HER WAY TO A COMIKET.
SISTER
SIGH--
BUT THEIR CREW ARE ALL SO HANDSOME. ♥
LIKE PRINCES ON WHITE HORSES--
BAGGAGE-- ALL DOUJINSHI.
...
WHY THE HELL SHOULD I HAVE TO RIDE AN AIRLINE LIKE A.N.A.L.--
KOHH--
THEY'RE ALL IN SWEATS?!
WELCOME ABOARD!
A.NAL
FLINCH!
ACK!
WELCOME ABOARD!
WELCOME ABOARD A.N.A.L.!

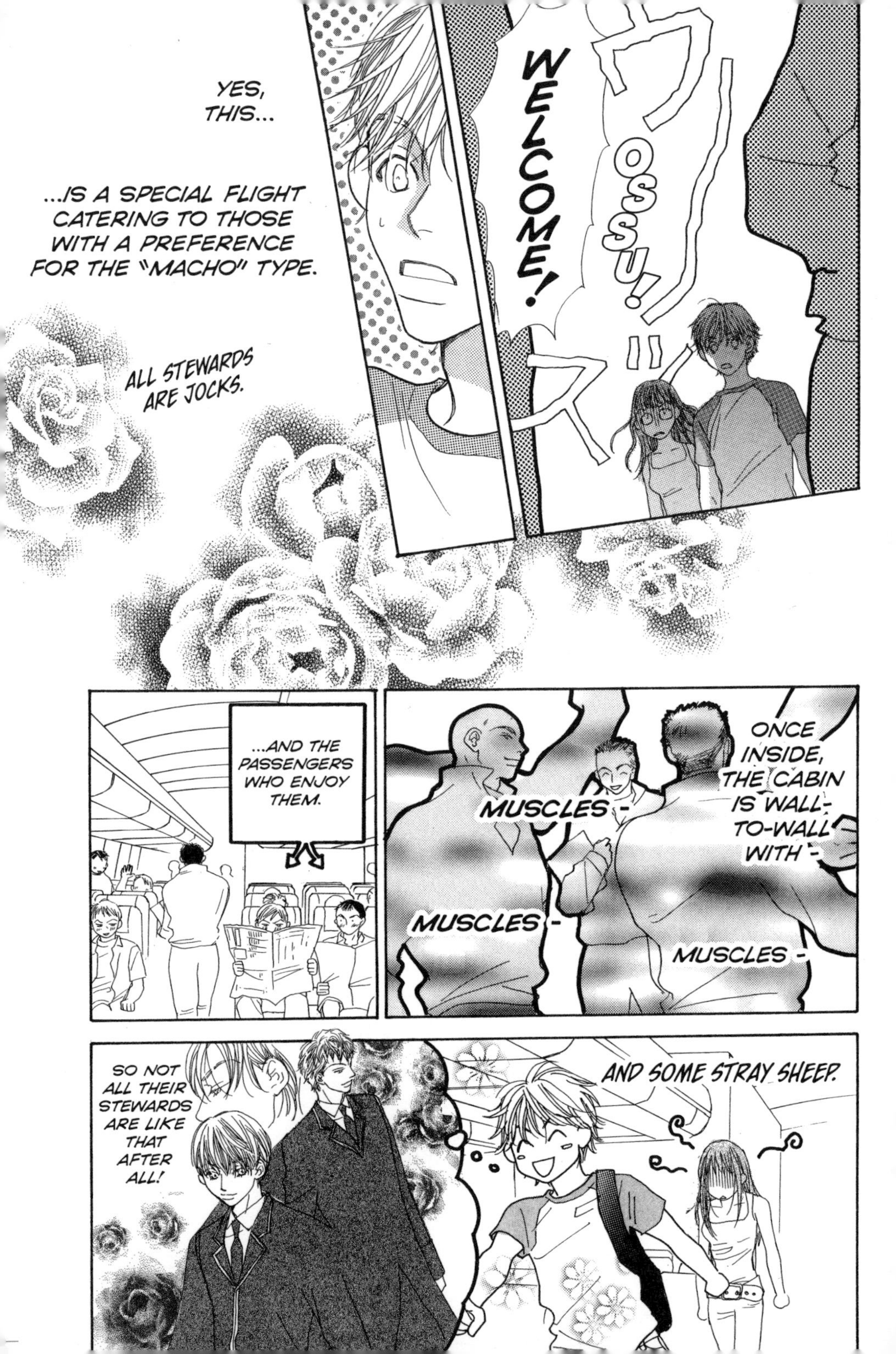
OSSU!
WELCOME!
YES, THIS...
...IS A SPECIAL FLIGHT CATERING TO THOSE WITH A PREFERENCE FOR THE "MACHO" TYPE.
ALL STEWARDS ARE JOCKS.
ONCE INSIDE, THE CABIN IS WALL-TO-WALL WITH -
MUSCLES -
MUSCLES -
MUSCLES -
...AND THE PASSENGERS WHO ENJOY THEM.
AND SOME STRAY SHEEP.
SO NOT ALL THEIR STEWARDS ARE LIKE THAT AFTER ALL!

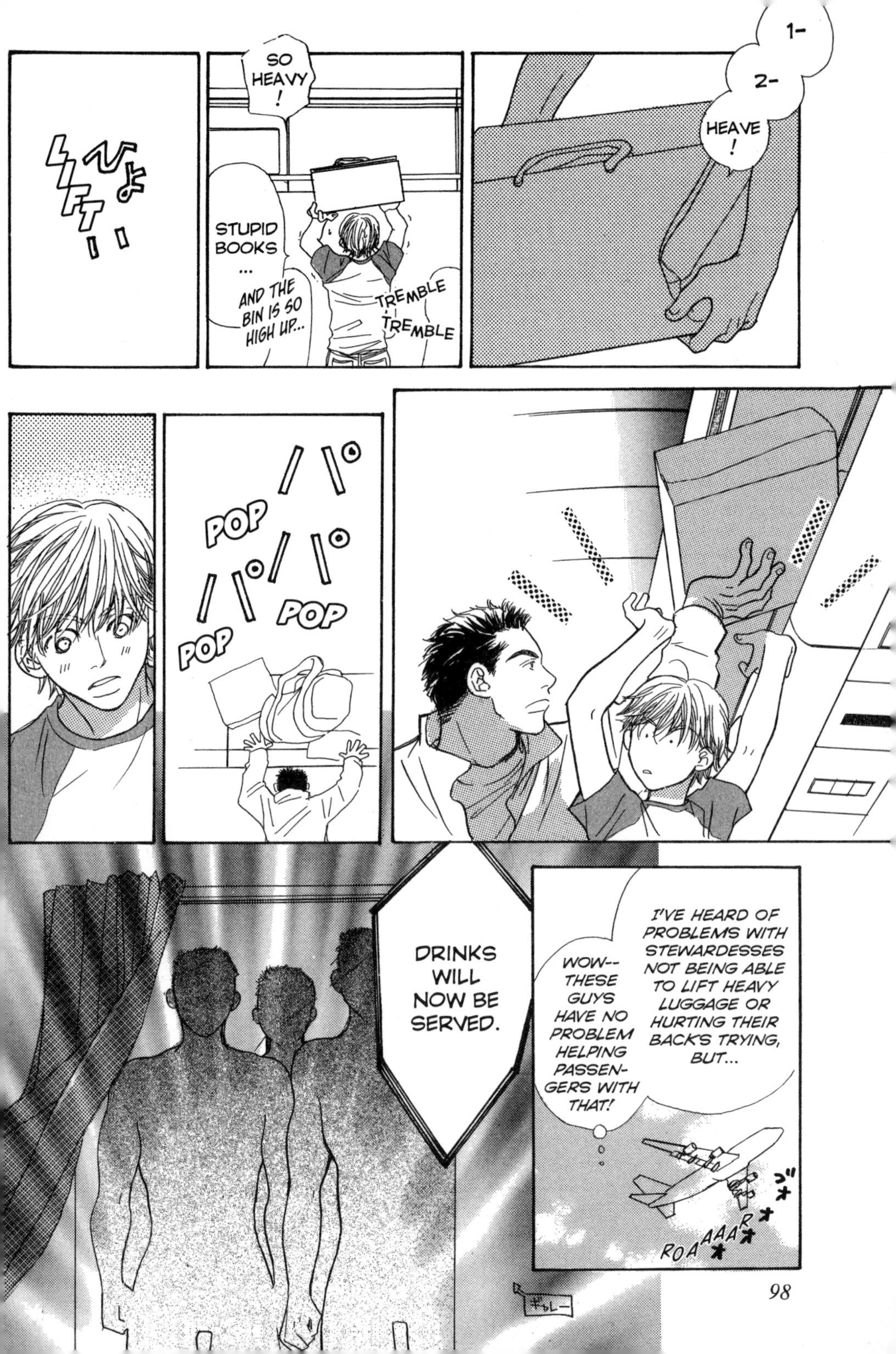
1-
2-
HEAVE!
SO HEAVY!
STUPID BOOKS...
AND THE BIN IS SO HIGH UP...
TREMBLE TREMBLE
LIFT
POP
POP
POP
I'VE HEARD OF PROBLEMS WITH STEWARDESSES NOT BEING ABLE TO LIFT HEAVY LUGGAGE OR HURTING THEIR BACKS TRYING, BUT...
WOW-- THESE GUYS HAVE NO PROBLEM HELPING PASSENGERS WITH THAT!
ROAAAAR
DRINKS WILL NOW BE SERVED.

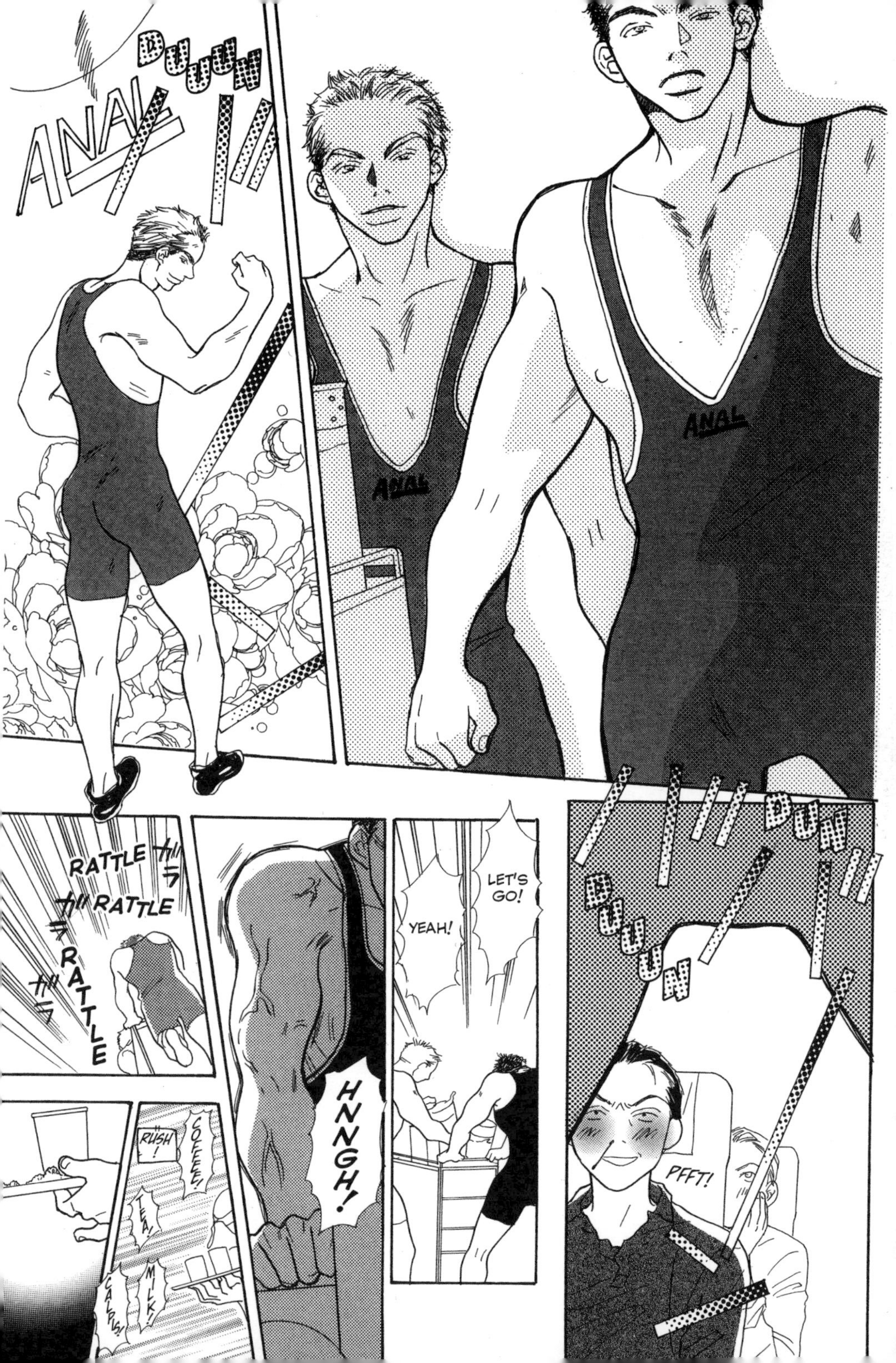

ANAL
ANAL
ANAL
DUUUN
DUN
DUUUN
PFFT!
LET'S GO!
YEAH!
HNNGH!
RATTLE RATTLE RATTLE RATTLE
RUSH!
COFFEE!
TEA!
MILK!
CALPIS!

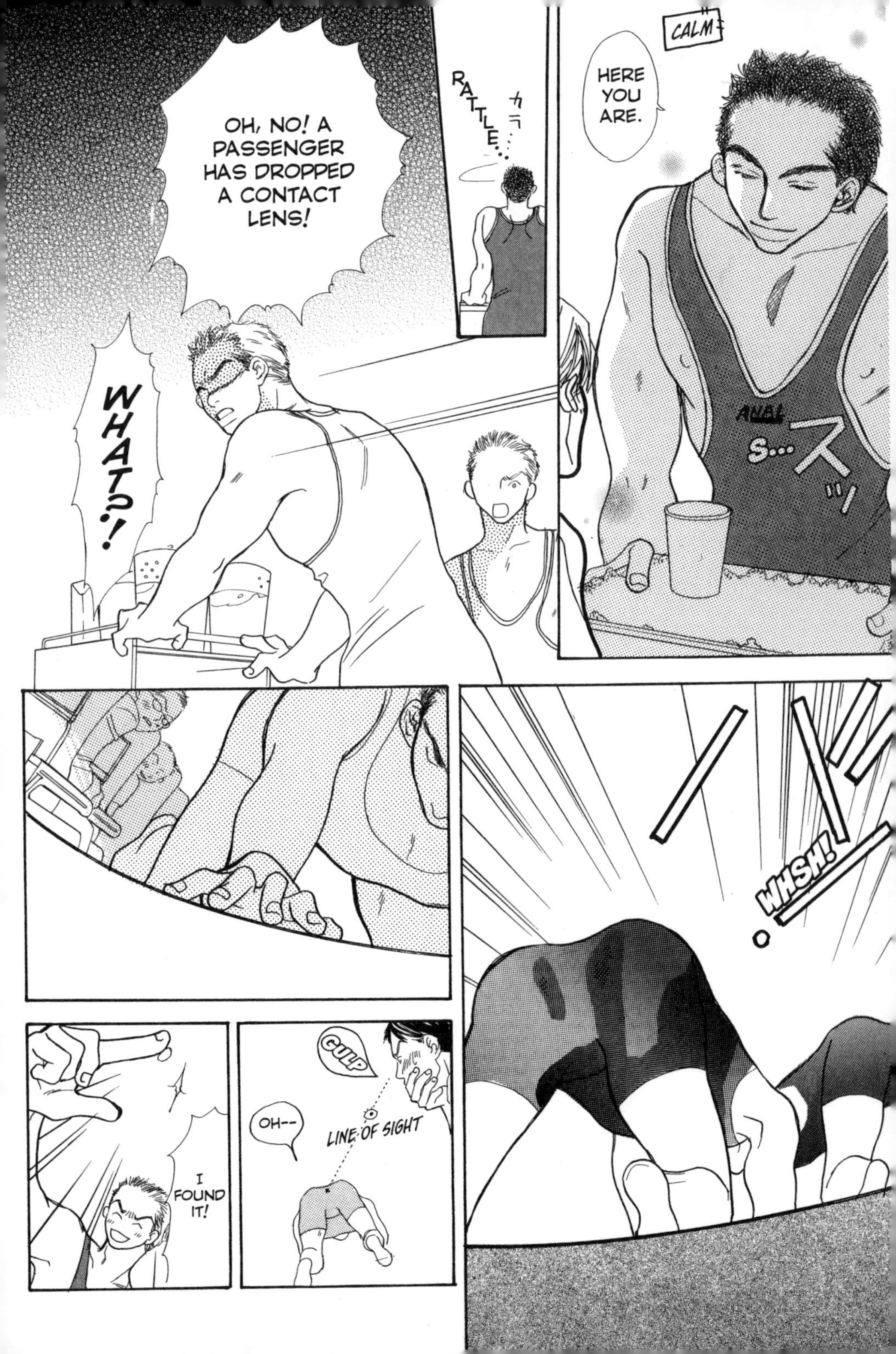
CALM
HERE YOU ARE.
ANAL S...
スッ
RATTLE...
カラ
OH, NO! A PASSENGER HAS DROPPED A CONTACT LENS!
WHAT?!
WHSH!
GULP
OH--
LINE OF SIGHT
I FOUND IT!

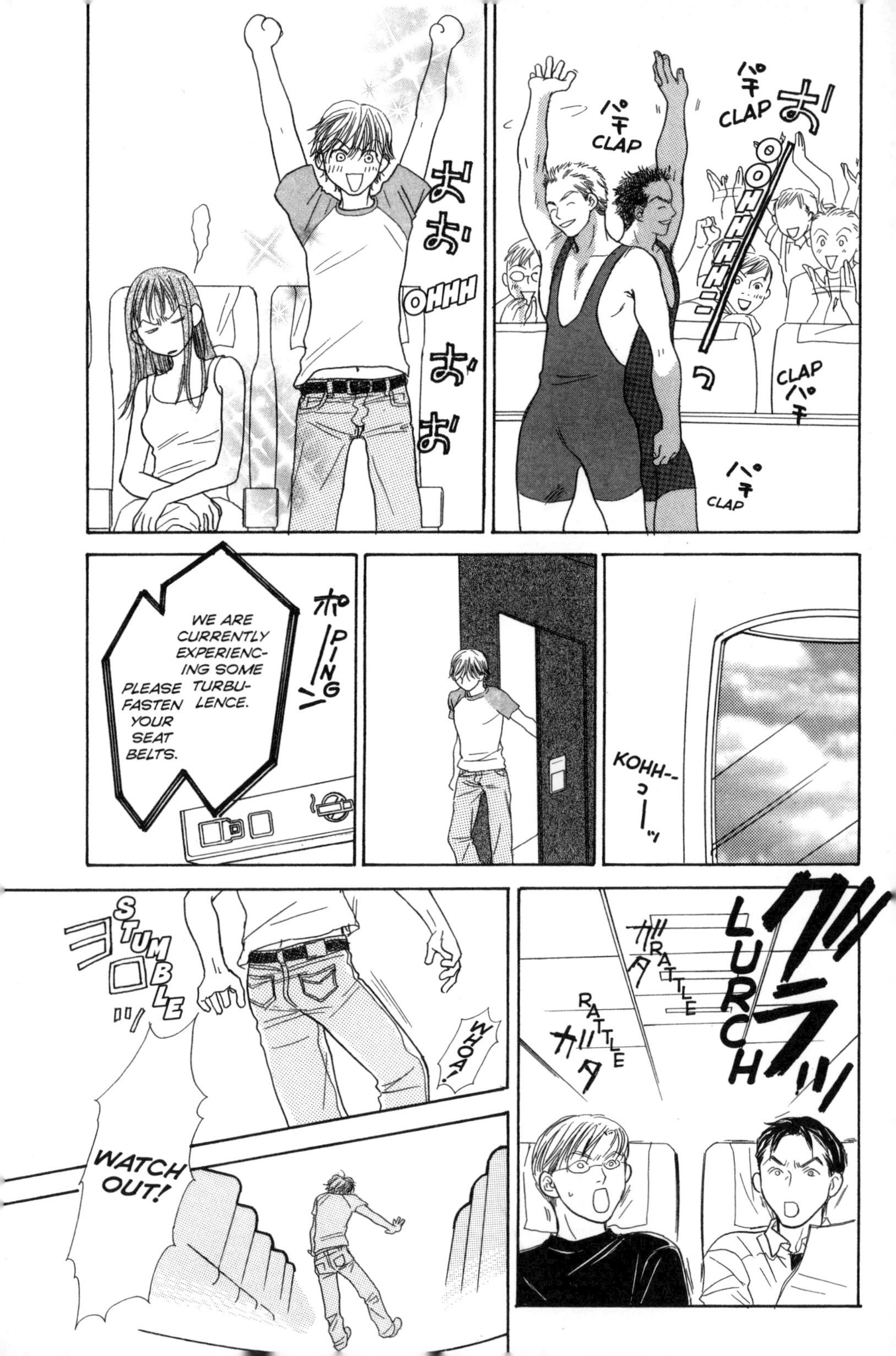
CLAP
CLAP
OOHHHHH!!
CLAP
CLAP
OHHH
KOHH--
WE ARE CURRENTLY EXPERIENCING SOME TURBULENCE. PLEASE FASTEN YOUR SEAT BELTS.
PING
LURCH
RATTLE
RATTLE
WHOA!
STUMBLE
WATCH OUT!

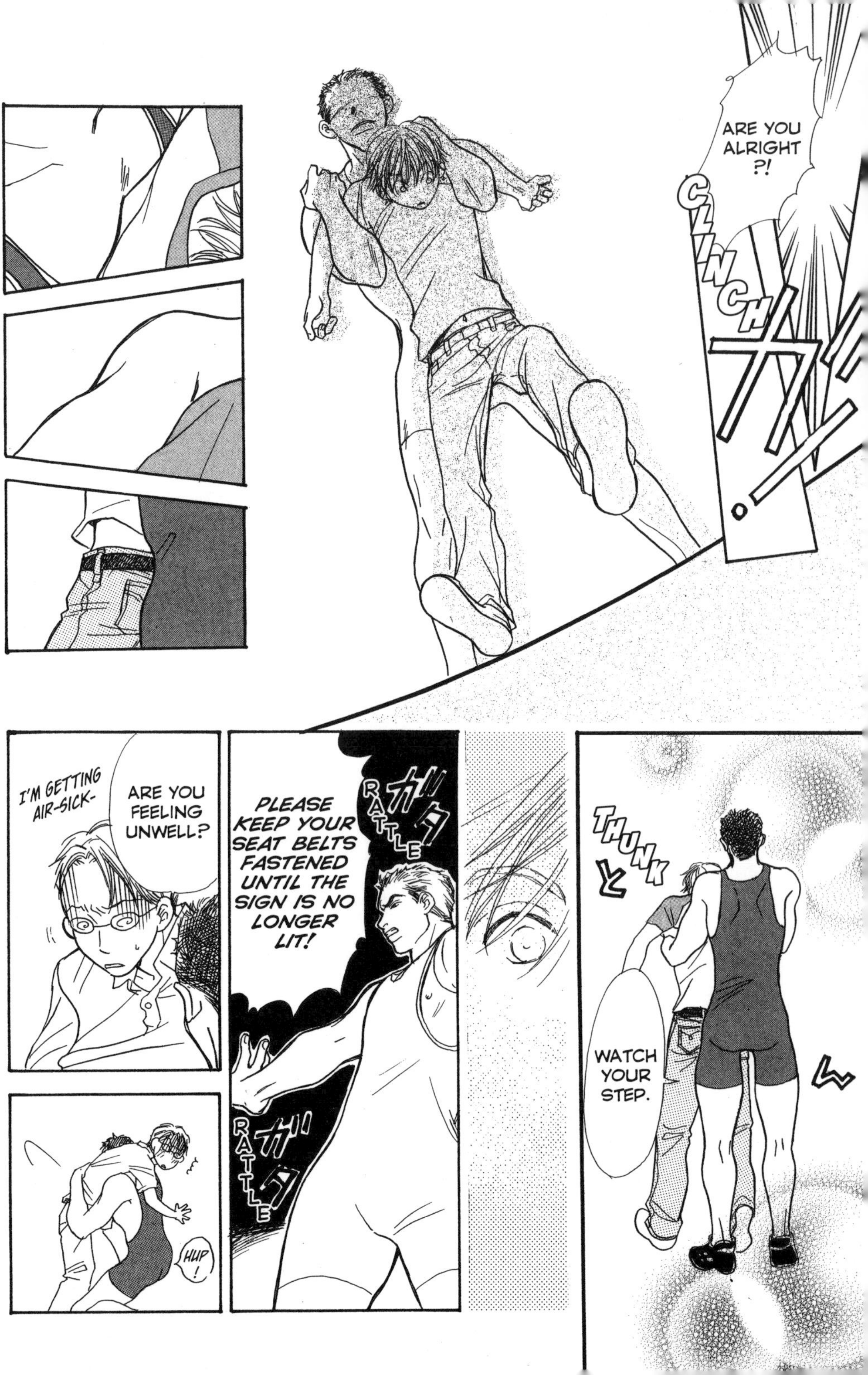
ARE YOU ALRIGHT ?!
CLINCH
THUNK
WATCH YOUR STEP.
PLEASE KEEP YOUR SEAT BELTS FASTENED UNTIL THE SIGN IS NO LONGER LIT!
RATTLE
RATTLE
ARE YOU FEELING UNWELL?
I'M GETTING AIR-SICK-
HUP!

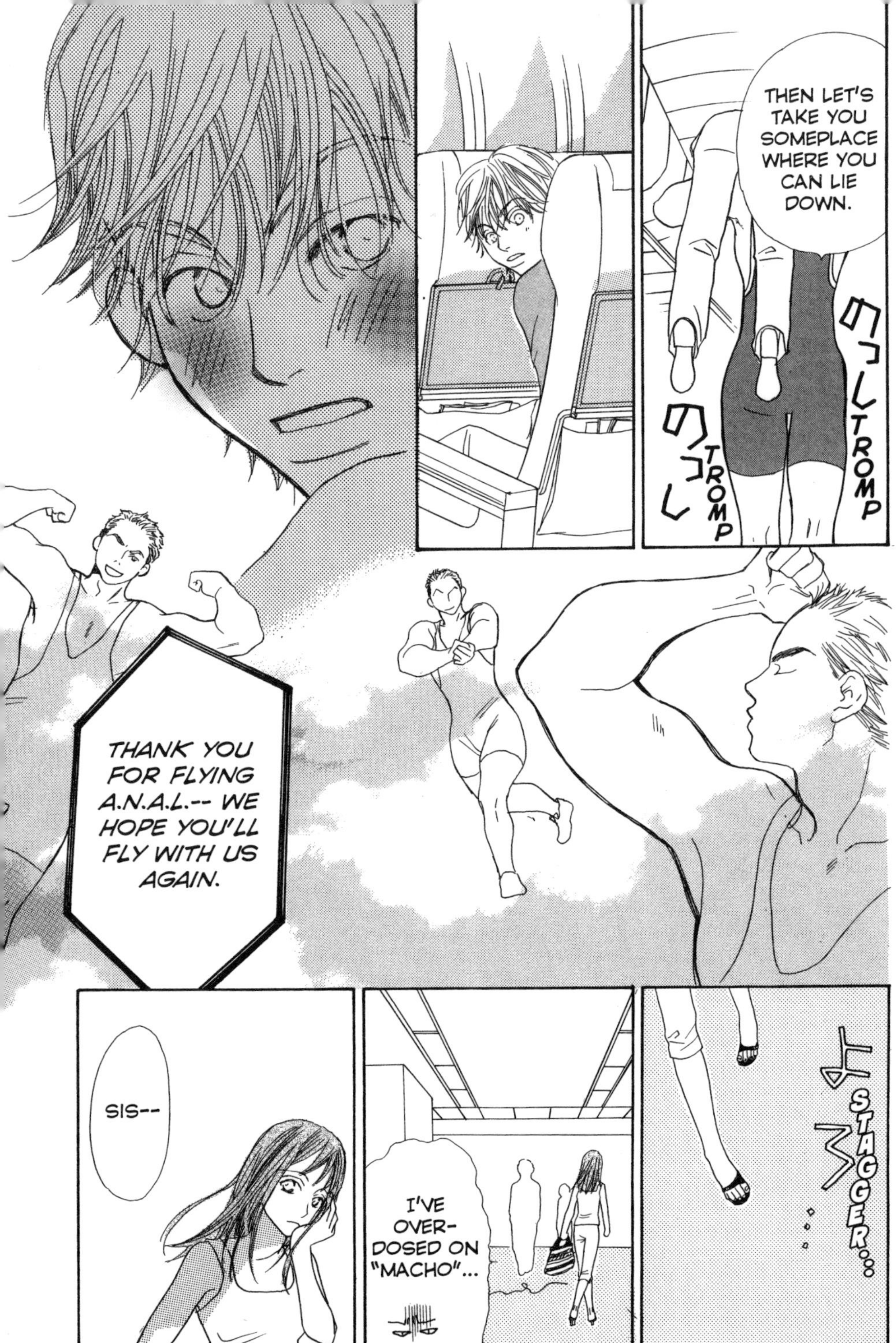
THEN LET'S TAKE YOU SOMEPLACE WHERE YOU CAN LIE DOWN.
のっし
TROMP
のっし
TROMP
THANK YOU FOR FLYING A.N.A.L.-- WE HOPE YOU'LL FLY WITH US AGAIN.
よろ
STAGGER...
I'VE OVER-DOSED ON "MACHO"...
SIS--

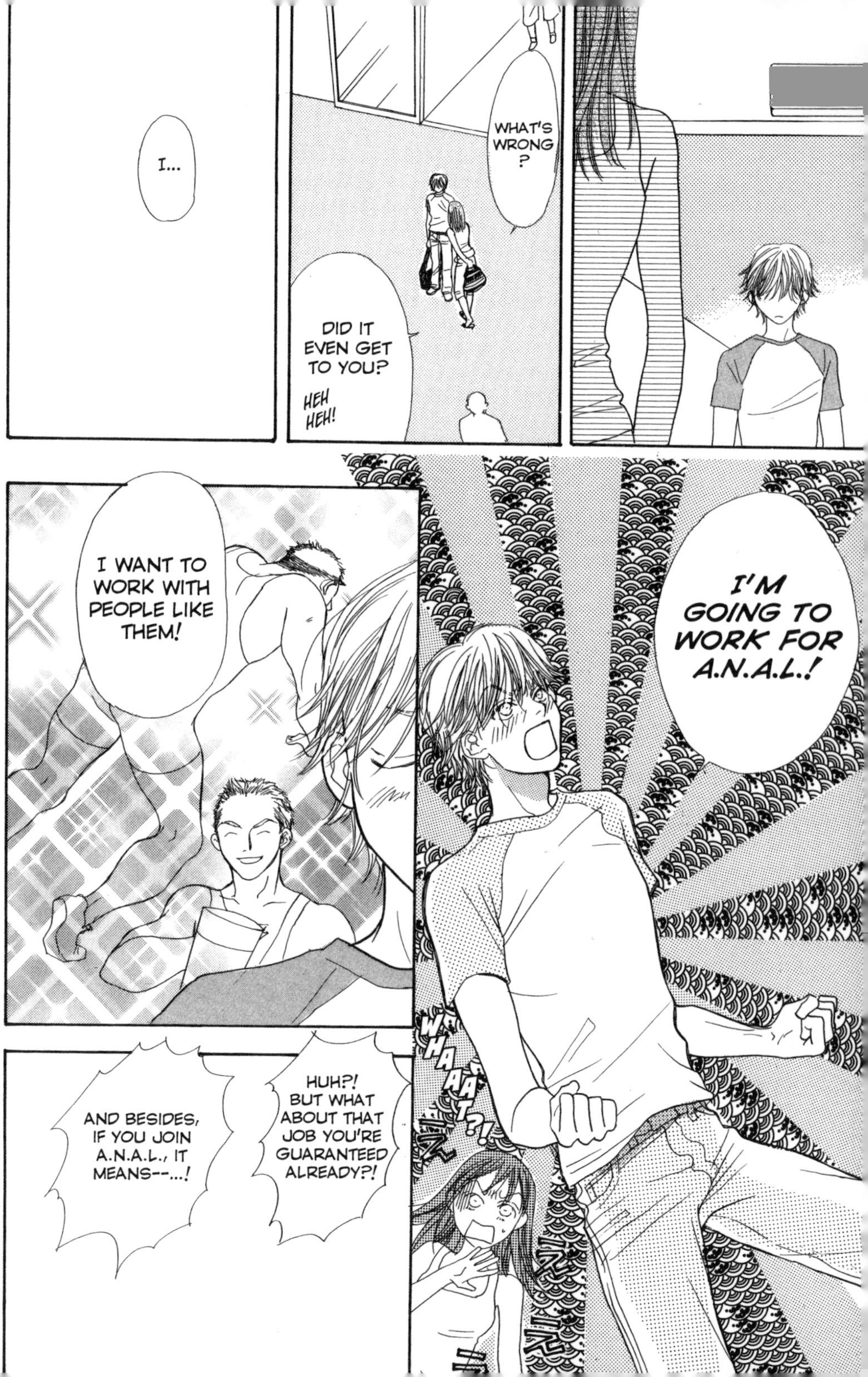
WHAT'S WRONG?
DID IT EVEN GET TO YOU?
HEH HEH!
I...
I'M GOING TO WORK FOR A.N.A.L.!
WHAAAT?!
I WANT TO WORK WITH PEOPLE LIKE THEM!
HUH?! BUT WHAT ABOUT THAT JOB YOU'RE GUARANTEED ALREADY?!
AND BESIDES, IF YOU JOIN A.N.A.L., IT MEANS--...!

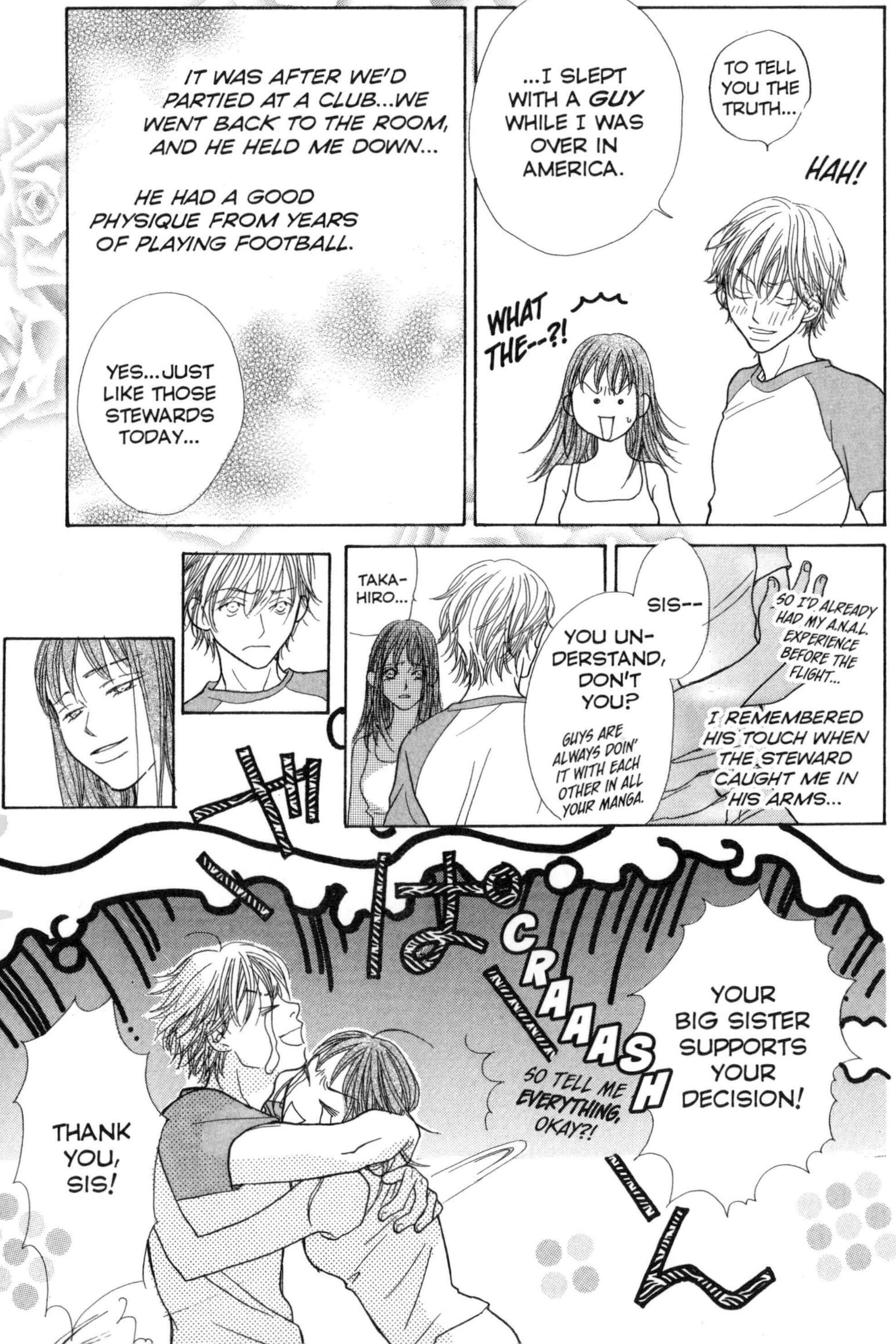
TO TELL YOU THE TRUTH...
HAH!
...I SLEPT WITH A **GUY** WHILE I WAS OVER IN AMERICA.
WHAT THE--?!
IT WAS AFTER WE'D PARTIED AT A CLUB...WE WENT BACK TO THE ROOM, AND HE HELD ME DOWN...
HE HAD A GOOD PHYSIQUE FROM YEARS OF PLAYING FOOTBALL.
YES...JUST LIKE THOSE STEWARDS TODAY...
SO I'D ALREADY HAD MY A.N.A.L. EXPERIENCE BEFORE THE FLIGHT...
I REMEMBERED HIS TOUCH WHEN THE STEWARD CAUGHT ME IN HIS ARMS...
SIS--
YOU UNDERSTAND, DON'T YOU?
GUYS ARE ALWAYS DOIN' IT WITH EACH OTHER IN ALL YOUR MANGA.
TAKA-HIRO...
CRAAAASH
YOUR BIG SISTER SUPPORTS YOUR DECISION!
SO TELL ME **EVERYTHING**, OKAY?!
THANK YOU, SIS!

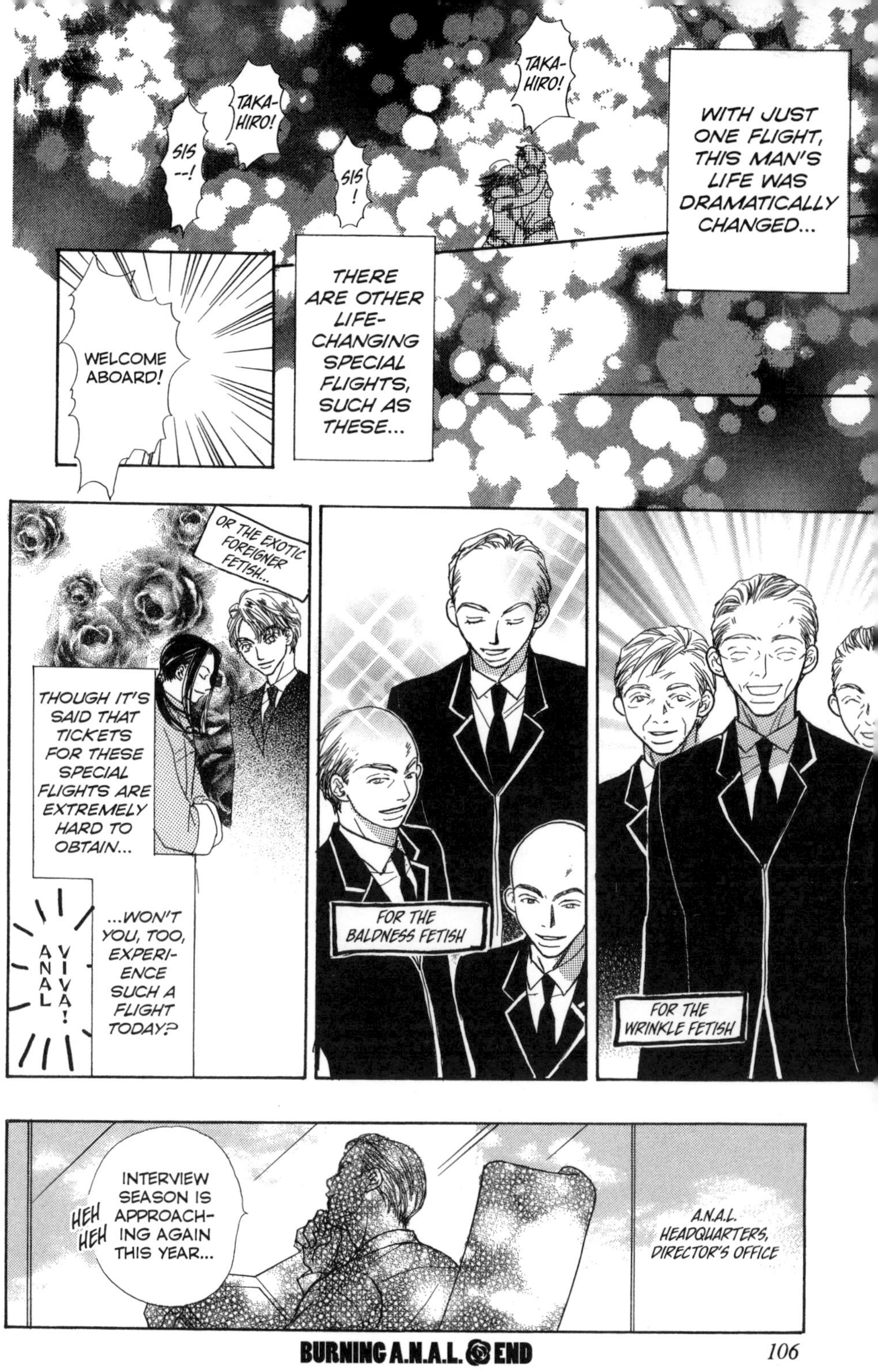

WITH JUST ONE FLIGHT, THIS MAN'S LIFE WAS DRAMATICALLY CHANGED...
TAKA-HIRO!
SIS!
TAKA-HIRO!
SIS--!
THERE ARE OTHER LIFE-CHANGING SPECIAL FLIGHTS, SUCH AS THESE...
WELCOME ABOARD!
FOR THE WRINKLE FETISH
FOR THE BALDNESS FETISH
OR THE EXOTIC FOREIGNER FETISH...
THOUGH IT'S SAID THAT TICKETS FOR THESE SPECIAL FLIGHTS ARE EXTREMELY HARD TO OBTAIN...
...WON'T YOU, TOO, EXPERI-ENCE SUCH A FLIGHT TODAY?
VIVA! ANAL
A.N.A.L. HEADQUARTERS, DIRECTOR'S OFFICE
INTERVIEW SEASON IS APPROACH-ING AGAIN THIS YEAR...
HEH HEH


BURNING A.N.A.L. END

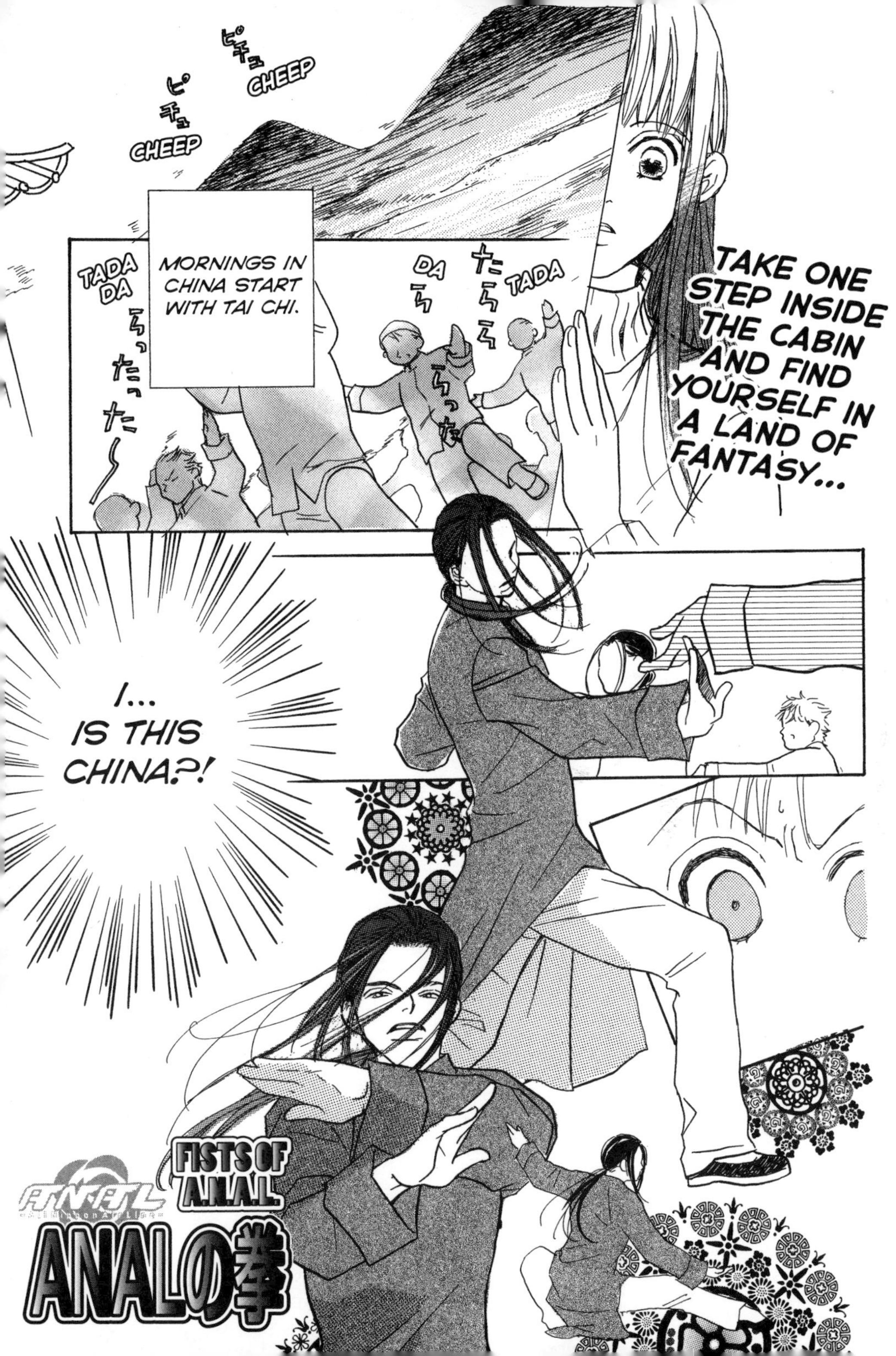

TAKE ONE STEP INSIDE THE CABIN AND FIND YOURSELF IN A LAND OF FANTASY...
ピチュ
CHEEP
ピチュ
CHEEP
たらら
TADA
DA
ら
らったっ
MORNINGS IN CHINA START WITH TAI CHI.
TADA DA
らったったー
I... IS THIS CHINA?!
FISTS OF A.N.A.L.
ANALの拳

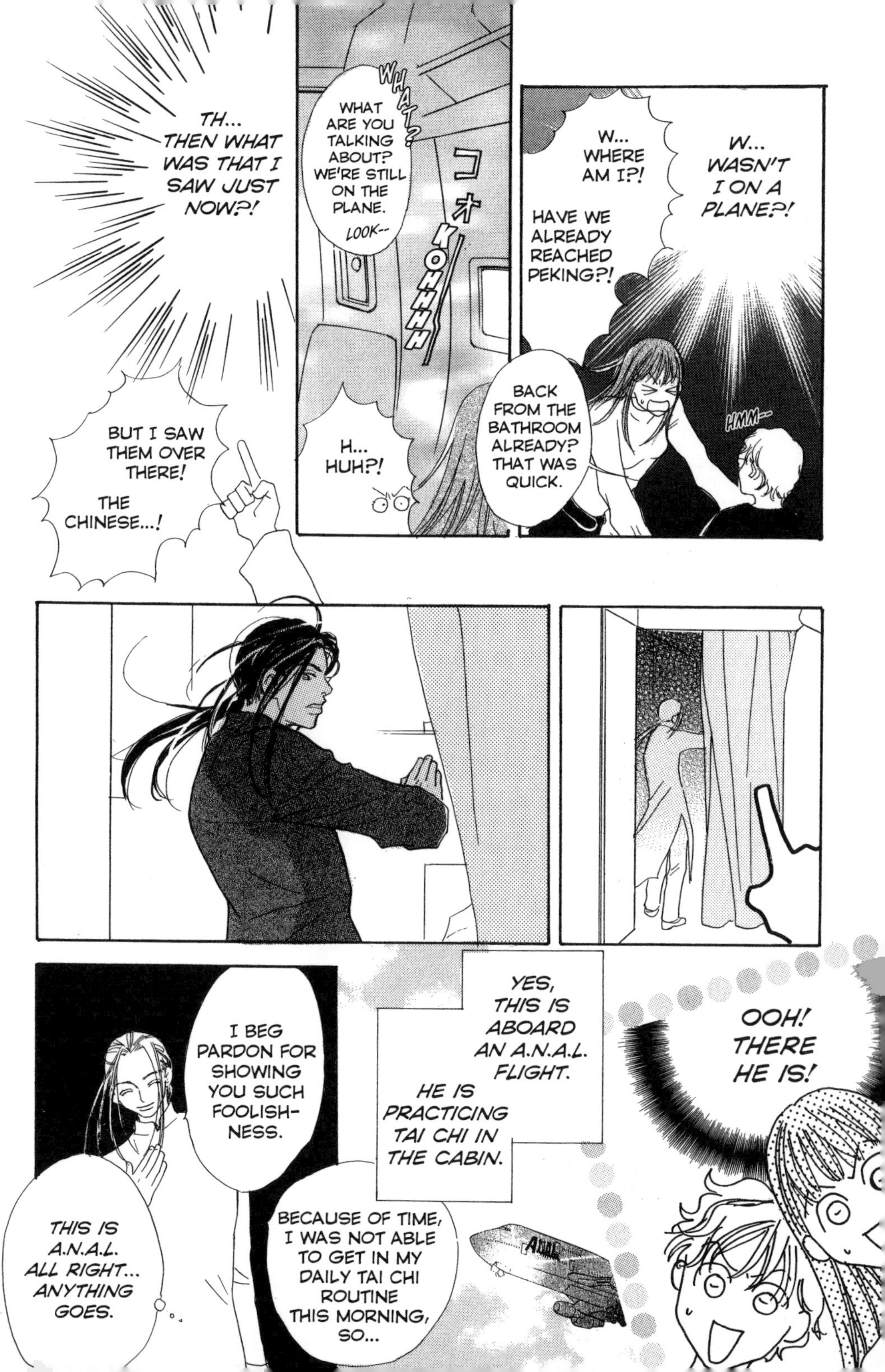
W... WASN'T I ON A PLANE?!
W... WHERE AM I?!
HAVE WE ALREADY REACHED PEKING?!
BACK FROM THE BATHROOM ALREADY? THAT WAS QUICK.
HMM--
WHAT?!
WHAT ARE YOU TALKING ABOUT? WE'RE STILL ON THE PLANE.
LOOK--
コオ
KOHHHH
H... HUH?!
TH... THEN WHAT WAS THAT I SAW JUST NOW?!
BUT I SAW THEM OVER THERE!
THE CHINESE...!
OOH! THERE HE IS!
YES, THIS IS ABOARD AN A.N.A.L. FLIGHT.
HE IS PRACTICING TAI CHI IN THE CABIN.
I BEG PARDON FOR SHOWING YOU SUCH FOOLISH-NESS.
BECAUSE OF TIME, I WAS NOT ABLE TO GET IN MY DAILY TAI CHI ROUTINE THIS MORNING, SO...
ANAL
THIS IS A.N.A.L. ALL RIGHT... ANYTHING GOES.

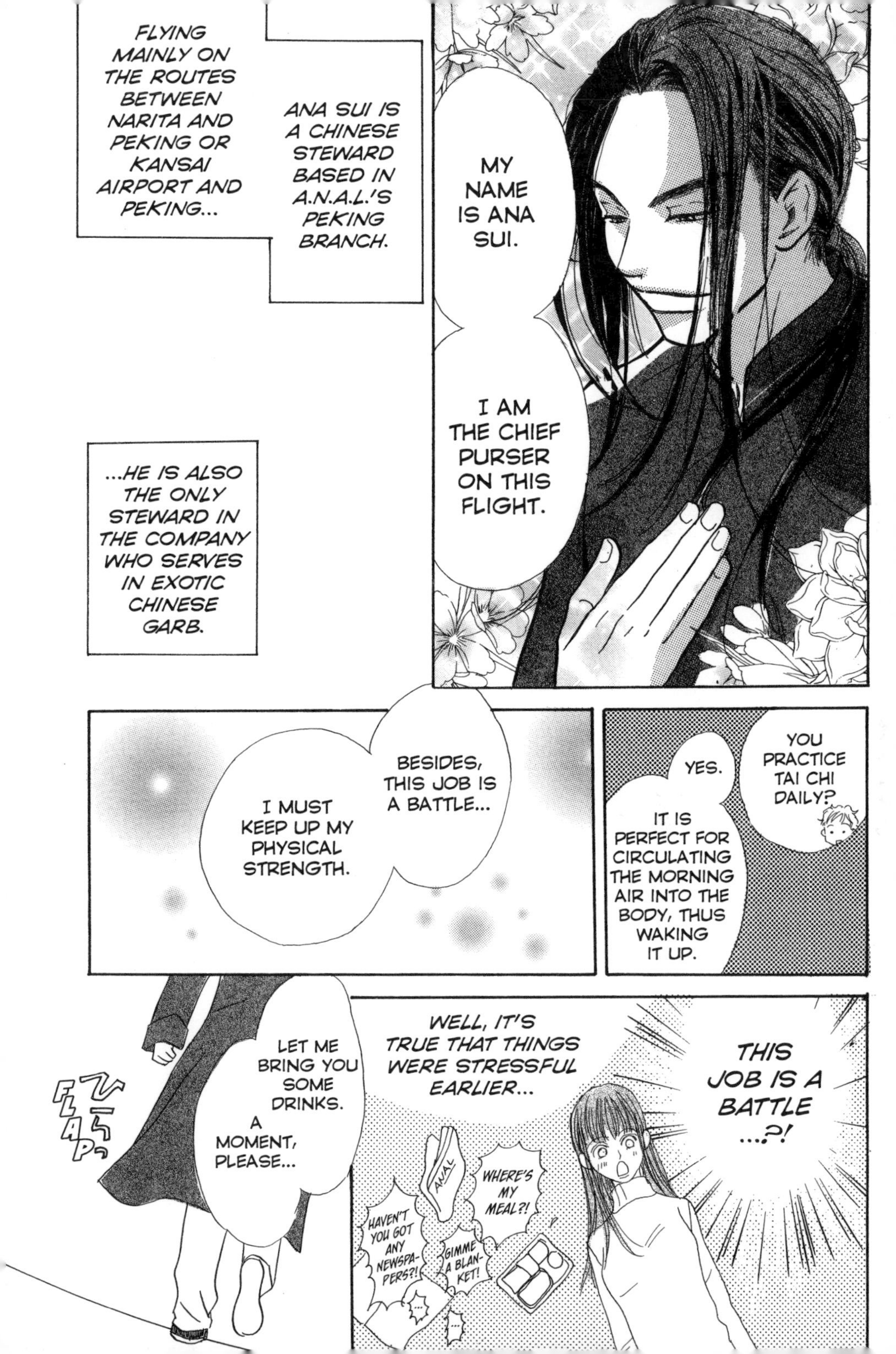
MY NAME IS ANA SUI.
I AM THE CHIEF PURSER ON THIS FLIGHT.
ANA SUI IS A CHINESE STEWARD BASED IN A.N.A.L.'S PEKING BRANCH.
FLYING MAINLY ON THE ROUTES BETWEEN NARITA AND PEKING OR KANSAI AIRPORT AND PEKING...
...HE IS ALSO THE ONLY STEWARD IN THE COMPANY WHO SERVES IN EXOTIC CHINESE GARB.
YOU PRACTICE TAI CHI DAILY?
YES.
IT IS PERFECT FOR CIRCULATING THE MORNING AIR INTO THE BODY, THUS WAKING IT UP.
BESIDES, THIS JOB IS A BATTLE...
I MUST KEEP UP MY PHYSICAL STRENGTH.
THIS JOB IS A BATTLE ...?!
WELL, IT'S TRUE THAT THINGS WERE STRESSFUL EARLIER...
WHERE'S MY MEAL?!
ANAL
GIMME A BLANKET!
HAVEN'T YOU GOT ANY NEWSPAPERS?!
LET ME BRING YOU SOME DRINKS.
A MOMENT, PLEASE...
FLAP

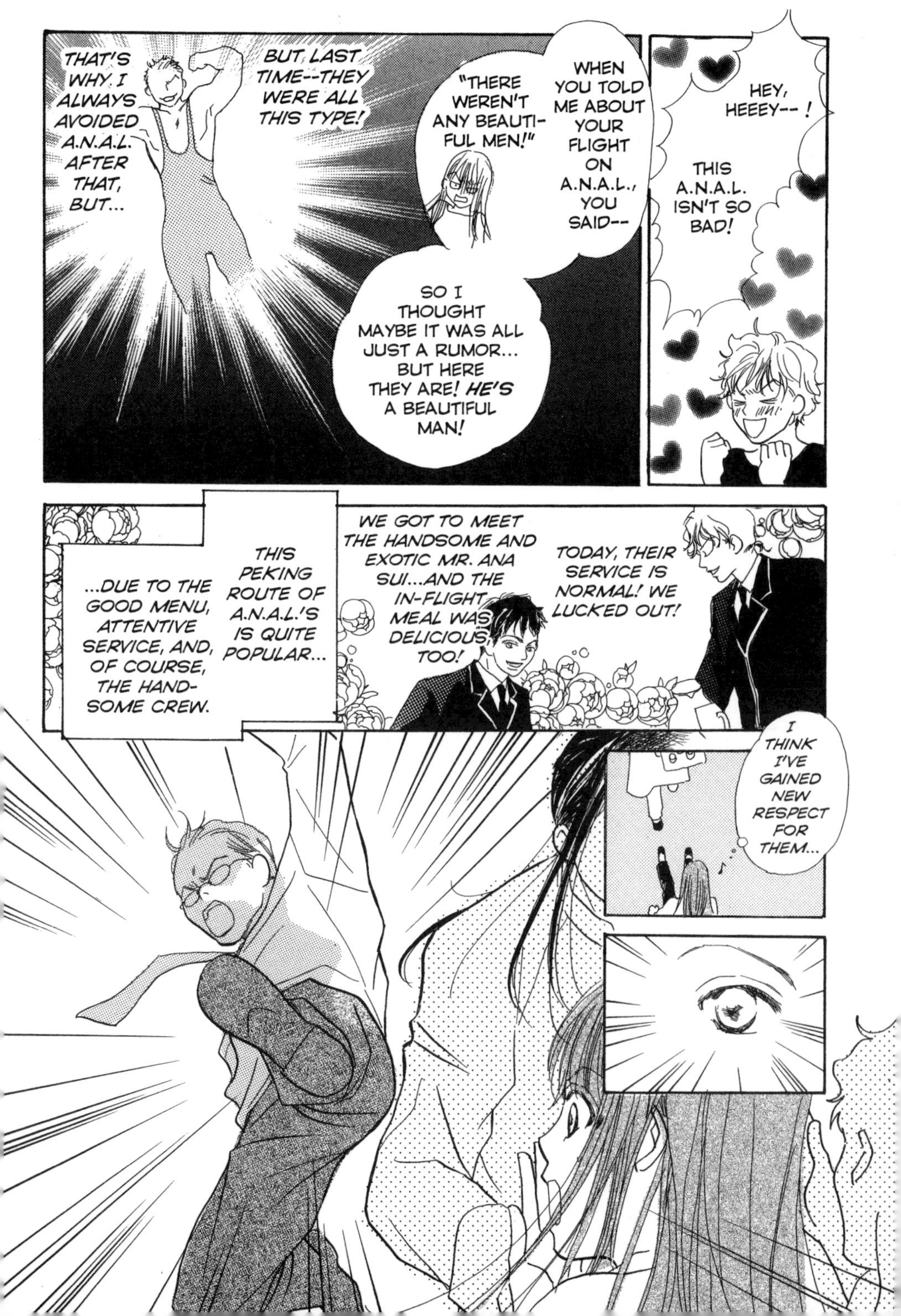
HEY, HEEEY-- !
THIS A.N.A.L. ISN'T SO BAD!
WHEN YOU TOLD ME ABOUT YOUR FLIGHT ON A.N.A.L., YOU SAID--
"THERE WEREN'T ANY BEAUTIFUL MEN!"
BUT LAST TIME--THEY WERE ALL THIS TYPE!
THAT'S WHY I ALWAYS AVOIDED A.N.A.L. AFTER THAT, BUT...
SO I THOUGHT MAYBE IT WAS ALL JUST A RUMOR... BUT HERE THEY ARE! HE'S A BEAUTIFUL MAN!
TODAY, THEIR SERVICE IS NORMAL! WE LUCKED OUT!
WE GOT TO MEET THE HANDSOME AND EXOTIC MR. ANA SUI...AND THE IN-FLIGHT MEAL WAS DELICIOUS, TOO!
THIS PEKING ROUTE OF A.N.A.L.'S IS QUITE POPULAR...
...DUE TO THE GOOD MENU, ATTENTIVE SERVICE, AND, OF COURSE, THE HANDSOME CREW.
I THINK I'VE GAINED NEW RESPECT FOR THEM...

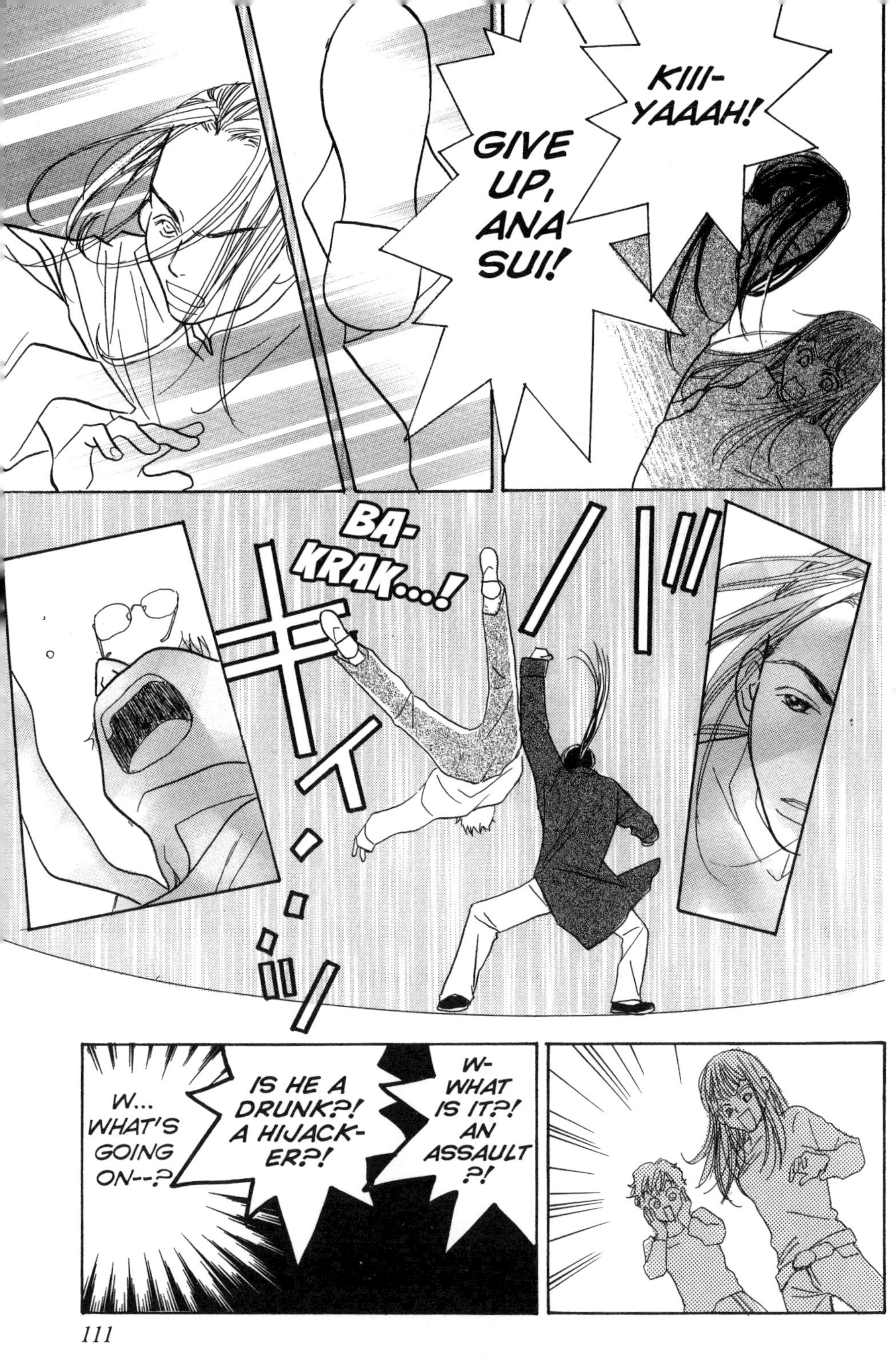
KIII-YAAAH!
GIVE UP, ANA SUI!
BA-KRAK...!
W-WHAT IS IT?! AN ASSAULT?!
IS HE A DRUNK?! A HIJACKER?!
W... WHAT'S GOING ON--?

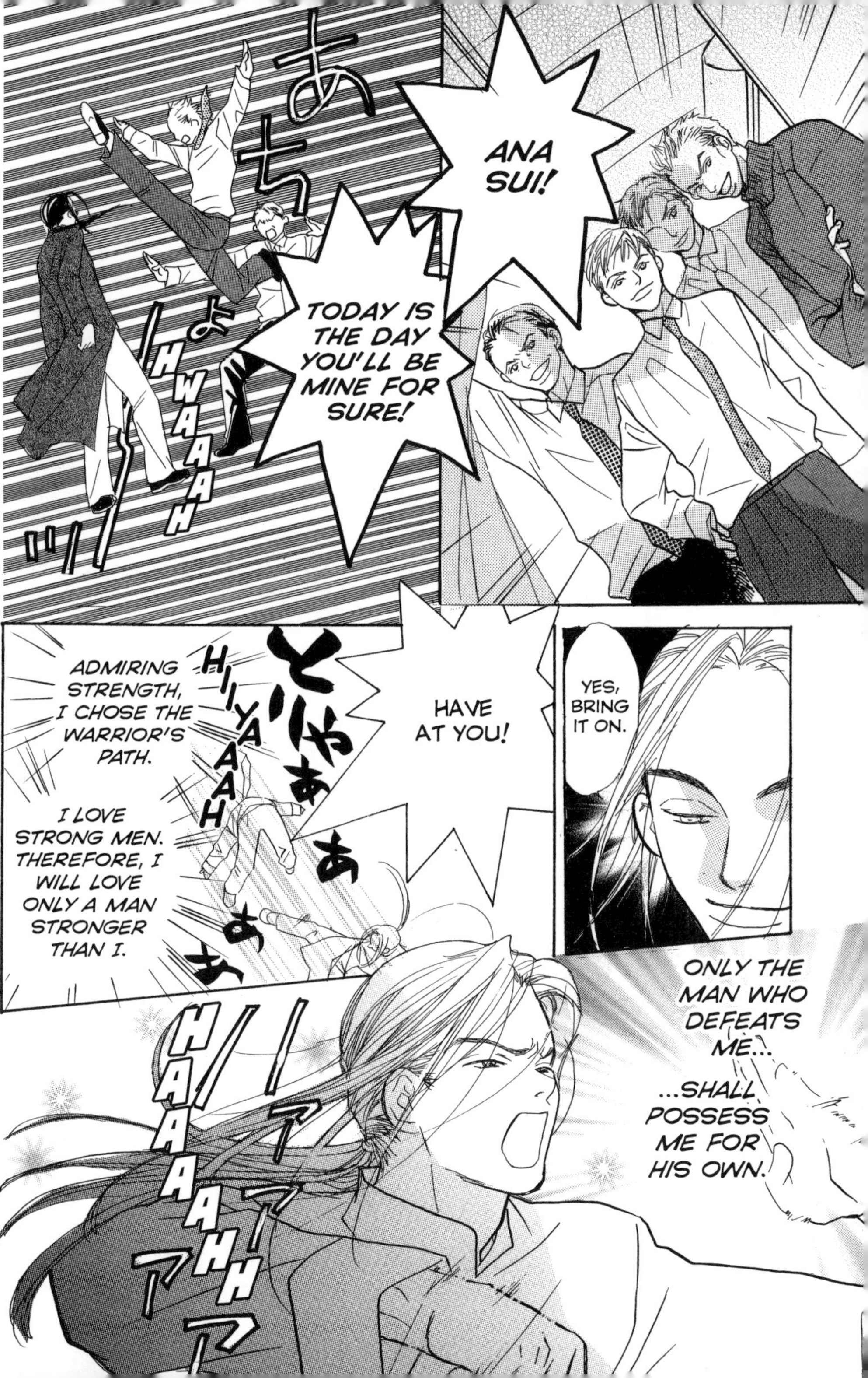

ANA SUI!
TODAY IS THE DAY YOU'LL BE MINE FOR SURE!
あちょ
HWAAAAAH
YES, BRING IT ON.
HAVE AT YOU!
とりゃああああ
HIIYAAAH
ADMIRING STRENGTH, I CHOSE THE WARRIOR'S PATH.
I LOVE STRONG MEN. THEREFORE, I WILL LOVE ONLY A MAN STRONGER THAN I.
ONLY THE MAN WHO DEFEATS ME...
...SHALL POSSESS ME FOR HIS OWN.
HAAAAAAAHH

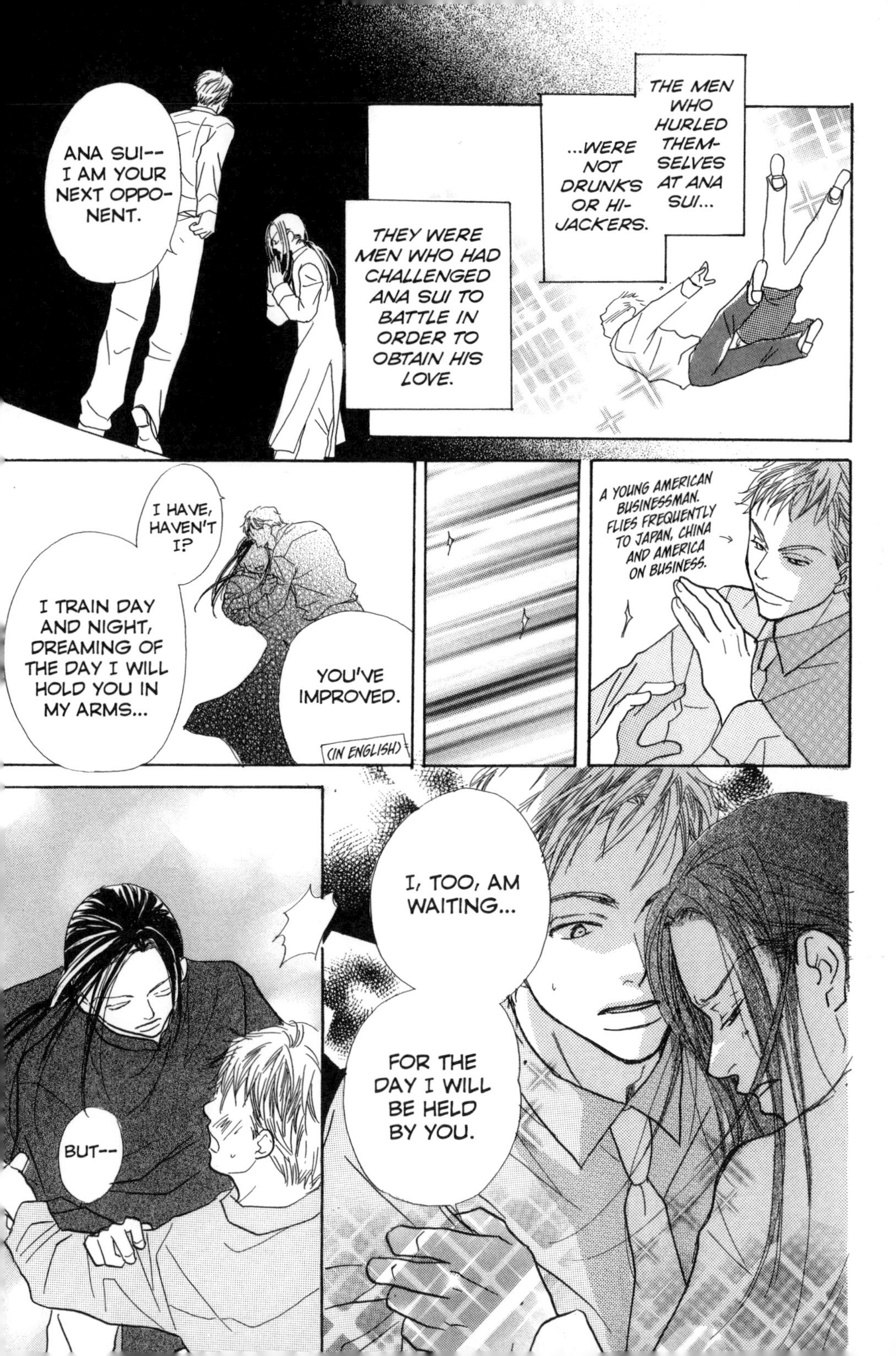
THE MEN WHO HURLED THEMSELVES AT ANA SUI...
...WERE NOT DRUNKS OR HIJACKERS.
THEY WERE MEN WHO HAD CHALLENGED ANA SUI TO BATTLE IN ORDER TO OBTAIN HIS LOVE.
ANA SUI-- I AM YOUR NEXT OPPONENT.
A YOUNG AMERICAN BUSINESSMAN. FLIES FREQUENTLY TO JAPAN, CHINA AND AMERICA ON BUSINESS.
YOU'VE IMPROVED.
(IN ENGLISH)
I HAVE, HAVEN'T I?
I TRAIN DAY AND NIGHT, DREAMING OF THE DAY I WILL HOLD YOU IN MY ARMS...
I, TOO, AM WAITING...
FOR THE DAY I WILL BE HELD BY YOU.
BUT--

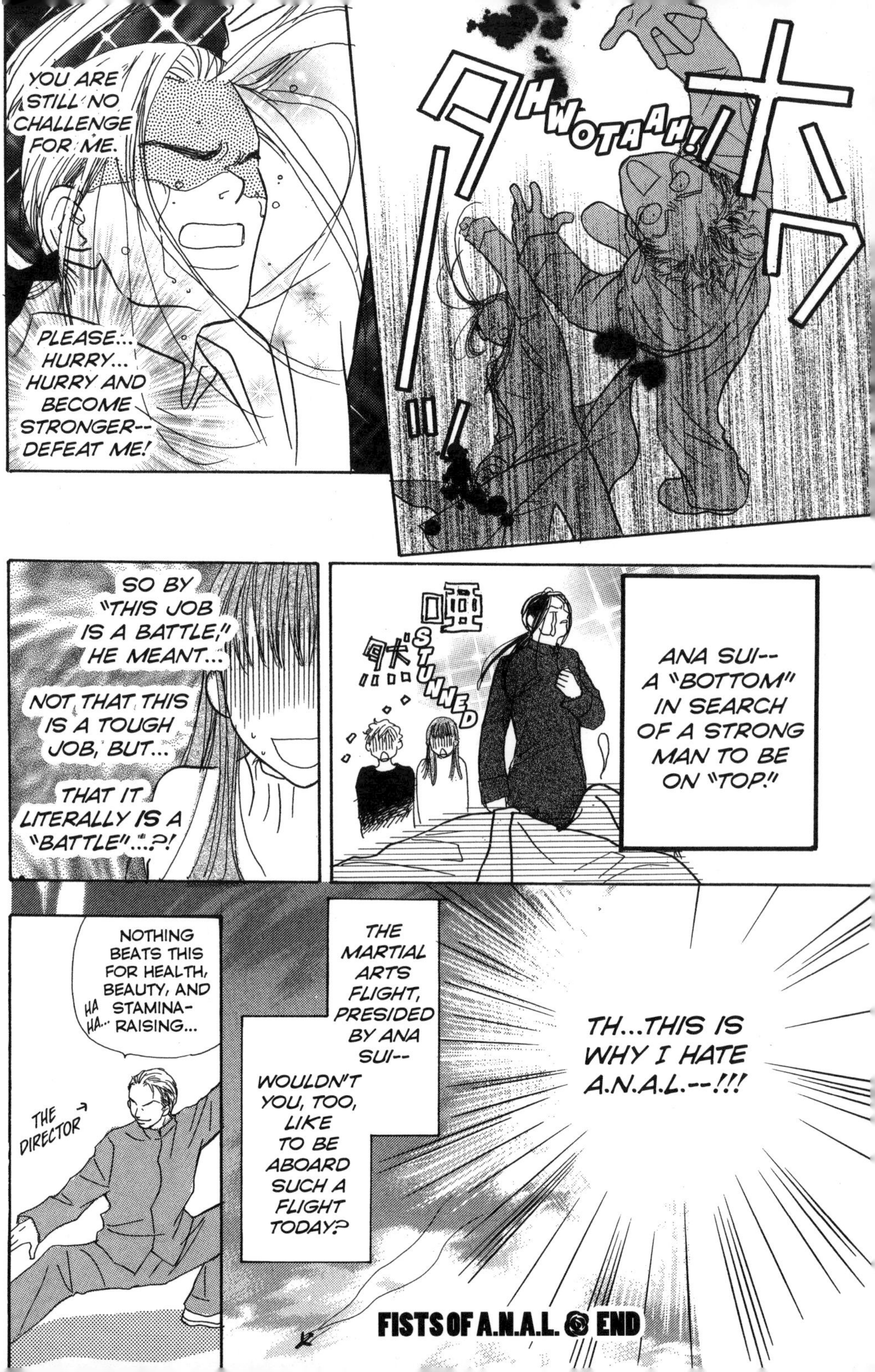
HWOTAAH!
YOU ARE STILL NO CHALLENGE FOR ME.
PLEASE... HURRY... HURRY AND BECOME STRONGER-- DEFEAT ME!
ANA SUI-- A "BOTTOM" IN SEARCH OF A STRONG MAN TO BE ON "TOP."
STUNNED
SO BY "THIS JOB IS A BATTLE," HE MEANT...
NOT THAT THIS IS A TOUGH JOB, BUT...
THAT IT LITERALLY IS A "BATTLE"...?!
TH...THIS IS WHY I HATE A.N.A.L.--!!!
THE MARTIAL ARTS FLIGHT, PRESIDED BY ANA SUI--
WOULDN'T YOU, TOO, LIKE TO BE ABOARD SUCH A FLIGHT TODAY?
NOTHING BEATS THIS FOR HEALTH, BEAUTY, AND STAMINA-RAISING...
HA HA...
THE DIRECTOR
FISTS OF A.N.A.L. @ END

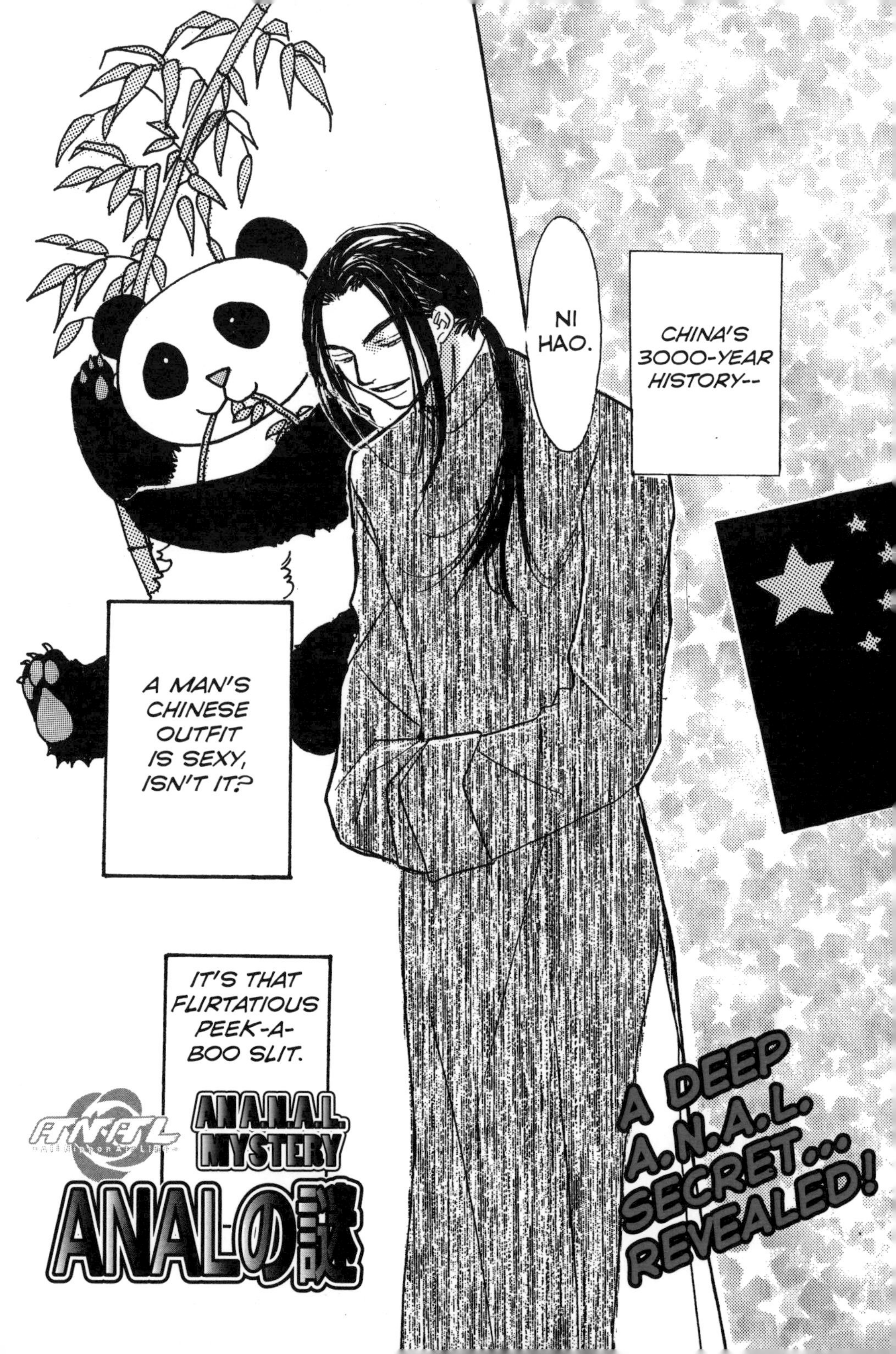
CHINA'S 3000-YEAR HISTORY--
NI HAO.
A MAN'S CHINESE OUTFIT IS SEXY, ISN'T IT?
IT'S THAT FLIRTATIOUS PEEK-A-BOO SLIT.
A DEEP A.N.A.L. SECRET... REVEALED!
A.N.A.L. MYSTERY
ANALの謎

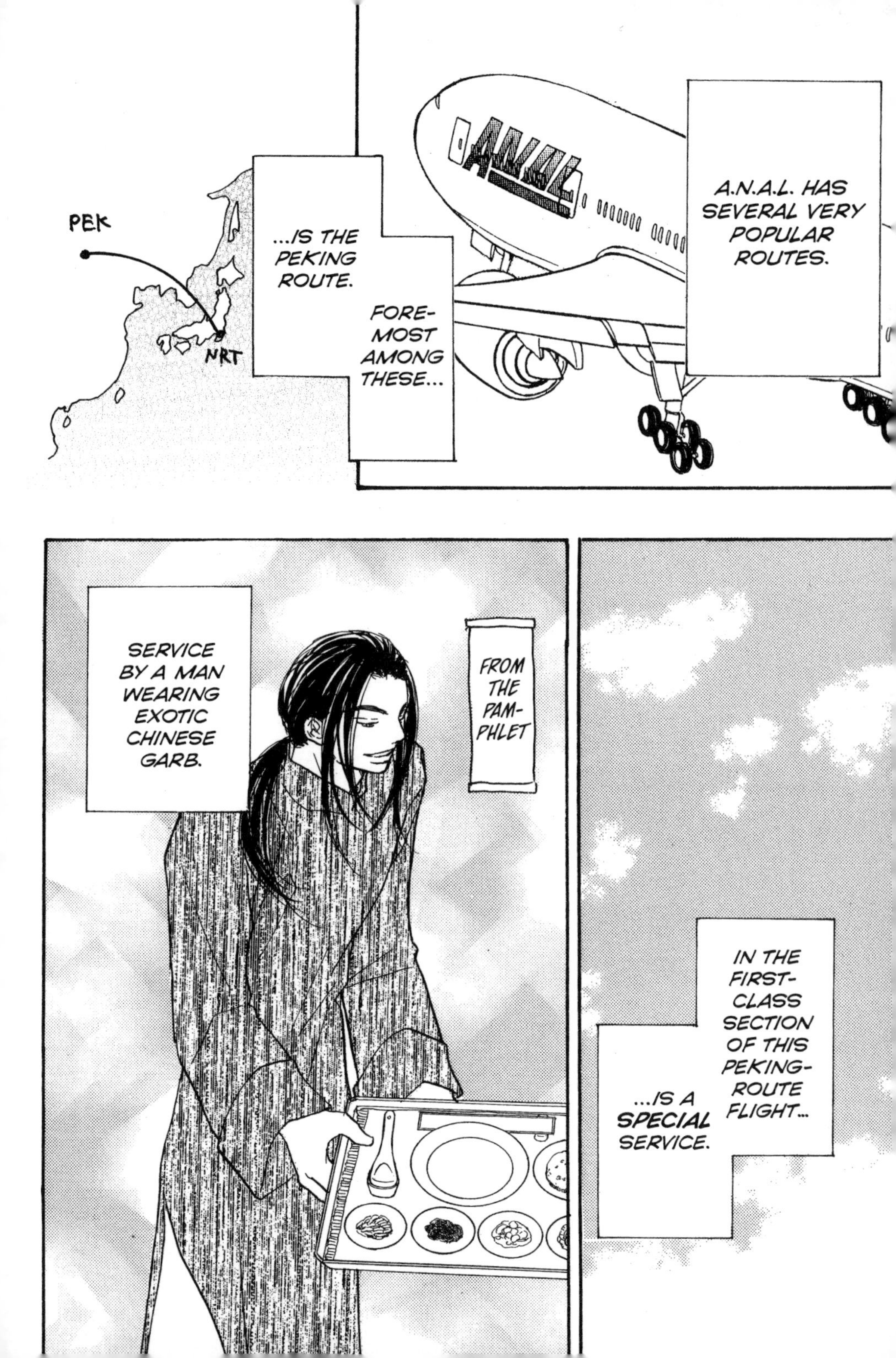
A.N.A.L. HAS SEVERAL VERY POPULAR ROUTES.
FORE-MOST AMONG THESE...
...IS THE PEKING ROUTE.
PEK
NRT
IN THE FIRST-CLASS SECTION OF THIS PEKING-ROUTE FLIGHT...
...IS A **SPECIAL** SERVICE.
SERVICE BY A MAN WEARING EXOTIC CHINESE GARB.
FROM THE PAM-PHLET

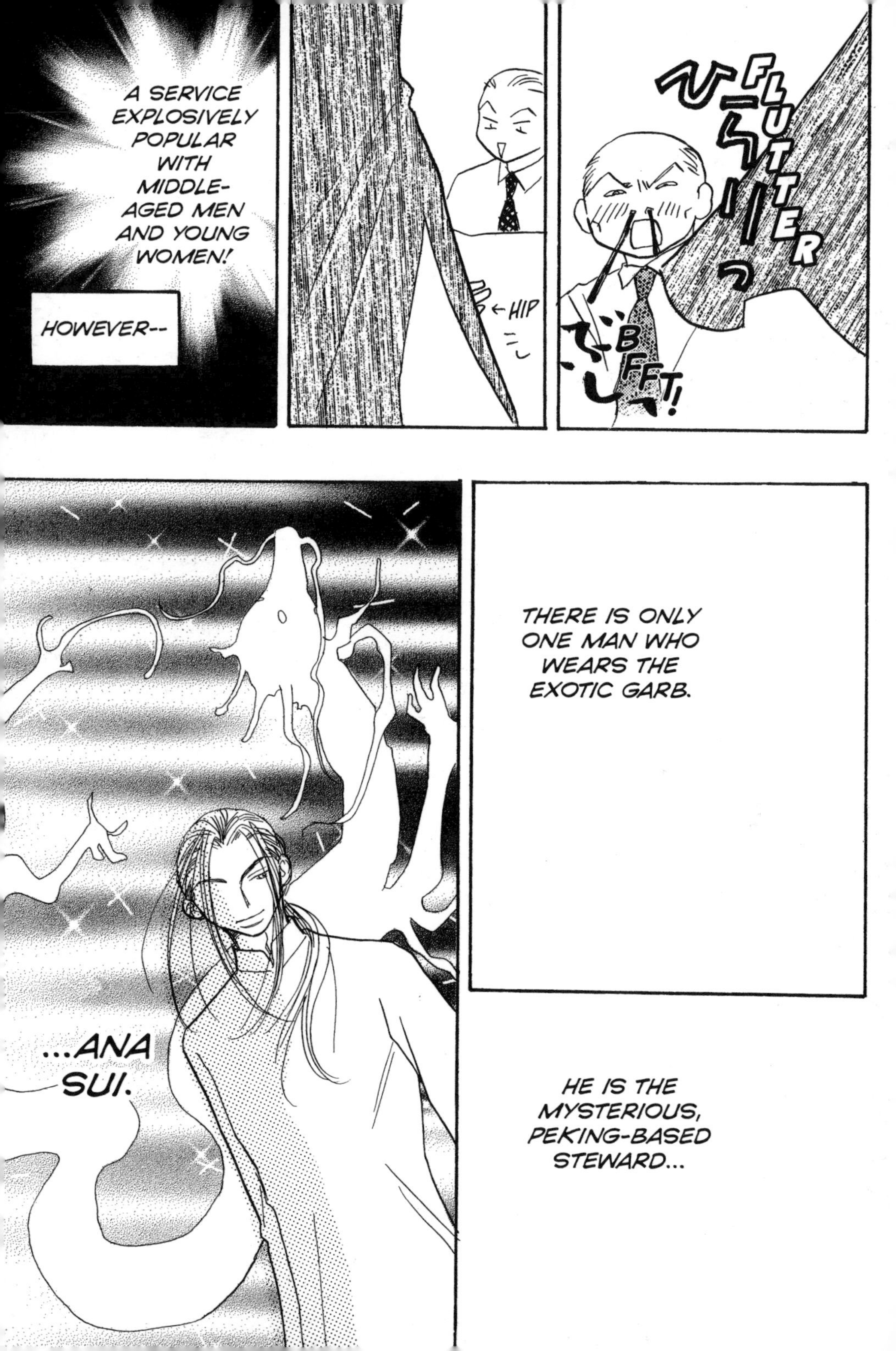
FLUTTER
BFFT!
HIP
A SERVICE EXPLOSIVELY POPULAR WITH MIDDLE-AGED MEN AND YOUNG WOMEN!
HOWEVER--
THERE IS ONLY ONE MAN WHO WEARS THE EXOTIC GARB.
HE IS THE MYSTERIOUS, PEKING-BASED STEWARD...
...ANA SUI.

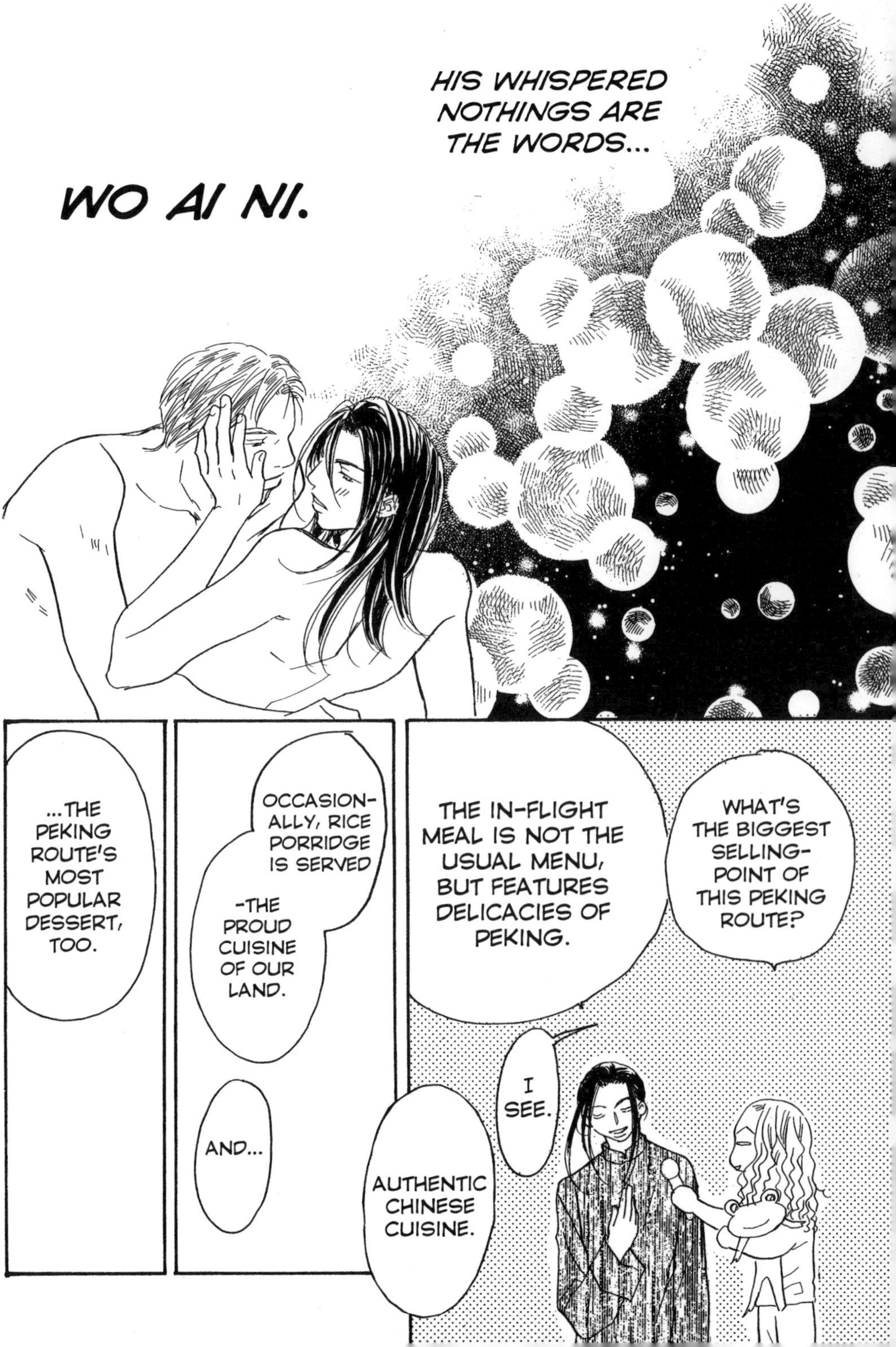
HIS WHISPERED NOTHINGS ARE THE WORDS...
WO AI NI.
WHAT'S THE BIGGEST SELLING-POINT OF THIS PEKING ROUTE?
THE IN-FLIGHT MEAL IS NOT THE USUAL MENU, BUT FEATURES DELICACIES OF PEKING.
I SEE.
AUTHENTIC CHINESE CUISINE.
OCCASION-ALLY, RICE PORRIDGE IS SERVED
-THE PROUD CUISINE OF OUR LAND.
AND...
...THE PEKING ROUTE'S MOST POPULAR DESSERT, TOO.

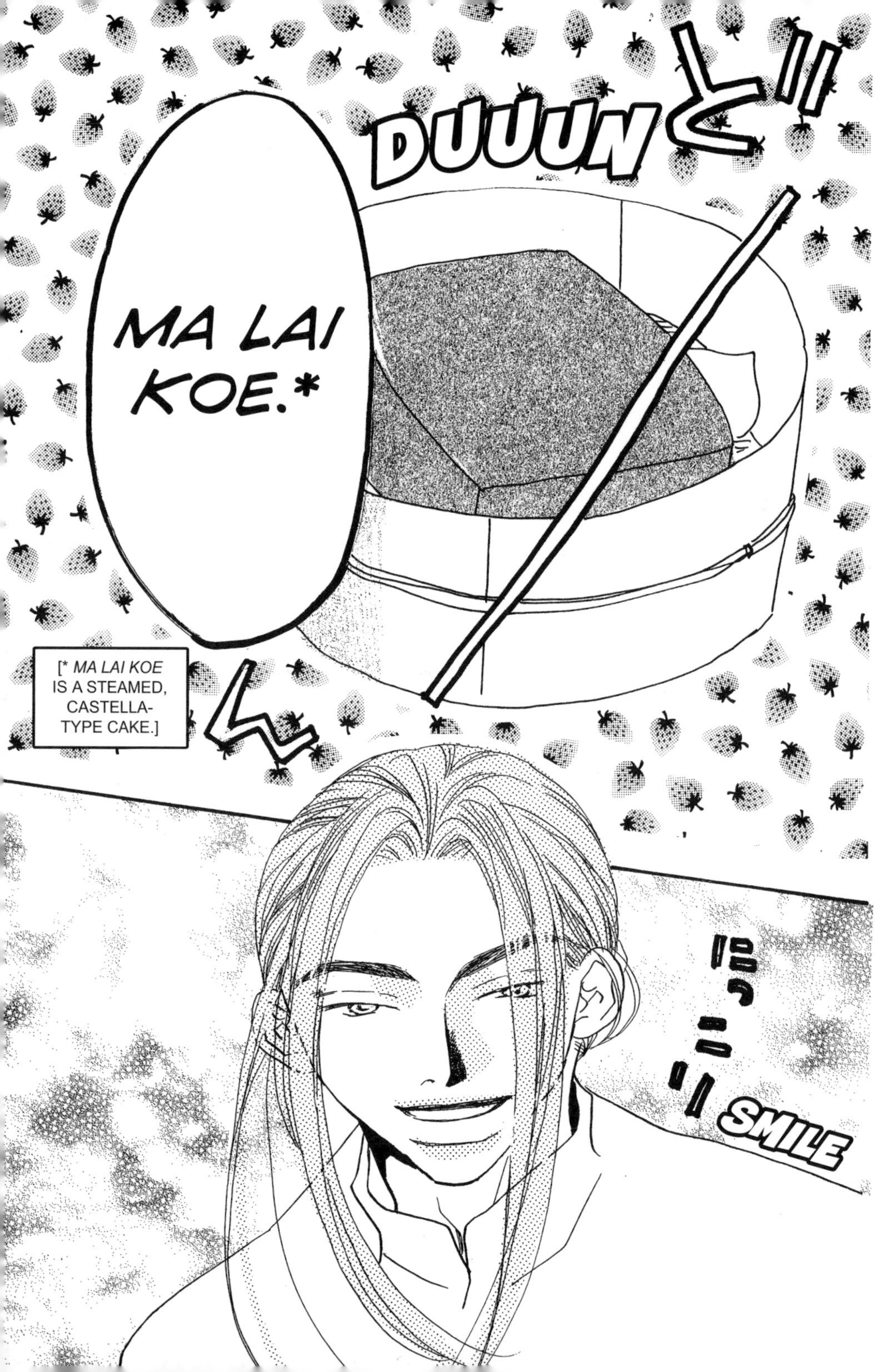
DUUUN
MA LAI KOE.*
[* MA LAI KOE IS A STEAMED, CASTELLA-TYPE CAKE.]
SMILE

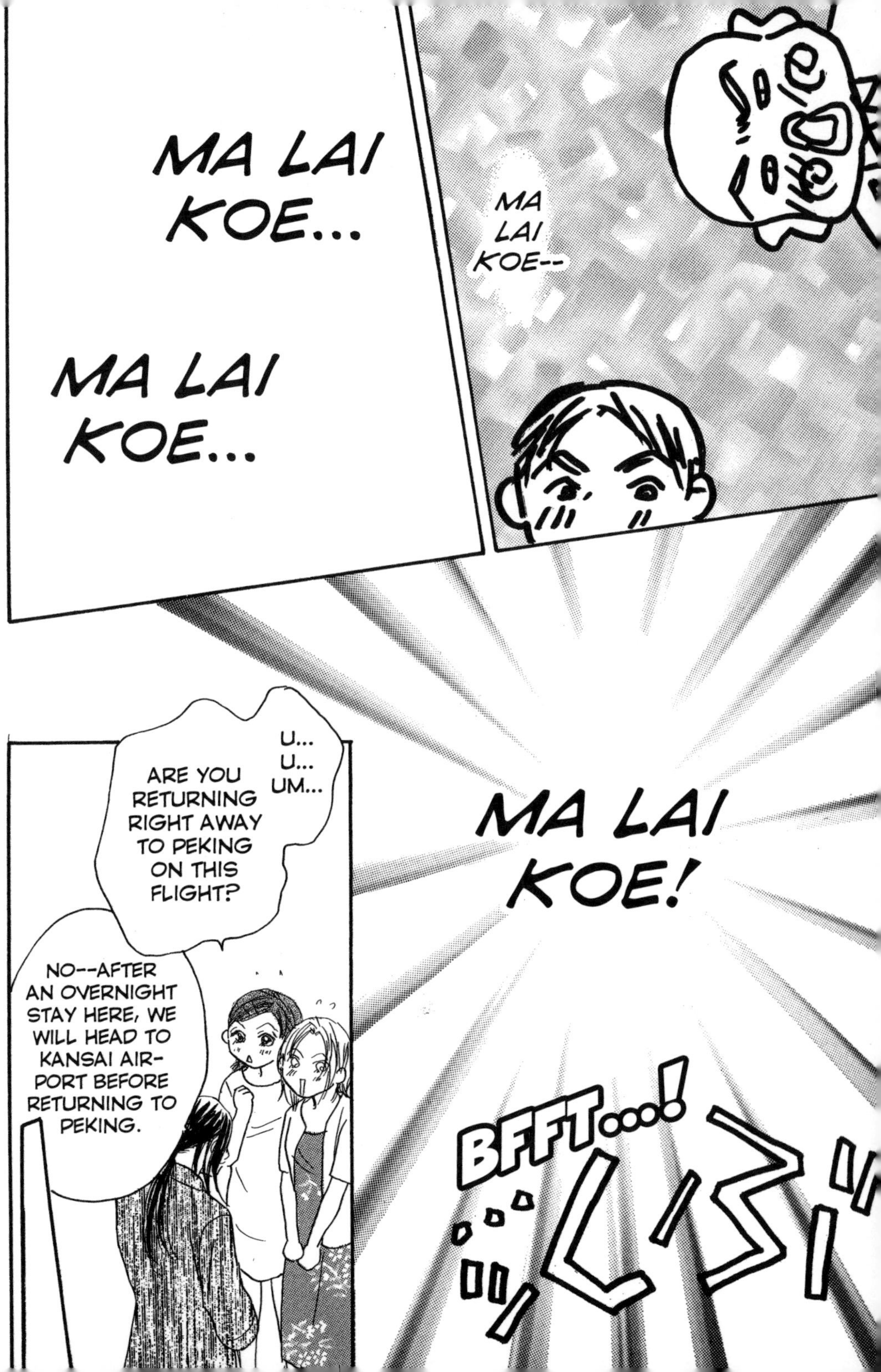
MA LAI KOE--
MA LAI KOE...
MA LAI KOE...
MA LAI KOE!
BFFT...!
U... U... UM...
ARE YOU RETURNING RIGHT AWAY TO PEKING ON THIS FLIGHT?
NO--AFTER AN OVERNIGHT STAY HERE, WE WILL HEAD TO KANSAI AIR-PORT BEFORE RETURNING TO PEKING.

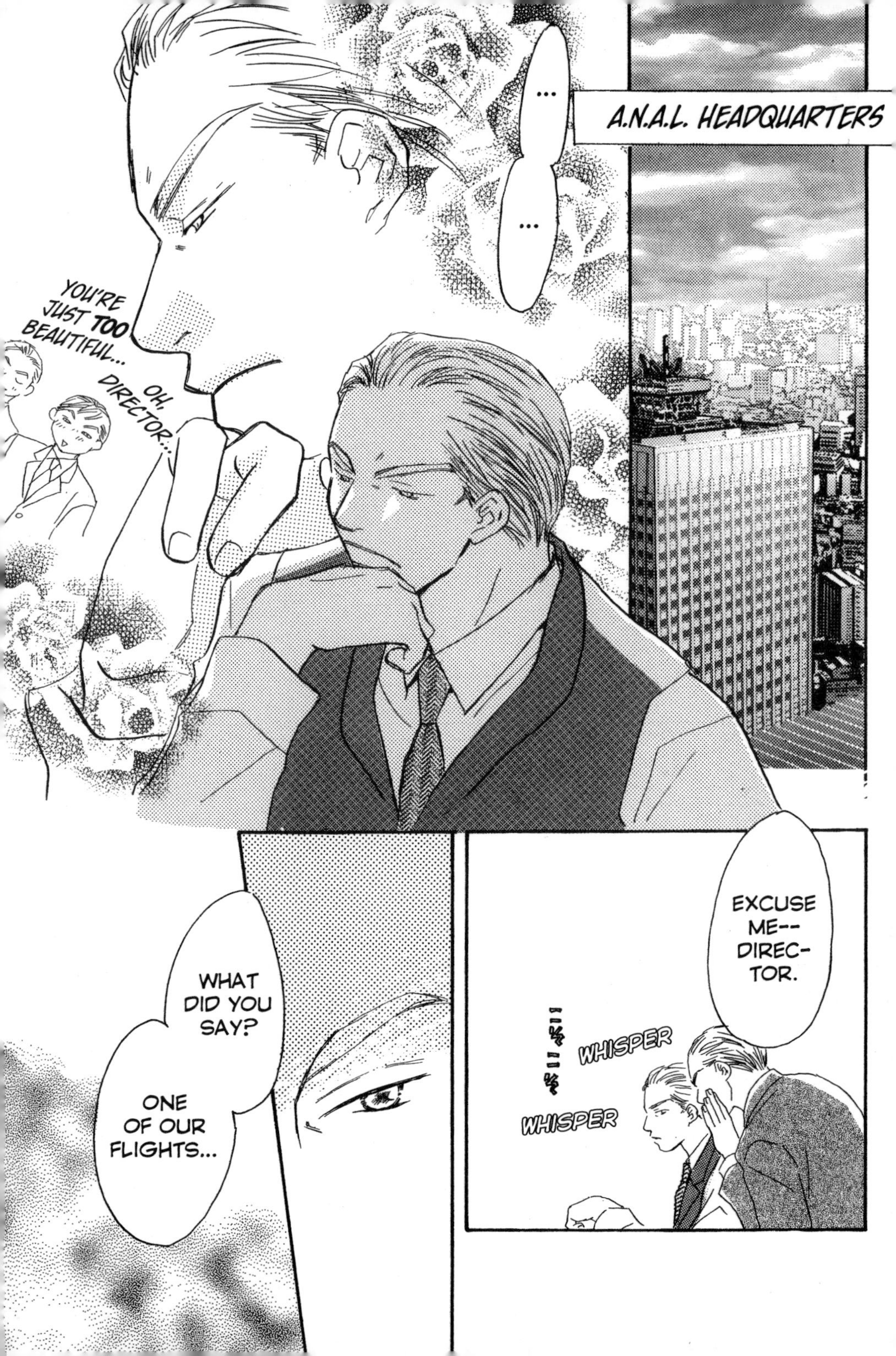
A.N.A.L. HEADQUARTERS
...
...
YOU'RE JUST TOO BEAUTIFUL...
OH, DIRECTOR...
EXCUSE ME-- DIREC-TOR.
WHISPER
WHISPER
WHAT DID YOU SAY?
ONE OF OUR FLIGHTS...

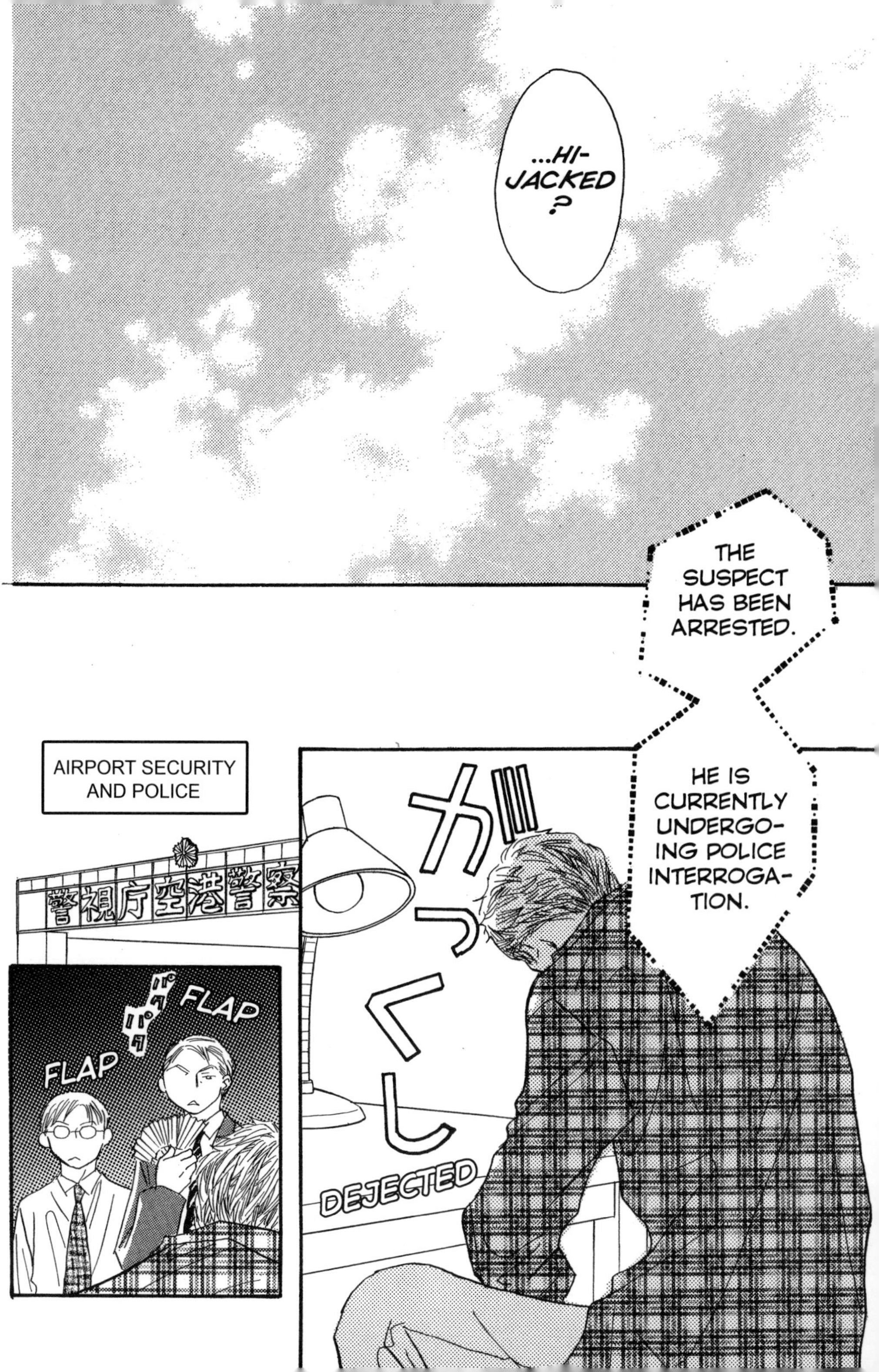
...HI-JACKED?
THE SUSPECT HAS BEEN ARRESTED.
HE IS CURRENTLY UNDERGOING POLICE INTERROGATION.
がっくし
DEJECTED
AIRPORT SECURITY AND POLICE
警視庁空港警察
FLAP
FLAP

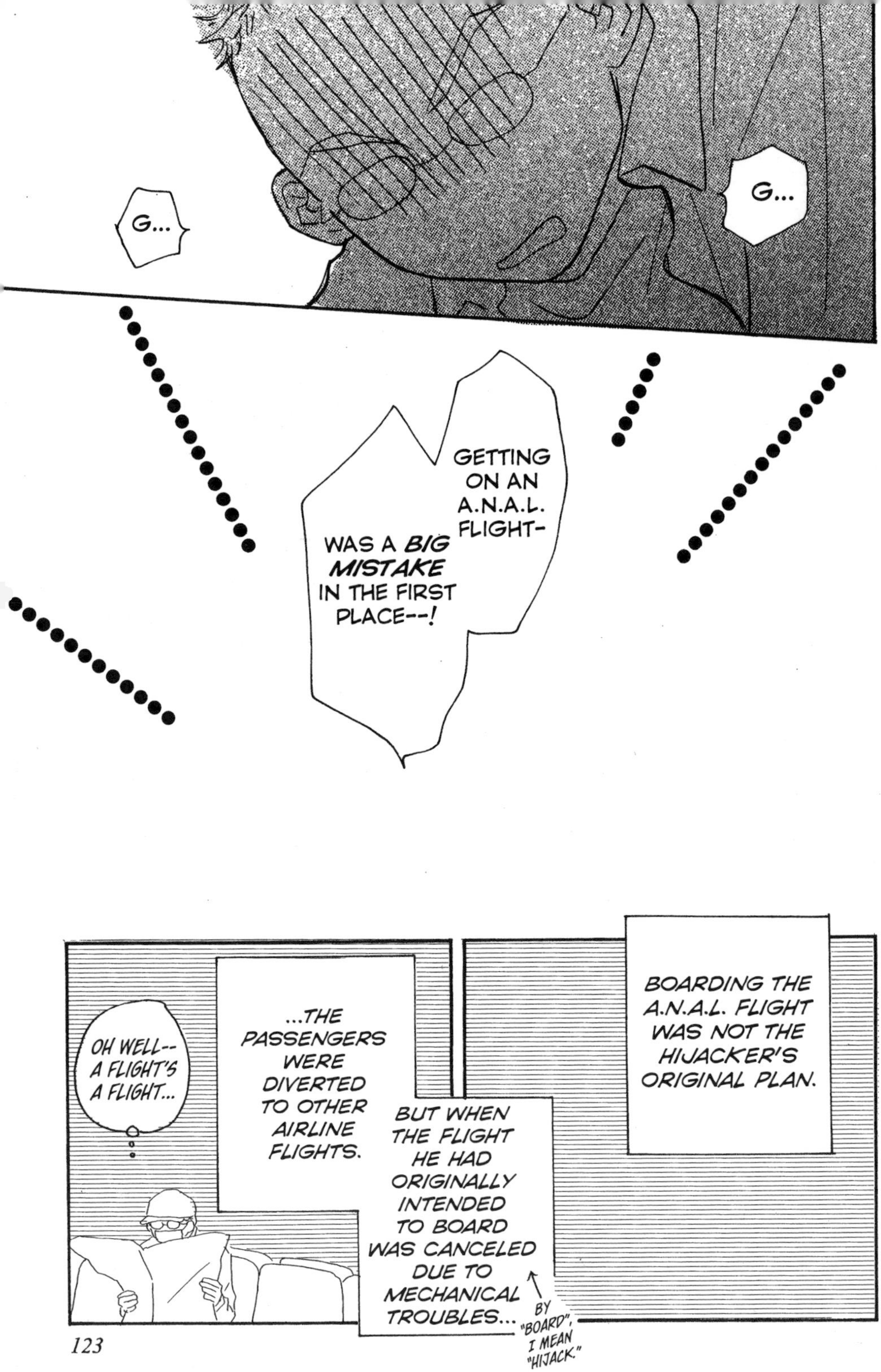
G...
G...
GETTING ON AN A.N.A.L. FLIGHT-
WAS A BIG MISTAKE IN THE FIRST PLACE--!
BOARDING THE A.N.A.L. FLIGHT WAS NOT THE HIJACKER'S ORIGINAL PLAN.
BUT WHEN THE FLIGHT HE HAD ORIGINALLY INTENDED TO BOARD WAS CANCELED DUE TO MECHANICAL TROUBLES...
BY "BOARD", I MEAN "HIJACK."
...THE PASSENGERS WERE DIVERTED TO OTHER AIRLINE FLIGHTS.
OH WELL-- A FLIGHT'S A FLIGHT...

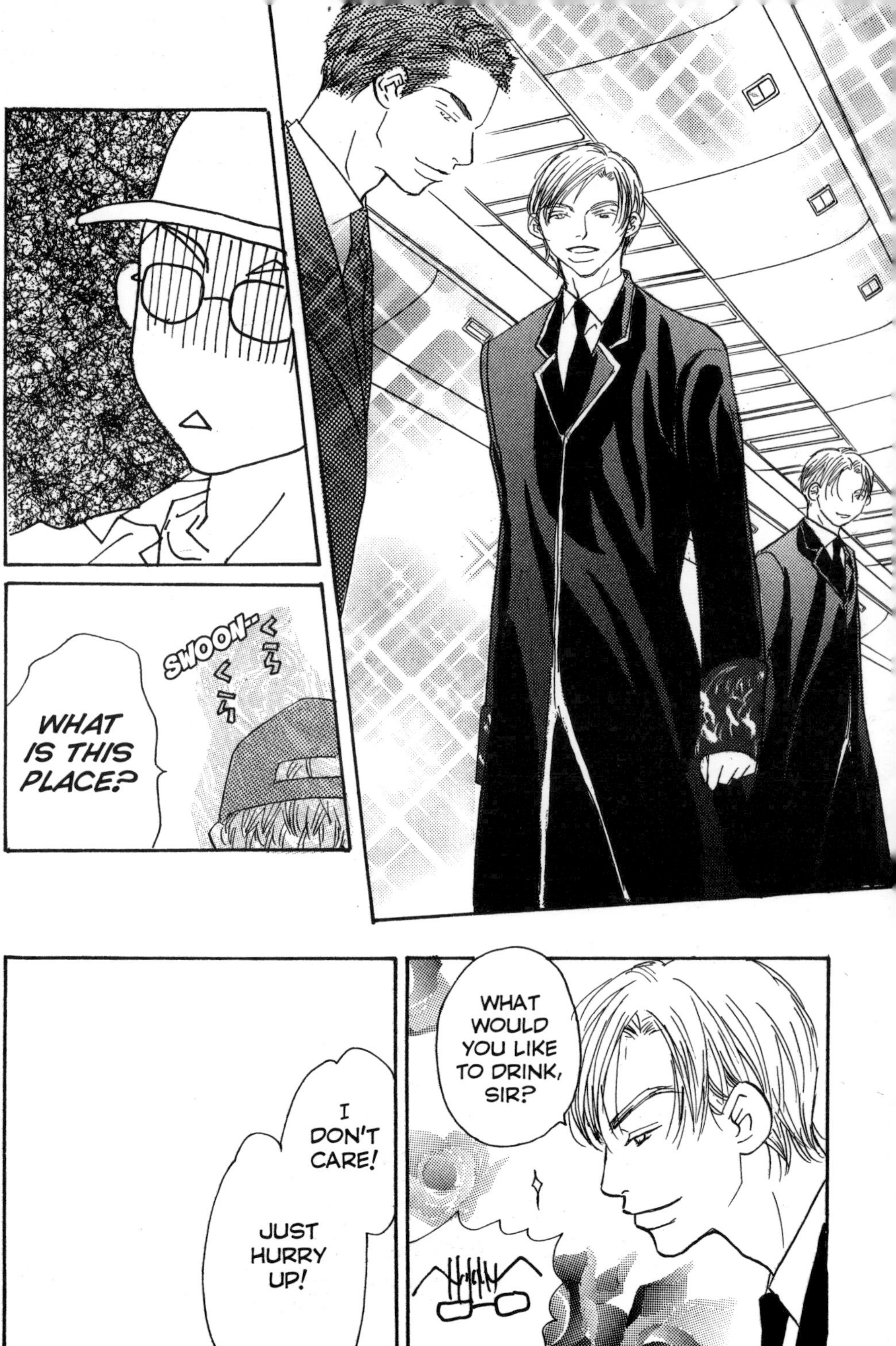
SWOON-
WHAT IS THIS PLACE?
WHAT WOULD YOU LIKE TO DRINK, SIR?
I DON'T CARE!
JUST HURRY UP!

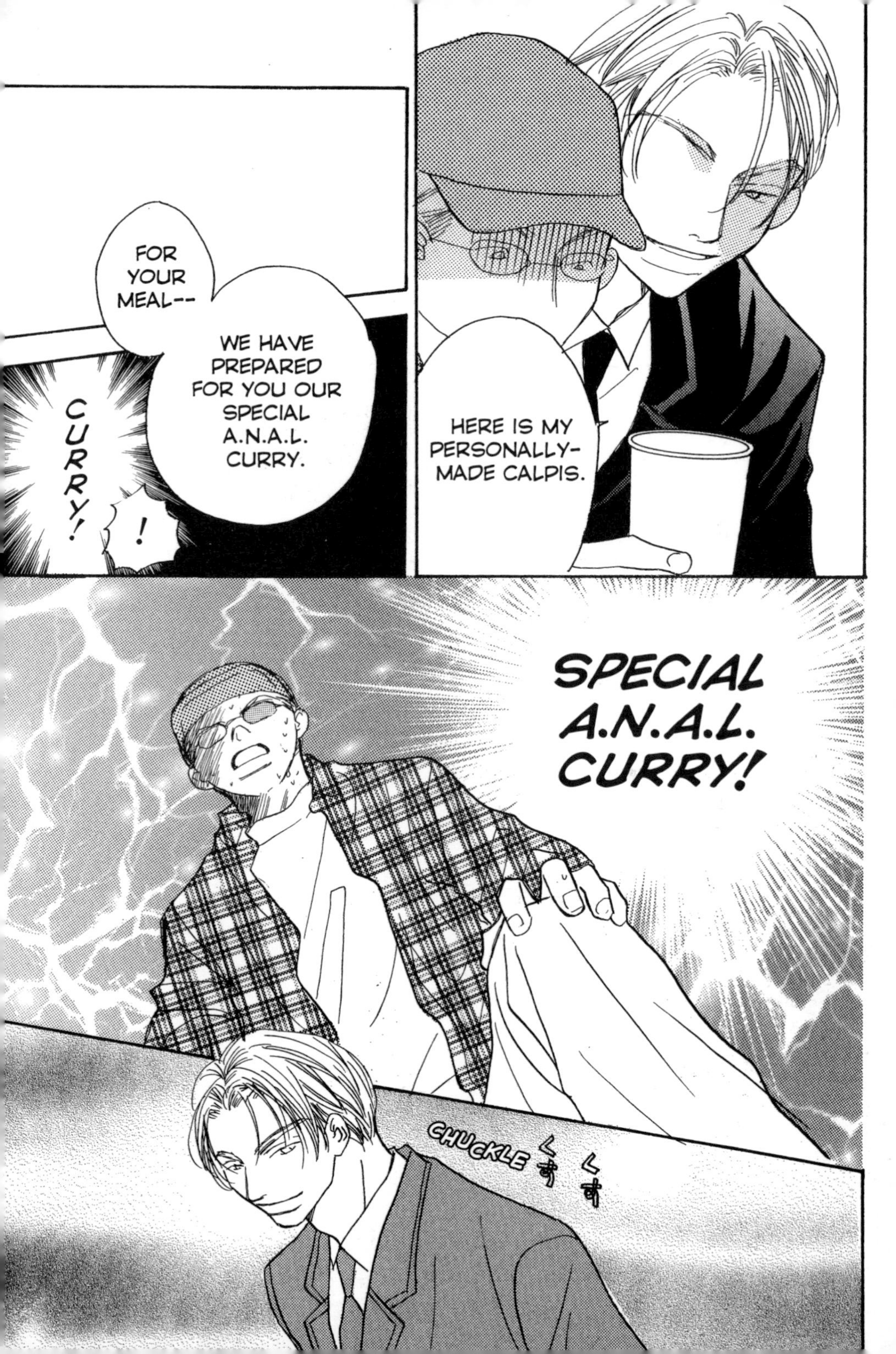
HERE IS MY PERSONALLY-MADE CALPIS.
FOR YOUR MEAL--
WE HAVE PREPARED FOR YOU OUR SPECIAL A.N.A.L. CURRY.
CURRY!
!
SPECIAL A.N.A.L. CURRY!
CHUCKLE
くすくす

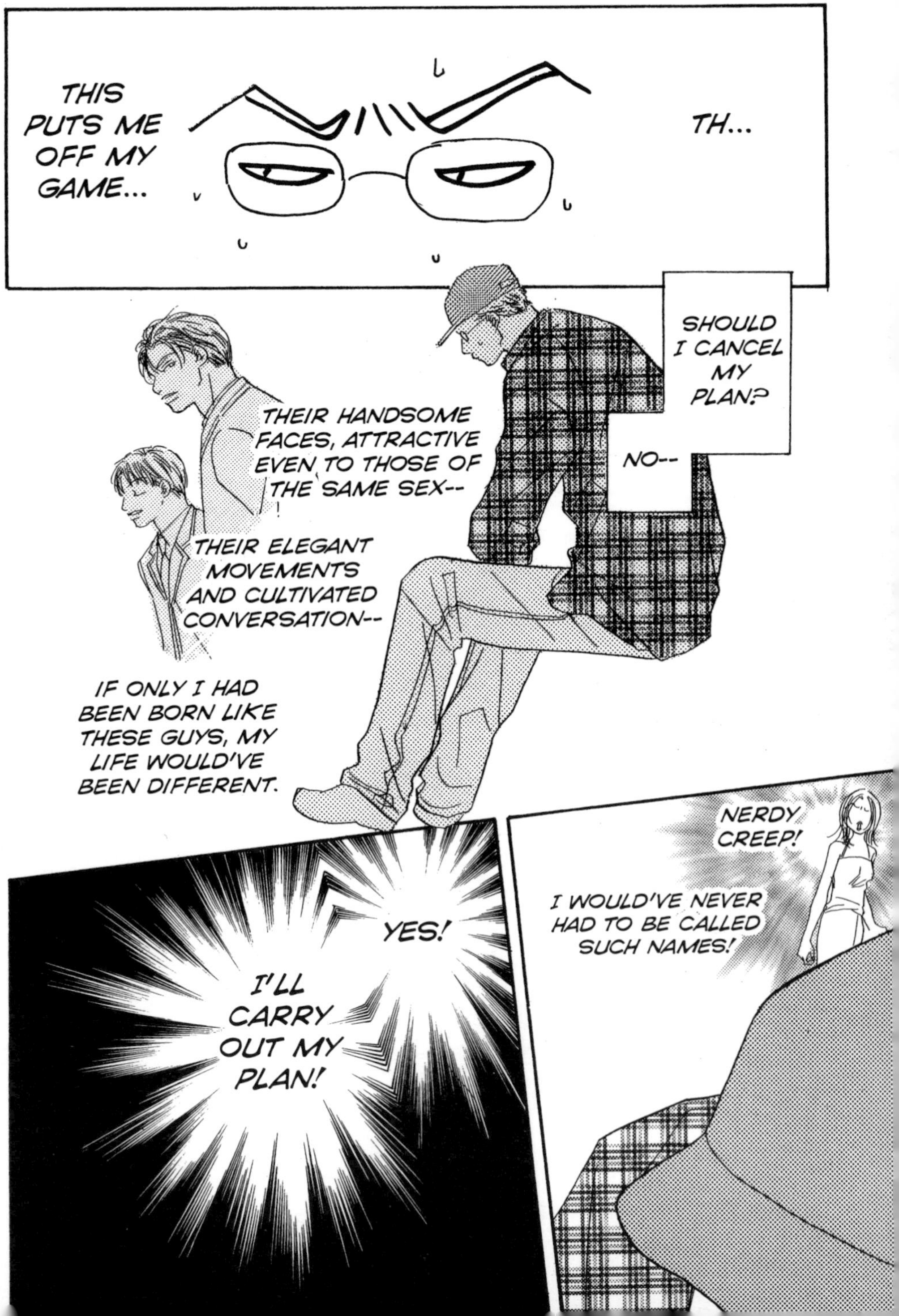
THIS PUTS ME OFF MY GAME...
TH...
SHOULD I CANCEL MY PLAN?
NO--
THEIR HANDSOME FACES, ATTRACTIVE EVEN TO THOSE OF THE SAME SEX--
THEIR ELEGANT MOVEMENTS AND CULTIVATED CONVERSATION--
IF ONLY I HAD BEEN BORN LIKE THESE GUYS, MY LIFE WOULD'VE BEEN DIFFERENT.
NERDY CREEP!
I WOULD'VE NEVER HAD TO BE CALLED SUCH NAMES!
YES!
I'LL CARRY OUT MY PLAN!

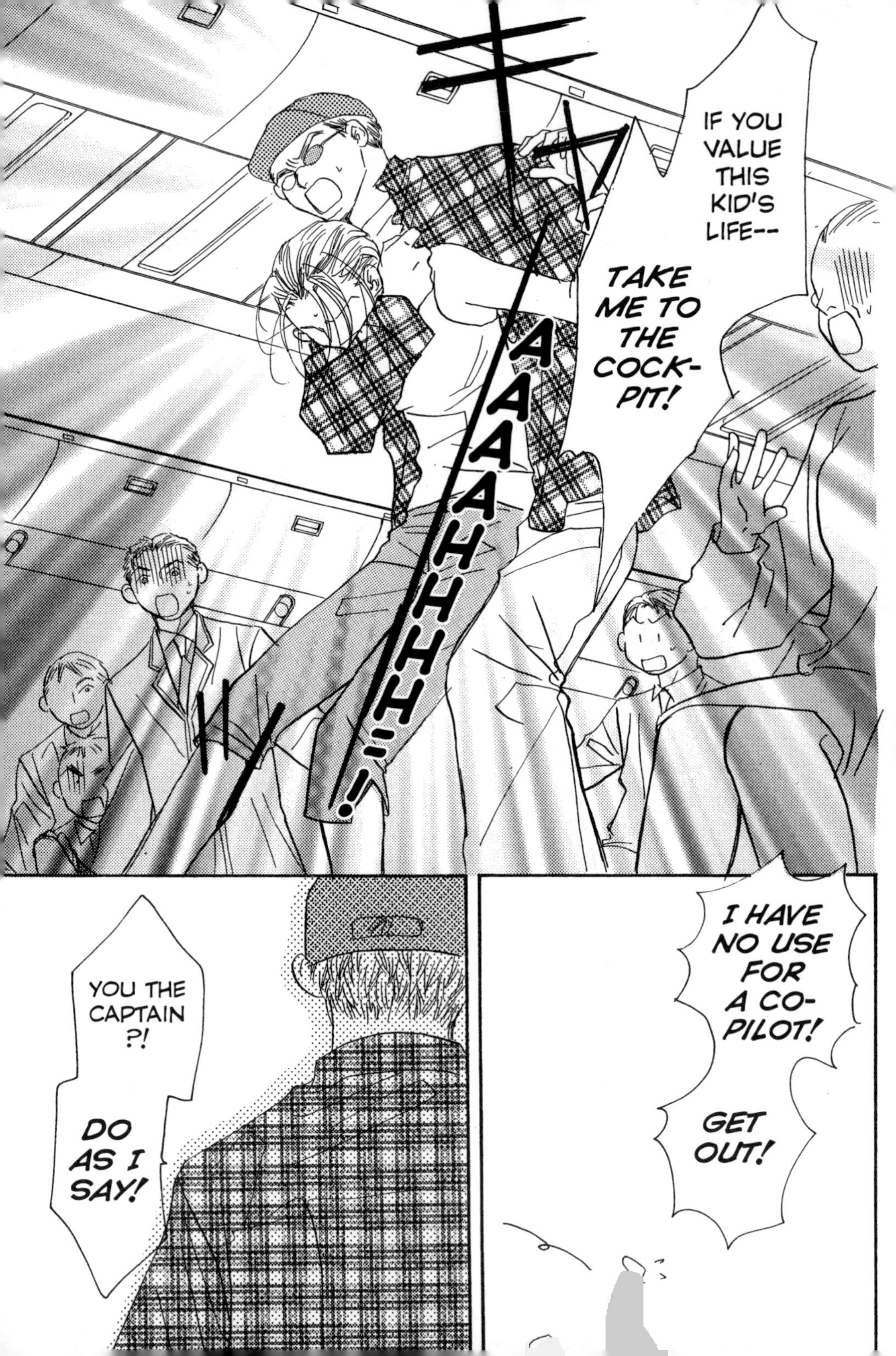
IF YOU VALUE THIS KID'S LIFE--
TAKE ME TO THE COCK-PIT!
AAAAHHHH--!
I HAVE NO USE FOR A CO-PILOT!
GET OUT!
YOU THE CAPTAIN ?!
DO AS I SAY!

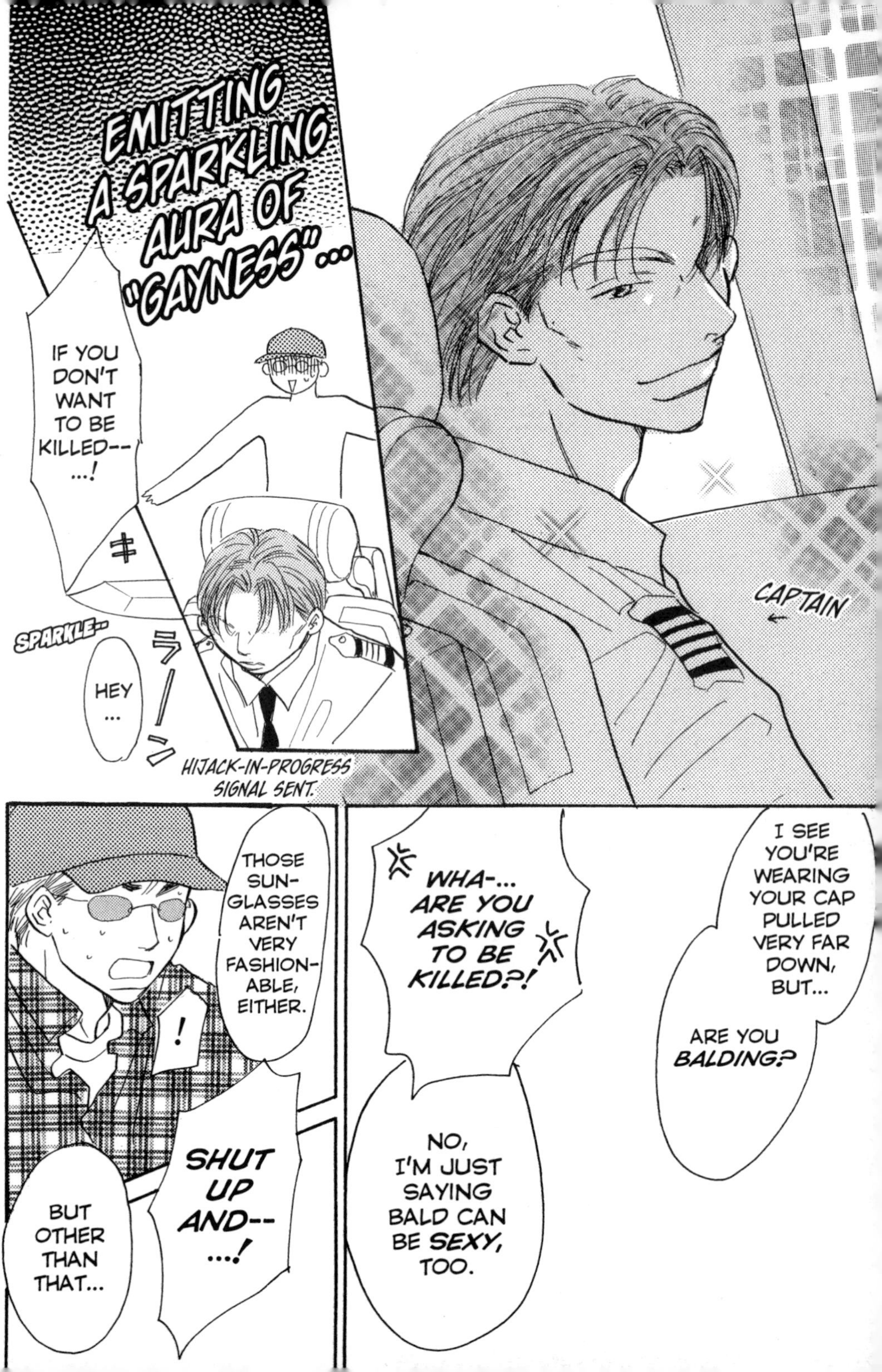
CAPTAIN
EMITTING A SPARKLING AURA OF "GAYNESS"...
IF YOU DON'T WANT TO BE KILLED-- ...!
SPARKLE--
HEY...
HIJACK-IN-PROGRESS SIGNAL SENT.
I SEE YOU'RE WEARING YOUR CAP PULLED VERY FAR DOWN, BUT...
ARE YOU BALDING?
WHA-... ARE YOU ASKING TO BE KILLED?!
NO, I'M JUST SAYING BALD CAN BE SEXY, TOO.
THOSE SUN-GLASSES AREN'T VERY FASHION-ABLE, EITHER.
!
SHUT UP AND-- ...!
BUT OTHER THAN THAT...

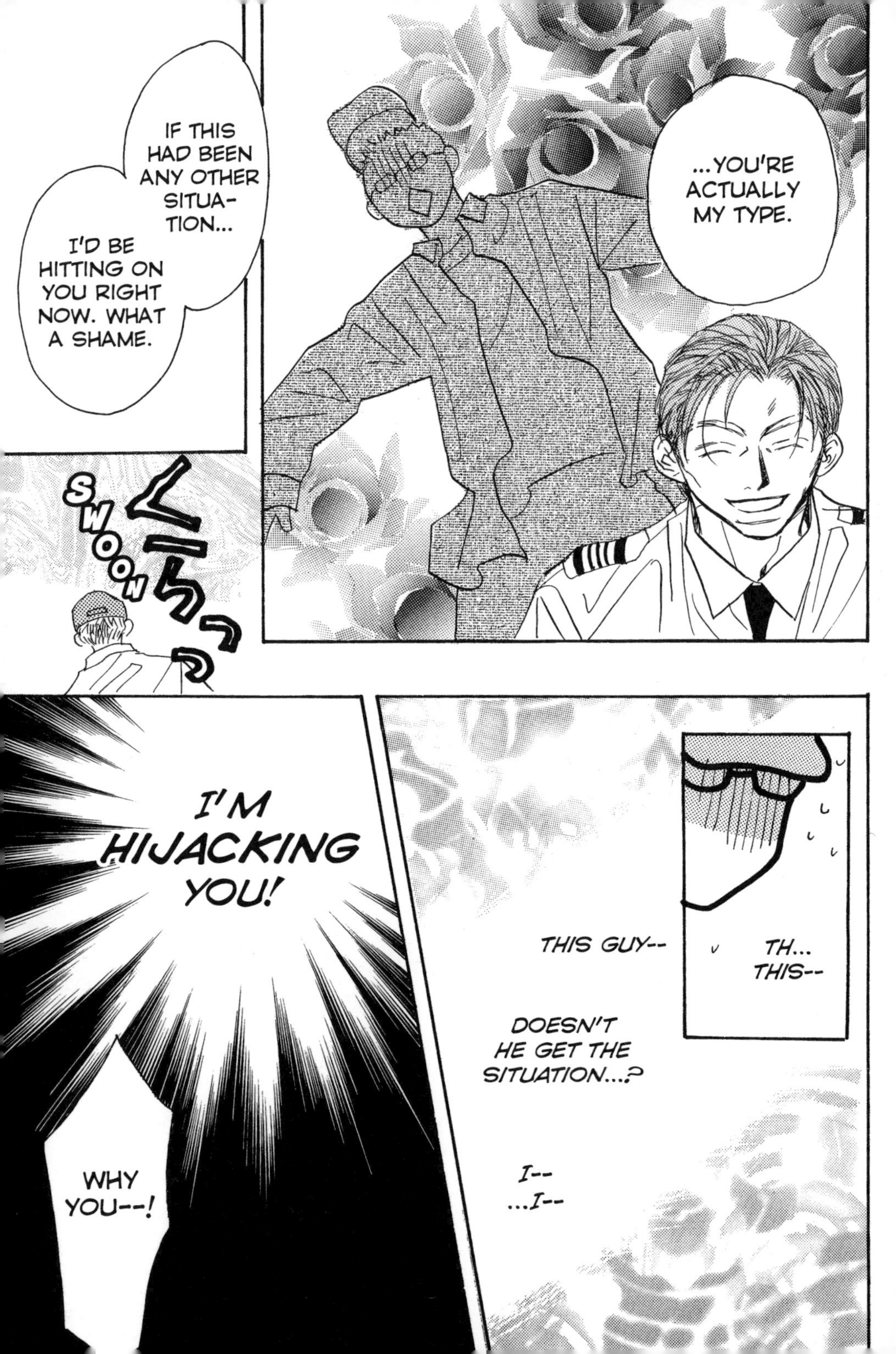
...YOU'RE ACTUALLY MY TYPE.
IF THIS HAD BEEN ANY OTHER SITUATION...
I'D BE HITTING ON YOU RIGHT NOW. WHAT A SHAME.
SWOON
TH... THIS--
THIS GUY--
DOESN'T HE GET THE SITUATION...?
I-- ...I--
I'M HIJACKING YOU!
WHY YOU--!

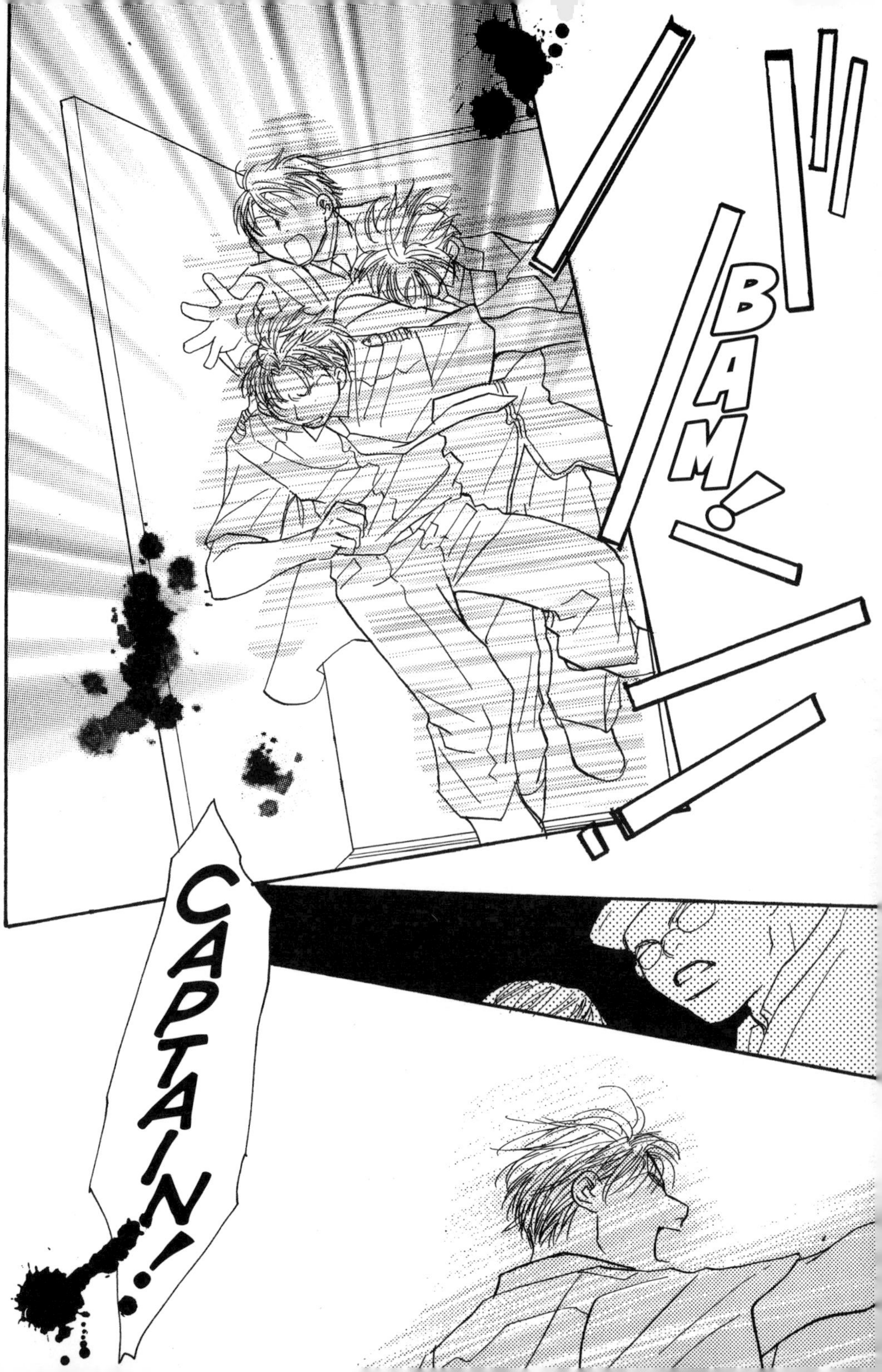
BAM!
CAPTAIN!!

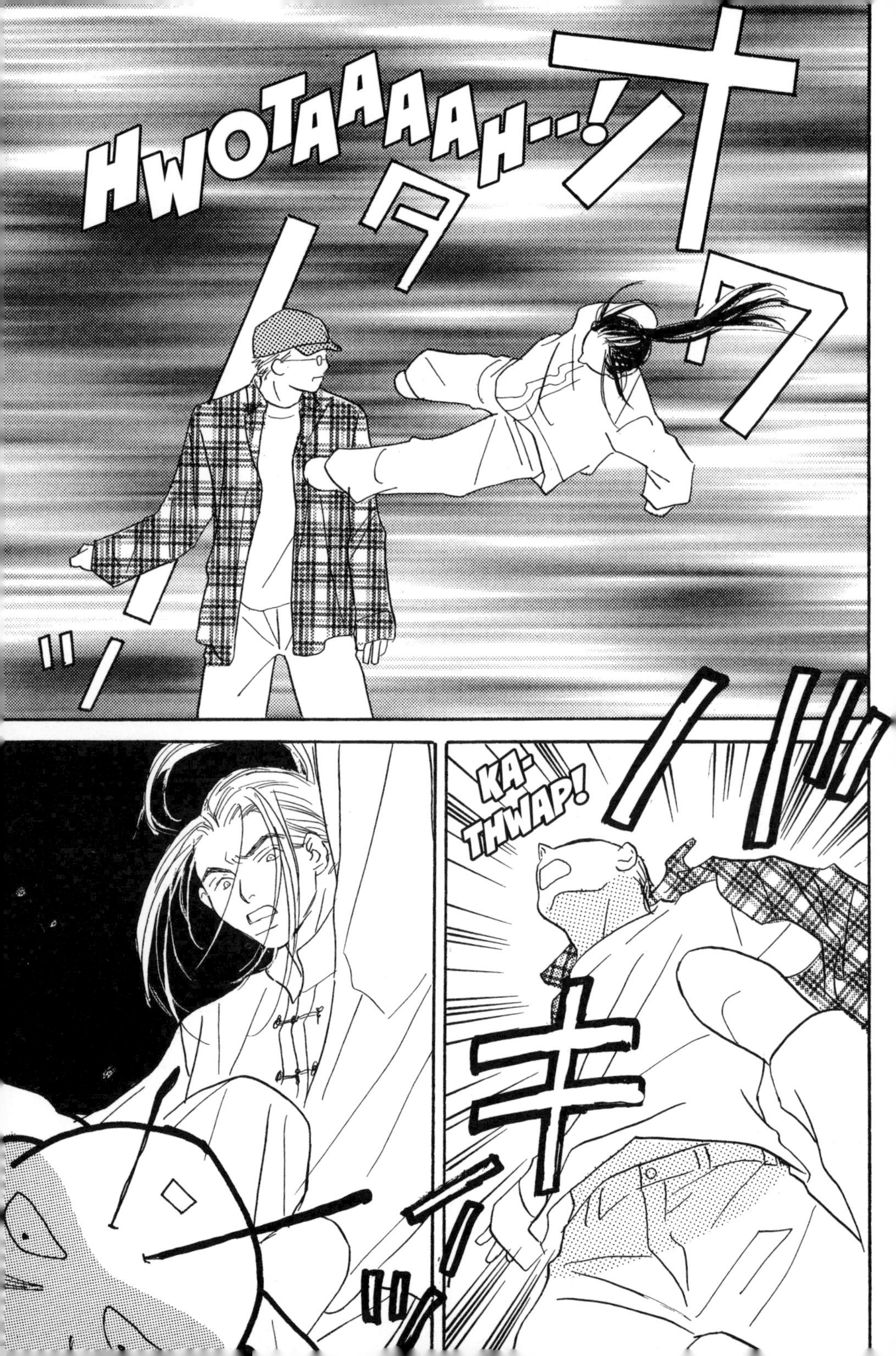
HWOTAAAAAH--!
KA-THWAP!

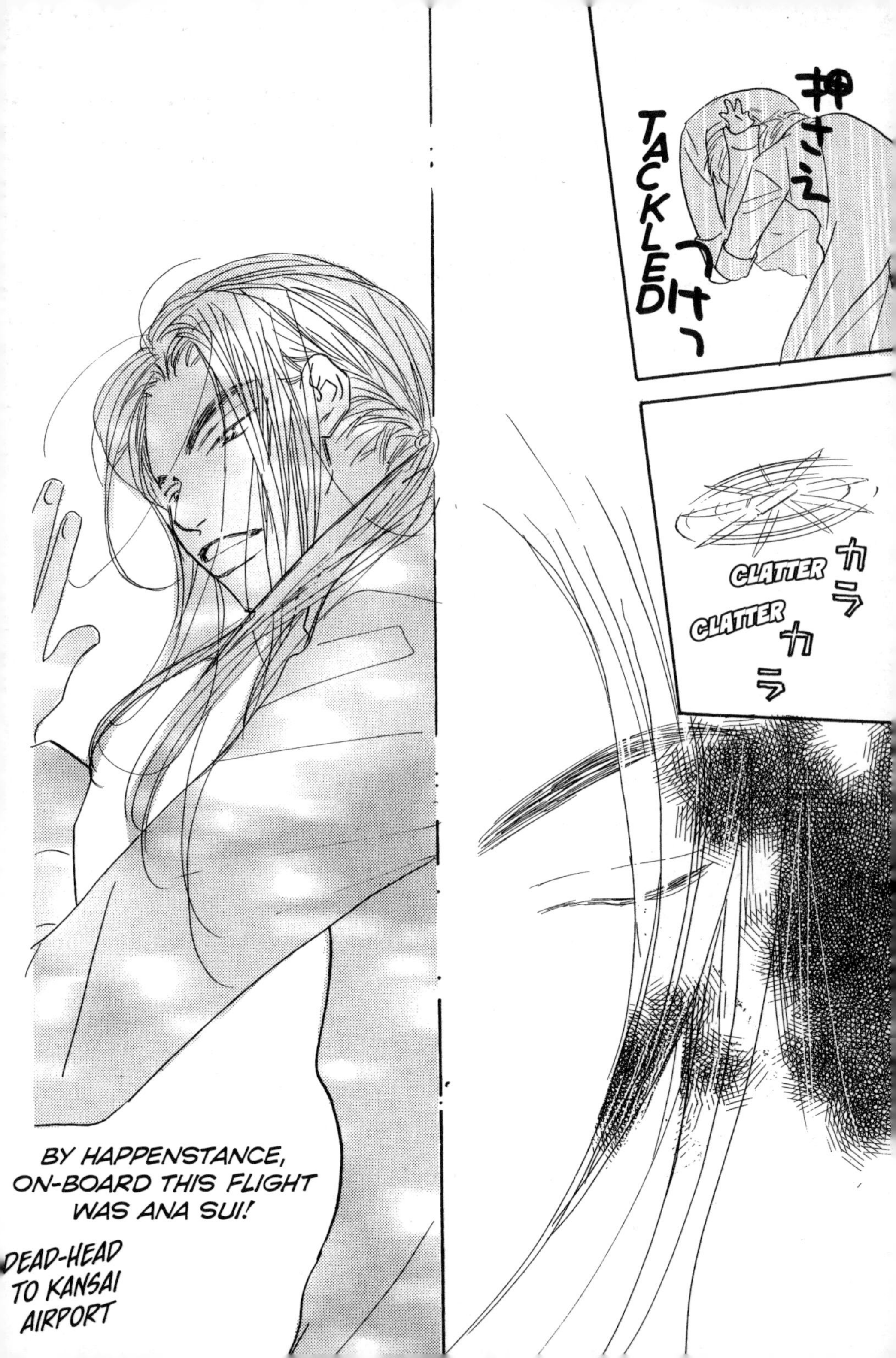
押さえつけっ
TACKLED
CLATTER カラ
CLATTER カラ
BY HAPPENSTANCE, ON-BOARD THIS FLIGHT WAS ANA SUI!
DEAD-HEAD TO KANSAI AIRPORT

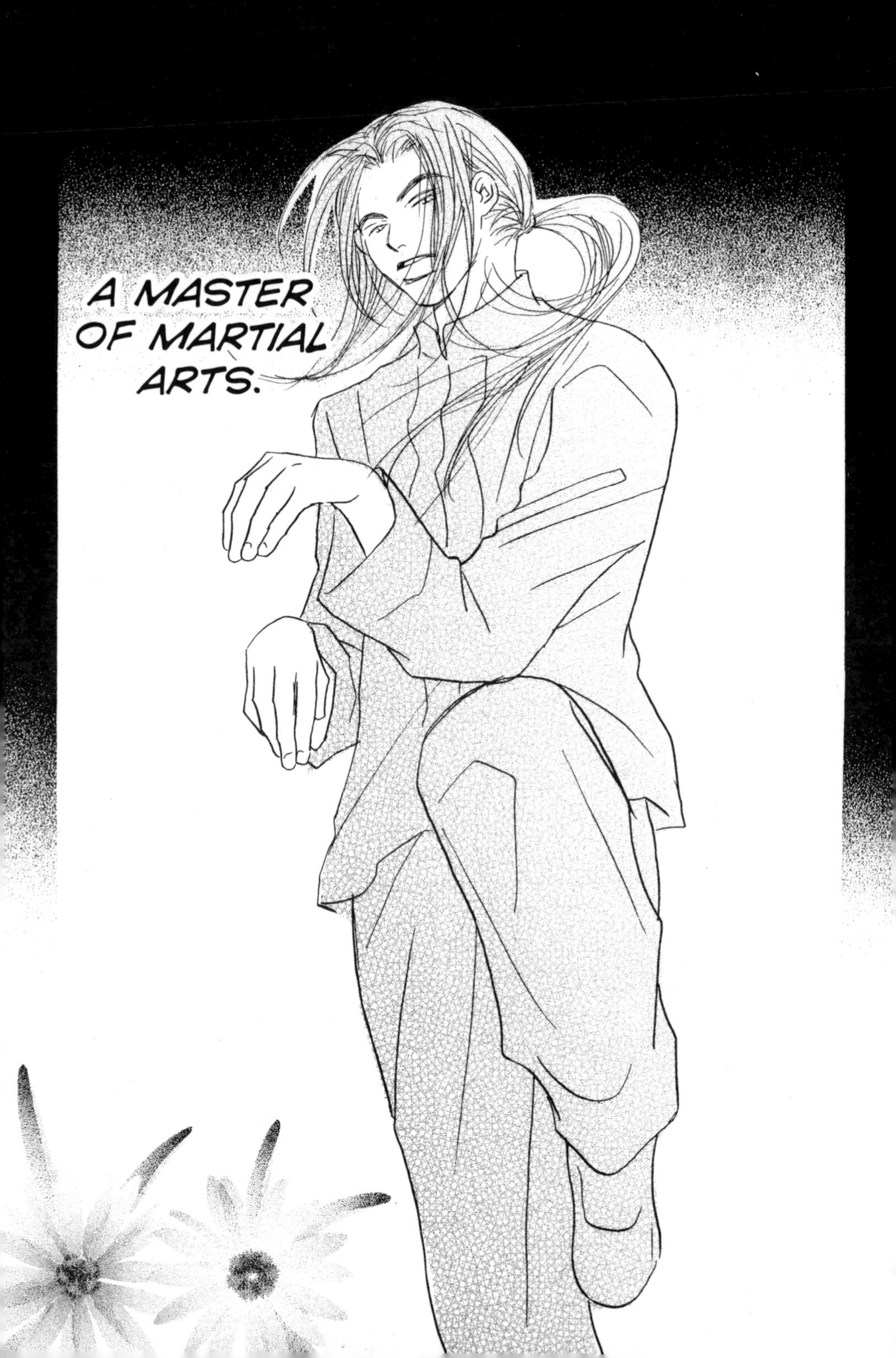
A MASTER OF MARTIAL ARTS.

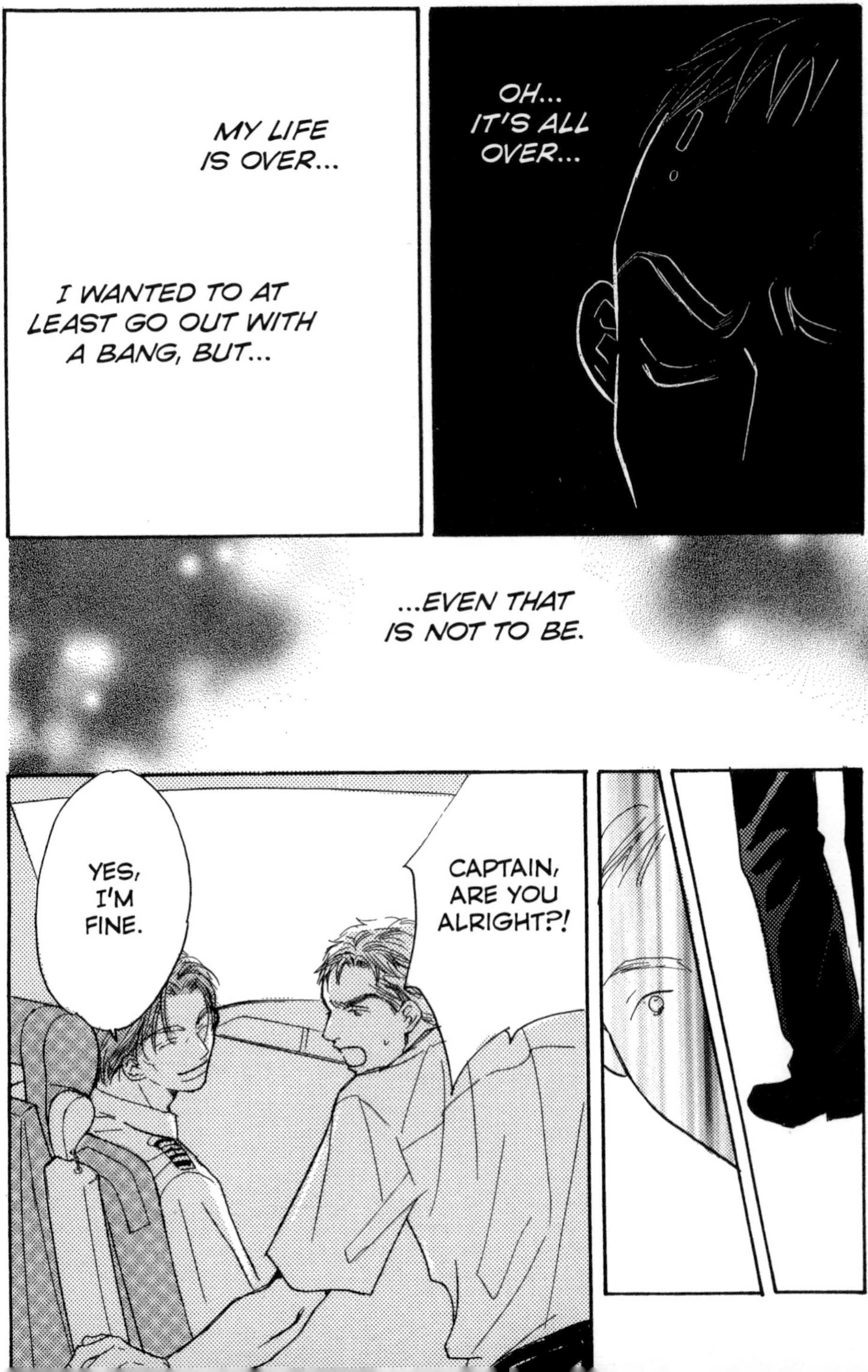
OH... IT'S ALL OVER...
MY LIFE IS OVER...
I WANTED TO AT LEAST GO OUT WITH A BANG, BUT...
...EVEN THAT IS NOT TO BE.
CAPTAIN, ARE YOU ALRIGHT?!
YES, I'M FINE.

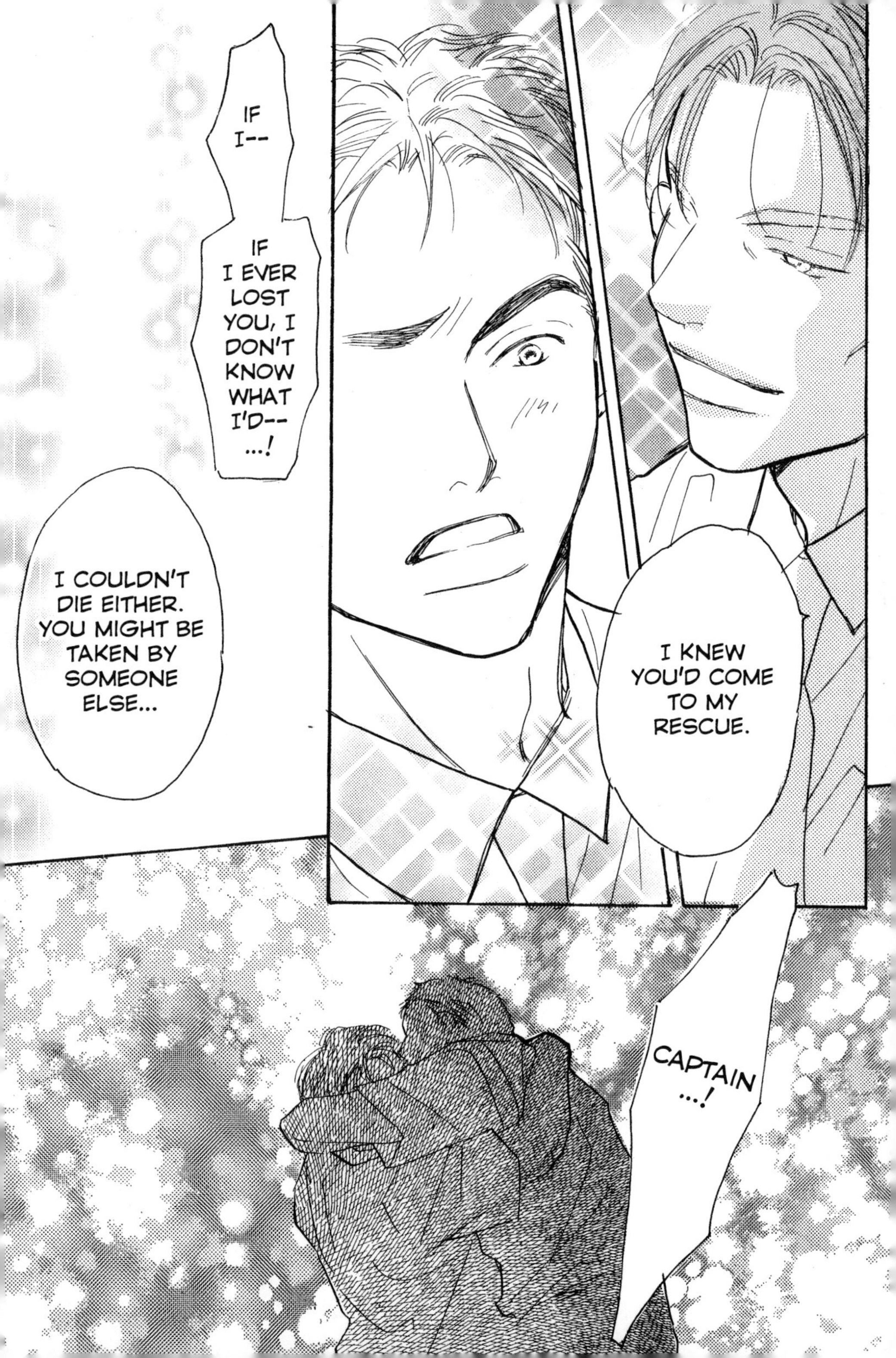
I KNEW YOU'D COME TO MY RESCUE.
IF I--
IF I EVER LOST YOU, I DON'T KNOW WHAT I'D-- ...!
I COULDN'T DIE EITHER. YOU MIGHT BE TAKEN BY SOMEONE ELSE...
CAPTAIN ...!

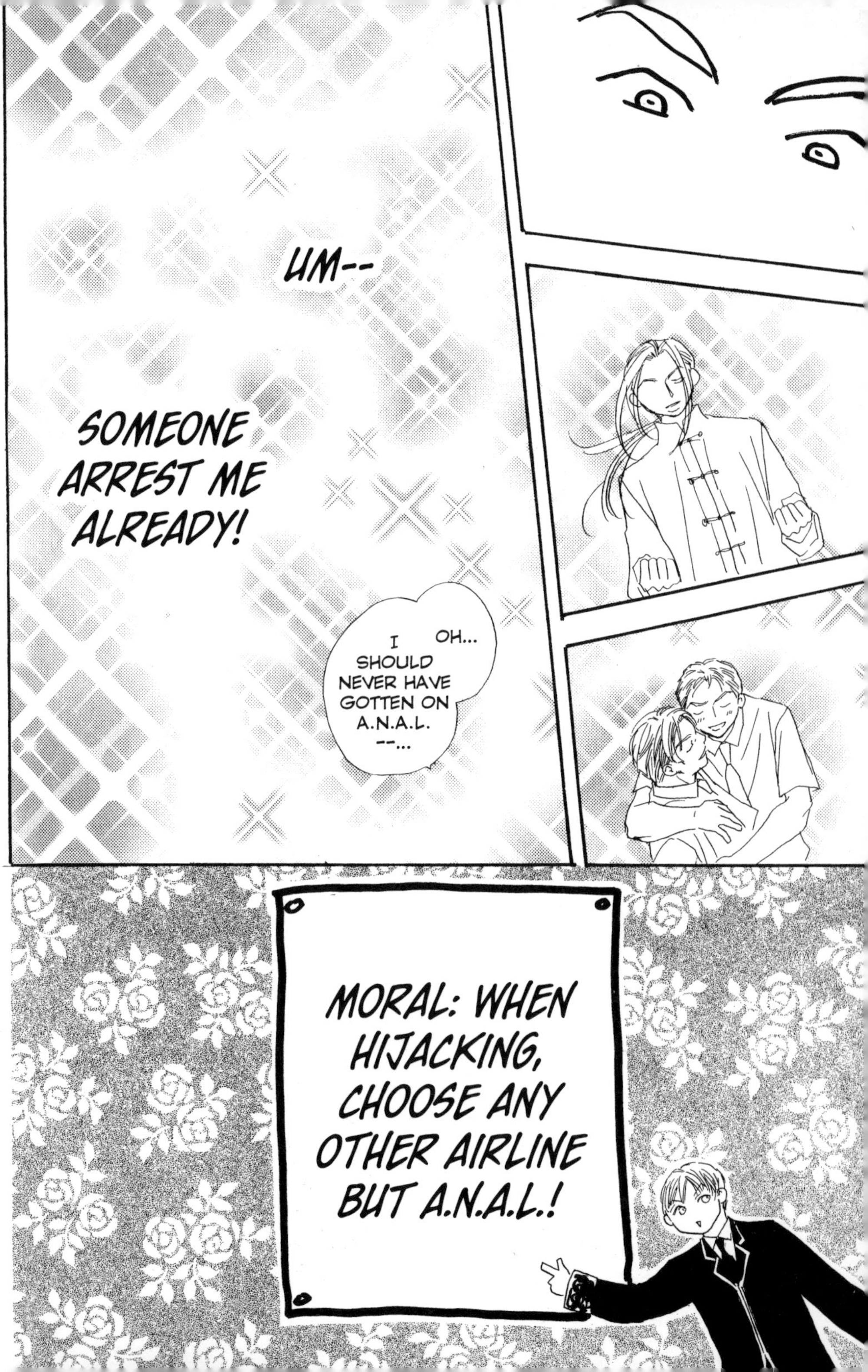
UM--
SOMEONE ARREST ME ALREADY!
OH... I SHOULD NEVER HAVE GOTTEN ON A.N.A.L. --...
MORAL: WHEN HIJACKING, CHOOSE ANY OTHER AIRLINE BUT A.N.A.L.!

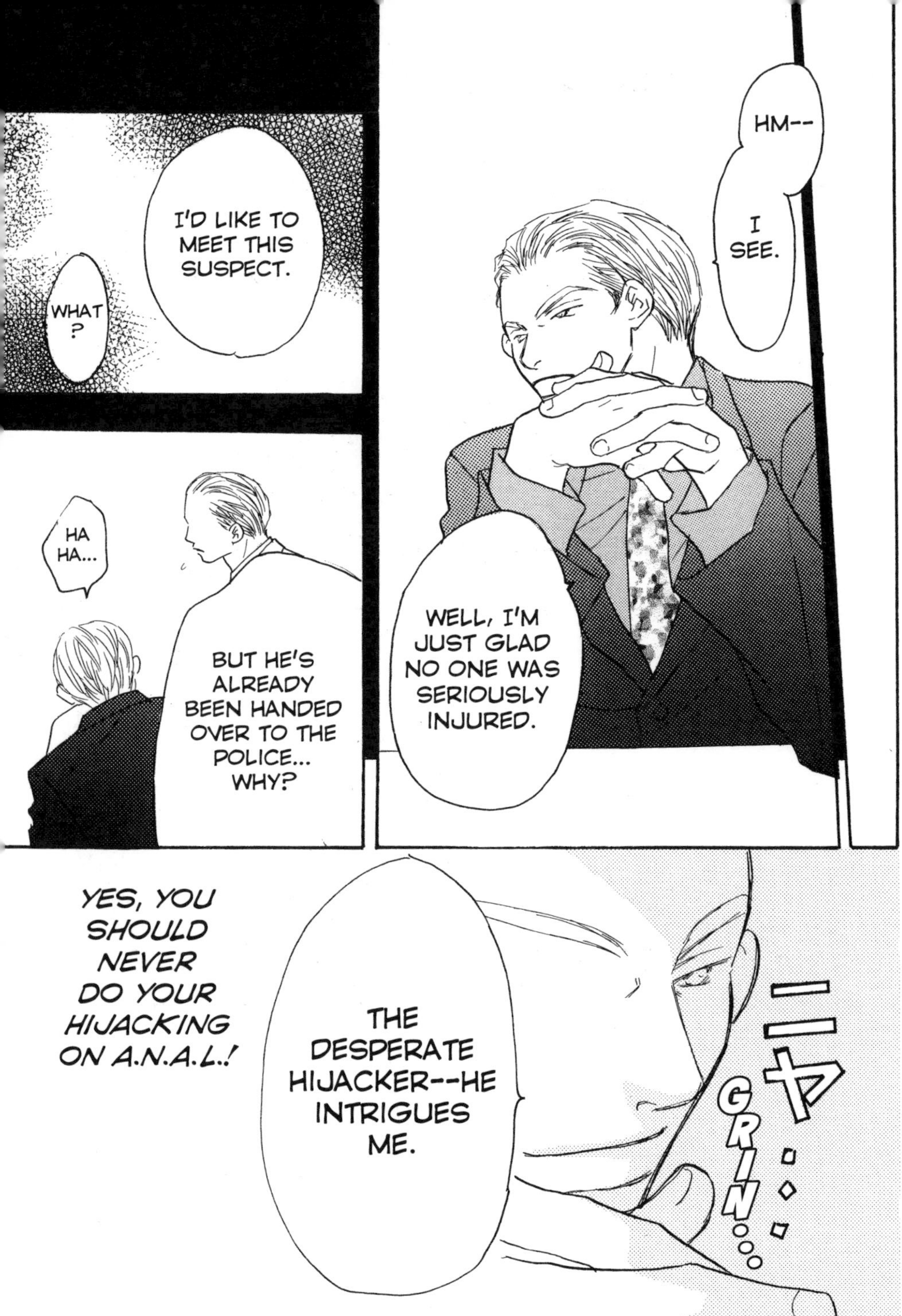
HM--
I SEE.
WELL, I'M JUST GLAD NO ONE WAS SERIOUSLY INJURED.
I'D LIKE TO MEET THIS SUSPECT.
WHAT?
HA HA...
BUT HE'S ALREADY BEEN HANDED OVER TO THE POLICE... WHY?
ニヤ
GRIN...
THE DESPERATE HIJACKER--HE INTRIGUES ME.
YES, YOU SHOULD NEVER DO YOUR HIJACKING ON A.N.A.L.!

**AN A.N.A.L. MYSTERY END**

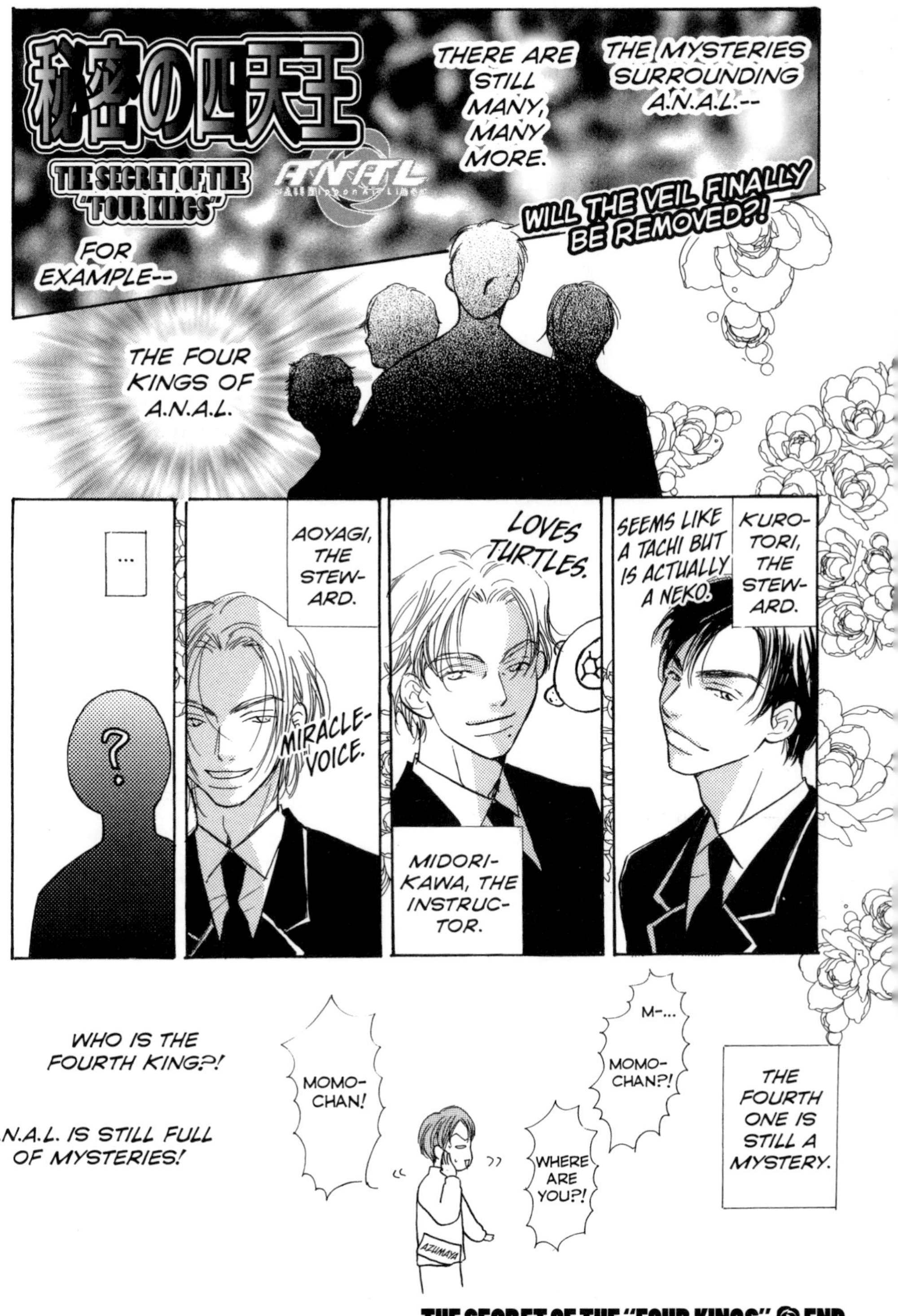
秘密の四天王
THE SECRET OF THE "FOUR KINGS"
THE MYSTERIES SURROUNDING A.N.A.L.--
THERE ARE STILL MANY, MANY MORE.
WILL THE VEIL FINALLY BE REMOVED?!
FOR EXAMPLE--
THE FOUR KINGS OF A.N.A.L.
KURO-TORI, THE STEW-ARD.
SEEMS LIKE A TACHI BUT IS ACTUALLY A NEKO.
LOVES TURTLES.
MIDORI-KAWA, THE INSTRUC-TOR.
AOYAGI, THE STEW-ARD.
MIRACLE-VOICE.
...
?
THE FOURTH ONE IS STILL A MYSTERY.
M-...
MOMO-CHAN?!
WHERE ARE YOU?!
MOMO-CHAN!
AZUMAYA
WHO IS THE FOURTH KING?!
A.N.A.L. IS STILL FULL OF MYSTERIES!

**THE SECRET OF THE "FOUR KINGS" END**

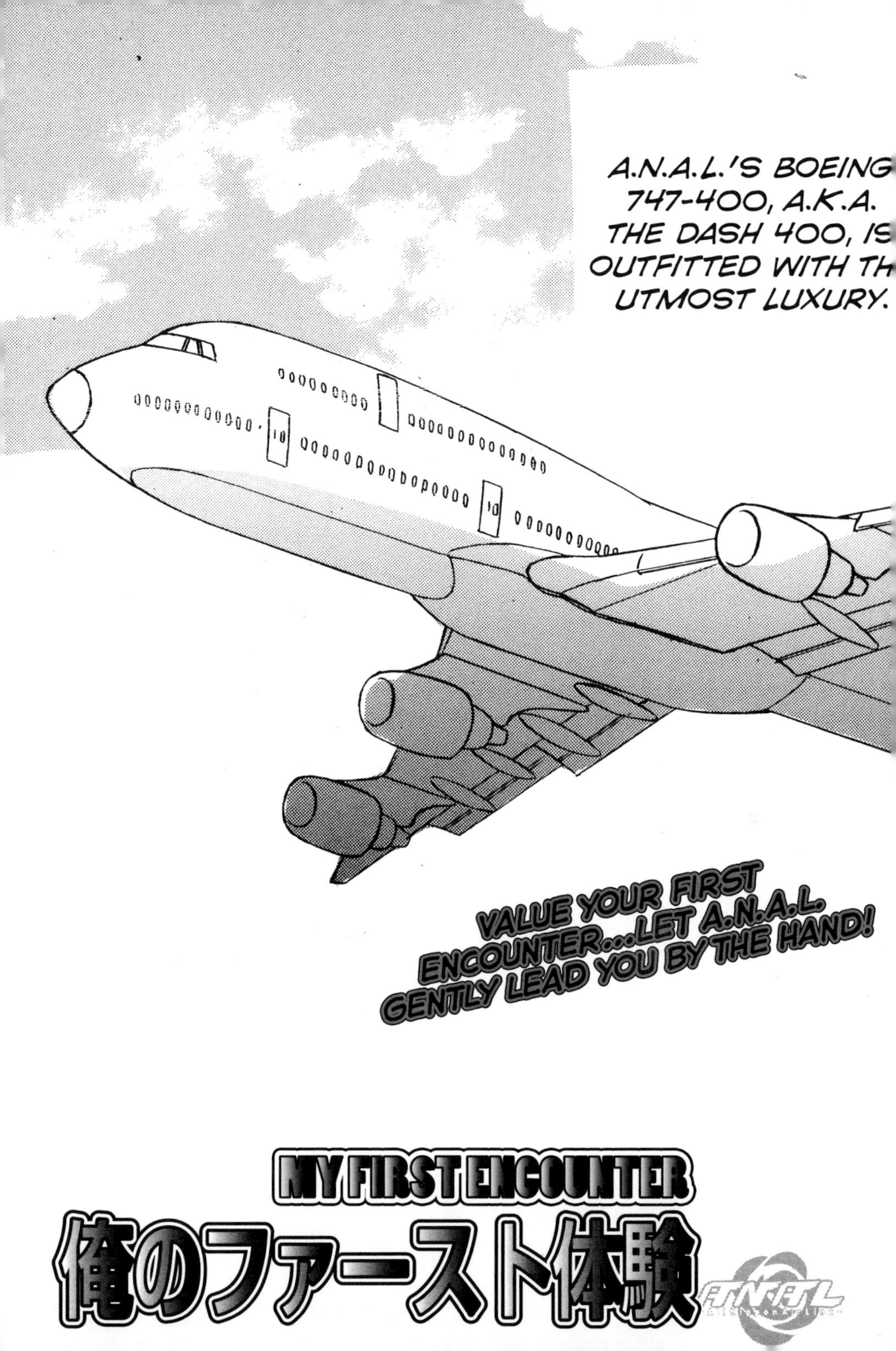
A.N.A.L.'S BOEING 747-400, A.K.A. THE DASH 400, IS OUTFITTED WITH TH UTMOST LUXURY.
VALUE YOUR FIRST ENCOUNTER...LET A.N.A.L. GENTLY LEAD YOU BY THE HAND!

# MY FIRST ENCOUNTER

# 俺のファースト体験

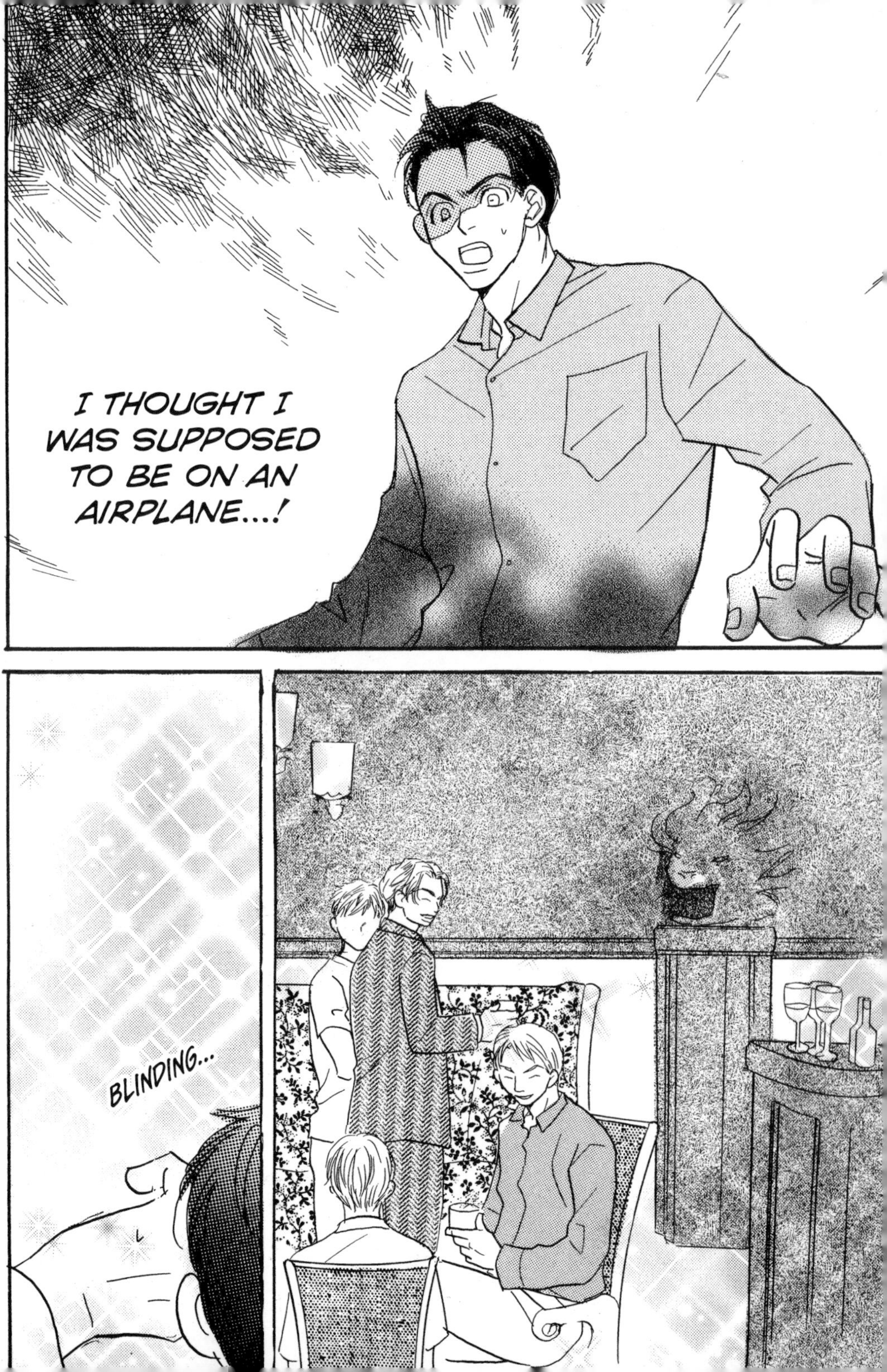
I THOUGHT I WAS SUPPOSED TO BE ON AN AIRPLANE...!
BLINDING...

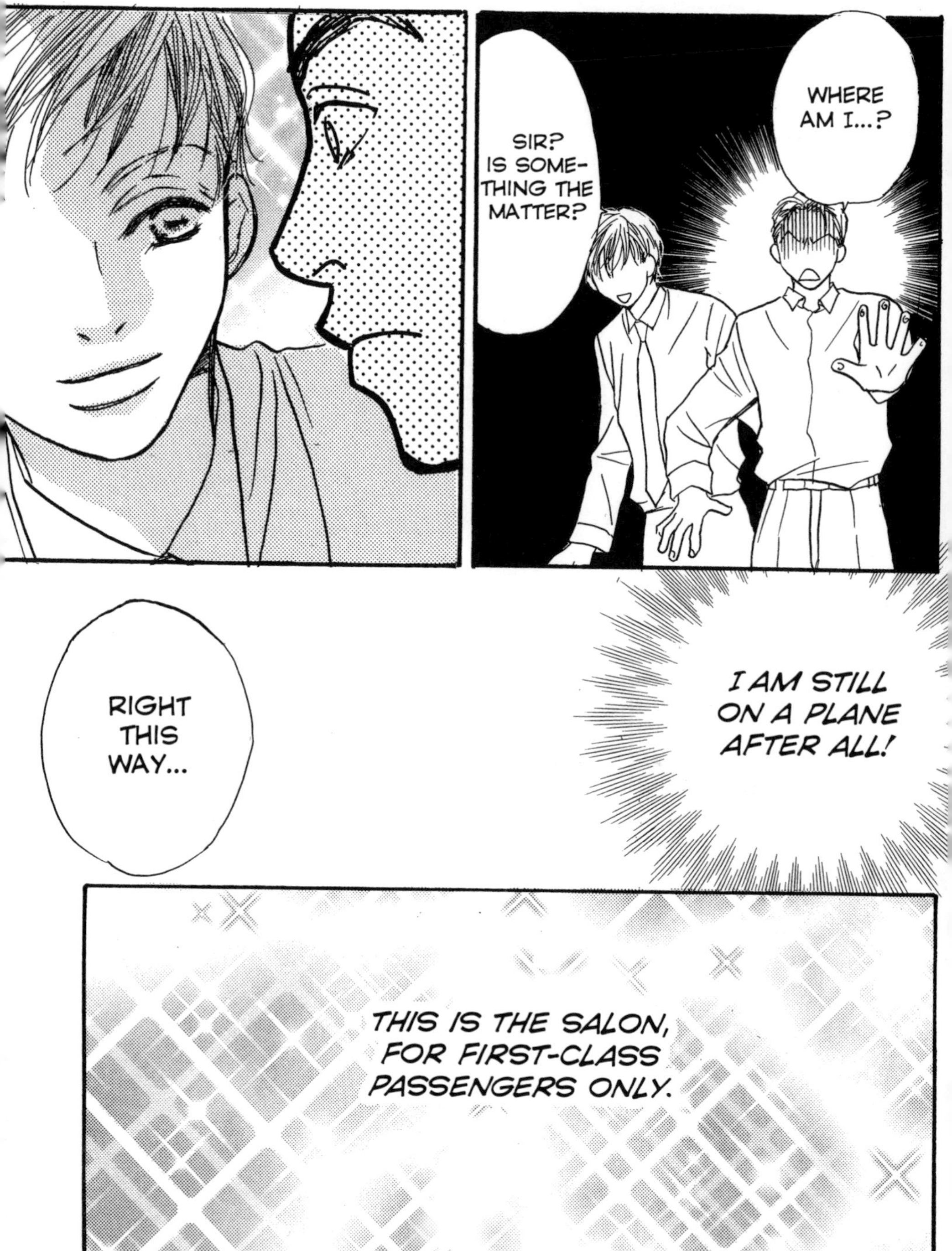
WHERE AM I...?
SIR? IS SOME-THING THE MATTER?
I AM STILL ON A PLANE AFTER ALL!
RIGHT THIS WAY...
THIS IS THE SALON, FOR FIRST-CLASS PASSENGERS ONLY.

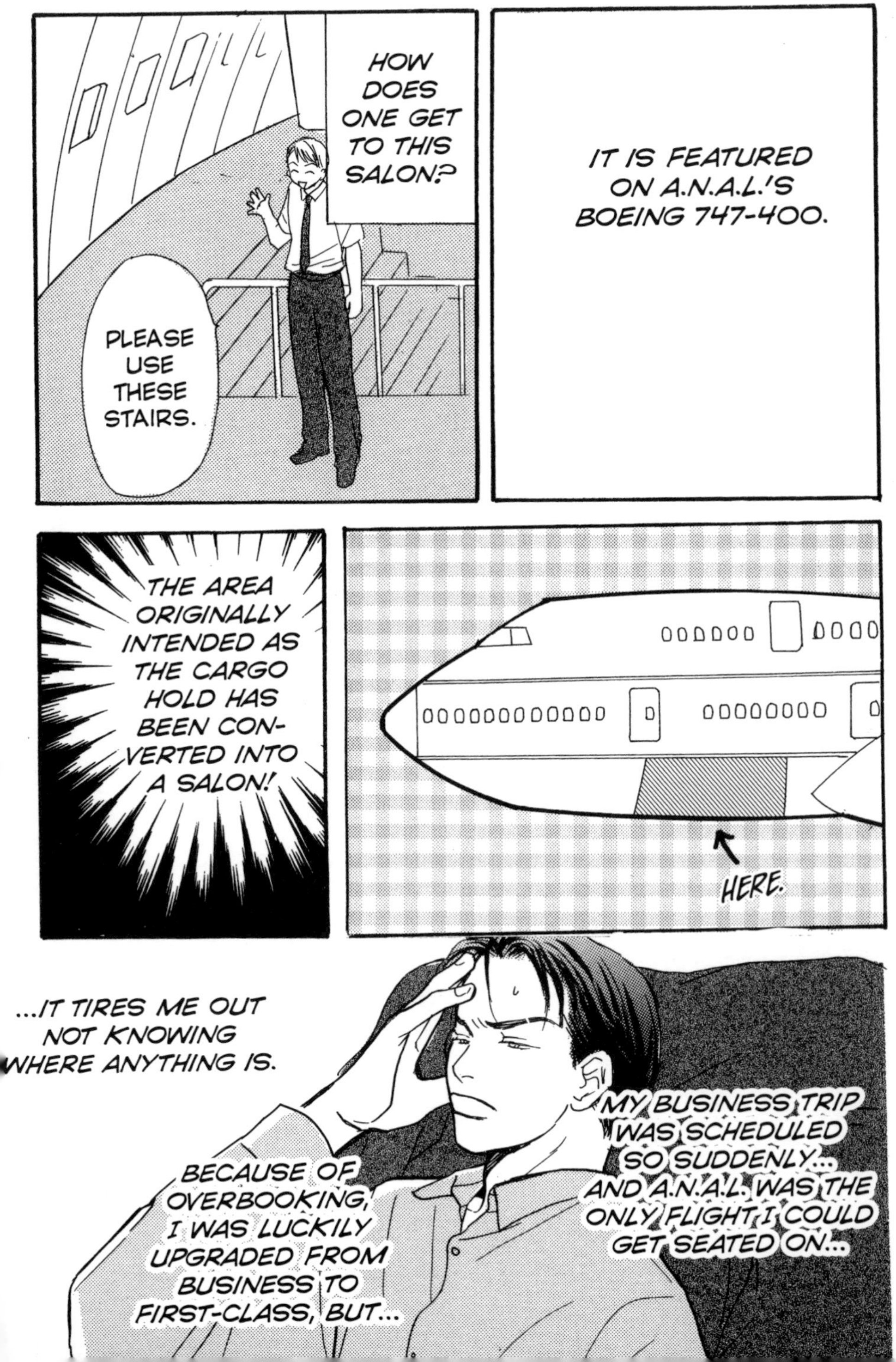
IT IS FEATURED ON A.N.A.L.'S BOEING 747-400.
HOW DOES ONE GET TO THIS SALON?
PLEASE USE THESE STAIRS.
HERE.
THE AREA ORIGINALLY INTENDED AS THE CARGO HOLD HAS BEEN CON-VERTED INTO A SALON!
MY BUSINESS TRIP WAS SCHEDULED SO SUDDENLY... AND A.N.A.L. WAS THE ONLY FLIGHT I COULD GET SEATED ON...
BECAUSE OF OVERBOOKING, I WAS LUCKILY UPGRADED FROM BUSINESS TO FIRST-CLASS, BUT...
...IT TIRES ME OUT NOT KNOWING WHERE ANYTHING IS.

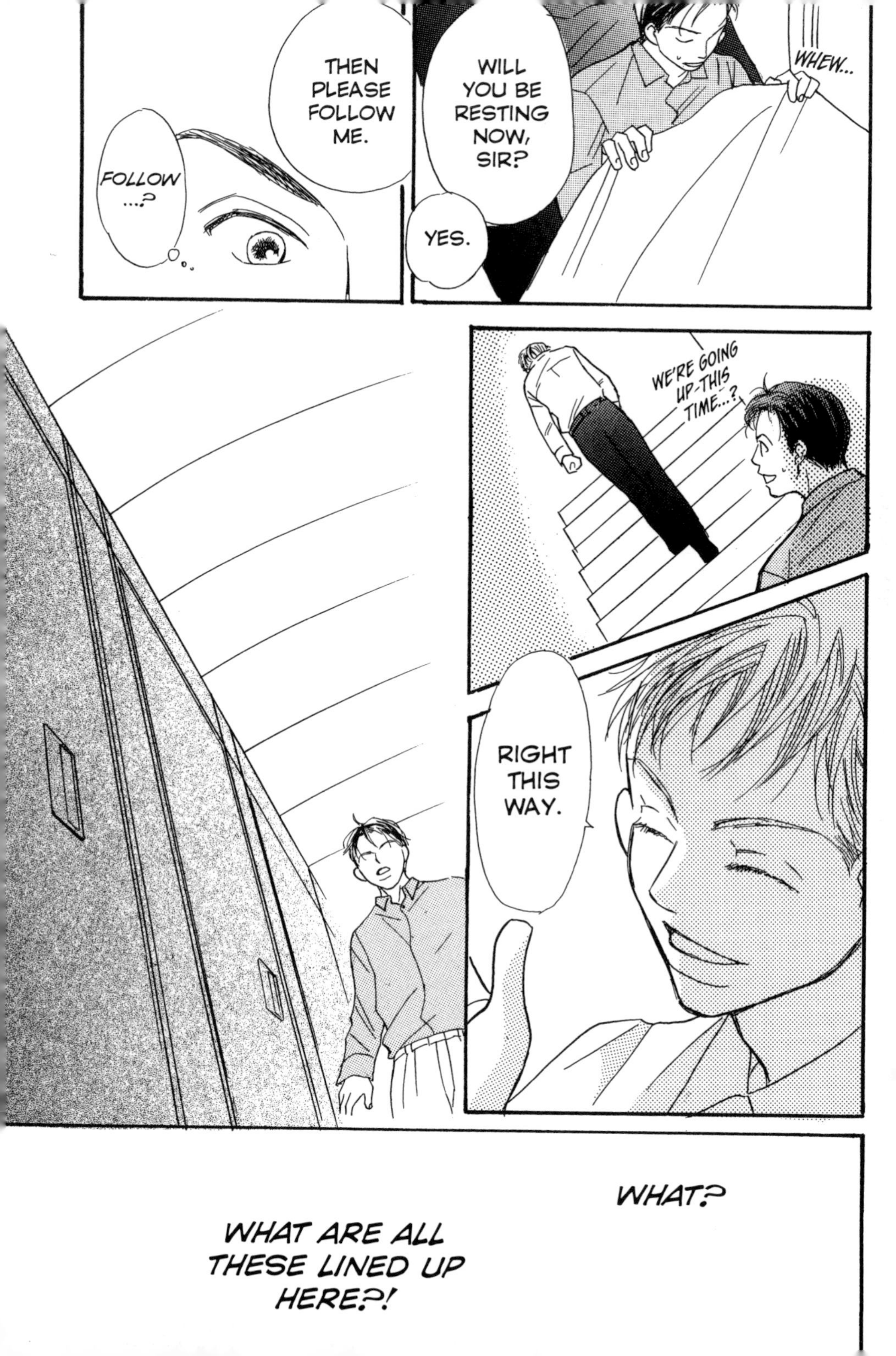
WHEW...
WILL YOU BE RESTING NOW, SIR?
YES.
THEN PLEASE FOLLOW ME.
FOLLOW ...?
WE'RE GOING UP THIS TIME...?
RIGHT THIS WAY.
WHAT?
WHAT ARE ALL THESE LINED UP HERE?!

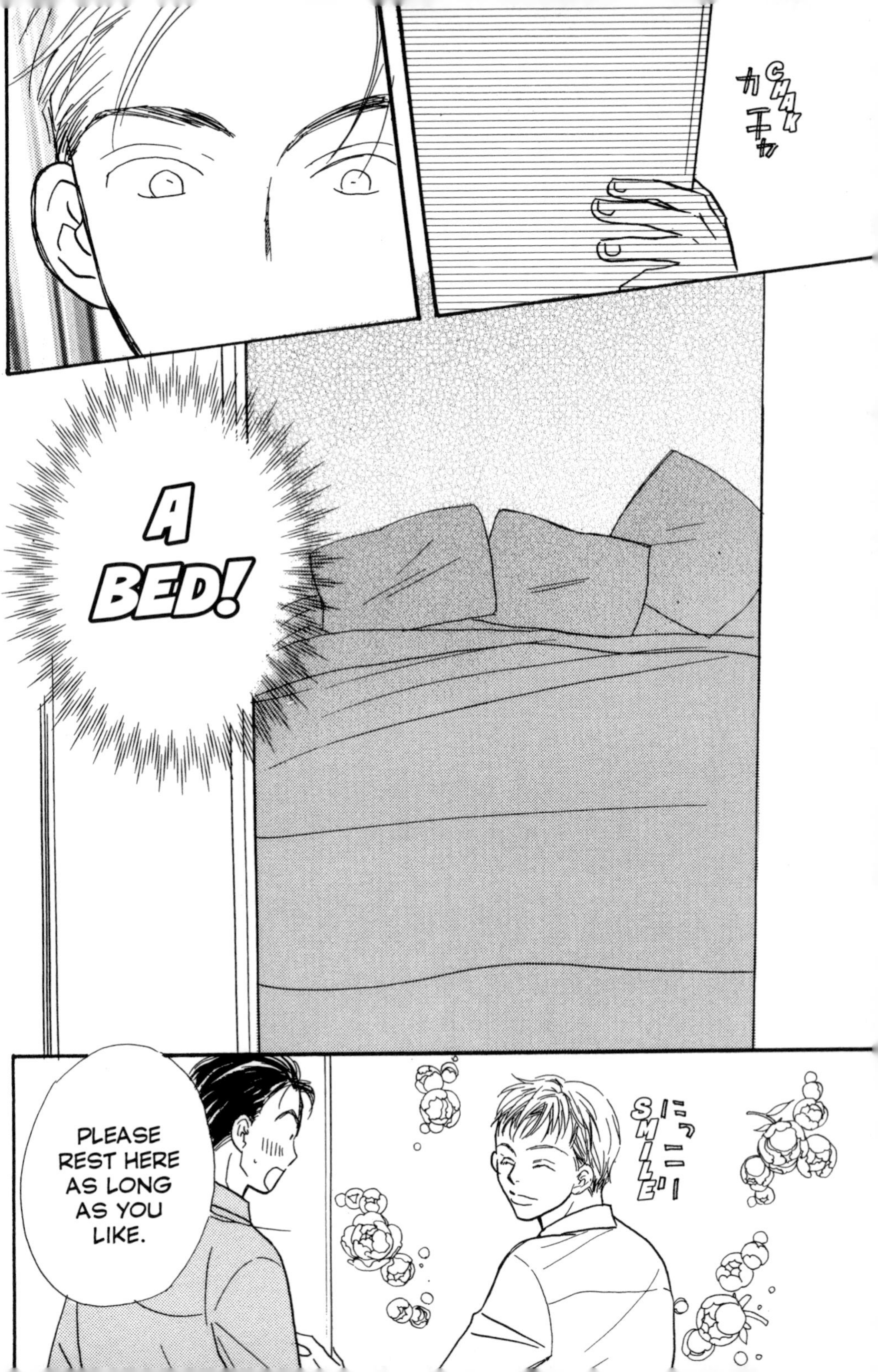
CHAK
A BED!
SMILE
PLEASE REST HERE AS LONG AS YOU LIKE.

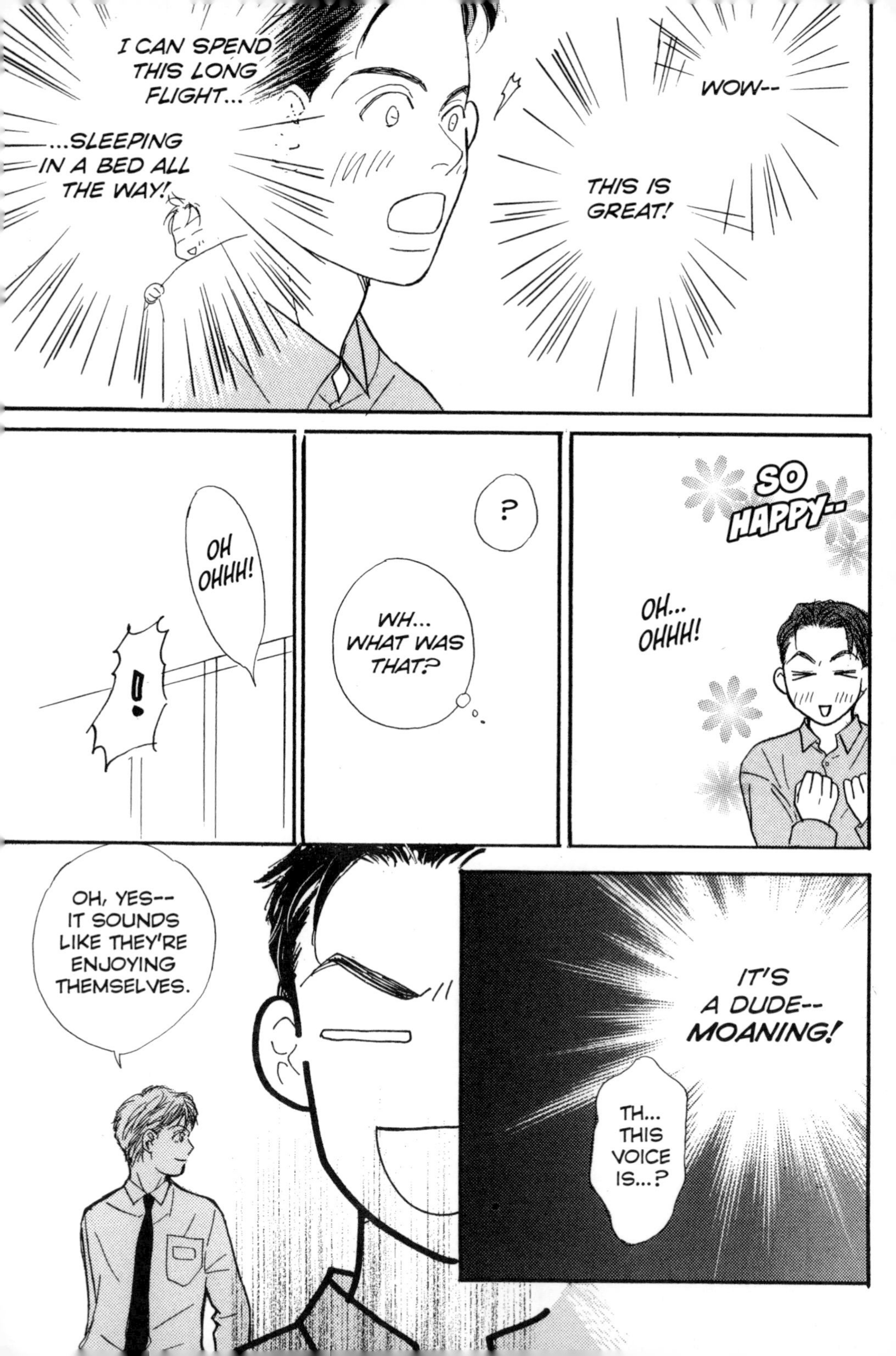
WOW--
THIS IS GREAT!
I CAN SPEND THIS LONG FLIGHT...
...SLEEPING IN A BED ALL THE WAY!
SO HAPPY--
OH... OHHH!
?
WH... WHAT WAS THAT?
OH OHHH!
!
IT'S A DUDE-- MOANING!
TH... THIS VOICE IS...?
OH, YES-- IT SOUNDS LIKE THEY'RE ENJOYING THEMSELVES.

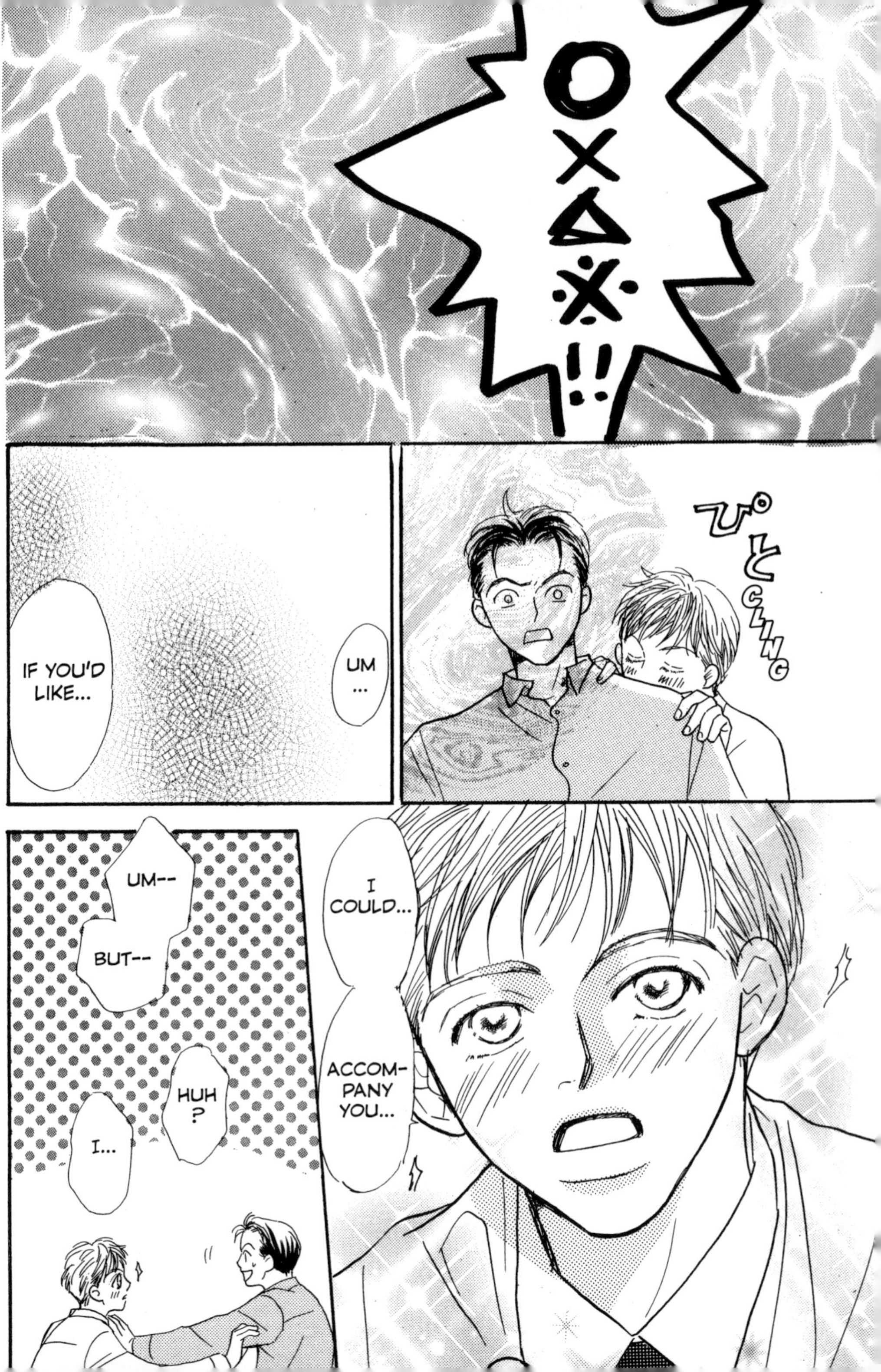
○×△※!!
ぴと
CLING
UM ...
IF YOU'D LIKE...
I COULD...
ACCOMPANY YOU...
UM--
BUT--
HUH?
I...

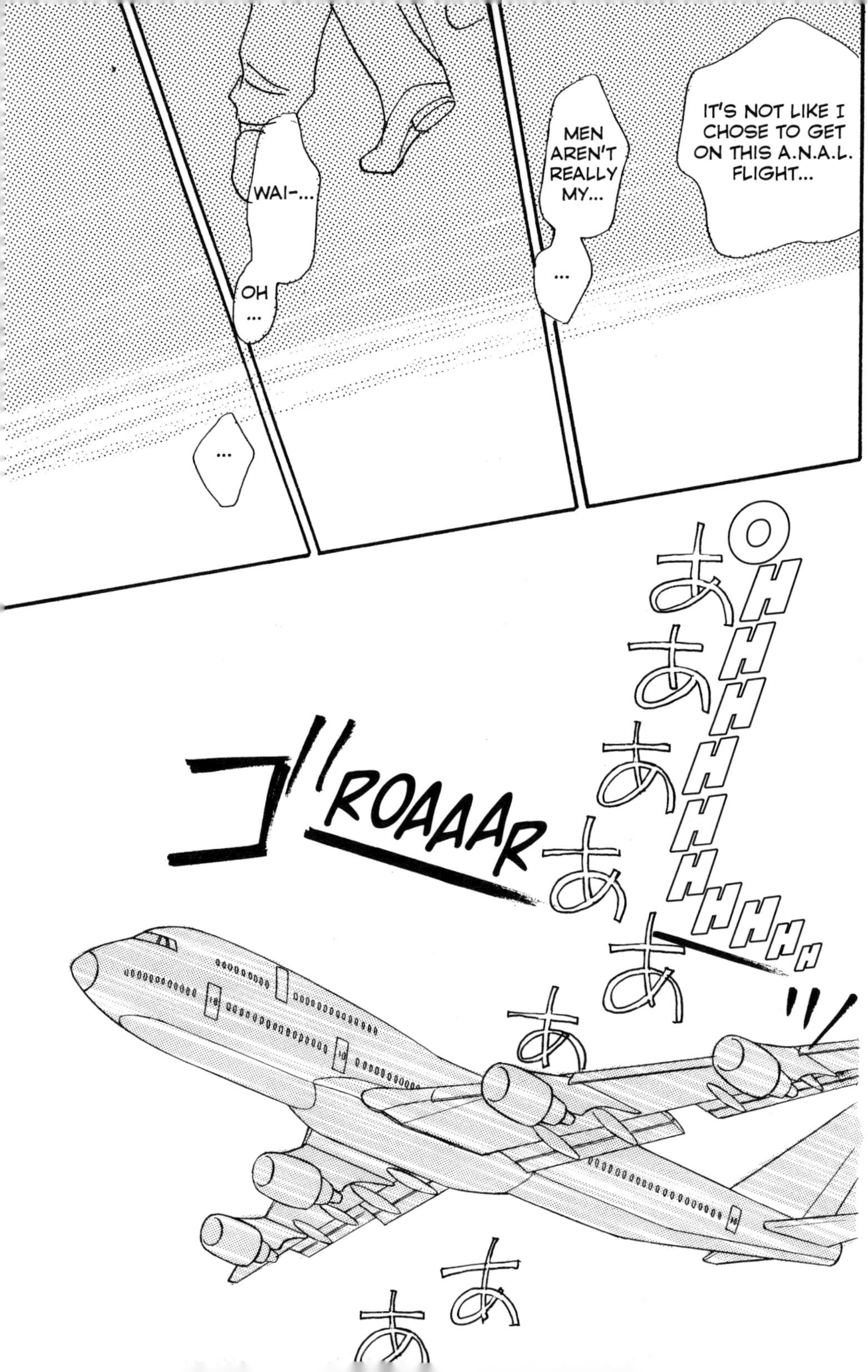
IT'S NOT LIKE I CHOSE TO GET ON THIS A.N.A.L. FLIGHT...
MEN AREN'T REALLY MY...
...
WAI-...
OH ...
...
OHHHHHHHHHH
ああああああああ
ゴ
ROAAAR

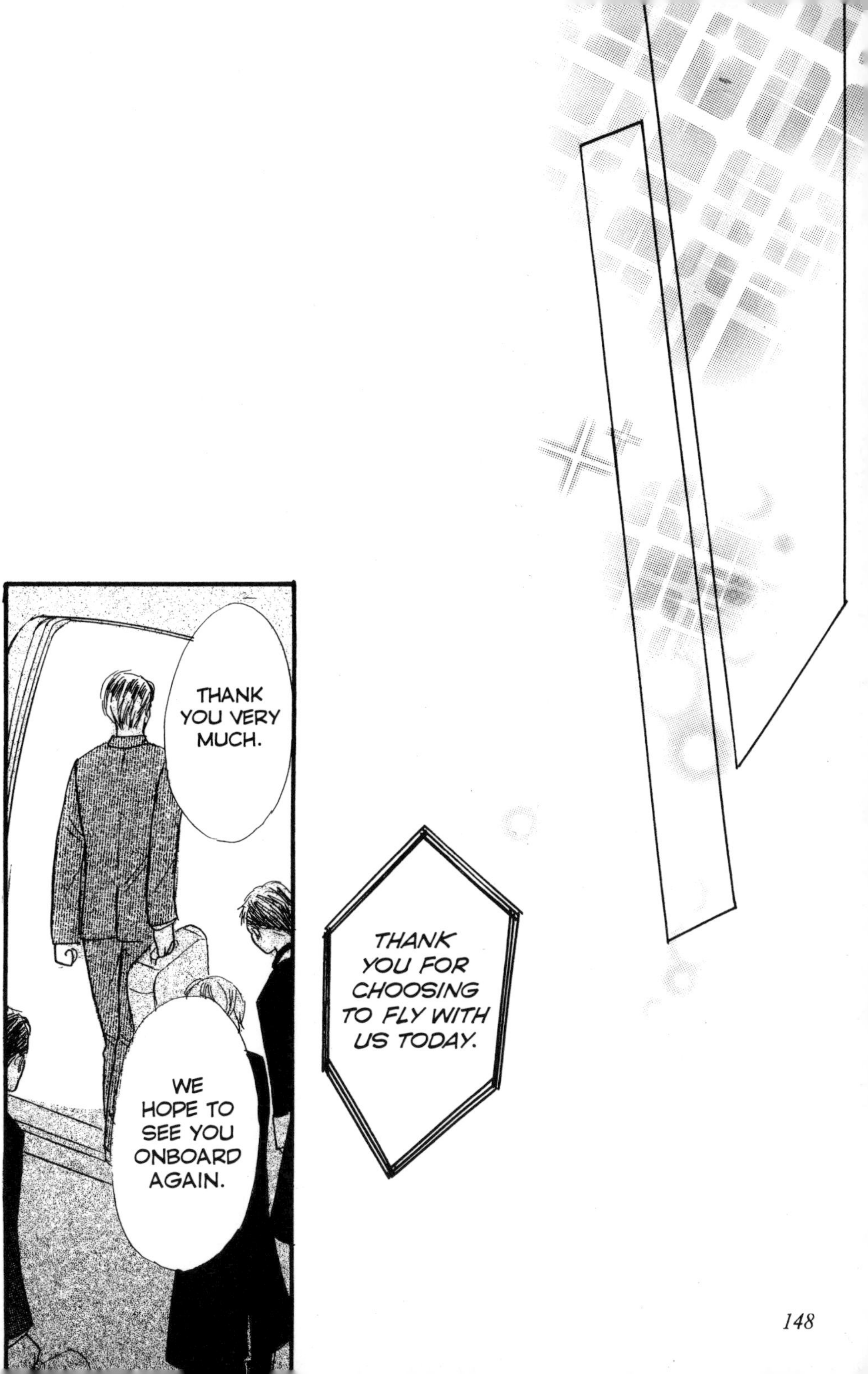
THANK YOU FOR CHOOSING TO FLY WITH US TODAY.
THANK YOU VERY MUCH.
WE HOPE TO SEE YOU ONBOARD AGAIN.

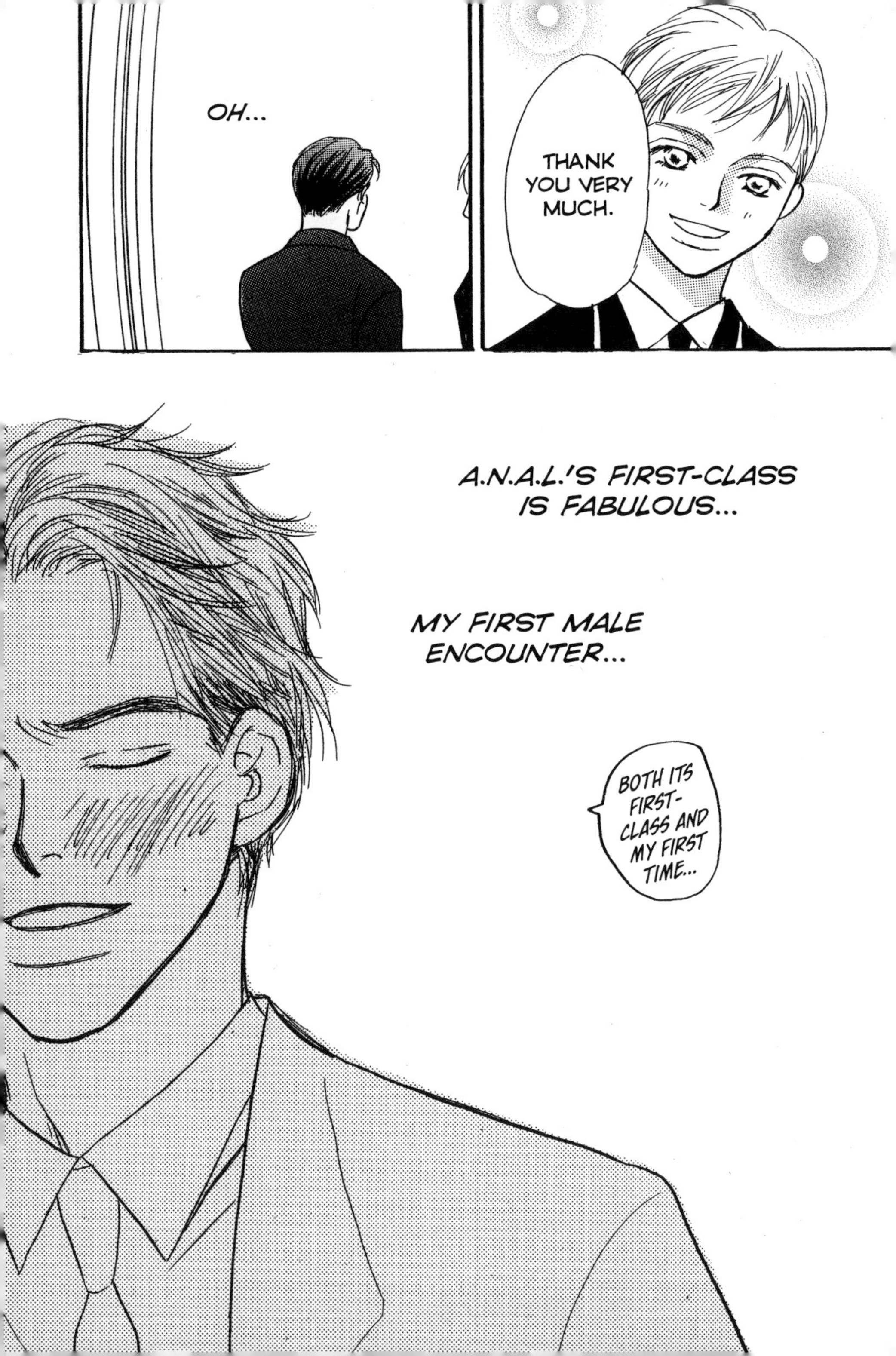
THANK YOU VERY MUCH.
OH...
A.N.A.L.'S FIRST-CLASS IS FABULOUS...
MY FIRST MALE ENCOUNTER...
BOTH ITS FIRST-CLASS AND MY FIRST TIME...

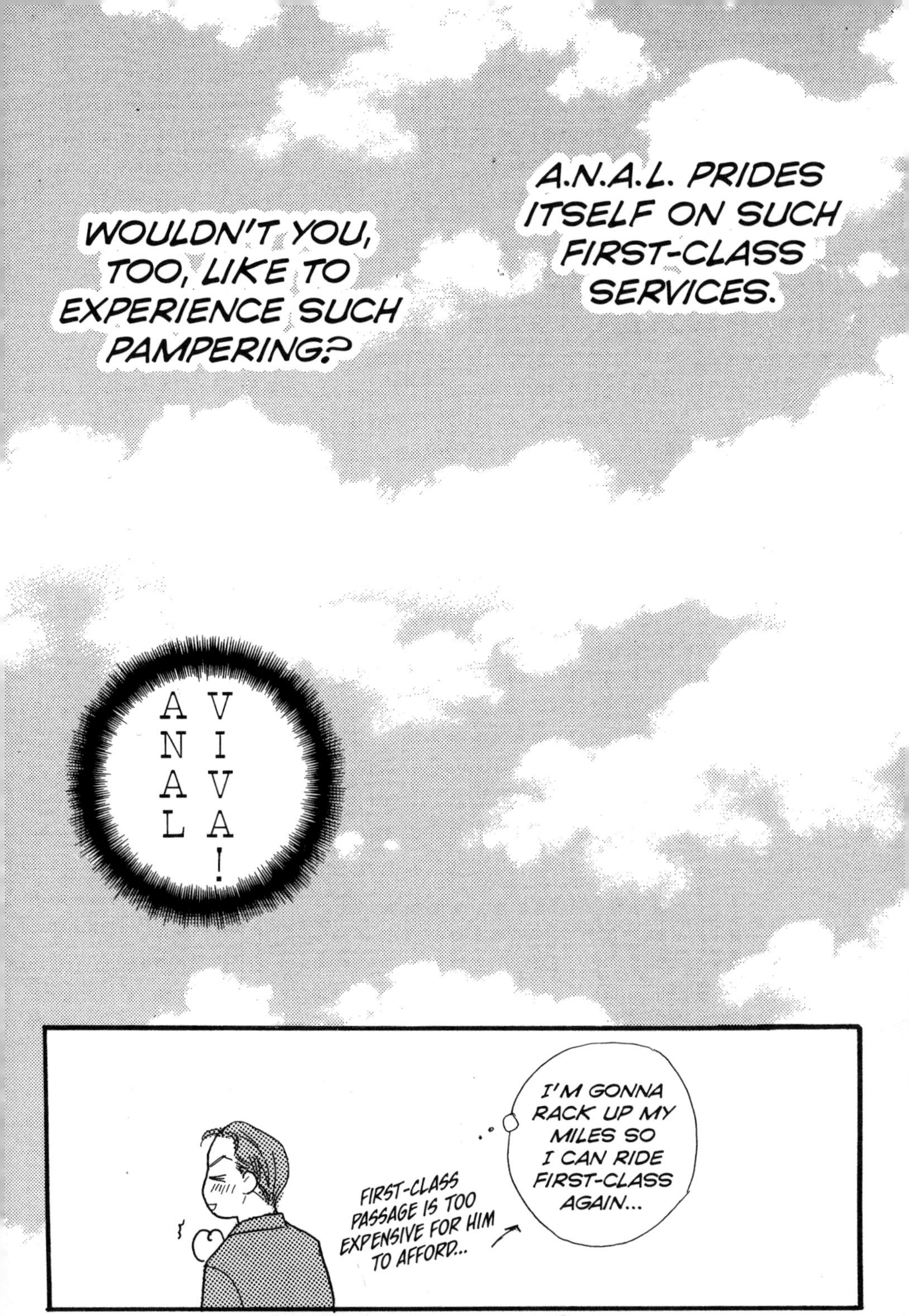
A.N.A.L. PRIDES ITSELF ON SUCH FIRST-CLASS SERVICES.
WOULDN'T YOU, TOO, LIKE TO EXPERIENCE SUCH PAMPERING?
VIVA ANAL!
I'M GONNA RACK UP MY MILES SO I CAN RIDE FIRST-CLASS AGAIN...
FIRST-CLASS PASSAGE IS TOO EXPENSIVE FOR HIM TO AFFORD...

**MY FIRST ENCOUNTER END**

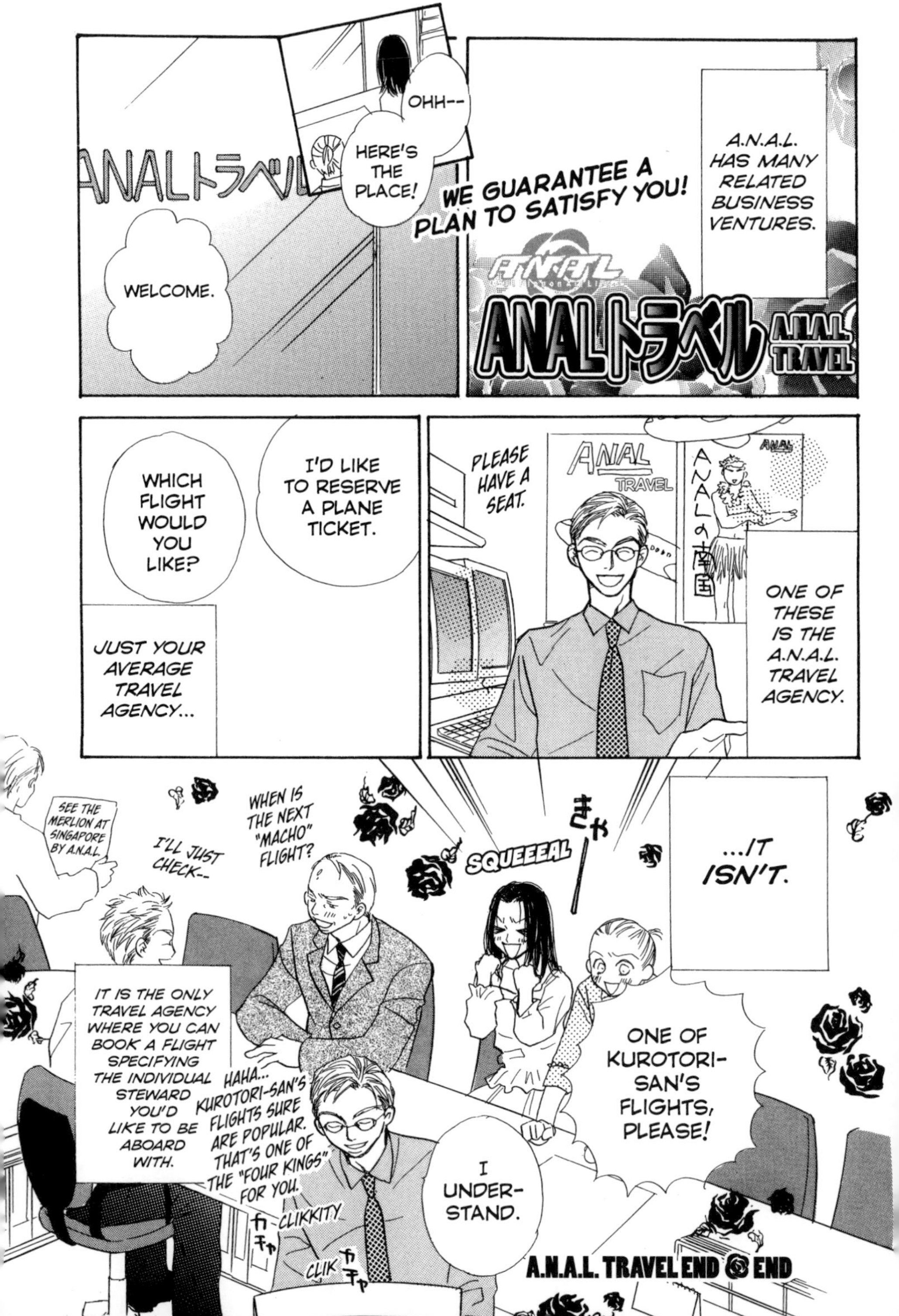
A.N.A.L. HAS MANY RELATED BUSINESS VENTURES.
WE GUARANTEE A PLAN TO SATISFY YOU!
ANALトラベル
A.N.A.L. TRAVEL
OHH--
HERE'S THE PLACE!
ANALトラベル
WELCOME.
PLEASE HAVE A SEAT.
ANAL TRAVEL
ONE OF THESE IS THE A.N.A.L. TRAVEL AGENCY.
I'D LIKE TO RESERVE A PLANE TICKET.
WHICH FLIGHT WOULD YOU LIKE?
JUST YOUR AVERAGE TRAVEL AGENCY...
...IT ISN'T.
きゃ
SQUEEEAL
ONE OF KUROTORI-SAN'S FLIGHTS, PLEASE!
WHEN IS THE NEXT "MACHO" FLIGHT?
I'LL JUST CHECK--
SEE THE MERLION AT SINGAPORE BY A.N.A.L.
I UNDERSTAND.
HAHA... KUROTORI-SAN'S FLIGHTS SURE ARE POPULAR. THAT'S ONE OF THE "FOUR KINGS" FOR YOU.
IT IS THE ONLY TRAVEL AGENCY WHERE YOU CAN BOOK A FLIGHT SPECIFYING THE INDIVIDUAL STEWARD YOU'D LIKE TO BE ABOARD WITH.
カチャ CLIKKITY
カチャ CLIK
A.N.A.L. TRAVEL END @ END

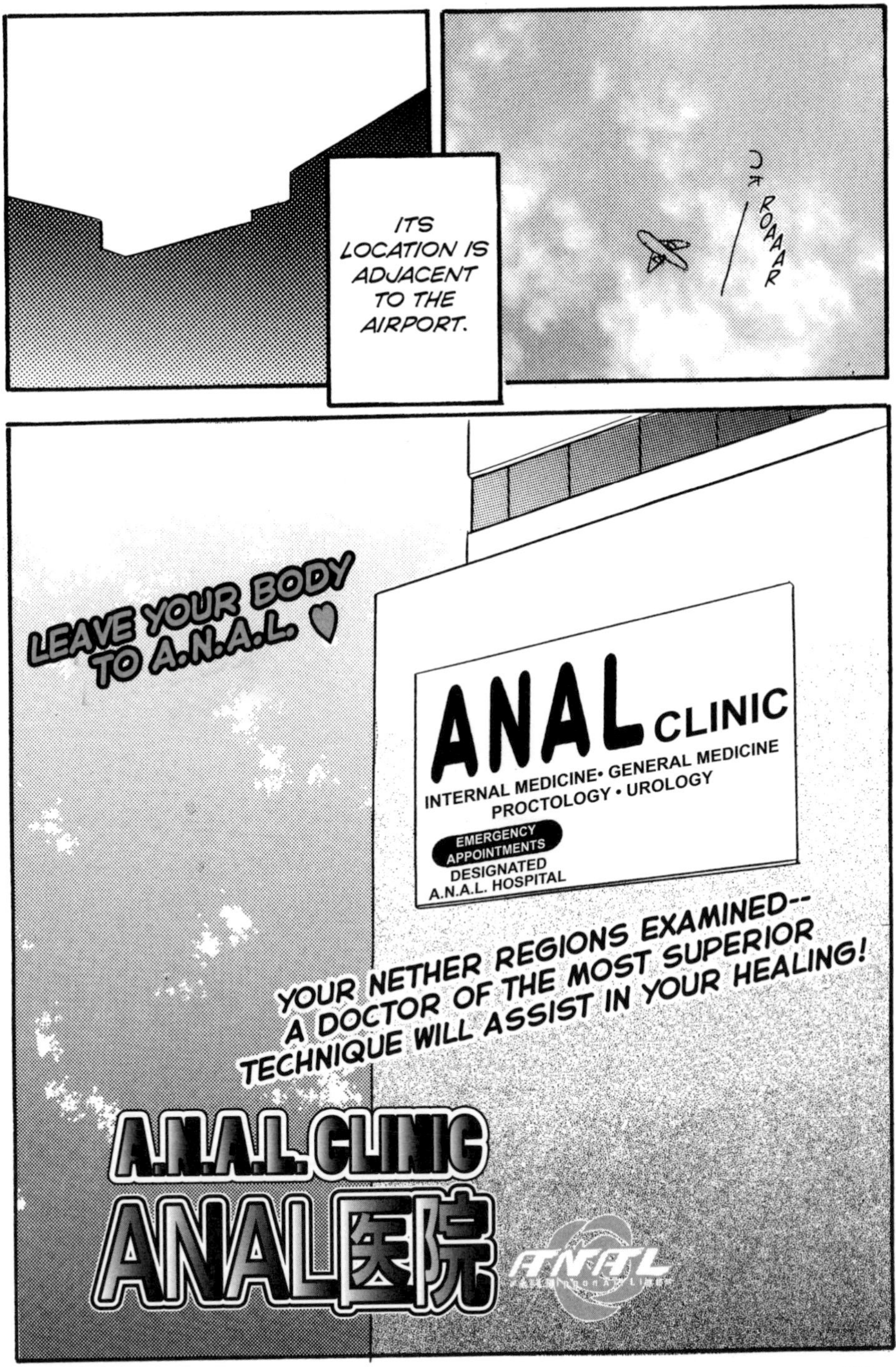
ROAAAR
ITS LOCATION IS ADJACENT TO THE AIRPORT.
LEAVE YOUR BODY TO A.N.A.L. ♥
ANAL CLINIC
INTERNAL MEDICINE• GENERAL MEDICINE
PROCTOLOGY • UROLOGY
EMERGENCY APPOINTMENTS
DESIGNATED A.N.A.L. HOSPITAL
YOUR NETHER REGIONS EXAMINED-- A DOCTOR OF THE MOST SUPERIOR TECHNIQUE WILL ASSIST IN YOUR HEALING!
A.N.A.L. CLINIC
ANAL医院

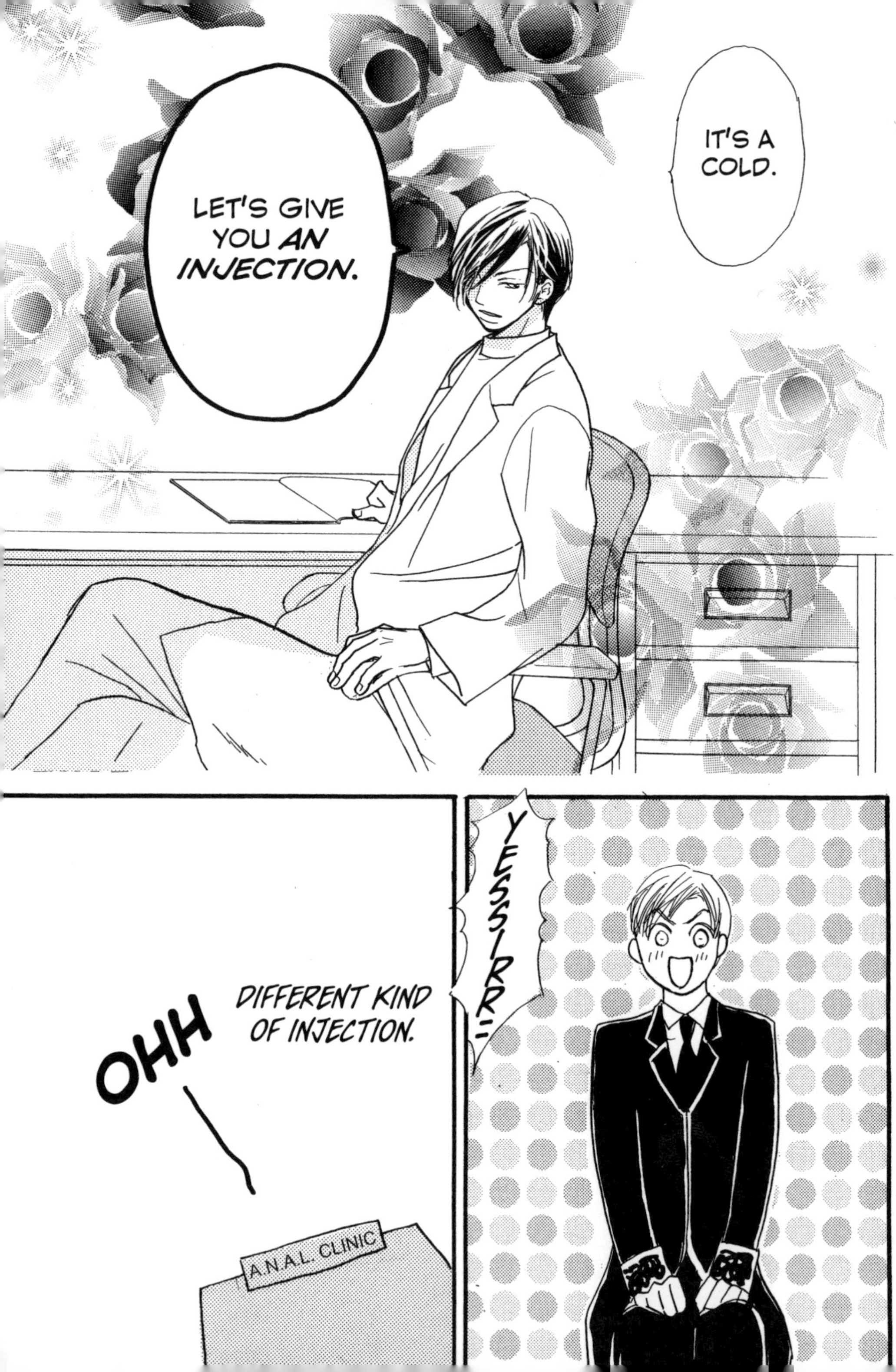
IT'S A COLD.
LET'S GIVE YOU *AN INJECTION*.
YESSIRR!!
DIFFERENT KIND OF INJECTION.
OHH
A.N.A.L. CLINIC

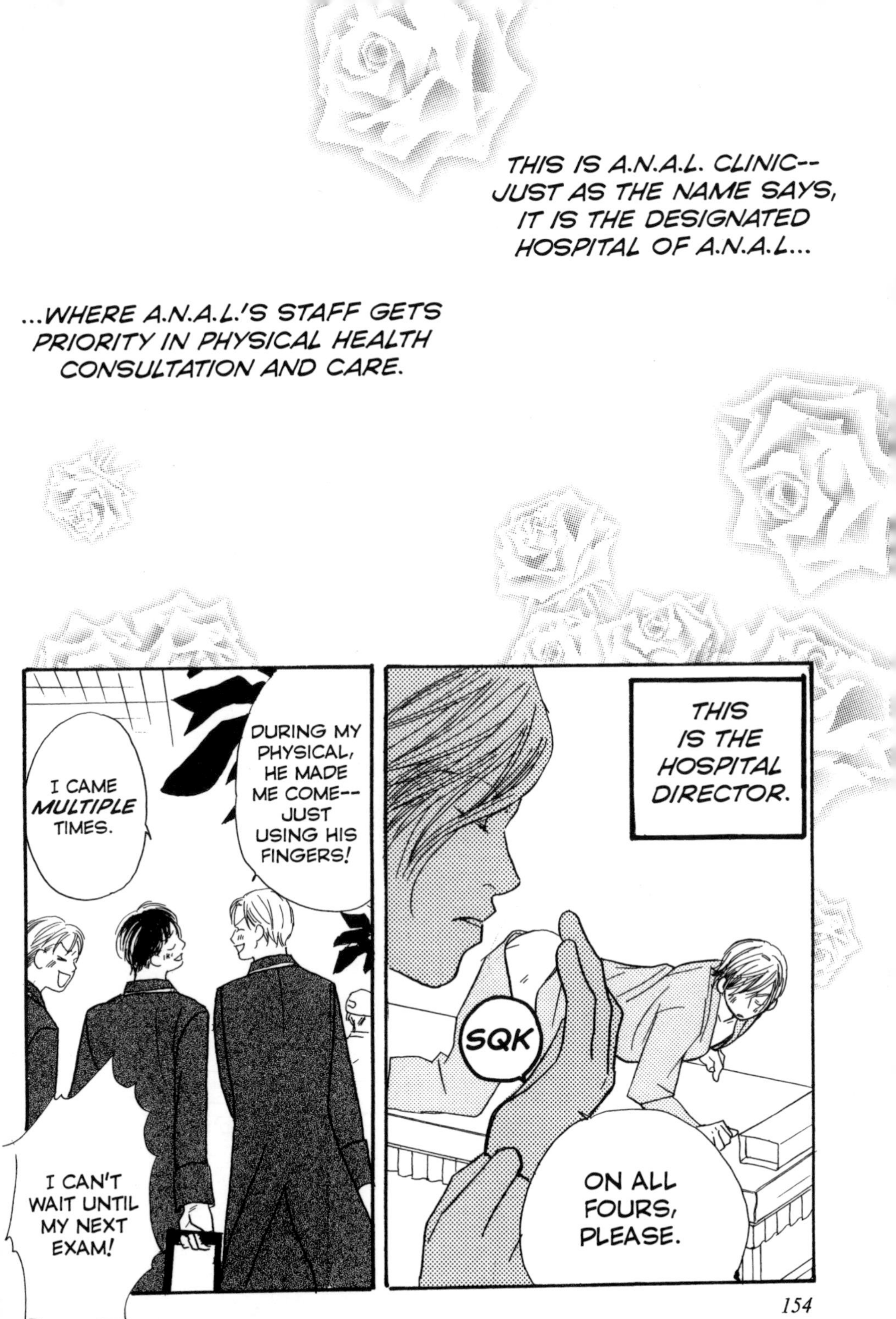
THIS IS A.N.A.L. CLINIC-- JUST AS THE NAME SAYS, IT IS THE DESIGNATED HOSPITAL OF A.N.A.L...
...WHERE A.N.A.L.'S STAFF GETS PRIORITY IN PHYSICAL HEALTH CONSULTATION AND CARE.
THIS IS THE HOSPITAL DIRECTOR.
SQK
ON ALL FOURS, PLEASE.
DURING MY PHYSICAL, HE MADE ME COME-- JUST USING HIS FINGERS!
I CAME *MULTIPLE* TIMES.
I CAN'T WAIT UNTIL MY NEXT EXAM!

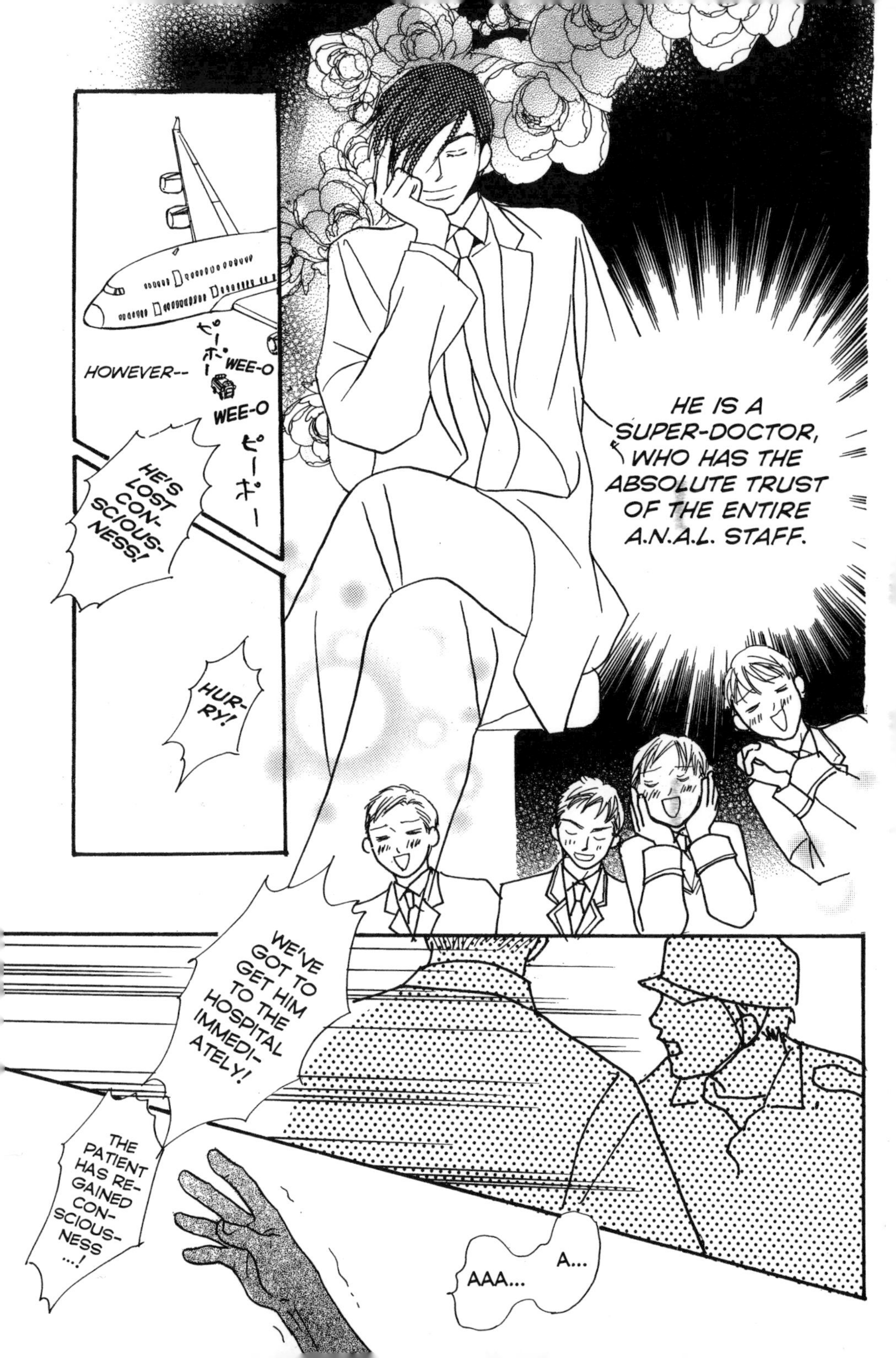

HE IS A SUPER-DOCTOR, WHO HAS THE ABSOLUTE TRUST OF THE ENTIRE A.N.A.L. STAFF.
HOWEVER--
ピーポー WEE-O
ピーポー WEE-O
HE'S LOST CONSCIOUSNESS!
HURRY!
WE'VE GOT TO GET HIM TO THE HOSPITAL IMMEDIATELY!
A... AAA...
THE PATIENT HAS REGAINED CONSCIOUSNESS...!

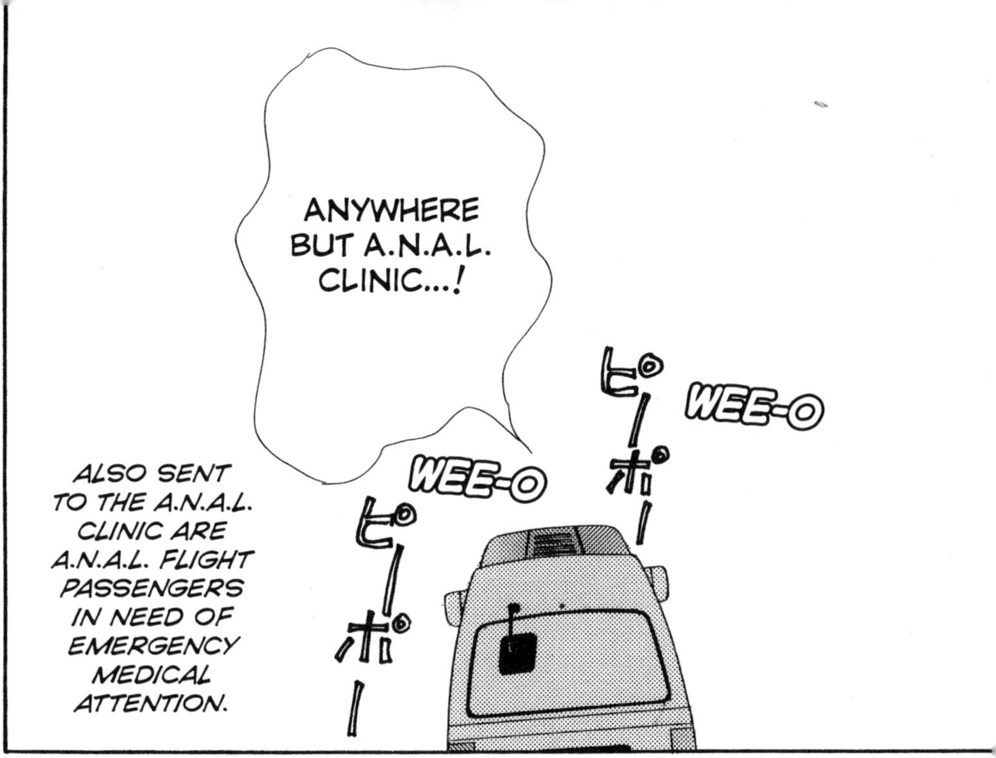
ピーポー
WEE-O
ANYWHERE BUT A.N.A.L. CLINIC...!
WEE-O
ピーポー
ALSO SENT TO THE A.N.A.L. CLINIC ARE A.N.A.L. FLIGHT PASSENGERS IN NEED OF EMERGENCY MEDICAL ATTENTION.

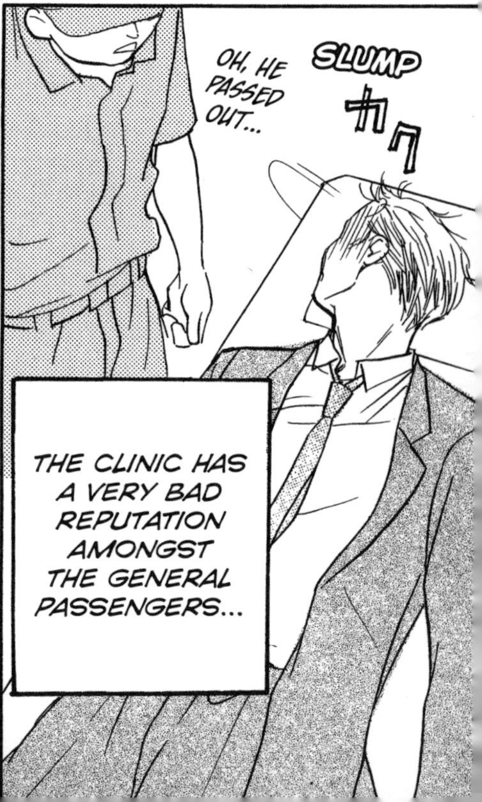
SLUMP
カク
OH, HE PASSED OUT...
THE CLINIC HAS A VERY BAD REPUTATION AMONGST THE GENERAL PASSENGERS...

MORAL: NEVER FALL ILL ON AN A.N.A.L. FLIGHT.

A.N.A.L. CLINIC END

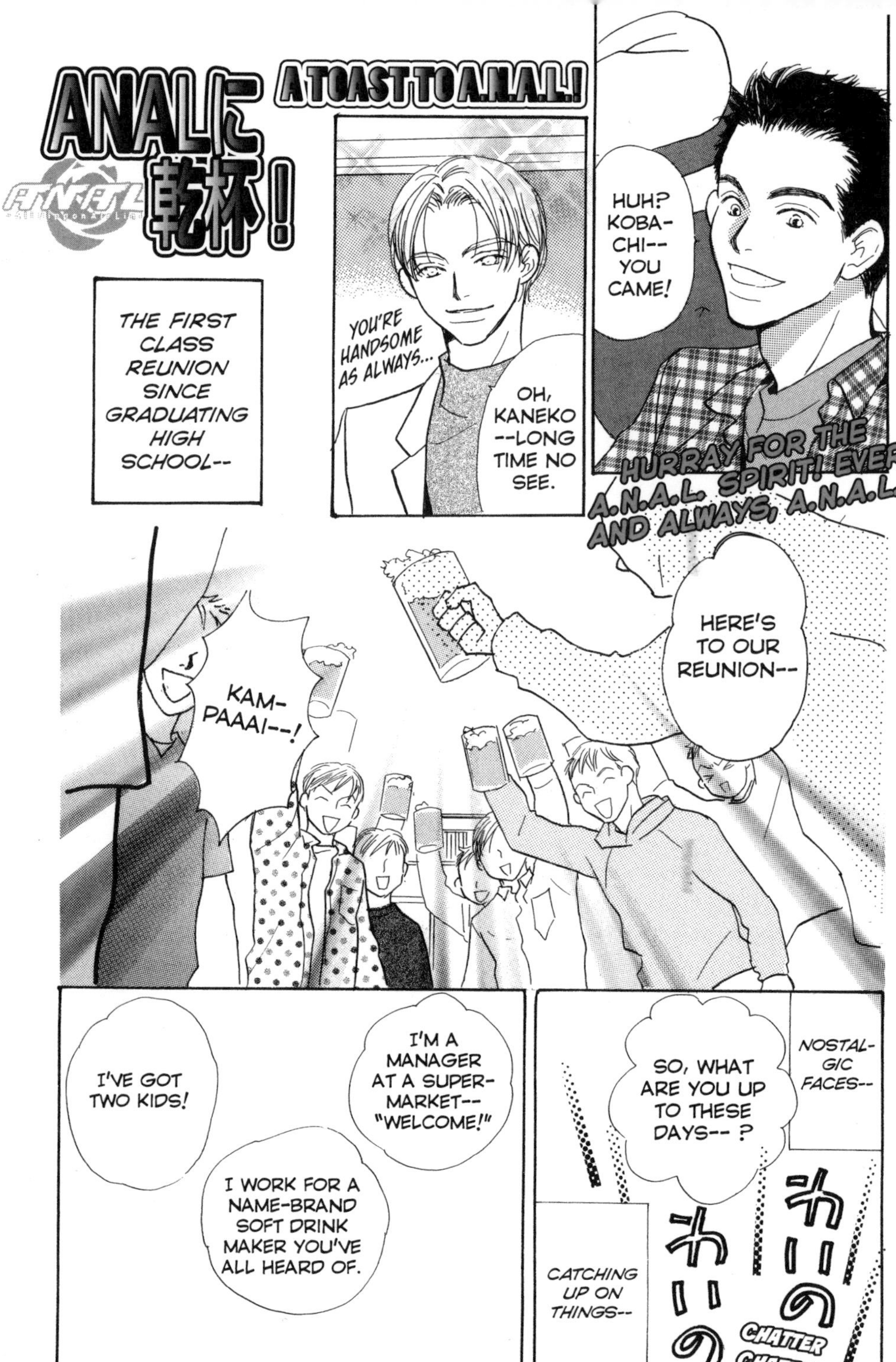
HUH? KOBA-CHI-- YOU CAME!
OH, KANEKO --LONG TIME NO SEE.
YOU'RE HANDSOME AS ALWAYS...
A TOAST TO A.N.A.L.!
ANALに乾杯!
THE FIRST CLASS REUNION SINCE GRADUATING HIGH SCHOOL--
HURRAY FOR THE A.N.A.L. SPIRIT! EVER AND ALWAYS, A.N.A.L.!
HERE'S TO OUR REUNION--
KAM-PAAAI--!
NOSTAL-GIC FACES--
SO, WHAT ARE YOU UP TO THESE DAYS-- ?
わいのわいの
CHATTER CHATTER
CATCHING UP ON THINGS--
I'M A MANAGER AT A SUPER-MARKET-- "WELCOME!"
I'VE GOT TWO KIDS!
I WORK FOR A NAME-BRAND SOFT DRINK MAKER YOU'VE ALL HEARD OF.

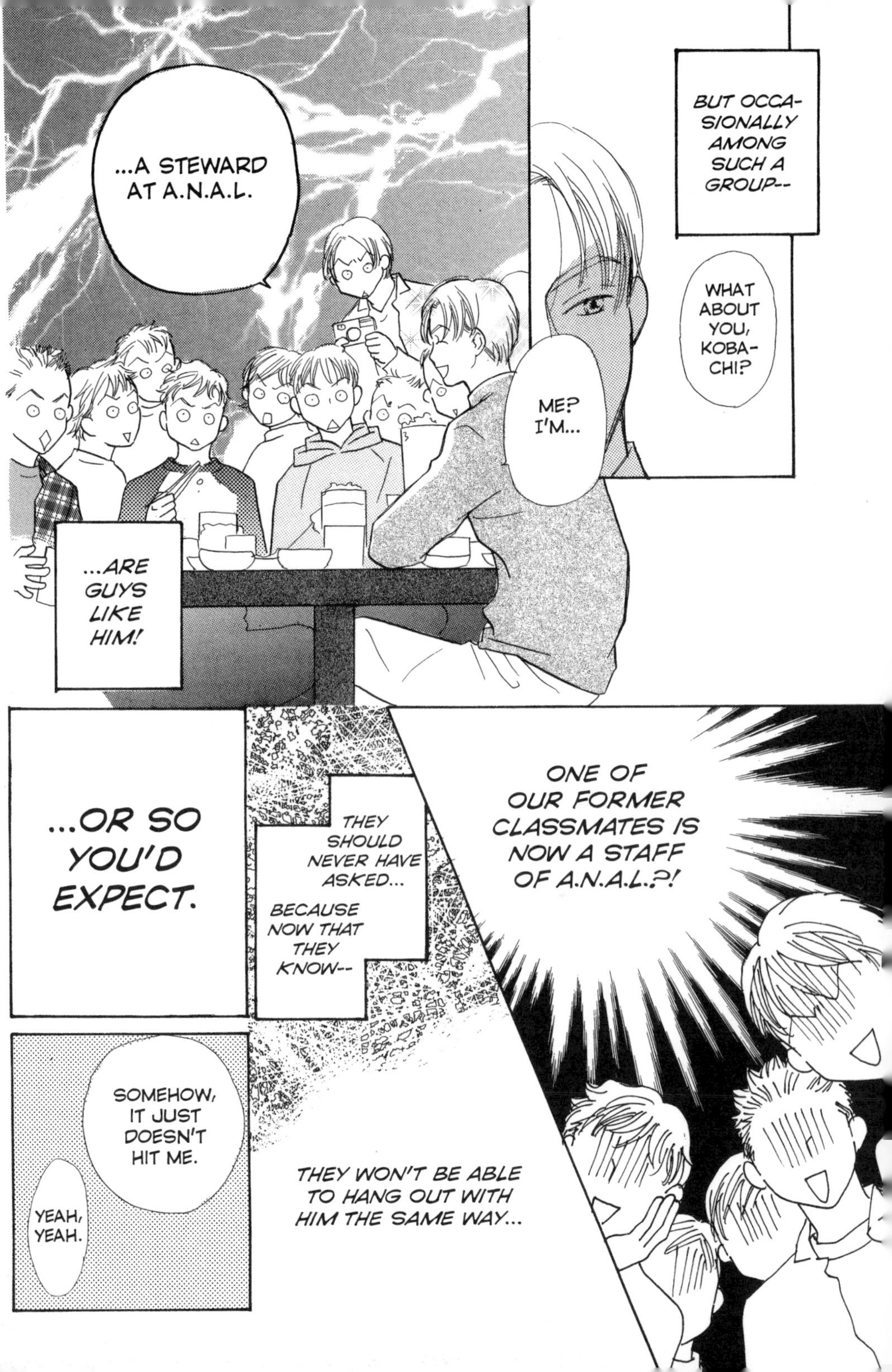

BUT OCCASIONALLY AMONG SUCH A GROUP--
WHAT ABOUT YOU, KOBACHI?
ME? I'M...
...A STEWARD AT A.N.A.L.
...ARE GUYS LIKE HIM!
ONE OF OUR FORMER CLASSMATES IS NOW A STAFF OF A.N.A.L.?!
THEY SHOULD NEVER HAVE ASKED...
BECAUSE NOW THAT THEY KNOW--
THEY WON'T BE ABLE TO HANG OUT WITH HIM THE SAME WAY...
...OR SO YOU'D EXPECT.
SOMEHOW, IT JUST DOESN'T HIT ME.
YEAH, YEAH.

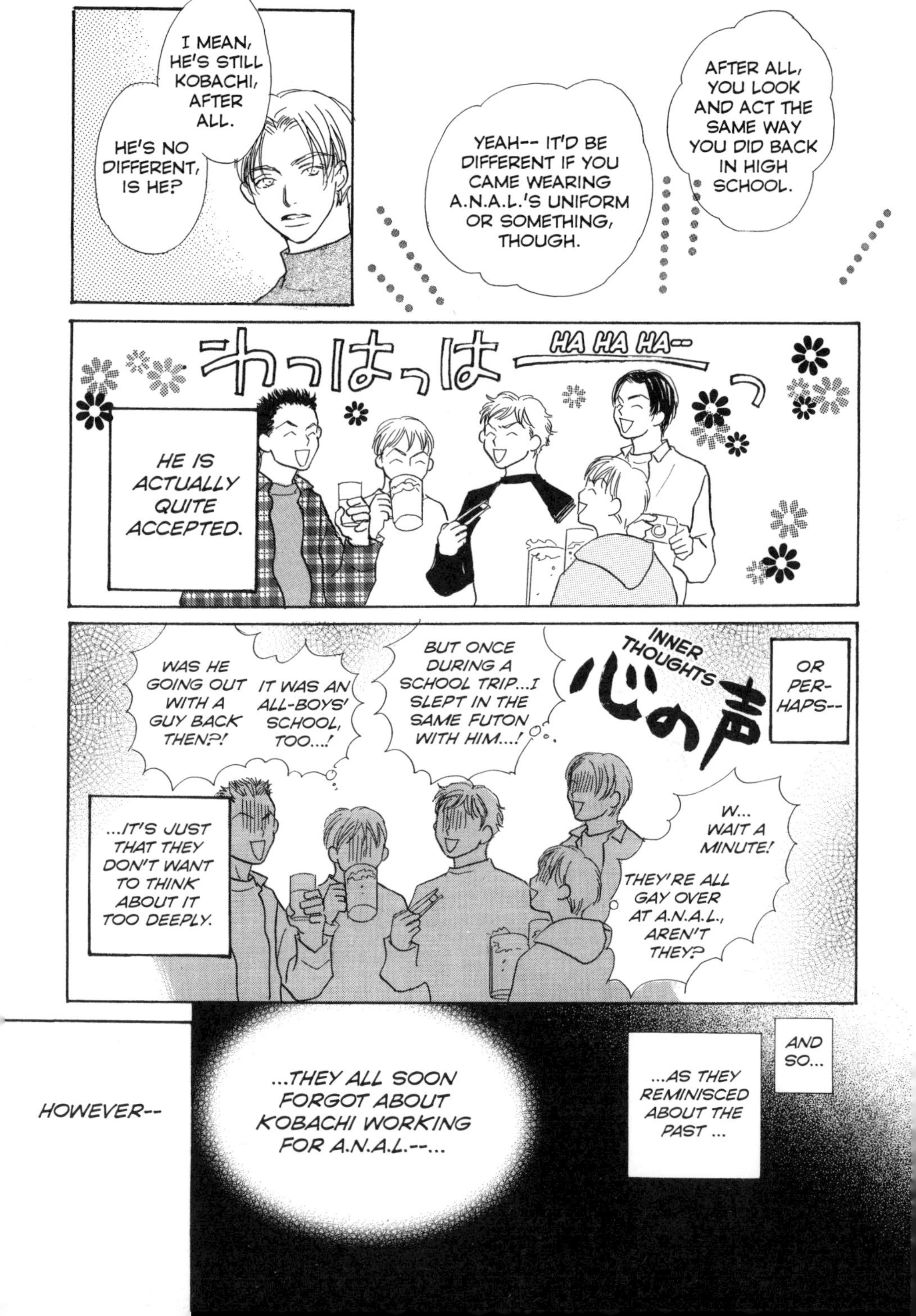
AFTER ALL, YOU LOOK AND ACT THE SAME WAY YOU DID BACK IN HIGH SCHOOL.
YEAH-- IT'D BE DIFFERENT IF YOU CAME WEARING A.N.A.L.'S UNIFORM OR SOMETHING, THOUGH.
I MEAN, HE'S STILL KOBACHI, AFTER ALL.
HE'S NO DIFFERENT, IS HE?
わっはっはーっ
HA HA HA--
HE IS ACTUALLY QUITE ACCEPTED.
OR PER-HAPS--
心の声
INNER THOUGHTS
BUT ONCE DURING A SCHOOL TRIP...I SLEPT IN THE SAME FUTON WITH HIM...!
IT WAS AN ALL-BOYS' SCHOOL, TOO...!
WAS HE GOING OUT WITH A GUY BACK THEN?!
W... WAIT A MINUTE!
THEY'RE ALL GAY OVER AT A.N.A.L., AREN'T THEY?
...IT'S JUST THAT THEY DON'T WANT TO THINK ABOUT IT TOO DEEPLY.
AND SO...
...AS THEY REMINISCED ABOUT THE PAST ...
...THEY ALL SOON FORGOT ABOUT KOBACHI WORKING FOR A.N.A.L.--...
HOWEVER--

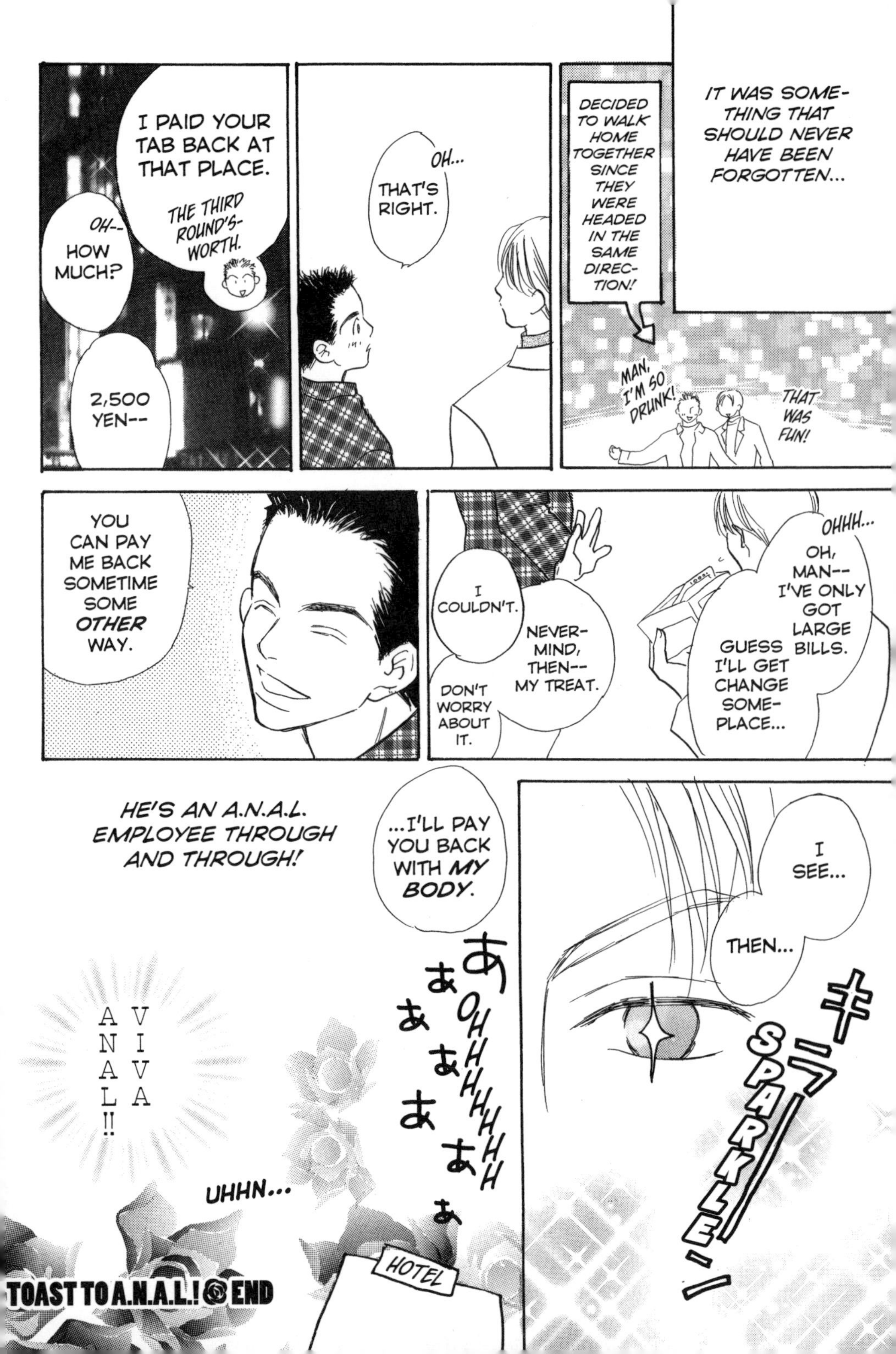
IT WAS SOMETHING THAT SHOULD NEVER HAVE BEEN FORGOTTEN...
DECIDED TO WALK HOME TOGETHER SINCE THEY WERE HEADED IN THE SAME DIRECTION!
THAT WAS FUN!
MAN, I'M SO DRUNK!
OH...
THAT'S RIGHT.
I PAID YOUR TAB BACK AT THAT PLACE.
THE THIRD ROUND'S-WORTH.
OH-- HOW MUCH?
2,500 YEN--
OHHH...
OH, MAN-- I'VE ONLY GOT LARGE BILLS.
GUESS I'LL GET CHANGE SOMEPLACE...
NEVERMIND, THEN-- MY TREAT.
I COULDN'T.
DON'T WORRY ABOUT IT.
YOU CAN PAY ME BACK SOMETIME SOME OTHER WAY.
I SEE...
THEN...
キラーン
SPARKLE
...I'LL PAY YOU BACK WITH MY BODY.
HE'S AN A.N.A.L. EMPLOYEE THROUGH AND THROUGH!
あぁぁぁぁぁ
OHHHHHHHHH
UHHN...
HOTEL
VIVA ANAL!!
TOAST TO A.N.A.L.! END

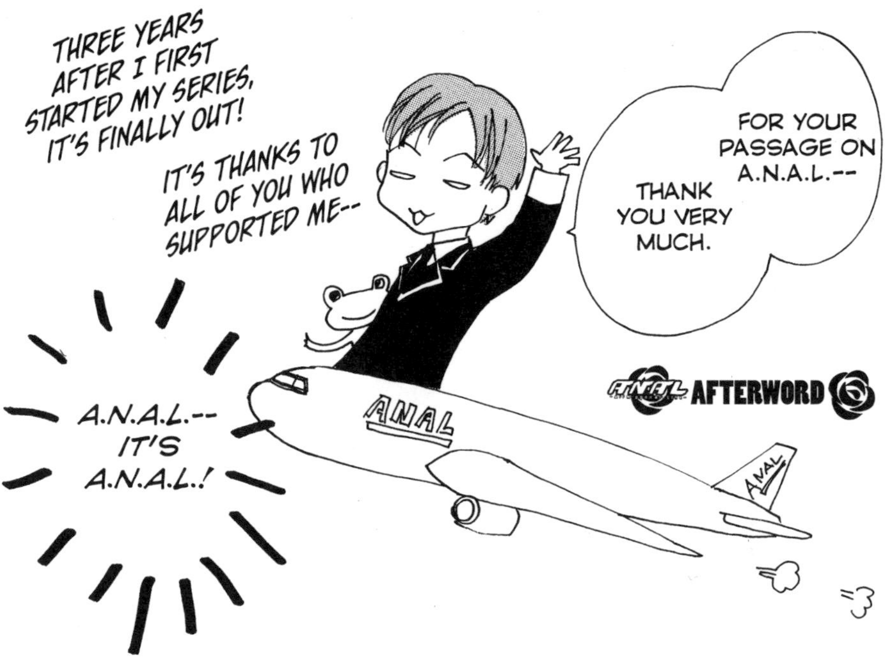
FOR YOUR PASSAGE ON A.N.A.L.--
THANK YOU VERY MUCH.
AFTERWORD
THREE YEARS AFTER I FIRST STARTED MY SERIES, IT'S FINALLY OUT!
IT'S THANKS TO ALL OF YOU WHO SUPPORTED ME--
A.N.A.L.-- IT'S A.N.A.L.!
ANAL


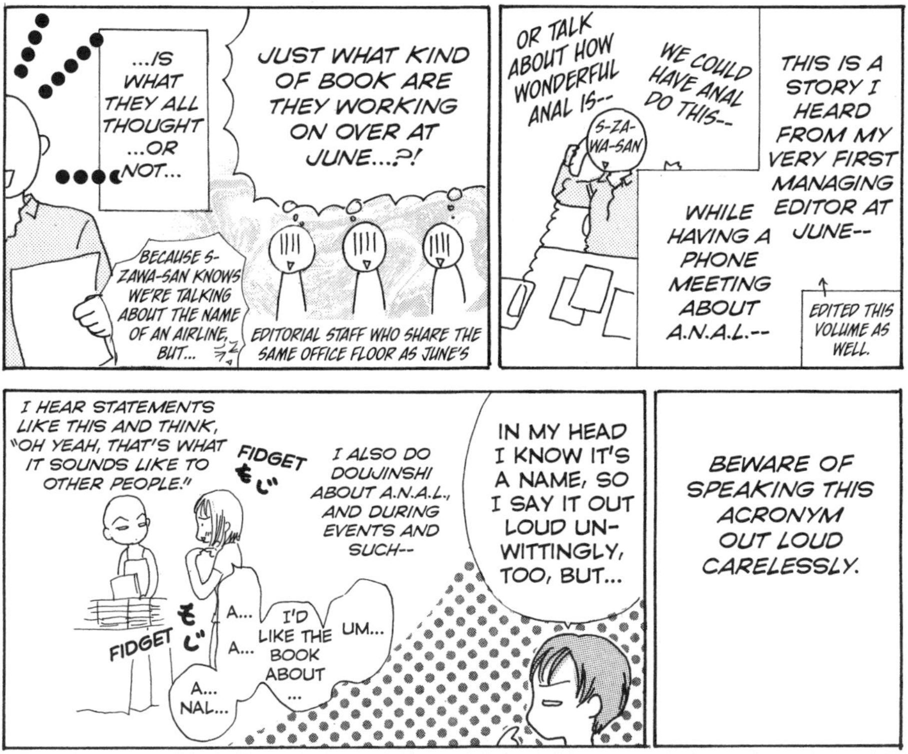
THIS IS A STORY I HEARD FROM MY VERY FIRST MANAGING EDITOR AT JUNE--
EDITED THIS VOLUME AS WELL.
WHILE HAVING A PHONE MEETING ABOUT A.N.A.L.--
WE COULD HAVE ANAL DO THIS--
OR TALK ABOUT HOW WONDERFUL ANAL IS--
S-ZA-WA-SAN
JUST WHAT KIND OF BOOK ARE THEY WORKING ON OVER AT JUNE...?!
...IS WHAT THEY ALL THOUGHT ...OR NOT...
BECAUSE S-ZAWA-SAN KNOWS WE'RE TALKING ABOUT THE NAME OF AN AIRLINE, BUT...
EDITORIAL STAFF WHO SHARE THE SAME OFFICE FLOOR AS JUNE'S
BEWARE OF SPEAKING THIS ACRONYM OUT LOUD CARELESSLY.
IN MY HEAD I KNOW IT'S A NAME, SO I SAY IT OUT LOUD UN-WITTINGLY, TOO, BUT...
I ALSO DO DOUJINSHI ABOUT A.N.A.L., AND DURING EVENTS AND SUCH--
I HEAR STATEMENTS LIKE THIS AND THINK, "OH YEAH, THAT'S WHAT IT SOUNDS LIKE TO OTHER PEOPLE."
FIDGET もじ
UM...
I'D LIKE THE BOOK ABOUT ...
A... A...
A... NAL...
FIDGET もじ




YOU CAN GET INFORMATION ABOUT THE DOUJINSHI AT: HTTP://WWW.NE.JP/ASAHI/KEI/GOODLIVING/

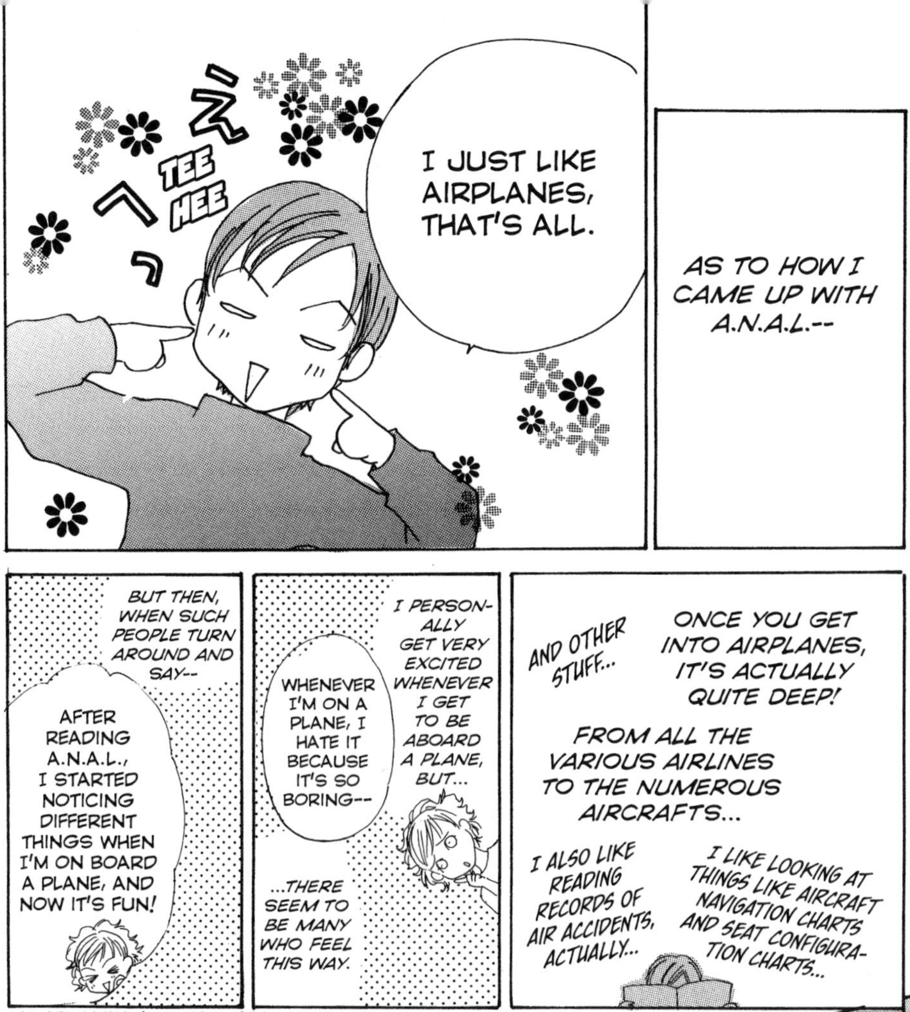
AS TO HOW I CAME UP WITH A.N.A.L.--
I JUST LIKE AIRPLANES, THAT'S ALL.
TEE HEE
ONCE YOU GET INTO AIRPLANES, IT'S ACTUALLY QUITE DEEP!
FROM ALL THE VARIOUS AIRLINES TO THE NUMEROUS AIRCRAFTS...
I LIKE LOOKING AT THINGS LIKE AIRCRAFT NAVIGATION CHARTS AND SEAT CONFIGURATION CHARTS...
I ALSO LIKE READING RECORDS OF AIR ACCIDENTS, ACTUALLY...
AND OTHER STUFF...
I PERSONALLY GET VERY EXCITED WHENEVER I GET TO BE ABOARD A PLANE, BUT...
WHENEVER I'M ON A PLANE, I HATE IT BECAUSE IT'S SO BORING--
...THERE SEEM TO BE MANY WHO FEEL THIS WAY.
BUT THEN, WHEN SUCH PEOPLE TURN AROUND AND SAY--
AFTER READING A.N.A.L., I STARTED NOTICING DIFFERENT THINGS WHEN I'M ON BOARD A PLANE, AND NOW IT'S FUN!

KEI AZUMAYA'S HOMEPAGE: HTTP://WWW2.GATEWAY.NE.JP/~KEI-A/

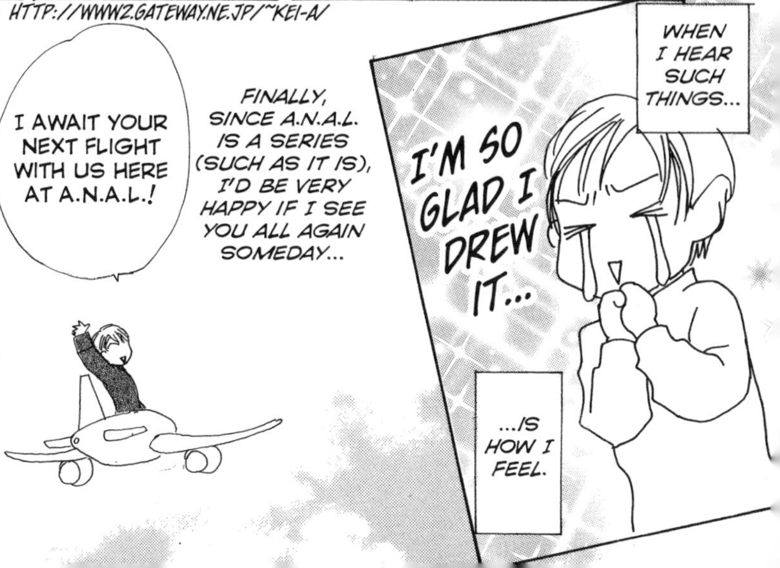
WHEN I HEAR SUCH THINGS...
I'M SO GLAD I DREW IT...
...IS HOW I FEEL.
FINALLY, SINCE A.N.A.L. IS A SERIES (SUCH AS IT IS), I'D BE VERY HAPPY IF I SEE YOU ALL AGAIN SOMEDAY...
I AWAIT YOUR NEXT FLIGHT WITH US HERE AT A.N.A.L.!

Special Thanks!!

TO MY ASSISTANTS: JIZO-SAN, AIHARA-SAN, AND AYAKO-SAN

AND MY EDITORS: SAZAWA-SAN, SHIMODA-SAN, MAKIYAMA-SAN, AND TAKAHASHI-SAN

AND TO ALL YOU READERS!

## FIRST PUBLICATION DATES

| | |
|---|---|
| PARADISE 30,000 FT. | *IN "SHOSETSU JUNE" 1999 JUNE* |
| FROM A.N.A.L. WITH LOVE '99 | *NOVEMBER* |
| THE BIRTH OF A.N.A.L. | *2000 AUGUST* |
| MY LOVER IS SANTA CLAUS | *JANUARY* |
| ROMEO & JULIET, A.N.A.L. VERSION | *APRIL* |
| A STEWARD'S STORY | *JUNE* |
| THE JOB INTERVIEW | *JUNE* |
| THE NARROW GATES OF A.N.A.L. | *REPRINTED FROM DOUJIN "A.N.A.L."* |
| A CHRISTMAS FANTASY | *IN "SHOSETSU JUNE" 2001 JANUARY* |
| LOVE A.N.A.L. | *REPRINTED FROM DOUJIN "BETSU ANA"* |
| THE DIRECTOR VS. MIRACLE-VOICE | *REPRINTED FROM DOUJIN "BETSU ANA"* |
| BURNING A.N.A.L. | *IN "SHOSETSU JUNE" 2001 AUGUST* |
| FISTS OF A.N.A.L. | *2002 FEBRUARY* |
| AN A.N.A.L. MYSTERY | *REPRINTED FROM DOUJIN "TSUBASA NO OUKOKU"* |
| THE SECRET OF THE "FOUR KINGS" | *ORIGINAL CONTENT* |
| MY FIRST ENCOUNTER | *REPRINTED FROM DOUJIN "JET STREAM"* |
| A.N.A.L. TRAVEL | *ORIGINAL CONTENT* |
| A.N.A.L. CLINIC | *REPRINTED FROM DOUJIN "JET STREAM"* |
| A TOAST TO A.N.A.L.! | *ORIGINAL CONTENT* |
| AFTERWORD | *ORIGINAL CONTENT* |

~All Nippon Air Line~

**THANKS FOR FLYING WITH US**

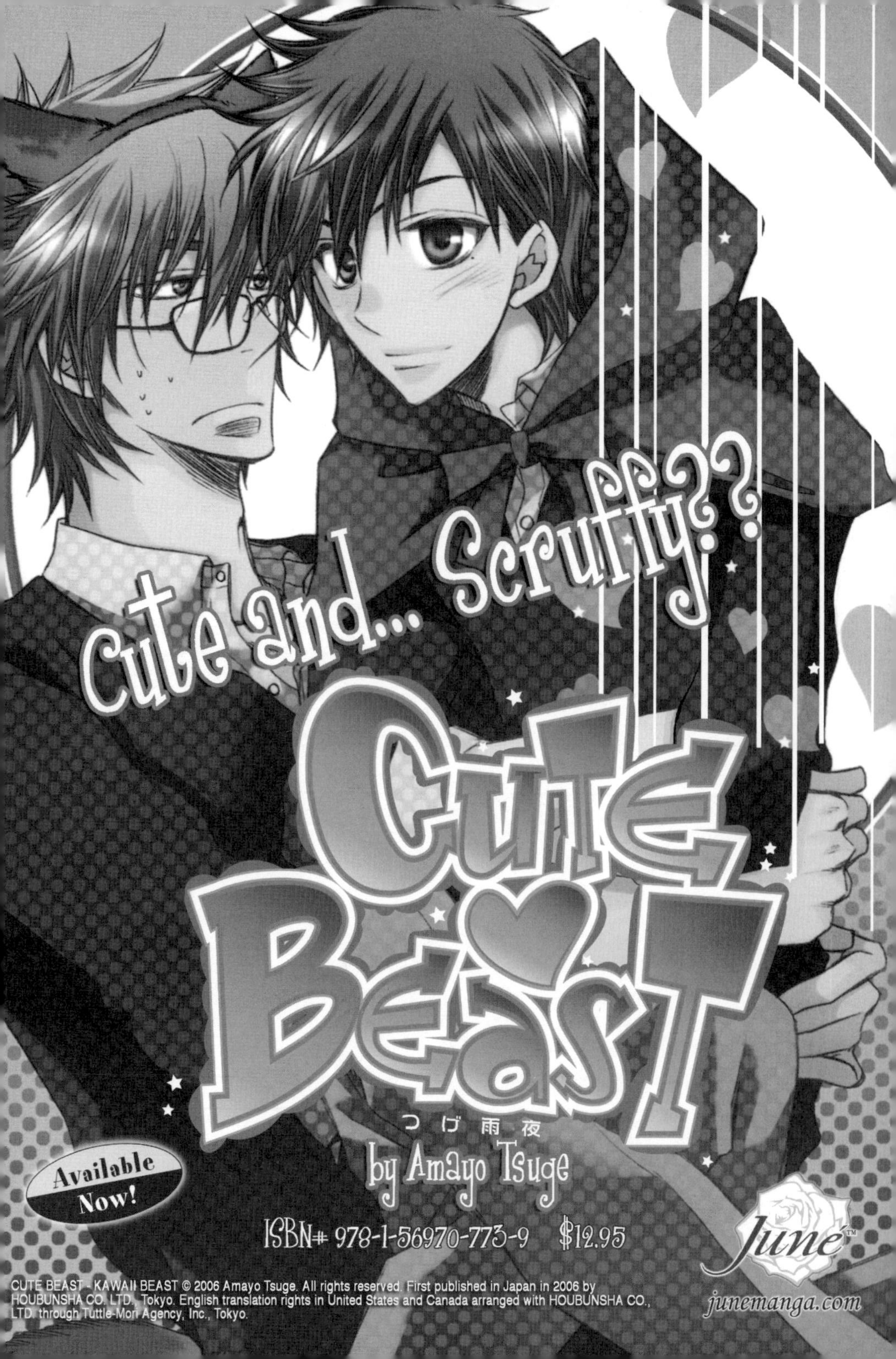
Cute and... Scruffy??
Cute Beast
つげ雨夜
by Amayo Tsuge
Available Now!
ISBN# 978-1-56970-773-9 $12.95
June™
junemanga.com
CUTE BEAST - KAWAII BEAST © 2006 Amayo Tsuge. All rights reserved. First published in Japan in 2006 by HOUBUNSHA CO. LTD., Tokyo. English translation rights in United States and Canada arranged with HOUBUNSHA CO., LTD. through Tuttle-Mori Agency, Inc., Tokyo.

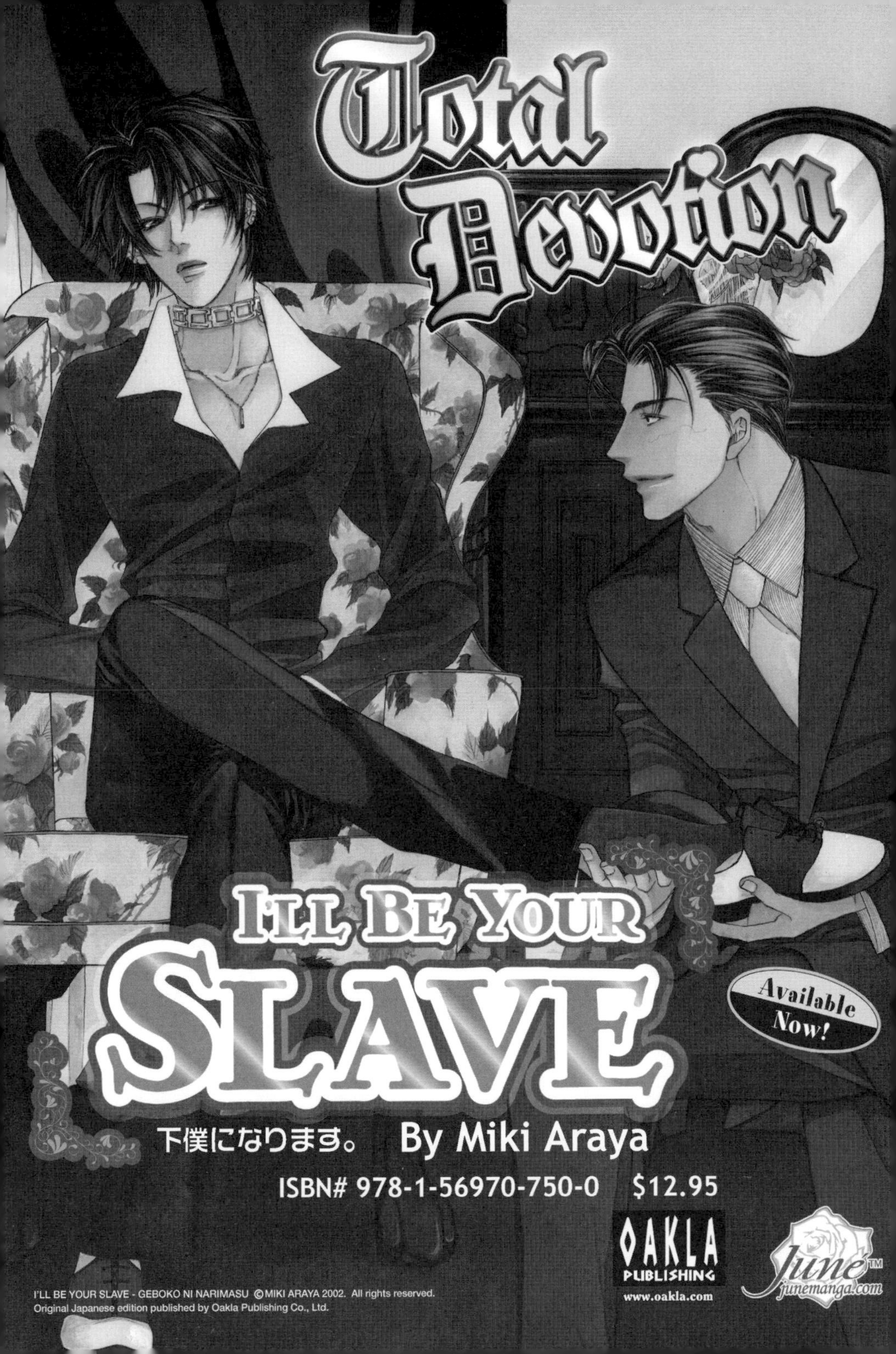
Total Devotion
I'LL BE YOUR
SLAVE
Available Now!
下僕になります。 By Miki Araya
ISBN# 978-1-56970-750-0 $12.95
OAKLA PUBLISHING
www.oakla.com
June™
junemanga.com
I'LL BE YOUR SLAVE - GEBOKO NI NARIMASU ©MIKI ARAYA 2002. All rights reserved.
Original Japanese edition published by Oakla Publishing Co., Ltd.

# LAUGH
## UNDER · THE SUN
太陽の下で笑え。

By Yugi Yamada

Pro
Boxer
...or
Punching Bag?

Available Now!

ISBN# 978-1-56970-776-0   $12.95

*june*™

junemanga.com

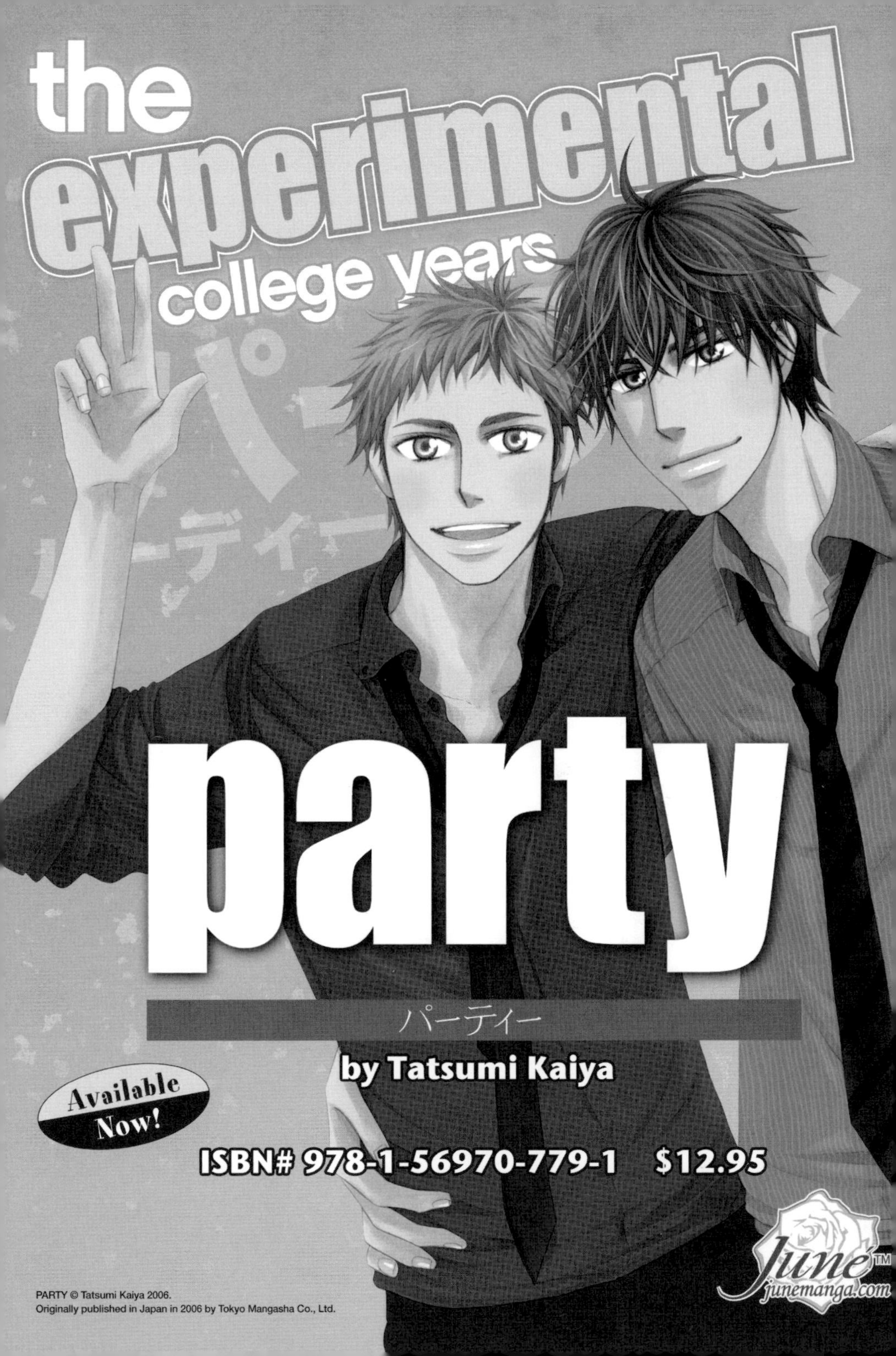
the experimental college years
パーティー
party
パーティー
by Tatsumi Kaiya
Available Now!
ISBN# 978-1-56970-779-1 $12.95
June™
junemanga.com
PARTY © Tatsumi Kaiya 2006.
Originally published in Japan in 2006 by Tokyo Mangasha Co., Ltd.

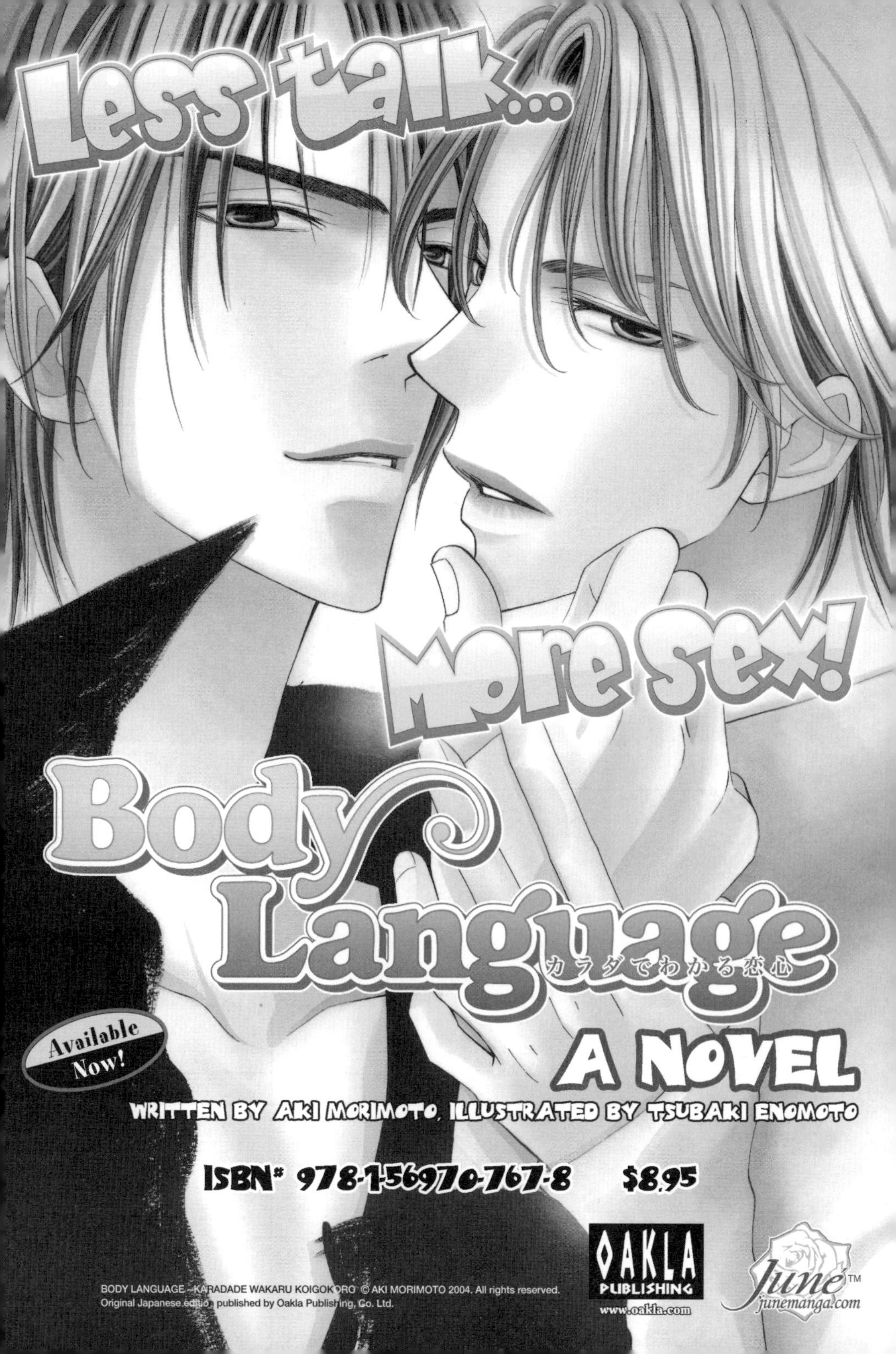

Less talk...
More sex!
Body Language
カラダでわかる恋心
A NOVEL
Available Now!
WRITTEN BY AKI MORIMOTO, ILLUSTRATED BY TSUBAKI ENOMOTO
ISBN# 978-1-56970-767-8
$8.95
OAKLA PUBLISHING
www.oakla.com
June™
junemanga.com
BODY LANGUAGE - KARADADE WAKARU KOIGOKORO © AKI MORIMOTO 2004. All rights reserved.
Original Japanese edition published by Oakla Publishing, Co. Ltd.

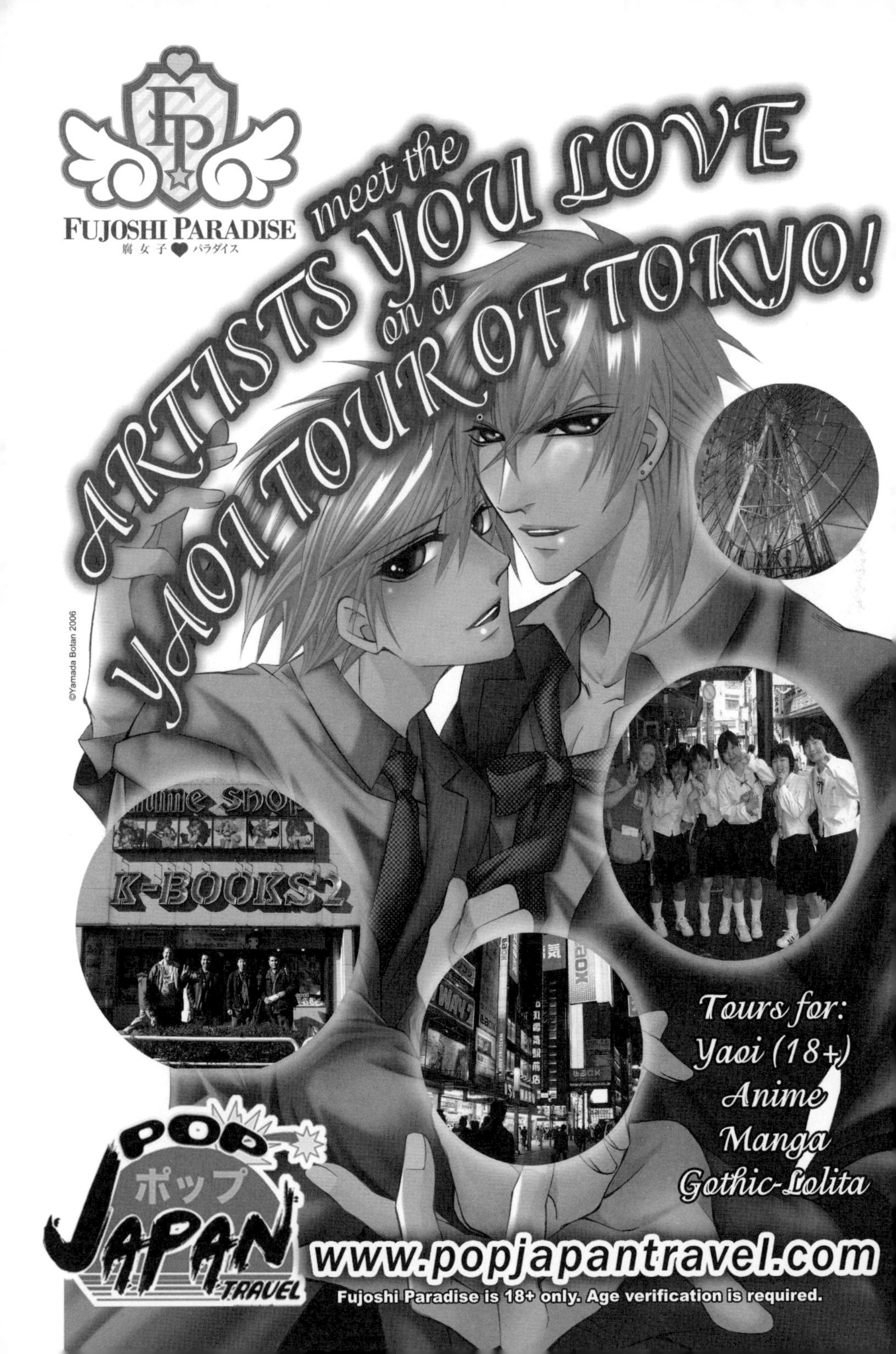
FP
FUJOSHI PARADISE
腐女子❤パラダイス
meet the
ARTISTS YOU LOVE
on a
YAOI TOUR OF TOKYO!
©Yamada Botan 2006
K-BOOKS 2
Tours for:
Yaoi (18+)
Anime
Manga
Gothic-Lolita
POP
ポップ
JAPAN
TRAVEL
www.popjapantravel.com
Fujoshi Paradise is 18+ only. Age verification is required.

then the novels...

now the

MANGA!

# HIDEYUKI KIKUCHI'S

## Vampire Hunter D

In 12,090 A.D., a race of vampires called the Nobility have spawned. Humanity cowers in fear, praying for a savior to rid them of their undying nightmare. All they have to battle the danger is a different kind of danger...

Visit the Website:
www.vampire-d.com

Available Now!

DMP

DIGITAL MANGA
PUBLISHING

VOLUME 1 - ISBN# 978-1-56970-827-9    $12.95

www.dmpbooks.com

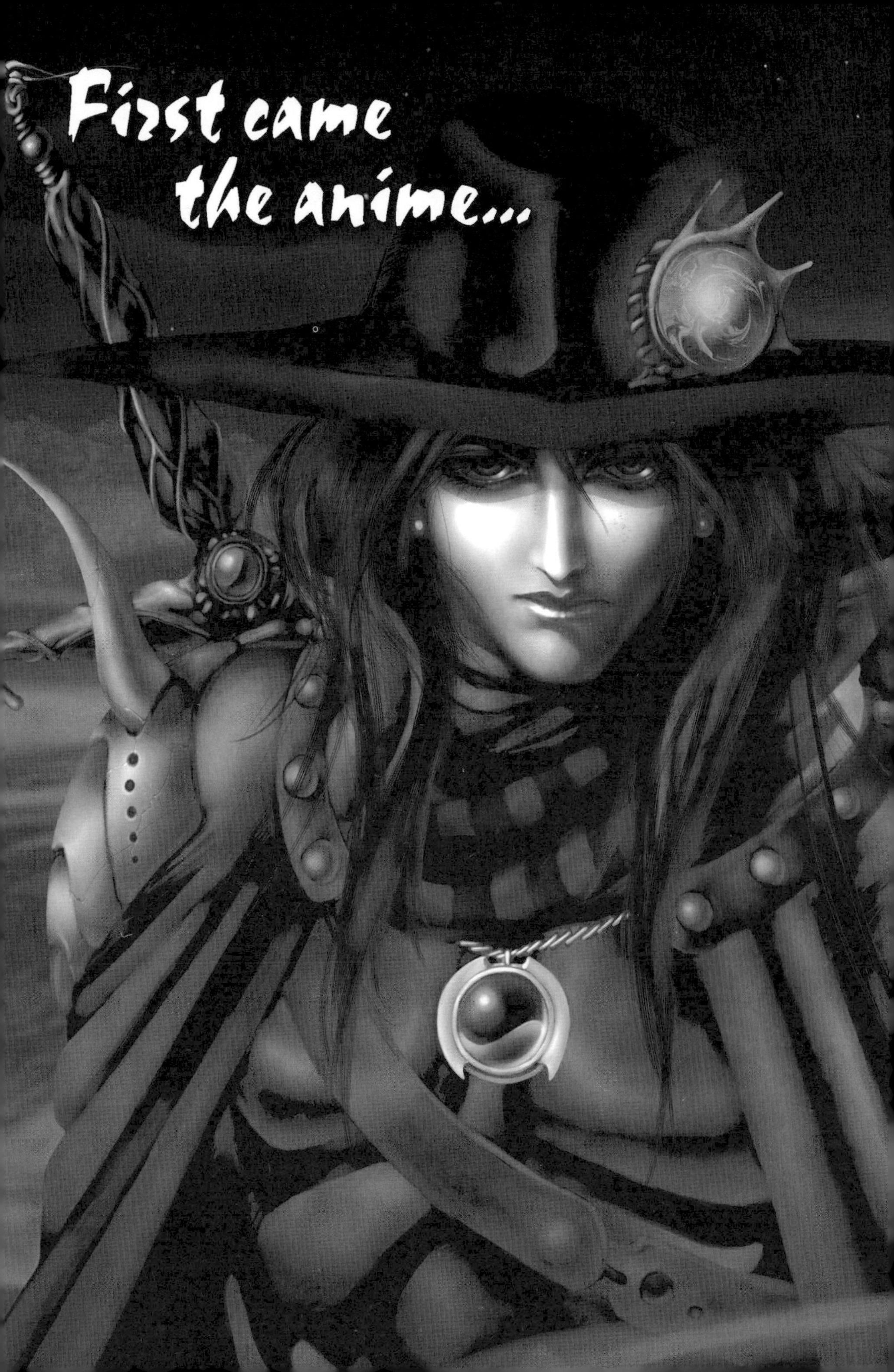
First came
the anime...

# STOP

## This is the back of the book! Start from the other side.

**NATIVE MANGA** readers read manga from **right to left**.

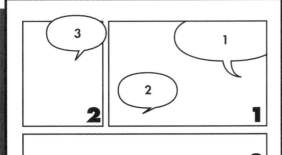

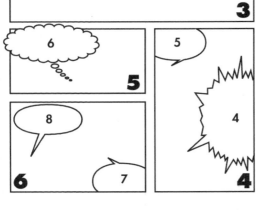

If you run into our **Native Manga** logo on any of our books... you'll know that this manga is published in it's true original native Japanese right to left reading format, as it was intended. Turn to the other side of the book and start reading from right to left, top to bottom.

Follow the diagram to see how its done. **Surf's Up!**

NATIVE MANGA

READ RIGHT TO LEFT